qui plane, qui domine.

25
Centuries
Of
Language
Teaching

An inquiry into

the science, art, and

development of language

teaching methodology

500 B.C. – 1969

NEWBURY HOUSE PUBLISHERS, rowley, massachusetts

25 Centuries of Language Teaching

Louis G. Kelly, Ph. D.
Faculty of Arts
University of Ottawa

25 CENTURIES OF LANGUAGE TEACHING

Library of Congress Catalogue Card Number 79-96466

CONTENTS

ILLUSTRATIONS

A NOTE ON THE BIBLIOGRAPHY

The bibliography is in three parts:

The first is an alphabetical index of abbreviations used in referring to periodicals, anthologies and encyclopedias in the other part of the bibliography.

The second is a numbered alphabetical list of primary sources.

The third contains secondary sources. In the text, all books are referred to by their numbers. Numbers referring to secondary sources are preceeded by an asterisk.

When a book is in one volume only, the page number is given immediately after the book number. However, if a book is in more than one volume, the volume or part number is given in Roman numerals after the book number. Passages from classical works are given in the normal manner. The symbol "§" refers to the section.

PREFACE

As a field of scholarly research and theorizing, the study of language teaching is claimed to be new. Specialists point out that whereas during the twentieth century it was developed into a separate discipline under the impetus of applied linguistics and psychology, in previous centuries language teaching was merely an outgrowth of linguistic scholarship. The all-important stages of learning a language were developed by two sorts of amateur. One was the professional grammarian who, for various reasons, found himself in the classroom; the other was the professional educator who, because of an interest in language, turned to teaching languages. Erasmus is a good example of the first and Comenius of the second. So it is that most present-day specialists are firmly convinced that in no other age has the body of knowledge underlying language teaching been so well organized, so complete, or in pragmatic terms so effective.

Nobody really knows what is new or what is old in present-day language teaching procedures. There has been a vague feeling that modern experts have spent their time in discovering what other men have forgotten; but as most of the key documents are in Latin, moderns find it difficult to go to original sources. In any case, much that is being claimed as revolutionary in this century is merely a rethinking and renaming of early ideas and procedures, so that on the practical plane, if this book can provide teachers and researchers with points of departure, it will have served one purpose and justified the years spent in writing it.

My main concern is not merely an account of teaching ideas, but an explanation of why at various times in the last two and a half thousand years some ideas were preferred to others. To this end teaching ideas are related to their social and intellectual context.

Apart from the interest such an aspect lends to language teaching itself, this book tries to show in another light the training of literary men and scholars. As languages were a basic part of education until well into the nineteenth century, the stock of ideas and procedures educated men carried with them was largely derived from the study of foreign languages and literatures, with a preponderance, one must add, of concepts drawn from the classics.

Although there are proportionately more sources from the twentieth century for a book such as this, it does not thereby follow that over the last seventy years more original or more constructive thinking has been done than during the preceding two thousand. My primary sources include discussions of language-teaching principles and practice; the secondary sources, histories of education, scholarship, and human sciences. As far as possible these have been supplemented by textbooks. For the seventeenth century, and to a lesser extent the sixteenth, I was fortunate in having access to copies that had been used in classrooms of the time and had been annotated by their users. In most cases translations of extracts from these books are my own.

The list of those who helped me with this study is long. I am indebted to Professor W. F. Mackey of Laval University, Quebec, for suggesting the subject and guiding the research. Part of the work was made possible by the generosity of the Canada Council, which gave me a grant in 1964. Likewise the work would not have been possible without the help of the staffs of the various libraries in which I did the research: those of Laval, le Petit Séminaire de Québec, le Collège des Jésuites de Québec; and in the United States, those of Harvard University, especially the Widener and Houghton Libraries. Many other organizations, such as the British Museum, the BBC, and the United States Information Service of Ottawa often gave more than I asked. I owe much to Dr. John Gallup of the Faculté de philosophie of Laval for guidance in interpreting medieval textbooks on grammar and for help in relating them to philosophy and theology. I am grateful to the Reverend Father Jacques Tremblay, S.J., of the College des Jésuites for several illuminating discussions of the *Ratio studiorum.* Last of all, I pay tribute to the patience and encouragement of my wife, perhaps the severest critic of all those who read the manuscript. Without her help my Canadian adventures would not have achieved their purpose. To all of these, and to the many I have not mentioned, I offer my thanks.

Ottawa, April, 1969

INTRODUCTION

It is through ignorance of languages that the world of learning fell on evil days and even came close to extinction . . . .

1529 (Erasmus) in 377: 501D

In a coherent system of education the approach to any discipline is governed by four factors: the aim of the system as a whole, the relevance of the discipline under discussion, theoretical findings in the sciences on which the discipline rests, and the availability of research results to teachers in the classroom. These four factors are really facets of a larger reality, the intellectual temper of the time. Scholars of all periods tend to accept certain groups of ideas as their own, slanting students almost unconsciously toward the accepted canon. In spite of this attempt to apply blinkers, there are always rebels who try to find applications for ideas from the past, or who strike out into the unknown, laying the foundation for future developments.

A glance at the bibliography will show that histories of method exist. This book is not designed to duplicate them, but to go one step beyond, isolating and describing the ideas that make up teaching methods. The word "idea" is taken in its widest possible sense: it is anything that affects teaching, whether it relates to the classroom itself, to the teacher's study, or to the researcher's workroom. Hence, as well as teaching ideas, there are included here accounts of the development of teaching resources, and treatments of the evolution of psychology and linguistics as they affect language teaching. As we have set our bounds at teaching, which is not automatically linked to learning, we have had to neglect the informal learning of languages that did not achieve scholarly and political acceptance. Though languages other than Greek and Latin were learned before the thirteenth century, they were not formally taught and thus they find no place here. Likewise, methods are of little interest. For this reason the arrangement of the book is not chronological, but thematic. To classify the ideas which govern the teacher's professional behavior we have adopted the schema used by Mackey in his Language Teaching Analysis. *In this way it is possible to relate each idea to its times, and to comment on the way it has been modified to fit into various types of methods.*

We do not pretend to a world-wide coverage: only the countries whose intellectual traditions are derived from Greece are included. Though these are usually identified with Western Europe and the former colonies, Alexandria, an important center of intellectual life in the Roman Empire, receives some mention; and Soviet Russia, which despite its political differences with Western Europe is really in the same intellectual tradition, has its place beside countries like the United States.

Outside general histories of education, the history of language teaching itself has hardly been treated. Some historians of education have written on the teaching of languages in specific places, but ideas have been hidden behind names and techniques. Some scholars, in compiling histories of ideas or of literary scholarship, have included accounts of language teaching, especially of classical languages. Apart from those like J. E. Sandys, who was genuinely interested in the history of scholarship, the teachers who entered this field often had one of two purposes in mind. Some were concerned with showing that their pet methods had their roots in sound theory and practice. Others wished to show that their own methods were superior to those in fashion. Comenius is an example of the first group[252:chapter 8] *and Lemare of the second.*[655:introduction]

Theories have been put forward about every aspect of language teaching: the matter of the course, the methods of transmission, and the media of teaching. The matter of the course and its arrangement are determined by the procedures of selection and gradation. Both are essential as, on the one hand, it is unnecessary and impossible to learn an entire language, and, on the other, for learning to take place the items to be absorbed must be arranged in some order.

Methods of transmission fall under the headings of presentation and repetition. Each of these processes has a different purpose. By the procedures of presentation the material of the language is introduced to the pupil, the main preoccupation of the teacher being the inculcation of the four systems of language: semantic, lexical, grammatical, and phonological. On the other hand, by repetition the teacher initiates the pupil to language use. Thus, this process is concerned with the four skills of listening, speaking, reading, and writing. In practice it is difficult to separate the two, as the type of presentation is usually chosen in view of the repetition techniques which are to follow.

As the techniques of presentation and repetition are shaped by the means of transmission at hand, the media of teaching come into a history of ideas. The teacher is the oldest, but the characteristics required of him vary according to the goal of the whole language-teaching process. As a teaching tool the book has been in common use only since the Renaissance. Machines are a modern invention, dating from the beginning of this century. All these media have had an important effect on the evolution of ideas, acting as catalysts for new ideas and guardians of the old. Underlying these three is the environment in which language teaching takes place, and the use to which the teacher or learner wishes to put it.

Matter, methods, and media relate ultimately to the provenance of ideas. Though ideas can be conveniently grouped according to the modern sciences of linguistics and psychology, their roots are to be found in the traditional disciplines of grammar and philosophy, even when their development is totally independent of abstract research. The gradual crystallization of the ancient sciences into linguistics, education, philosophy, and the natural sciences took place independently of the classroom, but in time deeply affected the thought and practice of language teachers (see schema on page 394). Through language teaching these sciences had a formative influence on philosophical and literary studies, which in turn have had a reciprocal effect on teaching. It is only during the last hundred years that scholars have divorced these disciplines one from another.

Seeing that education is a function of society, acceptance and rejection of ideas is largely due to social attitudes. Language teaching was a central part of education until the mid-nineteenth century, because it satisfied the aims of the society outside the school. When languages no longer supplied the needs felt by the public, they were tolerated only insofar as their teaching contributed to the formation of skills pupils could use in adult life. In an effort to keep their discipline respected and alive, teachers were forced to choose their methods accordingly.

To claim that one ensemble of ideas is the best would inevitably demand approval of the aims held at one time in history and, more serious, would imply that one was judging one period by the standards of another. In a sense, all ideas we treat are good in that they contributed to achieving the educational purpose of the time. In this we must be guided by the normal pragmatism of the teacher facing his class. Therefore we are concerned only with recording the evolution of ideas and accounting for the changes they have undergone. It is not our place to evaluate any of the ideas treated in this book.

PART I

GETTING THE LANGUAGE ACROSS

INTRODUCTION

The first steps in teaching, i.e., the stage known as "presentation," are concerned with transmitting to the pupil the four systems of language: semantics, lexicon, grammar, and phonology. Ideas on the presentation of semantic and lexical systems are studied together in the chapter on meaning, whereas those on grammatical and phonological presentation are treated separately.

Throughout the history of language teaching, methods of presentation have varied according to the type of mastery required of the pupil. During the Middle Ages and the eighteenth and nineteenth centuries, languages were usually presented through the codifications of grammarians. It was expected that skill in using languages would follow from an intellectual knowledge of their formal analyses. However, during the classical era, the Renaissance, and the early twentieth century, it was intuitive command of the target languages that was required, formal knowledge being seen as a mere reinforcement of practical mastery.

There are two themes to be traced in the development of presentation. The first is an alternation between formal and informal approaches to the problem; the second is a marked difference between classical and modern languages. In general, classicists have tended to be more formal than teachers of modern languages; and each group has distrusted the other. The depth of feeling was illustrated at the end of the nineteenth century by the Direct Methodists, who were inclined to reject classical languages out of hand, the intensely formal methods of presentation in vogue at the time being taken as a pretext for a wholesale condemnation of the discipline of classics. In spite of the early efforts of W. H. D. Rouse to apply the Direct Method to Latin and Greek, it was only during the 1960's that the gap in communication began to close, as it had closed once before, during the late Renaissance.

Presentation is a purely pedagogical procedure, not to be confused with language analysis. Though the linguist or grammarian produces a workable analysis of language, it is not his place to determine how this is to be presented. It is up to the teacher to adapt the grammarian's material to his own purposes. Failure to do this, or even to see the need for it, is at the root of most of the trouble in language teaching, whether the methods of presentation used draw their raw material from traditional Latinate analyses or recent types of language analysis designated as more "scientific."

1

TEACHING MEANING

In order to know Latin one must learn:
1. the meaning of the Latin words;
2. the inversions usual in Latin, or the transpositions of words that are not placed in the "natural order";
3. the ellipses;
4. the turns of phrase peculiar to the Latin language.

1722 (Du Marsais) in 347 : 96

Meaning is the most obvious aspect of language, and its transmission is that which first comes to mind in any consideration of language learning. Teaching word meaning presents two aspects—familiarizing the pupil with the connection between a concept and its linguistic sign, and acquainting him with the other linguistic, emotional, and material associations of the sign itself. To better demonstrate this we shall divide this treatment of the teaching of meaning according to Harold Palmer's classification: material association, context, translation, and definition.[836:77] In the classroom these four headings are represented by associating words of the foreign language with the things and actions they signify, with pictures, with corresponding lexical units of the first language, and with units in the second language.

1.1 GESTURES AND OBJECTS

A child starts learning language by direct association between objects and words, and this, as the most natural way of learning, can be found in the classroom as early as St. Augustine. Indeed, in spite of the predominance of other types of demonstration during the Middle Ages and the nineteenth century, it would be extremely rash to assume that it has ever fallen out of use.

1.1.1 Mime and Demonstration

During the second third of the twentieth century the concept of situation caught the attention of linguists and language teachers. Though the impetus for this development originally came from the work of Saussure,[317:99] linguists seized on the idea, making words depend for their meaning on verbal and situational context. Thus the stage was set for the linking of meaning, structure, and situation that was at the root of twentieth-century methods. A typical development was the methodology of the Ecole normale de St-Cloud, which used contextual ideas from the work of Peter Guberina in the late 1950's. New linguistic material was always introduced by illustrating or reproducing the social situation in which it would most probably be found.[490:435]

This approach, though rediscovered this century, was far from new, confirming as it did the opinions and practice of St. Augustine:

> We do not learn from words as mere words, that is as sound and noise. Those which are not signs cannot be words. If I hear a word I do not know whether it is a word or not until I know what it means. Once we establish its link with things, we come to know its meaning.
>
> A.D. 389 (St. Augustine) 60: §xi

It seems that in his own classroom in North Africa he did use direct methods, but the evidence is very slim. The staid medieval classroom failed to continue this development, as language was taught mainly for literary purposes. The result was that words came to be linked directly with other words, and only indirectly with reality.

It was the Moravian bishop, Comenius, who refocused educators' attention on the possibilities of demonstration and activity in the classroom. The Comenian classroom, judging from his later educational treatises, was one in which both teacher and pupils were in constant activity. Teacher demonstration was followed by pupil imitation: Comenius had little use for static learning in anything.[260:288] As far as languages were concerned, he regarded it a waste of time and energy to learn a language for its own sake, and assumed that at the same time he was acquiring Latin, a pupil would be forming new concepts and associations. The principle of demonstration by the teacher was now clear, and was continued in the schools of Pestalozzi.

But those following Pestalozzi seemed to emphasize teacher activity at the expense of pupil imitation. Thus Lemare, a nineteenth-century admirer of Pestalozzi, places the main emphasis on pupil observation:

> When for the first time a child hears the sentence: 'Shut the door,' if he does not see a gesture accompanying the order, if he does not see it carried out immediately, he will not know what it means. . . . But if a voice from somewhere shouts, 'Shut the door,' and someone rushes up to close it . . . , he perceives the sense of the expression he has heard.
>
> 1819 (Lemare) 655: viii

Active demonstration became one of the most important principles of the Natural Method, so called because its adherents believed that they were following the way in which a child learned his language from his family and environment. To traditional-minded teachers, its demonstration techniques often became the object of sardonic amusement:

> I have it from a very trustworthy authority that in some New England town a teacher of the 'Natural Method' gambols around the room to express the idea *to run.* If this be the general case, school committees will no longer be called upon to deliver certificates of proficiency to teachers of Languages: this duty will devolve on P. T. Barnum.
>
> 1878 (Lévy) 665: 16

While so far mime and demonstration had remained occasional tools for language teaching, with the work of Gouin mime became an essential part of teaching. In introducing and drilling his cycles, which were merely accounts of simple processes, he reinforced the impact of words by miming the action described, expecting the pupils to mime in their turn. The early twentieth-century psychologists who were attempting to justify or refute teaching methods on psychological grounds approved of Gouin, remarking that the link between meaning and activity was stronger if the action was being described while it was being performed.[614:77]

Though the Gouin techniques were not transmitted to the Direct Method, the idea behind them was. This was not untypical, as the Direct Method differed from the Natural Method only in its attempts to find a scientific rationale for its procedures. Like the Natural Method the Direct Method aimed at presenting language to the pupil without making him resort to grammatical analysis. But Direct Methodists had recourse to psychology, phonetics, and new types of structural analysis (see Palmer's "Ergonics") to build their courses.

Hence the sociological bias of both methods was one of their notable features. Paul Passy, for instance, remarked that "one could imitate rationally, i.e., use the expressions heard in the circumstances in which they were met."[848:17] Thus, while looking back to Gouin, he anticipates Palmer. For Palmer the key concept was the idea of *spatialization:* a word was remembered by relating it to the place in which it had been learned. Two words learned in the same "place" were easily confused; if learned in separate "places" they could be easily kept apart.[836:85] As he makes clear elsewhere, "place" has a very wide series of parameters, time and circumstance being of as much importance as space in differentiating the "place" in which a thing is learned. While modern methodologists like those of St-Cloud chose pictorial representation to delineate "place," Palmer had already opened the way to actions, objects, and other types of representation as well.

The sense of mission with which the pioneers of each idea put it forward left little room for a trace of humor, so necessary to the protection of a teacher. While the English Association of Assistant

Mistresses warned that attempts at humor could misfire,[54:9] West pointed out that a vivid, dramatic, or amusing situation was a powerful aid to memory.[1149:66] Even so, the need for caution was evident.

1.1.2 Objects and *Realia*

The use of objects to teach meaning probably goes back to the very beginning of language learning, being more common in informal situations than formal. Until the advent of the Direct Method, objects were used in the classroom to illustrate vocabulary which related to things common to the pupil's own culture and that of the new language. Under the Direct Method, such objects were termed *realia* or *realien.* However, certain teachers used this term to distinguish between objects of general relevance and those peculiar to the foreign culture. The literature of the twentieth century shows some confusion in the use of the term. While some, Breul for instance, use the word in the restricted sense, others, like Cole, make it denote pictures, films, plays, and other aids as well as objects peculiar to the foreign country. We prefer to take it in the narrow sense.

The first clear information on the use of objects of general relevance comes from Tudor England. Sir Thomas Elyot, for instance, remarks, "there can be nothyng more convenient than by little and little to trayne and exercise them in speaking of Latin; infourmyng them to know first the names in latin of all thynges that cometh in syght, and to name all the parts of their bodies."[364:33] In the famous scene from *Henry V* in which Princess Katharine's maid tries to teach her some English, we see a little of the practical application of Elyot's advice in the Tudor classroom.

Despite the formalistic tendencies of the time, this tradition lasted through the seventeenth century. Comenius, though more famous for his use of pictures, clearly regarded them as substitutes for the real thing: "Words must not be learned separately from things, for the word can neither exist nor be understood without the thing. But to the extent that word and thing are joined, they exist somewhere and fulfill a certain function."[253:162] The Comenian approach had a particularly enthusiastic following in England, and his doctrines were linked with those of earlier writers like Lubinus, who remarked that only by direct knowledge of an object or action could a child learn its name.[689:25] Outside England, isolated teachers like Lamy (1645-1715) carried on the Comenian tradition, but they gradually slipped away from the main stream. See de Bigault-d'Harcourt[289:64]

Only after two hundred years of verbally oriented teaching was this thread picked up. The Natural Methodists had empirically proved to their own satisfaction that demonstration of meaning through objects was superior to other methods, and in order to justify adopting the practice the Direct Methodists felt impelled to explain it scientifically. To illustrate the connection between a concept (C), the native word (N) and the foreign word (F), Felix Franke drew up the following diagram:

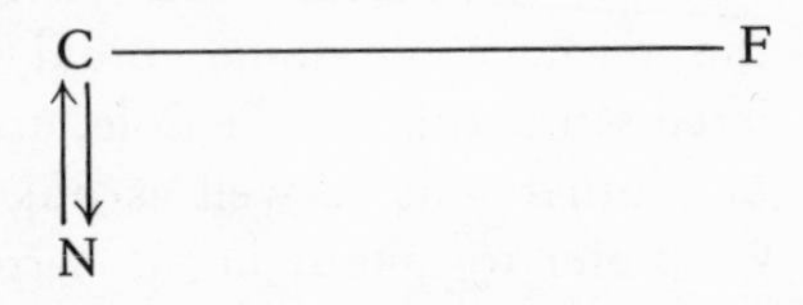

He rejected translation on the grounds that it took the long way round, i.e., FNC. To establish the direct connection between C and F that existed in the mind of the foreign speaker, he suggested object lessons. He saw no reason why the native word should intervene at all.[422:31] There was heartfelt agreement from most of the Direct Methodists.

From the 1900's, these techniques of demonstration were submitted to experiment. The results seemed to indicate that foreign words were more easily learned if they were presented in object lessons than if they were first taught by translation.[1007:163] Later teachers, especially those in the ASTP (Army Special Training Program), which was developed in the United States during the Second World War, adopted the idea. As there was no close supervision, they were free to use their own ingenuity. Angiolillo describes lessons in which the trainees were taught German automotive terms by examining wrecked cars and trucks and railway terms by observing the activity of a marshaling yard.*[5:126] Similar approaches were subsequently developed in the secondary classroom.

In defining the concept of *realia*, the inventors of the Direct Method found a use for the souvenirs that tourists bring home from a foreign country. Insignificant objects of daily life, like tickets, stamps, and coins, became teaching aids around which to build a knowledge of the language and its cultural setting. Breul was one who distinguished this type of object from the others, noting that illustrations of coins and stamps were better than nothing.[153:45] The idea remained alive until the 1960's, but was not given the emphasis it had received earlier.

A similar idea appeared in the kindergartens of Alsace. German-speaking children were taught their French vocabulary by playing with plastic toys shaped like animals and household objects. However, while this worked well with older children, younger children tended to specialize the French word to the toy and retain the Alsatian word for the real thing. But once the child was old enough to recognize that real things could have French names, the words concerned had been thoroughly learned.

1.2 PICTORIAL PROCEDURES

Though modern book illustrations and wall charts have a sophistication of concept and use that is directly traceable to twentieth-century technology, teaching through pictures was done by the ancient Chinese. In the West it is not found consistently before the Renaissance, though there is some evidence of it during the Middle Ages.

In the early Middle Ages it seems to have been an accidental offshoot of the practice of illuminating manuscripts and illustrating them with little line drawings in the margin. It seems that the first books to be so treated were psalters and liturgical books, cheap copies of which often found their way into the classroom.*[174] Copies from the schools of the early Middle Ages, e.g., those of Jarrow and the Carolingian court, were usually not illustrated, but in the centuries following there is some evidence that illustrated copies of vocabularies, psalters, and editions of classical works were used in the classroom.

These drawings were executed primarily for ornament and, in sacred books, secondarily as an aid to devotion. There was little attempt at historical accuracy, the figures being costumed in medieval dress and equipped with medieval tools. But this did have an advantage in that a reader or learner would link the word to something with which he was familiar. In most psalters the link was strengthened by putting the illustration in the margin or even in the text. There are some manuscripts in which the text intrudes on the illustration space for lack of room.

Perhaps the first deliberate point-by-point linking of illustration to text was effected by the illustrators of the bestiaries, books dealing with animals described by travelers and in the Bible. The artist had little to go on besides the text and gave his imagination full rein. The drawings doubled as headings to the appropriate section and were often labeled, a device going back to early hagiographical drawings. Every feature of the animal depicted was derived from a passage in the text (see Figure 1).

Humanist recommendations for the free use of illustrations were based on some implications of medieval practice.[1108:vv391-394] Other subjects in the curriculum used both charts and direct observation of phenomena in teaching. But the Renaissance classroom did not offer ideal conditions for the use of visual aids. All classes were taught in the same room under the control of one master, and effective displays were not easy to arrange. However, contemporary evidence shows that pictures were used, at least in private tutoring: "It is a greate forderance in lerning as well to know the names of things as the things self by their pictures and . . . the want of a painter causeth both him and me to stay." Palsgrave (1530).[*96:113] At about the same time the Dutch grammarian, Vossius, recommended the use of cheap woodcuts to teach pupils the names of things without recourse to the vernacular.[289:18] In the context of the quotation it is certain

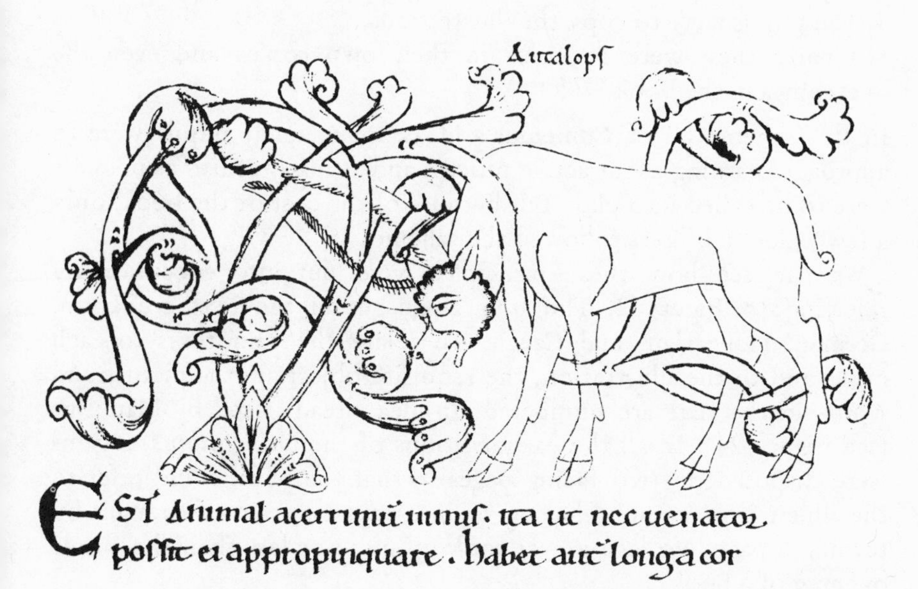

Figure 1. Antelope from Twelfth-century Bestiary (Bodl. MS. Laud. Misc. 247) from T. S. R. Boase, *English Art 1100-1216*, Clarendon Press, Oxford, 1953.

that this method of teaching was considered more useful in private tutoring than in school.

The first fully thought-out scheme of teaching vocabulary with pictures was that of Comenius, whose *Orbis sensualium pictus* first appeared in 1654. It was a development of his *Ianua linguarum reserata*, which was merely a vocabulary ordered by centers of interest. In the *Orbis sensualium pictus* each section was headed by a picture, correlation between text and illustration being assured by numbering the parts of the picture that were specifically referred to in the text. Comenius envisaged five steps in using the book:

1. The pupils were to familiarize themselves with the book itself;
2. They were to make sure they knew the vernacular names of everything depicted in the book;

3. If possible, the teacher was to show them the real thing;
4. The pupils were to copy the illustrations;
5. Finally they were to color in their own copies and even the etchings in the book.[257:6]

In this scheme all of Comenius's ideas are merged: pupils were to approach learning as an active process and as many senses as possible were to be called into play. But because of the cost of the book, only a few ardent admirers followed the scheme.

We can see how these principles were put into execution by referring to Figure 2. The four languages in the text are Latin, German, Hungarian, and Czech. To relate the four texts to each other and to the illustration, the requisite objects in the picture and words in the text are numbered, an idea already used by Manutius (see Figure 24). In all the early editions of the *Orbis pictus*, lessons were disposed on two facing pages so that the pupil could refer to the illustration without having to interrupt his train of thought by turning a page. No lesson ever took up more or less than the whole opening of a book.

Beyond occasional references, wall charts do not figure largely in the educational literature of the time. However they seem to have been used extensively by the Oratorians who kept schools in Paris during the seventeenth century.[*58:177] Our authorities specifically mention that these charts were in color, as if this was a new departure; but the evidence available does not allow us to draw firm conclusions. As the bilingual dictionary developed, pictorial methods disappeared from the classroom. But with the slow return of direct methodology during the nineteenth century came an equally slow development of charts and pictures. By 1868 teachers were using charts in the classroom and improved methods of commercial production were assuring a supply in the schools.

Despite these early experiments two centuries of almost total neglect of pictures followed Comenius. Illustrations slowly drifted back into the language text during the first half of the nineteenth century, but without any real plan. For instance, the only illustration in Sadler's English grammar (1879), reproduced here as Figure 3, is

(286)

CXL.

Miles. Der Soldat.
A' Vitéz. (Katona fegy veres.)
Wogak [Zoldnÿř]

Si bellandum est,
scribuntur milites. 1

Horum arma sunt,
galea f. I. (cassis) 2
f. III.
(quæ ornátur
cristâ)
armatúra, f. I.
cujus partes sunt,
torques III. ferreum, 3
m. II.
thorax, 4 m III.
brachialia, 5
ocreæ ferreæ, 6
mánicæ, 7
cum loricâ, 8
& scuto (clypeo:) 9
hæc sunt arma defensiva,

Wañ man kriegen soll/
werden geworben Sol-
[daten. 1

Deren Waffen sind/
der Helm (Bickelhaube) 2
(welcher gezieret wird
mit dem Federbusch)
der Harnisch (Rüstung)
dessen Stücke sind/
der Kragen/ 3
der Brustharnisch/ 4
die Armschienen/ 5
die Beinschienen/ 6
die Blechhandschuhe/ 7
sambt dem Pantzer 8
und Schild: 9
dieses sind Schutzwaf-
fen.

Hogyha hadakozni kell
katonákat 1 (hadat) fo-
gadnak,

Ezeknek fegyverek
a' sisak (vas süvëg) 2
(a' mely felékesíttetik
ezinimerrel, tollal)
a' vas-fegyver derék
mellynek részei,
a' vas-gallér, 3
a' mely (derék-vas, 4
a' karvasok, 5
a' vas-saruk, 6
a' plëhes kesztyűk, 7
a' pánczéllal 8
épayssal eggyütt: 9
ezek az óltalomra való
fegyverek.

Kdy wogna ma byti,
werbugi (popisugi)
wogaküw/ 1
Tychto zbroge sau/
ssissak/ 2
(ktery se prjozdobuge
Pérem)
Rystunk
kterého častky sau/
Galjři železny 3
Presnik 4 (kabat železny)
karwasse 5
Nákoleni 6
rukawice železne 7
z Pancyrem 8
a pawezau: 9
tato gest Braň pro o-
branu.
Offen-

Figure 2. Soldier from Comenius, *Orbis pictus* (1658).[257a:286] Copy in the Widener Library, Harvard

Figure 3. Diagram from P. Sadler, *Grammaire pratique de la langue anglaise.*[987] Copy from le Petit Séminaire de Québec

the prototype of many later representations of prepositional relationships: birds are pictured in or near a cage and the various spatial relationships are shown with the appropriate prepositions. Later users of this device managed to refer the whole picture to only one central point, a refinement Sadler misses. Sauveur too uses pictures, but they are more pegs on which to hang a story or a reading exercise, and to this end, like the bestiary illustration, they were linked fairly carefully with the text.

At the end of the nineteenth century a renewed interest in Comenius prompted a reissue of his works, the *Orbis pictus* attracting the most attention. The 1887 edition of J. W. Bardeen followed the English edition of 1727 very closely, but Bardeen seems to assume that the book would be used solely for the inspiration of the teacher. Four years before, a modernized edition, presumably for pupil use, had been published in Prague: the copperplates of the original had been replaced by water colors in the ruling style, and both the text and the content of the pictures had been brought up to date (see Figure 4). But the effect of this revival of interest was negligible.

As the Direct Method began to influence the style and content of the textbooks, illustrations showed the effect of both old and new styles. The English grammar of F. Berger adopted the Comenian idea of basing a text on a picture, the parts of which were numbered. The book also included maps and photographs of English coins. Such illustrations were merely miniatures of wall charts. In general, the theme was that of a limited center of interest, pictures of the time mostly depicting an improbable agglomeration of household articles, school equipment, clothes, or common tools. Charts and pictures of this type lasted well into the 1960's. It is worth noting that this sort of thing existed in books to teach in classical languages as well as in modern language texts, the turn-of-the-century editions of classical authors including line drawings, rubbings, and photographs of classical *realia.*

In spite of the availability of certain types of pictures, teachers faced with special problems had to improvise. During the First World War the United States Army had to deal with many groups of conscripts drawn from minorities that did not speak English. In order to find suitable material, the instructors carried out research resembling the language and area studies, which later became current in the 1950's, summarizing their results by making charts out of photographs cut from the *National Geographic Magazine.*[636] As these conscripts were, in many cases, totally ignorant of anything outside their immediate environment, these charts taught the learners about real things as well as about language, thus putting into practice the basic approach of Comenius to language teaching.

In the field of pictorial charts no advance was made until after the Second World War. Researchers at the Ecole normale de St-Cloud and at universities in the United States worked independently on the

MILES. — VOJÁK. — DER SOLDAT. — LE SOLDAT. 205

antehac mercede con-ducti, nunc conscri-buntur delectu e civibus.	ondy za plat najati jsouce, nyní vybí-rají se odvodem z občanů.	ehemals wurden sie um Lohn geworben, jetzt werden sie durch Conscription aus Bürgern ausgehoben.	autrefois on les enrôlait à la solde, aujourd'hui on les recrute parmi les citoyens par conscription.

XCIII.

Miles.	Voják.	Der Soldat.	Le Soldat.
Milites sunt aut pedites	Vojáci jsou buď pěší	Der Soldat ist entweder Fusssoldat	Les soldats sont ou d'infanterie

206 MILES. — VOJÁK. — DER SOLDAT. — LE SOLDAT.

aut equites, etiam tormentarii et a., et vestiuntur cultu militari.	nebo jízdní, také dělostřelci a j., a odívají se stejno-krojem.	oder Reiter, auch Kanonier u. a.; sie sind mit Uniformen bekleidet.	ou cavaliers ou canonniers etc., et portent l'uni-forme.
In capite gerunt petasum militarem [1]) vel galeam [2]), quae ornatur crista [3]);	Na hlavě nosí čáku [1]) nebo přilbici [2]), která jest okrášlena chocholem [3]);	Auf dem Kopfe tragen sie den Czako [1] oder Helm [2]), welchen ein Federbusch [3]) ziert;	Sur la tête ils ont le shako [1]) ou le casque [2]), orné d'un panache [3]);
corpus protegit vestis militaris [4]), pannis coloratis [5]) decorata, super quam equites loricati gestant cata-phractam [6]), tum bracae [7]), quae interdum desinunt in caligis [8]), et sagum [9]).	tělo kryje kabá-tec [4]), opatřený výložky [5]), přes nějž kyrysníci mají brnění [6]), dále spodky [7]), jdoucí časem do bot [8]), a plášť [9]).	den Körper deckt der mit Aufschlägen [5]) versehene Waffenrock [4]), über welchem die Kürassiere Harnische [6]) tragen, ferner die Beinkleider [7]), welche manchmal in den Stiefeln [8]) stecken, und der Mantel [9]).	le corps se couvre de la tunique [4]) garnie de parements [5]), par-dessus laquelle les cuirassiers portent la cuirasse [6]), puis des pantalons [7]), quelquefois fourrés dans les bottes [8]), et du manteau [9]).
Eorum arma sunt: apud pedites	Jejich zbraň jest: u pě-choty	Ihre Waffen sind: bei der Infanterie	Voici leurs armes: chez l'in-fanterie

Figure 4. Soldiers from *Orbis pictus* (1883).[258:205] Copy from the Widener Library, Harvard

problem and, as is not uncommon in teaching research, came to much the same conclusion. The aim was to make pictures that could teach or exercise structures. Both groups of researchers found that certain situations lent themselves to teaching specific structures: buying and selling, for instance, taught dative constructions.[787:55] They both relied heavily on Palmer's theory of spatialization, seemingly without acknowledgment. The method of realization was different in each case. Whereas the Americans constructed wall charts without integrating them into a connected course, the French put out a complicated series of filmstrips which were intended to be used with tapes. The best known course using this approach was *Voix et Images de France*; there were, as well, several less ambitious *méthodes audio-visuelles* for other languages.

Though the use of pictures and objects was meant to prevent translation, many teachers were aware that a pupil would automatically work out his own translated equivalent of the native word denoting the object. This point Harold Palmer had made thirty years before the appearance of the *méthodes audio-visuelles.* This uneasiness over pictures was heightened by the postwar consciousness of differences in the meaning of pictures, gestures, and objects according to cultural milieu. One of the first exhaustive treatments of this problem in relation to language teaching was that of Lado.[639] In Europe, consciousness of cultural disparity caused some uneasiness over the validity of audio-visual methods. There was some doubt about the effectiveness of the picture in conveying meaning to pupils of a culture different from that of the artist who drew it: Greimas notes in an article on TV teaching that audio-visual methods seemed to assume that everybody had the same vision of the world, and expressed his doubts about its truth.[482:141] Following the lead of American and French teachers some experimenters developed a method of language teaching based on comic strips, which was related to the Gouin cycle. As well as teaching word meaning, such textbooks acted as an introduction to composition.[135:17] Though the first experiments were carried out in the late 1930's, this procedure was not popular until after the Second World War.

1.3 NATIVE-LANGUAGE EQUIVALENTS

When faced with an unfamiliar word, one's first reaction is to find out what it "means," and the answer usually comes in the form of another word or in a verbal expression. It is natural that this procedure should be used in learning foreign languages; and, indeed, it is one of the oldest techniques of demonstrating word meaning, being found as far back as the schools of the Roman Empire. Two variants of the technique have been in common use: exact translation and paraphrase in the pupil's own language.

1.3.1 Exact Translation

During the twentieth century the *avant-garde* of language teachers refused to consider translation as a valid procedure in teaching meaning. The majority attitude was well put by West: "Every time a child refers to an English-Vernacular dictionary his mind is switched out of English and he is encouraged to translate instead of thinking in English."[1154:1] Others claimed that the vernacular word was useful as long as it did not become a permanent crutch.[207:35] There are very few periods of teaching that have resolved this conflict of opinion.

Though bilingual lexicography first appeared among the Akkadians in 2500 B.C., as far as the West is concerned, it was a Roman invention. But apart from isolated references in treatises on rhetoric, little is known about it. Greek-Latin glossaries were used in the schools of Alexandria and Gaul, and between the end of the Empire and the beginning of the eighth century there seems to have been further activity in the field. Vernacular-Latin glosses take their place beside the Greek-Latin; but whether they are classroom documents or monuments to intellectual curiosity cannot often be determined. According to W. M. Lindsay, extant glossaries, such as the Epinal, Leyden, and Erfurt, were compiled from vernacular glosses written into the margins of manuscripts.[*116:vi] The arrangements of these early glossaries varied; some were alphabetical, others arranged to a primitive concept of the semantic field. By the ninth century, the field arrangement had become standard, being used by Aelfric and the monastic teachers of the later Middle Ages.

The full-scale dictionary made its appearance during the Renaissance. Owing to the prevailing custom of learning several languages at once through the intermediary of Latin, these were often multilingual, including as many as seven languages (see 78). At the same time, dictionaries were published in which Latin did not figure. The multilingual approach came to an end in the seventeenth century as polyglot texts like the *Ianua linguarum* went out of fashion. In his treatise on translation, Etienne Dolet writes: "And this technique is (as far as I have seen in my reading) not to follow the aphabetical order, as most teachers do, but to relate things to things, and to link words of similar meaning."[333:II:iii]

Only from the late eighteenth century did the bilingual dictionary become a standard part of the teacher's arsenal. From the mid-seventeenth century, however, bilingual vocabularies became a normal aid in grammars and readers. Usually they were arranged according to semantic fields or centers of interest, probably because alphabetical indexes are not such effective learning tools as vocabularies arranged according to subject. Dictionaries, however, being works of reference rather than tools of learning, were arranged alphabetically. Publishing dictionaries that translated in both directions, i.e., from the first to the second language and vice versa was, it seems, a nineteenth-century development.

Nineteenth-century teachers, in general, saw translation as the only sure method of transmitting meaning. This article of faith was challenged first by the Natural Methodists, then by the Direct Method. Yet there were many Direct Methodists who considered translation to be of considerable value:

> As any hint of exaggeration must be avoided, I must add that it would not be good to reject, absolutely and systematically, all recourse to the mother tongue. In exceptional circumstances it could happen that one might be in too much of a hurry to use gestures and explanations in the foreign language.
>
> 1899 (Passy) 848: 16

Later commentators on the Direct Method were inclined to agree, Peter Hagboldt even remarking of Franke (see §1.1.2) that, in connecting a familiar concept with foreign word, it was almost impossible to avoid some recall of the native words to act as a prop.[502:21] Yet one can understand the extremism of the later Direct Methodists, who, stung by the scorn of traditional teachers, rejected every part of the old approach.

Unfortunately for the Direct Method, rejection of translation became its trademark, Palmer even going so far as to describe this opinion as the "fallacy of the Direct Method." Palmer held that the use of translated equivalents was a necessary preventative for mistakes.[836:99] Though both these opinions lasted well into the second third of the twentieth century, some degree of accommodation was reached. F. G. French summed up the compromise by laying down that if translation led to mistakes, it should be avoided, but that it should be used if it helped to avoid mistakes.

1.3.2. Explanations in the First Language

There are many cases in which the foreign word cannot be translated directly, either because the object or concept does not exist in both languages, or because a periphrasis is demanded by the circumstances of teaching: "When English is used it should be by the teacher and only when needed to paraphrase new material before beginning practice in French."[1019:7] As a teaching procedure this is undoubtedly very ancient, but the fluctuations in the meaning of the word "translation" make the separation of this technique from that of ordinary translation quite difficult. One can see in Aelfric the modern technique as described above, and there seems to have been no discernible development since.

1.4 EXPLANATIONS IN THE SECOND LANGUAGE

This falls under three heads: inference from context, definition, and etymology. All three can be traced back to classical practice, their only period of eclipse being the eighteenth and nineteenth centuries.

1.4.1 Inferences from Context

Twentieth-century teachers treated the sentence as the unit of teaching in order to give pupils a base from which to infer the meaning of words new to them. Close connection with the situation involved in the sentence was also an important feature of the approach. Thus the audio-visual methods developed by CREDIF presented all linguistic items to the pupil by means of real situations. As a first step, these were depicted by pictures accompanied by oral texts; then the pupil was made to take part in the situation by repeating the text himself.[490:12] But this was far from new, having its roots in the sound practice of former times.

Illustration of fine shades of meaning by placing the word in a meaningful context is a most natural way of clarification. During the first century B.C. it was a common Alexandrian practice, and was taken over by the Roman grammarians in their *orthographiae,* a form of textbook that continued during the Middle Ages. Despite the title, spelling was only one of the interest of the genre: usage and nuances of meaning were accorded equal importance. The *orthographiae* were distinguished by the elegance of their language and the pithiness of their examples:

> *Comminus* per duo m, *eminus* per unum m. Comminus cum gladiis pugnamus; eminus cum lanceis. (*Comminus* is spelt with two ms, *eminus* with one. We fight at close quarters (comminus) with swords, and at some distance (eminus) with spears.)
>
> 775 (Alcuin) 24: 906A

Obviously, little improvement is possible in a technique such as this.

A thousand years later Palmer sounded a warning against uncritical acceptance of any one way of teaching meaning, preferring to combine procedures and giving precedence to inferential methods like the above.[836:91] Except among fanatical adherents to the Direct Method, this was the orthodox position, representing a return to the philosophy behind the medieval *orthographiae*. An illustration of this development is given by the dictionaries, both unilingual and bilingual, which list examples of usage under head words. Yet context has hardly ever been used alone as a means of demonstrating meaning; it is usually coupled with some type of definition.

1.4.2 Definition

Being an integral part of lexicography in the mother tongue, definition is a very ancient means of transmitting meaning. In the *orthographia* of Palaemon (A.D. 75), we find the following: "*ludibrium* and *ludicrum: ludibrium* implies insult to another person; *ludicrum* is enjoyed by the perpetrator without amusement at another's expense."[834:315] Until the Renaissance it was not felt necessary to separate the three aims of illustrating meaning, establishing the difference between synonyms, and regulating spelling. In fact, the distinction between paronyms and synonyms was the most frequent mode of definition, and as hairsplitting became more to the medieval taste, this method of defining meaning grew in importance. For example, Remigius of Auxerre wrote: "There is this difference between *perpetuus* and *aeternus: perpetuus* denotes lacking beginning, end, and succession of time; *aeternus* lacks beginning and end, but takes into account the passing of time."[940: §7.15] There has been little further development since his time in this technique.

The Renaissance teacher was concerned with expanding vocabulary and evolved a technique in the *copiae* by which the technique of definition was reversed: the word defined was that known and it was the definition which was new. Erasmus was a particular expert at this, being able to produce two hundred ways of saying "I was delighted with your letter."[368: book 2 § 33] But the pupil more usually met something like the following:

Es mihi charissimus:
Nemo est omnium, in quem magis, quam in te mea sit propensa benevolentia,

qui mihi te sit charior, quem ego vehementius quam te diligam: quam ego maiore quam te benevolentia prosequar; magis ex animo quam te diligam.[1]
1571 (Manutius) 713: 7

What is notable here is that it was the point of books like this to expand vocabulary and enable pupils to write in a more telling fashion. The evil days on which composition fell in the next century effectively destroyed this type of introduction to the riches of vocabulary.

In the twentieth century, the names most closely connected with definition in language teaching are those of Michael West and C. K. Ogden. Ogden was one of the inventors of Basic English, and West used some of his principles in writing the *Definition Vocabulary* (1935) and the *New Method Dictionary* (1941). West adopted the idea that all adequate definitions could be based on about 1,500 words of very wide meaning. His theory was that in order to survive in a foreign-language environment, a person needs to ask questions about a very broad range of necessities of daily life, not merely to make remarks about the commonplaces at the head of the frequency lists. To gain their effect such questions have to be descriptive: Thus if a learner wants to find a faucet he will ask for something that water comes out of when you turn a handle. Though few lexicographers have worked out the theory with the rigor of Michael West, this technique of definition is that of many dictionaries.

1.4.3 Etymology

One feature of traditional teaching that drew the anger of the Direct Methodists was its reliance on etymology as a tool for teaching spelling and meaning.

During the classical era etymology had been considered the most accurate court of appeal on word meanings and shapes:

Etymology, which investigated the origin of words, was called 'marking' (*notatio*) by Cicero because Aristotle used the word *σύμβολον*, which means mark (*nota*). For Cicero himself, who used to coin words, held in great

1 "There is nobody for whom I feel more affection than you, who is dearer to me than you; whom I love more deeply than you; of whom I think with more tenderness; who is closer to my heart."

respect the scholarship involved in tracing one word to another as this was one way of discovering truth.

A.D. 100 (Quintillian) 923: I.vi.28

However, as far as modern scholars are concerned, classical etymology was not exact enough to inspire confidence. Varro and other professional grammarians were not sure what relation Greek had to Latin, and some even tried to cover all possibilities by working out two etymons for Latin words–one based on Italic dialects and one on Greek. This confusion did not, however, prevent inspired insights: Varro connected the Latin *harena* with the Sabine *fasena*, for instance. But during the sixth century, owing to the increased tendency towards archaism in scholarship, etymology took a central place in regulating spelling, usage, and meaning.

Allegory ruled the scholarship of the time; and it seems that the more fanciful an etymology was, the more acceptable it was to the scholars. For example, Isidore of Seville (550) claimed that: "*Meridies* is used to refer to midday as the day is then purer. *Meros* means *pure. Meros* is Greek, and *purus* is Latin."[*12:31] This and similar tendencies to break up words and find etymologies for their dismembered parts dominated the Middle Ages, reaching their height in the grammarian, Vergilius Maro. It is not at all unlikely that his work is satirical:

Whether compound or simple, what does *verbum* mean? It is a compound of two corrupt words, *ver* from *verbere* [sic] to beat, and *bum* from *bucina*, a trumpet. This is Vergil's ruling: *verbum* comes from two roots, *ver* from *verbere*, the blow the tongue gives the mouth, and *bum* from *bucina*, the cavity in which the sound resonates.

seventh century (Vergilius) 1106: 196

Despite this sort of tomfoolery, there was some imaginative etymological scholarship being done: "*Dius fidius* seems to mean *the son of Jupiter*. The Greek for Jupiter is *Dius, fidius* is a transformation of *filius*, because the ancients often replaced an *l* by a *d*, saying *fidius* for *filius*, and *sedda* for *sella.*"[711:410] During the Renaissance the importance of etymology did not diminish, remaining an important tool in the *copiae* and vocabulary manuals. Interest in living languages and the realization that Romance languages were direct descendants of Latin, and thus related genetically, prompted the application of etymology to the problems of teaching French, Italian, and Spanish. By the early seventeenth century it had become one of the key disciplines in language teaching. Comenius, while realizing that the approach was of considerable value, counseled caution, preferring even to avoid the procedure if he felt a reasonable doubt about the accuracy of the results.[257:58] His attitude did little to reduce the vogue of etymology in class.

Etymology was regarded as more important in classics than in modern-language teaching. During the next two centuries, the concept of the "root" or "primitive" held a key position in the expansion of vocabulary. An eighteenth-century pupil noted in the copy of Schickard held at the Petit Séminaire de Québec: "By comparing the different significations of a Hebrew word in all its several shapes, we may arrive at the most proper and precise or the original sense of it." This approach dominated Latin and Greek. The "root" was not what modern philologists take it to be, but rather a head word from which a family of derivatives was seen to come:

	Adj.
Macer, dénué, ou peu gras,	cri, crae
Maceria, mur ou plâtras	ae. f.

1789 (Duplan) 351: 80

In this case *macer* (thin) is taken as the root. This concept was abandoned during the nineteenth century. The editor of the 1861 edition of the Port-Royal *Jardin des racines grecques* remarks on the difference in conception between him and original authors:

> We do not take the word *root* in the same way as Lancelot who meant by it a word which forms derivatives. For us the root is not a word but merely the essential part of a word, and this fundamental part is to be found in derivatives as well as in primitives. Thus, Lancelot considers the word λύω

as a root, while for us the syllable λυ-, which we find in λύσις etc., is the root.

1861 (Regnier) 49: 10

During the nineteenth century, etymology had its vogue in both modern languages and the mother tongue. A revival of interest in Anglo-Saxon resulted in short-lived missionary efforts in the schools of England. As far as foreign languages were concerned, similarity in vocabulary and grammatical system brought about etymological orientations of self-teaching courses of German for English speakers. As justification of his etymological approach, F. Thimm, the author of a number of modern-language grammars popular during the 1870's, stated somewhat rashly: "German and English have a connecting link in both being based on Anglo-Saxon, which induced a greater similarity in the methods of expression than exists between any other living languages."[1073:v]

Though there was little place for it in the Direct Method, teachers treated etymology with some respect: "The linguistic relation of English to French and German should be carefully explained. The relation of numerous words like *finir* and *finish* or *leib* and *life*, might very well be shown."[153:29] Twentieth-century teachers tended to be cautious, modern-language teachers more than classicists, as it was now accepted that differences in meaning between etymon and derivative were not the result of linguistic decay, but a normal process. The literature tends to emphasize the dangers of cognates as emphatically as the teachers of earlier centuries proclaim their usefulness. But this caution did not exclude etymology from the classroom altogether. Many teachers found that incidental references to philology both aroused and held interest, and helped to give a rational background to difficult spellings, irrational paradigms, and semantics.[913:78] The idea does not seem to have been widely accepted by teachers of the time: first, the methods in vogue did not allow for it; second, memories of nineteenth-century abuse of etymology were still alive among older teachers. So it tended to remain a scholastic discipline, and it was not reintegrated into the language teacher's range of techniques.

Thus the teaching of vocabulary and its meaning has passed from the classical and medieval approaches, based on definition and etymology, to the "modern" methods of associating word and thing. To the verbally orientated ways of the previous fifteen centuries, the Renaissance added object lessons, and generalized the first tentative uses of translation. During the next two centuries, owing to the importance of general grammar and the dogma that languages differ only in word-stock, translation was practically the only means of demonstration used in the classroom. With the rise of the Natural and Direct Methods, more than four hundred years after the Humanists first conceived such a full range of teaching approaches, educators reintroduced them, firmly believing that these discoveries were new.

But control of foreign language barely begins with mastery of its vocabulary. For any sort of command, one must be able to manipulate the frame on which the language is built. In other words, vocabulary without grammar is of little practical value.

2

TEACHING GRAMMAR

> Language teachers have always tended to apply language analysis to the teaching of a language; in fact, some of the first descriptions of a language were made for the purpose of teaching it.
>
> 1964 (Mackey) in 698: 30

Since the beginning of language teaching the manner of learning the syntax and flexions of language has been disputed. Accepted methods have ranged from the inductive, by which the pupil himself arrives at rules from examples, to the deductive whereby one proceeds from rules to a knowledge of the language. At all periods of language teaching both have existed, but never on an equal footing. Inductive methods were most fashionable during the late Renaissance and early twentieth century, while deductive approaches reached their greatest development during the late Middle Ages and the eighteenth century.

2.1 INDUCTIVE METHODS

As early as 500 B.C. the inductive principle was recognised by Greek philosophers as the basis of scientific discovery. The Romans, a more practical people, extended its use to the discovery of techniques and the establishment of skills: "...to worry out the various arts by pondering on their practical uses" (Vergil, Georgics I.133). But it was probably St. Augustine who first saw the utility of the principle in the classroom. He conceived learning as a process of passing by abstraction from particular to universal: skills were to be implanted by practice and use. To learn words and meanings one must have the symbolized thing present, at least by representation:

> Once things are known knowledge of words follows. Hearing words does not result in learning. We do not learn words we know; but we can not hope to learn words we do not know unless we have grasped their meaning. This is not achieved by listening to the words, but by getting to know the things signified.
>
> 389 (St. Augustine) 60: XI; 36

Thus, knowledge of reality was more to be sought after than knowledge of words. In language, this implied that one was to seek a practical command of linguistic skills rather than memorize the rules. To meet this aim, St. Augustine popularized dialogued methods of teaching, making the pupil's role in the dialogue part of the act of discovery. Years later, during the Middle Ages, the externals of his methods were fused with the more classical style of rhetoric teaching, and its basic principle was forgotten. It was rediscovered just before the Renaissance.

Among the early attempts at inductive teaching during the fifteenth century were those of Vittorino da Feltre, who founded the *Casa Giocosa* in 1424. This school was formed in the household of Prince Gianfrancesco Gonzaga of Venice, primarily for the education of his two sons. The aim of da Feltre was "applied scholarship."[*186:71] His pupils were not to be scholars, but men of the world whose scholarship was to be a grace and not an obsession. He rejected both the linguistic standards accepted during the Middle Ages and the methods used: classical Latin and Greek were taught, not by formal methods, but through reading, speaking, and imitation.

There were many other revolts against the school grammars. In a letter to a pupil in 1405, Aretinus had pointed out that "we may gain much from Servius, Donatus and Priscian, but more by careful observation in our own reading, in which we must note attentively vocabulary and flexions. . . ."[*223:124] Two influences seem to have pushed this development into the background: the Ciceronianism of Petrarch and the efforts of Baptista Guarino and of da Feltre himself, who, in the name of good style, reacted violently against the Latin of the Middle Ages and imposed a norm based on the classics. As only the exceptional teacher attempted to follow the inductive method of da Feltre, the classical standard reinforced tendencies to follow the medieval methods of teaching by rule from the book.

Vivès carried the inductive approach into the sixteenth century, strongly influencing Rabelais. Vivès adopted da Feltre's method of teaching Latin by induction to small classes of carefully selected pupils. His subsidiary aim was passing on to the vernacular the graces of style he was teaching in Latin and Greek. But because his principles were of universal application, his contemporaries applied them to other subjects, even while excluding them from the language classroom. Owing to the powerful reaction against medieval standards of language, Renaissance teachers preferred to teach by the book to avoid barbarisms. At first nobody seemed to find this odd, although the teaching of other subjects was evolving away from the methods used in language teaching. Rabelais, for example, cast scorn on the bookish training of the old school, recounting how Gargantua was taught manual skills and science by observing nature and watching craftsmen at work. However, his ridicule of grammatical teaching was confined to that of the late Middle Ages: he did not see that what had replaced it was the same in method with different stylistic standards.

This undercurrent of resistance to the official trend persisted right through the Renaissance. For example, Georgius Haloinus Cominius, a minor member of the Erasmian circle, advocated completely abandoning grammar as a teaching method. He is quoted by Despauterius, a contemporary whose Latin and Greek grammars went through edition after edition: "The authority of a grammarian is, in itself, worth nothing. It is clear that the real discipline of grammar was evolved only by the observation of the most cultured orators, historians, poets, and other writers worthy of study" (1520).[*184:569] The reaction of Erasmus was far from favorable: in a letter of reproof dated June 21, 1520, he reaffirmed the necessity of formal grammar to beginners, but admitted that inductive methods could be used at an advanced level. It is tempting to see in the rather brusque Latin of the letter a doctrinaire rigidity. But Erasmus was a man who always chose the middle way. He makes it quite clear to Cominius that he regards rejection of grammar as an excess which was every bit as reprehensible as the opposed devotion to analysis. Probably owing to Erasmus's attitude, Cominius did not publish his *Restauratio linguae latinae* until 1533, though it was first drafted in 1506. One copy survived in a Copenhagen library until 1808.[*184:569]

The sixteenth and seventeenth centuries credited Ratke with the invention of the inductive principle: one can sense the smirk in Schickard's assumption of virtue: "Perhaps you expect me to follow Ratke in doing away with rules—you will be disappointed."[1001:11] The pioneer work was actually shared with Lubinus and Ramus, who started from the principle that "merely to know the universal rules without knowing particular usage is not real and absolute knowledge."[*52:212] Partisans of the formal method were making themselves ridiculous by the variation in standard accepted: Ramus reported bitterly that the learned doctors of the Sorbonne could not make up their minds which was correct, *ego amat* or *ego amo*.[928:15] To remedy the ills of which this was only a symptom, he reclassified Latin grammar along principles not very different from those of the twentiety-century structuralists, and laid down an approach to teaching built on a self-consistent framework which the learner had to discover for himself. His pupils were to be conscious of language as language; rules were to come later. Lubinus in turn attacked the contemporary fashion of teaching grammar as contrary to common sense:

> Now what and how monstrous an absurdity is it . . . to bid them give an account, why they speake Latine right, before they can in any wise speake properly, and of the *δία ὅτι* before they have knowledge of the *τό ὅτι*?
>
> 1550 (trans. Hartlib 1654) 519: 11

Lubinus's attack has a surprisingly modern touch: for him grammar repels the pupils and bores the master; its emphasis on rules encourages, rather than prevents, bad stylistic habits; it clutters the mind with reasons and connections before the facts to be reasoned out are known. His own system starts from two principles: using as many of the pupil's faculties as possible, and starting with the concrete facts of language before dealing with grammatical principles. These men laid the ground for the eighteenth-century insistence on the role of usage as a guide for correctness and elegance of language.

Induction was in the air, Francis Bacon having discussed it at some length:

> And Celsus acknowledgeth it gravely, speaking of the Dogmatic and Empirical Sects of Physicians, that Medicine and Cures were first found out, and then after the reasons and causes were discoursed: & not the Causes first found out, & by light from them the Medicines and Cures discovered.
>
> 1605 (Bacon) 68: 123

In 1626, after several appearances before the English Parliament, Joseph Webbe, an enthusiast for the work of G. H. Cominius, patented an inductive method of language teaching. He had prepared his ground by attacking the usual methods and by experimentation in his own school in London. However, he was unfortunate in that his teaching was verbally oriented and that he was primarily interested in laying a firm foundation for translation from and into the classical languages. His famous contemporary Comenius, who based his similar scheme on knowledge of things, was truer to Renaissance ideals, and his concern with living languages was more in harmony with contemporary fashion. Hence Webbe was overshadowed and forgotten.

Yet one must not exaggerate Comenius's support for inductive methods. In his early years he tried to combine the best of both approaches,[252: 2] though it is clear that for much of his career his sympathies did lie with the less formal school:

> xl. All things are taught and learned through examples, precepts, and exercises.

xli. The exemplar should always come first, the precept should always follow, and imitation should always be insisted on.

1648 (Comenius) 256: 111

In this Comenius was one with Erasmus. The key to effective learning was combining skill in use with as full understanding of the principle as possible. At the stage detailed by the above quotation, the rule was still treated as a prop, but in later years, it was imitation that became the prop to the rule.

In modern languages there was no need to champion inductive methodology, as exhaustive grammatical analyses of spoken languages did not exist—with the notable exception of Palsgrave's monumental treatment of the French language. This, however, was not a popular book; only one edition of a thousand copies was printed and it was greeted with some skepticism: according to Duwes, tutor to Mary Tudor, "I have nat neverthelesse founde rules infalibles because it is nat possible to finde any suche. . . ."[356:1] His own book, based on inductive grammar, went through three editions.

Inductive methodology continued into the seventeenth century. Lamy (1645-1715) put forward the idea later to become the keystone of nineteenth-century natural methodology: that languages were to be learned in the same way as one's mother tongue.[*58:94] Vocabulary was the first system to learn, then grammar by attempting to put words together by imitation of good models. This idea remained alive during the eighteenth century, but its currency was extremely limited: "Rules and general principles are absorbed by the brain following the study of good examples" (Pluche). See Lemare.[655:lxi] Since by the end of the eighteenth century translation had become the basis of language teaching, inductive schemes involving interlinear translation were suggested by Locke and put into practice by Jacotot and Hamilton. The pupil was to learn his foreign languages by dint of relating native equivalents to texts in the language he was learning. As each linguistic unit was learned it provided a base for expansion; Jacotot's comment was: "Learn something thoroughly, and refer everything else to it" (quoted in Payne).[854:1]

Lemare was struck by the learning theory of Rousseau: "We should like each pupil to make his own observations before reading ours, and to come to ordered knowledge himself instead of learning it."[655:xxv] In a footnote he comments: "A thought from Jean-Jacques' *Emile*." His own theory was that the mother tongue was learned by the "language of action," and he suggested that a second language could be learned in the same way. Thus he rules that, though sentences were made up of discrete units, only a fool would dream of teaching units of language one by one. No mother ever tried that approach with her children, so why try it in the classroom?[655:xxvi] The essence of the Lemare method was reliance on analogy. Rules were not to be presented to the pupils, but they were to generalize from imitation of type sentences (see §4.2.3). Where the teacher felt it necessary to formulate a rule, such formulations were based on transformations of type sentences: the rule came only when the pupil could handle a construction with considerable ease. Lemare did not believe that inductive behavior in the classroom excluded translation, his method being deliberately aimed at either free composition or translation from and to Latin.

Since rejection of translation was the watchword of the Natural Method, it is doubtful whether the pioneers of the movement took much notice of the developments already detailed. Acting as if nobody had thought of it before them, they laid out the principle with considerable rigor. Joseph Payne, a disciple of Jacotot, denied that explanation was a necessary part of teaching, claiming that the pupil should be made to discover for himself how to handle his new language.[854:iii] In 1823 this English attack on grammar was paralleled on the other side of the Atlantic by Dufief, who appealed to natural methods of language teaching: "It is evident that the rules of Grammar can not convey the art of language. . . . How then is language to be acquired? I answer by adopting the mode by which nature teaches children their mother tongue."[345:xci] Dufief envisaged saturating the pupil by conversation methods and allowing him to make his own generalizations about rules and customs.

Thirty years later, in 1853, Marcel detailed his concept of language learning, basing himself, like Dufief, on nature to prove his point.

Though he claims Locke as his master, he rejects translation, observing that no child learns his language by this method.[718:I:276] His method is purely empirical, resting on the observation and codification of principles. Its most interesting feature is the recognition of self-teaching as an application of induction, rather than as a necessity forced on one by the lack of a teacher.[718:I:216] Marcel conceives learning as generalization from examples and advocated practice in short concentrated sessions, which had been the position of St. Augustine. The most important contribution by Marcel, and one that was not generally adopted until the Direct Method was seeking to absorb the Natural Method, was precise definition of course aims, both immediate and long-term.

By the 1860's it was well accepted that the most natural method of teaching languages was through conversation. It was in this way that Gottlieb Heness taught standard German to dialect speakers. His friend and follower, Lambert Sauveur, built on the conversation aspect, as is shown by the title of his best-known book, *Causeries avec mes élèves.* Sauveur was not, however, one to ignore reading. In the *Causeries* he remarks that the best way of learning subjunctive constructions is through the study of authors like George Sand, adding, "Only great authors can give us a grasp of this grace of our language."[993:195] It was this approach he used in classics.

Though early Natural Methodists actively repudiated grammar, later adherents to the school sought to systematize the approach by producing textbooks based on induction. Worman and Rougemont's French grammar (1883) followed the Comenian approach to the letter, even to writing a preface that could almost have been written by the master himself. In classical languages, the Greek grammar of Harper and Waters (1888) boasts its inductive methodology.[515:iii] The time was now right, as Kappert was to see thirty years later, for the Direct Method to take over.[614:11]

Yet the impact of the Natural Method had been so slight that Vietor and the Direct Methodists could not rely on the pioneering efforts of the method they were replacing. While admitting that they took their inspiration from the Natural Method, they insisted that they added to it a sound theoretical basis and a systematic approach to language problems, especially the phonological.[1110:4] Perhaps one of the most damaging aberrations of the method was the exaggerated enthusiasm of its less knowledgeable followers, whose attitude was acidly summed up in a parody of a famous couplet from Goethe's *Faust:*

> Sobald die direkte Methode erklingt
> Die Seele in den Himmel springt.
>
> (As soon as the Direct Method blazes forth, the soul springs straight into Heaven.)
>
> quoted by Purin 920: 48

The claims of the Direct Method were met with a fair amount of skepticism, and during the first third of the twentieth century much of the exposition of Direct Method theory was mingled with polemic. In 1903 Schweitzer summed up a discussion of methodology with the claim that the Direct Method was the only easy and logical way of teaching grammar.[1006:7] Thirty years later Gustave Bénédict still found it necessary to accuse his critics of "ignoring the possibilities of mental intuition."[99:22] Yet the method did win fairly wide acceptance: France and Germany gave it official recognition, despite misgivings from a large section of the profession. And in England the method was also widely used. One of the most famous American applications was the "Cleveland Plan" of Emile de Sauzé, which in effect outlived the method itself.

Inductive teaching really caught the public fancy during the Second World War when the teaching profession was short-circuited by the governments concerned, who went to professional linguists for approaches suitable for giving soldiers a limited command of second languages. The most important concept from the Direct Method was the emphasis on inculcating language behavior and avoidance of rules in the classroom, even if they formed the basis of the course planner's thinking.[*5:15] After the war one of the most acute problems was adapting the ASTP program to civilian schools. The rigid avoidance of the mother tongue and of rules was to be relaxed by later theorists, especially when studies of bilingual interference became important in linguistics: Rondeau and Vinay write: ". . . interference must of course be avoided, . . . by bringing the matter to the attention of the student rather than by keeping him in the dark and hoping he does not 'catch on.' "[967:10]

The early Direct Methodists had regarded cultural content as a most important tool in inductive teaching: the pupil was to learn the foreign behavior patterns that went with the language.[*57:96] This aspect became even more important later in the twentieth century, being one of the keystones of the ASTP and the audio-visual approaches. The main teaching approach was through re-creation of typical situations involving formulas of politeness, social behavior in home and work environments, and inductive study of institutions. This, obviously, made teaching by grammatical rule even more unfeasible.

But in the 1960's psychologists began to return to the Erasmian position that both inductive and deductive approaches were relevant. Carroll, for instance, noted that conceptual learning is a part of language acquisition and drew the conclusion that in a school situation, both inductive and deductive learning had their place.[193:578] This point had already been known and used by contemporary teachers, and Carroll called for solid experimental proof.

2.2 GRAMMAR THROUGH RULES

While the inductive approach aimed at inculcating a set of skills, the deductive approach sought to teach analyses of language so that the requisite language skills would follow. Usually with this approach it was the written language that had priority, as the etymology of the word "grammar" shows. Grammar was first based on literature, and indeed it was not until the Renaissance that the study of grammar and literature were definitively separated. The cardinal preoccupation of teachers was correctness, not fluency of response; consequently much time was spent teaching flexions and structure. Explanation of rules was naturally an important factor in introducing them to the pupil. For centuries the usual language of explanation was Latin, explanation and introduction in the vernacular not becoming usual until the eighteenth century. Means of assuring retention were at first based on debating methods drawn from medieval philosophy, remaining so until they were displaced by the Grammar-Translation Method, an eighteenth-century development.

For this aspect of language teaching, the distinction between presentation and repetition is arbitrary, as there was no real methodological distinction between the two stages. Learning grammar was like drinking a glass of water, there being no difference in procedure between the first and the last sip. Looked at from another viewpoint, until the halcyon days of the nineteenth century when most teachers lost sight of the fact that grammar had to be applied, all grammar teaching is presentation, as the real linguistic practice comes from applying the rules in a linguistically relevant fashion.

2.2.1 Methods of Introduction

Grammar traditionally includes accidence (or morphology) and syntax (or structure). The first term covers flexions and the other characteristics of the isolated word that fit it to enter structures. Declining nouns and conjugating verbs is a legacy of the ancient grammarians. The case, tense, and mood names they coined were still in use in the 1960's in spite of determined efforts to displace them by Renaissance and modern grammarians. They had originally been developed to teach Greek and Latin speakers the formal skeleton of their own languages, but during the Middle Ages this aspect of the question was lost sight of and they became part of the process of introducing these languages to nonnative speakers. The seeming illogicality of this procedure was not apparent, as Latin was still a living language as late as the early eighteenth century.

The usual method was rote learning. It seems that medieval teachers were content with presenting the pupil with the morphology and syntax of Latin. Renaissance teachers tried to supplement this method by mnemonic devices. The declension systems of Greek and Latin were pictured as bunches of keys. In declining a noun or an

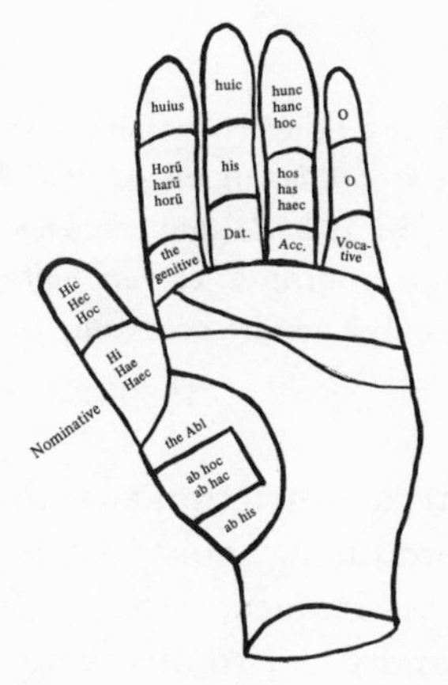

Figure 5. Tracing from John Holt, *Lac Puerorum* 548: 5 (1500?). Facsimile in the Houghton Library

adjective, cases were ticked of on the fingers of the left hand, as in the diagram from John Holt (Figure 5). The singular was declined by touching the top joint of each finger, starting with the thumb, the plural by going round the next joints. This worked well for Greek, which had only five cases, so that to accommodate Latin, the ablative was counted on the ball of the thumb.

Analogy has always held a place as an indispensable tool in this type of learning. Gilles Duwes remarks:

> The manner to form the present of the verbs infinitive mode here-after following is: that all those that end in *er* putting the *r* away: and making the *e* a consonant ye shall have the perfect of the indicative: as in these words: parler/ appeller/appaiser/appuier. Putting the *r* away ye have parle/ appelle/ appaise/appuie.
>
> 1534 (Duwes) 356: fII

By the word "consonant" Duwes here means sounding the vowel as [e]. In illustrating this he was hampered by the lack of the modern acute accent, which only arrived in French orthography about fifty years later. The temptation to place the rule above observation is one grammarians and linguists have always found hard to resist. Duwes's arch rival, John Palsgrave, underlined rather complacently instances where French conformed to the pattern he had deduced for it:

> All substantives ending in *on*, with any other consonant coming before *on*, be of the masculyn gendre: except *facon, lecon, chancon* and *plancon*. But whereas I find in Alayn Chartier: *En la belle dame sans merci ou il luy playst, et bon luy semble, guerdon contraint et renchiere,* it would be *contraint,* for guerdon is of the masculyn gendre according to my rule.
>
> 1530 (Palsgrave) 840: 165

This sort of thing developed into a conviction that the language had to follow the grammarian, producing abberations like Richard Bentley's notorious editions of Horace, where everything that seemed illogical was emended, and more to our point, leading to the enthronement of grammatical analysis during the eighteenth and nineteenth century.

Opinions varied on what should be learned by rote: Brinsley, for instance, advised learning just the endings, the idea not being abandoned until the eighteenth century.[155:64] In modern languages with grammatical gender, the idea of learning the article with the noun seems to date back to the Renaissance, and it was common practice during the seventeenth century. Rote learning of paradigms was unquestioned during the eighteenth and nineteenth centuries, but came under fire at the end of the period from Viëtor and his followers.[1110:15] But the principle of analogy in accidence was still vigorous during the twentieth century, probably encouraged by those Direct Methodists who did not reject grammar altogether: Duwes's idea on the *er* conjugation in French has been repeated countless times during this century.[2:357]

The usual introduction to rules themselves is explanation. For classical languages, until the eighteenth century the usual language of explanation was Latin; and even during the twentieth century there were a few Greek grammars published with explanations in Latin. In living languages too the language of explanation was often Latin during the Renaissance, successful vernacular grammars like that of Maupas's French grammar being published in Latin for the international market. During the nineteenth century a few teachers were convinced that grammatical explanations in the foreign language gave valuable insights into both language and grammar,[306:3] and some twentieth-century authors advocated the same procedure for advanced pupils.

Vernacular explanation of grammar first appears during the ninth century as a stated principle in the introduction to Aelfric's grammar and glossary: "I know that many will not be pleased that I was willing to work in this field and turn grammar into English. But I am convinced that this subject should be made suitable for ignorant little boys and not for old men."[11:1] This procedure reappeared in the sixteenth century in both classical and contemporary languages. The principle was not accepted without prolonged polemic from both supporters and opponents of the practice. However, during the mid-seventeenth century the Jansenist schools of Port-Royal adopted the custom of explaining Latin in French. As their grammars became popular, vernacular expositions of grammar became acceptable. The tendency was undoubtedly encouraged by the new interest in the grammar of the vernacular. By the end of the century it was taken as inevitable that a pupil's introduction to the grammar of foreign languages should come through a sound knowledge of the analysis of his own. Already by 1740 it was possible for Rollin, rector of the Sorbonne, to write: "It seems to me that there is, at present, general agreement that the first rules given to teach Latin should be in French. . . ."[965:II:149]

By the beginning of the nineteenth century, vernacular explanation was accepted by default by most authorities. The few who did otherwise were roundly condemned by the Direct Methodists, Kappert remarking that such teaching was contrary to common sense.[614:15] The main reason was that by such methods the pupil did not get a clear picture of the reality described, as extraneous difficulties with the language of exposition complicated the learning problem. Vernacular explanation was not regarded as inevitably evil by many Direct Methodists. Laudenbach, for instance, devoted a large section of his prize-winning essay to it.[*57:86] Palmer heartily agreed with this stand, while being under the impression that he was, in fact, contradicting the Direct Method.[810:169]

Few teachers in any period believed that vernacular explanation on its own was entirely desirable. Maupas, for instance, used such explanations only on points which he felt the pupil had missed.[*220:7-8] The need for meaningful examples is expressed again and again as an aid to effective learning. This was especially important when literary composition was one of the aims of the language course. But when this aim died, the mnemonic utility of the example became paramount, and indeed was almost its sole justification.

In spite of the large body of informed opinion to the contrary, many teachers in all periods of language teaching regarded the retention of grammar rules solely as a function of rote memory. The most ancient method of assuring perfect parrot retention was presenting rules in verse. Apart from a few epigrams, verse teaching of grammar was unknown in the classical period, though verse treatises in other aspects of learning were far from uncommon. Near the end of the Low Latin period verse grammars began to appear. It seems that at first they were not fully accepted, Donatus and Priscian holding the field. The first really successful verse grammars were the *Doctrinale* of Alexander de Villa Dei and the *Graecismus* of Evrard of Bethune, both owing so much to the great Latin grammarians that D'Andeli dubbed them Priscian's grandsons.[281:v.202] These two twelfth-century productions survived until the time of the early Humanists, the *Doctrinale* actually being recommended by Guarino.[*222:165] To medieval scholars presentation in verse "leads to easier memorization, to more elegant and pithy expression and to firmer retention."[*158:35]

This attitude was still to be found during the high Renaissance, the two grammars being replaced by a mixed group of prose and verse manuals. The verse grammar was especially popular in England, which had more reverence for medieval customs than the rest of Europe. The most important grammar written in this form was that of John Stanbridge, which appeared in two parts: *Libellus grammaticus latinus longe parvula* and *Accidence.* But as the Erasmian school gained a foothold in England through the work of John Colet, the verse grammar lost its popularity.

Though verse grammars as such were not revived, during the early seventeenth century manuals with rules laid out in verse were used to teach classical languages. The standard grammar in this form was that of Despauterius, which was modeled on the *Doctrinale.* Port-Royal adopted the general framework of Despauterius for its grammars, but used French verses instead of Latin. The jingle method of learning grammar spread to other languages without, however, putting down very deep roots. Yet it was sufficiently popular to draw the fire of Viëtor.[1110:20] As it was, nineteenth-century grammars used it sparingly and it survived rather grudgingly into the twentieth century, as in Mountford's edition of Kennedy's *Latin Primer.*[621:221-225]

2.2.2 Methods of Drilling Grammar

Retention of grammar involves two things: rote memory of the rules themselves, and functional retention. This difference was recognised as early as the seventeenth century:

> And therein to content ourselves, if we can but obtaine so much of many, as to be able to understand and make use of the rules, or to turn to them though they can not say them readily; for we see most schollers, when they come to the Universities, to forget that perfectnesse in their Grammars, and most learned men can not say the rules; yet so long as they have full understanding & remembrance to make use in resolving, writing or speaking, this sufficeth.
>
> 1627 (Brinsley) 155: 86

The ways of ensuring retention were, in the first instance, based on catechesis, then later on reference to the first language.

Moderns tend to think of catechesis as a method of teaching religious dogma: as it is based on a stock response to a stock cue, it provides for extremely firm control over pupil learning in the classroom. It originates in the philosophical dialogues of Greek and Latin classicism in which a great man is represented as leading an interested inquirer to wisdom. The Late Latin grammarians rid themselves of the fiction that their treatises represented a conversation, but often kept a question-and-answer form. In the medieval classroom grammar learning seems to have progressed to the disputation through rote learning.

Brinsley gives us a step-by-step account of Renaissance practice:

> Thus to goe forward in every rule:
> 1. Reading it over to the children;
> 2. Shewing the plaine meaning in as few words as you can;
> 3. Propounding every piece of it in a short question, following the words of the booke, & answering it yourself out of the words of the book;
> 4. Asking the same questions of them & trying how themselves can answer them, still looking upon their books. Then let them goe in hand with getting it amongst themselves.
>
> 1627 (Brinsley) 155a: 57

This procedure was also found in the Jesuit schools of the time. It remained normal until the early nineteenth century, the last real flourish of the method being Pinnock's catechisms, which appeared in 1822. After this it gradually died out as a method of exposition.

Catechetical exposition was formalized in the disputation, which was originally a philosophical exercise at the backbone of the medieval university course. From the testimony of Alcuin we know that by Carolingian times it was already a standard exercise,[26] and by the fourteenth century it was well established.[*38:182] By the sixteenth century the exercise had become so popular that boys used to engage spontaneously in such "appositions," interschool feelings running high enough to lead to riots. With the decline of spoken Latin in the classroom it died out.

The form of the disputation seems one-sided to those used to modern debating. One party to the debate undertook to defend a proposition, while the other tried to find faults in reasoning and argument. Erasmus implies that the debate could be done either orally or by writing,[367:6E] while for Brinsley one of its greatest values was the practice it gave in spoken Latin.[155a:206] The kind of argument is well shown by this extract from Brinsley's own disputations:

Q. If it be a proper name, belonging to the female kind or shees, what gender must it be?
A. The feminine.
Q. Where is your rule?
A. Propria femineum.
Q. What is the meaning of that rule?
A. All proper names belonging to the female kind are the feminine gender.

1633 (Brinsley) 158: 88

Brinsley was courageous enough to write his models in English, but most models existed in Latin. A pupil was introduced to the technique by being made to learn model disputations (Brinsley recommends those of Stockwood) and recite them in class. Once these were known, the pupil was expected to improvise.

At about the time disputations lost their importance, the Grammar-Translation Method appeared. Though the basis of the method had existed during the Renaissance, it did not appear in the form so hated by the Direct Methodists until the end of the eighteenth century. The *vulgaria* (see §6.3.1) of the Renaissance were translation exercises with the double aim of inculcating a sense of style and a knowledge of grammar. Translation as a language-teaching tool had had a brief trial during the third century of the Christian era in Alexandria and Gaul, and then had been abandoned until the late Middle Ages. The Renaissance attitude to it was summed up by Roger Ascham: "Translation is easy in the beginning for the scholar, & bringeth also much learning and great judgement to the master."[53:100] This remained one of the prime justifications of translation until our day, similar sentiments appearing in the writings of Thomas Arnold[*64:215] and in modern linguists like Jean Darbelnet. But one school of Renaissance thought, headed by Whittinton, regarded the *vulgaria* as aids to grammar-learning, and in his book Whittinton actually printed the rule to be observed at the head of each chapter. During the following century the discipline of general grammar (see §15.2.2.2) prepared the climate for translation methods in grammar learning by postulating that there was one basic system for all languages. But there was little use of translation in grammar learning until the grammars of Meidinger and Seidenstücker appeared at the end of the eighteenth century.

Port-Royal had insisted on the importance of knowing the grammar of one's own language, and had taught languages in such a way that there was a transfer of grammatical training between the classical languages and French. During the following century this practice was erected into a principle that underlay the Grammar-Translation Method. Condillac laid down that "it would be useless and even unreasonable to teach the arts of language to a child who had not yet learned how to handle the structures proper to his own language."[261:31] Following this principle, authors began to write grammars of European languages especially to prepare pupils for foreign-language study.

Though Meidinger's method was used in a good many modern-language classrooms during the early nineteenth century, it was not easily accepted by the classicists. Even if he had provided for translation in both directions instead of merely from the mother tongue, the long tradition of composition methods in classical languages and the avowed cultural aims based on a close knowledge of literature still acted for a time as a block to his method in the great schools. However, it was but a short step from the grammatical teaching of Latin and Greek by the aid of the "construe" to full Grammar Translation. The tendency was further strengthened by the loss of the spoken dimension of Latin and the declining importance of Latin composition.

The best known Grammar-Translation texts were those of Ollendorf, whose grammars first appeared in the 1840's and were widely imitated. The first editions followed Meidinger's technique, later ones adding translation from the foreign language as a supplementary exercise. The order he used in his lessons became standard: a statement of the rule, followed by a vocabulary list and translation exercises. At the end of the course translation of connected prose passages was attempted. As yet the content of the course was not unreasonable, but even then more importance was accorded to exceptions than would have been considered justified during the Renaissance.

Thus Grammar Translation did not enter classical language classes until the first decade of the nineteenth century. The practice seems to have come from the Prussian school system: an American classics teacher, B. Sears, published a method based on the "Prussian system" in 1845. The procedure consisted of learning the rules and then drilling them by translating snippets of Cicero. Composition and reading were excluded, as those did not encourage a word-for-word knowledge of the rules, and as, at times, Cicero is most unciceronian. With the appearance of the Ollendorf grammars for Latin and Greek the victory of Grammar Translation was complete.

During the second half of the nineteenth century the grip of Grammar Translation was tightened by Karl Plötz. In his system, which was basically that of Ollendorf, the disciplinary and analytical value of language study was paramount, and the linguistic aims quite secondary. The growing exactness of philological studies was reflected in the increased formalism of his grammatical description. Language teaching drifted further from the languages taught by reason of the abandonment of authentic specimens of literature for synthetic passages that were built around rules, exceptions, and restricted vocabulary selected for its congruence with grammatical rules. Language skill was equated with ability to conjugate and decline.

The reaction of the Direct Methodists to this "traditional" method was mixed. Jespersen distinguished ability to "feel at home in a language and skill in translation."[587:50] Others were not so charitable. Rouse was especially bitter:

> I will only add finally, that the current method is not older than the nineteenth century. It is the offspring of German scholarship, which seeks to know everything about something rather than the thing itself: the traditional English method which lasted into the nineteenth century was to use the Latin language in speech.
>
> 1925 (Rouse) 9.77: 2

Others had already gone further, questioning the very competence of the practitioners of the Grammar Translation Method:

> If the authorities of colleges and universities were really to insist upon good genuine English being rendered into good genuine French, as a test in all examinations prescribed by them, I dare say not a single candidate, perhaps not even a single examiner, would be able to comply with such a requirement in a satisfactory manner . . .
>
> 1893 (Rambeau) 927: 324

The traditionalist replied by pointing out that translation was an unrivaled way of comparing the resources of two languages. Since the Direct Methodists could not see how an ability to compare both languages was useful, neither side was convinced of the truth of the other's arguments. Palmer, as usual, tried to steer a middle course, pointing out that translation did have a role to play in connecting concepts drawn from two languages.[838:78] But by the 1940's Grammar Translation was irretrievably discredited in the drive to teach language as behavior and not as an assembly of abstractions.

2.3 DIFFERENTIAL GRAMMAR

From this point of view, teachers have fallen into two large groups: those who reject the mother tongue, and those who use it as a point of departure. Into the first group come, by necessity, most medieval teachers, the Natural Methodists, the later Direct Methodists and most of the teachers and policy makers of the twentieth century; the second group encompasses the rest.

It seems that only after the Renaissance did teachers exploit the differences between languages in teaching them. Three ways of approaching the problem were developed: the first rests on comparing the analysis of the mother tongue with one of the target languages. The second consists of teaching two foreign languages together, both ordered so that comparable and contrasting features throw each other into relief. Unlike these two which rest on comparing facts of structure, the third way is based on an examination of the means of expression open to different languages for the same idea.

The first is the most obvious; discussion goes back to Passy, but the approach is implicit in much earlier work. Elements of the idea had been current during the Renaissance:

> After that the child hathe ben pleasantly trained, and induced to knoe the parts of speech, and can separate one of them from another in his own language, it shall be time that his tutor or governour do make diligent search for a master. . . .
>
> 1531 (Elyot) 364: 50

But a systematic approach along these lines was not possible until living languages had been analyzed with the same rigor as classical. Thus it was that Port-Royal pioneered introduction to a foreign grammar through one's own. The only possible analytical scheme to follow was that which had been developed for Latin, so the illusion that all languages shared a basic grammar was complete. Books of vernacular grammar designed to help the learner of classical languages were very common in the two centuries following Port-Royal. As modern languages gained respectability they were treated in the same way: a learner was expected to be able to sort out from his grammar the rules like those of his own language and distinguish them from the others.[737:v]

Owing to the development of historical linguistics in the late nineteenth century, a considerable number of German methods for English speakers were based on family resemblances between the two languages. Some claims about this type of teaching tended to be unrealistic:

> [my method] is based on the fact that the German and the English [sic] are substantially one and the same language, a great, if not the greater part of the German vocables being found in the English speech. It is true that these vocables . . . have so changed their outward form that they are no longer recognisable by the eye or the ear—unless a knowledge of the principles which have determined these seemingly arbitrary metamorphoses has first been acquired.
>
> 1873 (Roehrig) 964: iv

As may be expected, the Direct Method was suspicious of this approach. Palmer went even further: "A pupil will be more docile and require fewer disciplinary measures when learning a language of a totally strange nature."[837:59]

The late nineteenth-century reaction against grammar caused denial of the value of comparison. Many teachers, during the heyday of the Direct and Natural Methods, considered this desirable. Fifty years later some teachers felt they were reaping the whirlwind: ". . . our professional woes come almost altogether from failure to condition students early to the things of our own language, so that foreign languages can be implanted."[1164:476] This feeling had been growing outside the traditional school since the 1930's,[1162:10] much to the delight of the traditionalists, who saw their claims for the efficacy of translation methods confirmed. The structuralists took it up in another way: Fries, for instance, called attention to the need for contrastive analyses in foreign-language teaching. What was emphasized was to vary according to the difficulties expected from the structure of the mother tongue.[432:15] Thus the emphasis was subtly changed: the effort of comparison was to be taken out of the hands of the pupils and left to the teacher and the writer of the textbook.

The second method, that of teaching languages in parallel, is, it seems, the oldest, being the method used to teach Greek during the Middle Ages and Renaissance. Its genesis lies in the parallel Greek-Latin texts used in the schools of the Roman Empire, especially those of Alexandria. Bilingual glossaries and grammars exist from the third century at least, and much of Priscian is based on comparison between Greek and Latin. In taking these texts over, medieval teachers never seemed to place much importance in the fact that originally one of these languages had been the pupils' first language. Thus the methodology of the schoolrooms of the monastery of St. Gall, for example, did not differ from those of the Greek East. Latin, being the first language introduced, was the basic language of comparison.

It was in this way that many Renaissance schoolboys learned their modern languages. In learning the literary registers of these languages formal comparison was the ruling method, Latin, not usually the vernacular, being taken as the norm. Though eighteenth-century teachers replaced the method in modern languages by grammatical analysis, it was kept for Latin, Greek, and Hebrew and certain other languages required for Biblical exegesis. The discovery of genetic relationships between Latin, Greek, and Sanskrit gave a sudden impetus to this arrangement, and between 1840 and 1900 a large number of grammars teaching both languages together were published. Roman-Cornut, the author of one of the earliest, claims that "this method of teaching will have immense advantages. The two languages thus brought together will be more easily learned and retained."[966:vi]

Modern teachers of Greek were not prepared to go so far as this, merely retarding the introduction of Greek until a solid basis had been laid in Latin.[795:v] Though the idea has rarely been applied to Germanic languages, during the twentieth century there have been many schemes for teaching Romance languages in tandem. Neither was it unusual to pair Latin with a Romance language, one language being intended to throw light on the other.[*127:29]

To these two structurally based approaches certain modern linguists and teachers added a third: a comparison of the various means at the disposal of different languages to express the same idea. The germ of this idea goes back at least to the Renaissance, but it is implicit in the inevitable recognition that every language has its own genius. In 1626, Webbe pointed out in his submission to Parliament that: ". . . though *un* be *an; cavallo, horse; di, of; buon, good; metallo, metall;* and *a horse of good metall* put together be good English; the Italian understands not *un cavallo di buon metallo* to be Italian but disclaims it."[*183:337] Little was said about this aspect of the matter during the next three centuries, as the whole notion ran counter to the prevailing grammatical approach. The germ of modern comparative stylistics was already current in the late 1930's:

> . . . the best way to tackle a language is to take an idea, let us say giving an order, and show how the language handles it, instead of taking the form called the 'imperative mood' and illustrating its uses.
>
> 1939 (Wilson) 1162: 44

The modern version of the idea was prompted by an implication of Saussure's dichotomy of *signifiant* and *signifié* within the linguistic sign: that grammatical structures are a reflection of thought structures.[317:185] The basis of comparison became sociological and psychological, instead of merely linguistic. Naturally, the approach was too sophisticated for the elementary stages of composition:

> The aim of comparative stylistics is not to set forth the facts of grammar and vocabulary, but to examine how the parts of the system interact to render the idea expressed in the other language.
>
> 1963 (Vinay and Darbelnet) 1112: 26

Thus translations like the following were proposed: "Ils grimperent des escaliers interminables," for, "They climbed flight after flight of stairs."[1112:150] The importance of finesse in handling the second language is a definite return to the Renaissance preoccupation with good style.

The utility of all three approaches was controverted. Palmer stated flatly that resemblances between languages led to "a vicious system of mechanical conversion."[837:59] The first two were attacked on the ground that they gave the impression that it was possible to compare languages point to point, when very often one has to change levels of analysis to compare expressive resources of language.[698:28] To the claim that differential linguistics can predict the mistakes that a pupil is likely to make, opponents replied that any experienced language teacher can do the same, and with much more sureness. Some mistakes, instead, are not due solely to interference but also to mistaken analogy.[698:28] The third came under the general attack on all methods which called on the first language. However, it was agreed that differential considerations should play an important part in establishing gradation.[639:59] It was also suggested that, even if the pupil did no translation, he should be encouraged to compare the resources of the foreign language with those languages he knows already.[404:92]

These three approaches acquired specialised functions during the twentieth century. The first two were found to be more appropriate to the elementary stages of language study where finesse was not required. The last was reserved for the first stages of teaching composition. But in spite of this many teachers used it to introduce isolated features in the early stages of foreign-language study, then to integrate the pupil's entire linguistic knowledge in the later stage of the course.

The changes in grammar teaching can be shown diagrammatically. In reading the following chart, one must remember that this shows only the main trends of thought and practice:

Era	Teaching Inductive	Teaching Deductive	Language Analysis (cf. Ch. 15)
Classical	X	X	Grammar
Medieval		X	Grammar, Grammatica Speculativa
Renaissance	X	X	Grammar
18th/19		X	General Grammar
19th/20	X	X	Linguistics, Grammar

It will be noticed that where grammar was approached through logic, the range of methods was reduced to teaching rules; but where inductive approaches were used, the deductive did not necessarily disappear.

3

TEACHING PRONUNCIATION

> Even supposing one has a perfect grasp of the theory it is the production of the sounds that counts.
>
> 1908 (Lockhart and Jones) in 685: 97

In comparison with the mass of material on teaching meaning and grammar, little has been written about teaching pronunciation, at least in the West, where comparatively little was known about the mechanisms of speech until modern times. This situation contrasts with that in India, where, in the millenium before Christ, the Sanskrit grammarians had developed a sophisticated system of phonology that provided some of the impetus for the European school of phonetics which flourished during the late nineteenth century. Phonetic descriptions which appear in Europe before that time are only partially accurate, and with a few exceptions, the teaching of pronunciation was based largely on imitation and approximations drawn from spelling.

In the teaching of classical languages, except for the placing of the accent, necessary because of the importance of verse composition, little attention was paid to the niceties of pronunciation, the phonemes of the local language being used to render the spelling. This custom was abolished in many places at the end of the nineteenth century with the introduction of the reformed pronunciation. In modern languages, however, pronunciation was accorded some importance, although it was regarded purely as correct articulation, the role of the ear not being fully understood until the 1930's. During the high Renaissance the approach was informal, so informal that beyond commonplaces about the necessity of good models little was said. The intense interest of the Renaissance scholar in spelling reform was expressed in many kinds of phonetic transcription, some of which were used to teach foreigners. Teachers of the seventeenth century relied a great deal on rules deduced from spelling and etymology, but during the nineteenth century pronunciation was neglected.

Linguists of the twentieth century showed that in pronunciation, correct articulation was impossible without some control by the ear. This prompted them to train the powers of perception independently, allowing the pupil to monitor himself while he was learning to speak. This, they claimed, is what happens in one's first language.[309:5]

The ways of teaching the skills of pronunciation fall into two groups: intuitive and analytical. The first group depends on unaided imitation of models; the second reinforces this natural ability by explaining to the pupil the phonetic basis of what he is to do.

3.1 INTUITIVE PROCEDURES

For the proper functioning of speech, reactions must be spontaneous and immediate. Thus imitative procedures have always been the backbone of pronunciation teaching. The development of analytical methods did not displace them, even in the Direct Method. Glauning, an early Direct Methodist, remarked that phonetics itself had no place in the classroom, despite the utility of the discipline to the teacher.[462:11] Teachers of the twentieth century shared this attitude, so that the imitative approach flourished in the face of competition from techniques based on phonetics and phonology. Imitation implies two stages: perception of speech and then production.

3.1.1 Perception

Though scholars have known since the sixteenth century that it is impossible to separate the skills of perception and production, the first pronouncements on the subject came from the Direct Method:

"Listen before you imitate is one of the axioms of practical phonetics" (Sweet).[1054:8] Jespersen elaborated this statement, pointing out how necessary to every language learner were highly developed skills in listening to and interpreting the sounds of another language.[587:145] At this stage, speaking followed very closely on the heels of listening, the more complicated skills of both being taught concurrently.

Without adverting to the full implications of the principle, teachers of the seventeenth and eighteenth centuries did insist on models, indirectly endorsing the separation of the two groups of skills:

> But as it is the voice which forms it [language], it is certain that it can not be well learnt except by hearing speech. Thus in one's contact with language one can not expect more from the book than the minimum of help and simple guidance which can be given by explaining the properties of the letters.
>
> 1701 (Anon.) 807: 2

It is noticeable that the author of the above textbook was suspicious of the phonetic analyses current during his time. Likewise the schools of Basedow and Pestalozzi relied entirely on imitation, thus forestalling the Natural Methodists, for whom phonetic analysis held no interest whatsoever. In the 1870's, Alexander Melvin Bell, in training deaf-mutes to speak, cast some doubt on the efficacy of the current analyses, which had survived from the eighteenth century. He traced the difficulties he ran into to the fact that though his pupils knew the exhaustive analyses he had taught them, they had no auditory means of checking their performance. It was from him that the Direct Method acquired both a philosophy of teaching pronunciation and a system of articulatory analysis.

It seems that Palmer was the first to advocate teaching receptive skills separately in recommending that pupils should not be allowed to attempt speech before a firm foundation of receptive skills had been laid. In its most extreme form, that in which Palmer applied it himself, it meant that pupils were exposed to foreign speech for about three months before being allowed to attempt it themselves (see §8.1.1). He did not envisage any other way of conditioning except exposure to speech. Scientific backing for this technique came from the Prague school, whose definition of the phoneme implied a mental reality to which the spoken sound was meant to conform.

By the usual process of independent research that takes no account of what went before, Tan Gwan Leong, Director of Education for Burma, and Robert Gauthier developed the Tan-Gau method which formalized Palmer's approach. They claimed that by exposing the pupil to foreign speech while allowing him to reply in his own language they were imitating the way in which one learns the first language, where understanding definitely preceded expression. The new element here was the active participation of the pupils, whose rate of learning was controlled by the quantity and type of reaction.

Such hit-and-miss methods of conditioning were called into question by Peter Guberina, professor of phonetics at Zagreb and Paris. Like Bell before him, his work with language pupils grew out of his main purpose, teaching the deaf. He postulated that many deaf-mutes are sensitive only to a limited range of sound frequencies. For him the process of conditioning fell into two parts: the pupils were to be trained to hear and then to interpret. Though he was by no means the discoverer of the phonological uses of rhythm, at the time he put it forward, his idea of teaching speech in rhythmic units seemed new and revolutionary. As he worked in the CREDIF team, his idea was almost their trademark. No sound was ever presented or drilled outside a phonological or grammatical structure, and, if possible, it was taught in a context involving some emotional or physical reaction. For instance, in *Voix et Images de France,* the phoneme /o/ was associated with the exhaustion of a man who has just climbed up four flights of stairs: "Quatrième étage! C'est haut!"

One of Guberina's techniques of conditioning that was not utilized by CREDIF was rhythmic conditioning without the use of phonemes as such. By the use of a machine called "Suvag lingua," he had the pupils listen to typical rhythms of the second language given out in low frequencies; these he regarded as being more stimulating, because they were in tune with the basic frequencies to which the body as a resonator would react. He followed this by lessons in which he used the technique described above. For him every sound had a definite emotional color or typical context in which it was best taught.

A different and more specific type of conditioning was evolved by the psychologists who worked on programed learning. They observed that the saturation type of conditioning was not entirely successful in the language laboratory, because the pupil did not discriminate between features of foreign sounds in the same way that native speakers did. This was one eventuality that the planners of laboratory courses had made no allowance for.[644:273] In an attempt to fill this gap, experimenters tested the effect of teaching discrimination between sibilants, and between voiced and unvoiced plosives. By a device known as "pattern playback," spectrograms of speech were converted into sound and played to the pupil for identification. When the pupil signaled the correct identification to the machine, it went on to the next stimulus. Phonemes were presented in all their possible realizations and positions within the word. The subjects of the experiment showed "significant improvement" in both discrimination and production of the sounds in question.[644:273-276] The same group of experimenters also noticed that attempts at vocalizing the sounds in question facilitated recognition. But their experimental results did not allow them to draw any firm conclusions.[644:276]

3.1.2 Mimicry

The goal of all phonetic conditioning is mimicry or imitation, which, especially in teaching children, was considered an essential part of all modern language methods. For example, in the preface to the teacher's books belonging to the *Parlons français* course, Mrs. Slack points out that "close imitation of the films is all-important, and you will encourage the children if you participate yourself. . . ![1019:I:6] Despite the attention drawn to it by the teachers of the twentieth century, mimicry is the oldest and simplest tool for teaching pronunciation. But its very simplicity prevented any sure treatment of it until the Renaissance:

> All languages, both learned and mother tongues, be gotten, and gotten only, by imitation. For as ye use to hear, so ye learne to speake; if ye hear not other, ye speak not yourself; and whom ye only heare, of them ye only learne.
>
> 1570 (Ascham) 53: 133

This quotation is also notable for its implication that receptive and productive skills are separate. Some exceptional schools of the eighteenth century, like the *Philanthropinum* and those of Pestalozzi, relied on imitation rather than rules; but this practice was not basic to any techniques of teaching until the Natural Methodists tried to restore inductive methodology in language teaching.

Various ways of guiding imitation were developed early. Those that did not introduce the pupils to scientific analyses of speech rested on some sort of "gymnastics" or utilization of sounds that were not strictly speech sounds. In the famous dictionary of Randle Cotgrave, we find the following directions for learning the French /y/: "U is sounded as if you would whistle it out, as in the word *a lute.*"[275:1] During the next two centuries, when teaching was oriented towards the written language, very little attention was paid to learning pronunciation, by imitation or by any other means.

The school of phoneticians which rose at the end of the nineteenth century boasted that its most important improvement on the Natural Method was basing the teaching of pronunciation on sound phonetic knowledge: according to Breul, "a teacher should possess a correct pronunciation and a sufficient knowledge of the auxiliary science of phonetics, to be able to teach the conscious imitation of foreign sounds."[153:97] This did not necessarily mean that phonetics itself was taught in the classroom. Indeed, on this precise point there was much discussion among the Direct Methodists. Textbook writers advised careful listening to the teacher to learn difficult sounds, backed up by learning devices such as trying to say [i] through rounded lips to produce the French and German. [y].[151:4]

Techniques of teaching by using existing phonetic habits in new directions was one practical outcome of nineteenth-century phonetics. For instance, Henry Sweet suggested teaching the Welsh sound[l̥] as in *Llanfair* by alternately pronouncing [vvffvvffvvff] until the mechanics of voicing and unvoicing were quite clear to the pupil. Then, by using the same muscular movements as far as possible, a similar sequence [lll̥l̥lll̥l̥lll̥l̥] could be pronounced fairly easily.[1054:7] Another method developed by an anonymous researcher of the time was that of repeating two extreme sounds quickly, harnessing human laziness to produce the intermediate sound. Thus, in teaching the English [æ] to a Frenchman one has the pupil repeat [ε-a] until the two sounds come together as varieties of [æ]. All of these methods are inductive, the pupil having to find out unconsciously how to produce the new sounds.

The main preoccupation of the Direct Methodists was individual sounds rather than systems, of which they had only a dim consciousness. But it was realized that pupils would learn much from observation of foreign accents in their own language:

> The teacher practices an English sentence pronounced as a Frenchman would pronounce it with French vowels, accent, etc. He may refer to this sentence now and again in speaking of the single sounds, and it will serve to warn the students against the kind of mistakes that they themselves are to avoid.
>
> 1904 (Jespersen) 587: 154

By this means, as well as the textbook pronunciation of individual sounds, rhythm and free variation were taken care of. This technique had been used, it seems, by the poet, Verlaine, during the 1880's. It remained a commonplace of the Direct Method, being mentioned by Kappert as one means of forming the psychological set required to speak the foreign language well.[614:69] Twenty-five years later the idea was still current, being found in the writings of Bloomfield. He advised learners of German to learn to speak English with a German accent to facilitate the task of learning the German phonemic system.[123:5]

Other methods of teaching pronunciation rest on distorting the sounds to be taught in order to minimize interference from native phonemes and phonological customs. The most widespread form of distortion has always been slowing the rate of delivery. It is impossible to trace this back in time, for it is an almost inescapable didactic tendency. With the advent of the language laboratory, some doubt was cast on the utility of slowing. It was pointed out that the natural rhythm of the language can be badly upset by this means, and that in any case, it is often difficult to accustom the pupils to a normal rate of delivery afterwards. For these reasons, many teachers refused to speak slowly, even for beginners, preferring to repeat.

One of the most original ways of distorting language to forestall interference was devised by an American teacher faced with the problem of teaching English juncture to Spanish speakers: "Let us say that we had to teach a set of sentences such as the following: 'It's a pencil; it's a table; it's an apple.' The trick consists of distorting the data to the point where the difficult cluster /ts/ was practically eliminated. Here is what we taught: 'It–sa pencil; it–sa table; it–san apple.' "[1165:1] As the pupil was made to repeat this with increasing speed he found that he could remake the clusters without inserting the usual Spanish supporting vowel.

The concept of language system was late in affecting the classroom teaching of pronunciation. During the 1940's the traditional emphasis on isolated phonemes began to give place to the consideration of melodic speech patterns. As one of the preoccupations of elocution teachers, this had already become standard in first language teaching, but had so far had little effect on second language teaching. Phonological research had made it clear that melodic and intonation patterns were an integral part of the system, causing many teachers to begin pronunciation training with sentence shapes instead of isolated phonemes. Guberina, for instance, as may be expected from his use of intonation patterns for conditioning, treated intonation and rhythm as the logical first step.[490:16] Mastery of such patterns would then facilitate acquisition of individual phonemes.[490:18] This scheme was put into practice by CREDIF in its audio-visual methods.

3.2 ANALYTICAL PROCEDURES

Many teachers have tried to give their pupils an understanding of the science of phonetics in order to guide them towards the correct way of forming foreign sounds. But until the twentieth century, the phonetic and phonological analyses current in Europe were far from complete and hardly rigorous enough to give more than a rough guide. The two periods in which analytical procedures were most important in teaching pronunciation, considering the state of knowledge at the time, were the sixteenth century and the late nineteenth and twentieth centuries: these procedures could be directed by the teacher either towards teaching discrimination or towards guiding imitation.

3.2.1 Teaching Discrimination

In teaching discrimination between the various phonological units of foreign languages, linguists have alternated between two approaches: the synchronic, which analyzes the language as it is at the time, and the diachronic, which is concerned with the development of the language. Both types of approach rest on some sort of differential analysis. The synchronic approach goes back to the Renaissance, being used almost exclusively in modern languages. Diachronic analysis has a longer history in teaching pronunciation, found as early as Roman times, and losing its importance only at the beginning of the nineteenth century.

3.2.1.1 Differential Analysis. Analysis of differences is a temptation few teachers or pupils can resist. Apart from giving free rein to intellectual curiosity, it is one approach to the unknown through the known.

Before the Renaissance very few authorities speak about this, but the amount of writing in "figured pronunciation" that was done shows that such analyses were known. Disputes over the relationship between spelling and pronunciation flourished with considerable verve during the early Roman Empire, suggesting that for classical grammarians it was a definite problem. But there was little appreciation of its ramifications before the Renaissance. Several scholars of the time began to realize that the phonetic habits of different linguist groups were limited: C. Estienne remarked on the difficulties Germans had with [d]: "*D* is pronounced thus by the Germans: *Tonum tie* for *Donum dei*."[388:23]

Some grammars, like those of César Oudin, used a thematic approach to the problem. Oudin's Italian grammar disposes quite quickly of sounds similar to French ones:

> ... it is certain that their *a* and *i* are no different from ours. As for the *u*, it is pronounced like our *ou*. ... Now for *e* there are two quite different sounds in Italian, one closed which resembles rather closely our *e* which is used in accented positions and to denote the masculine. The sound is the same as in the words *bonté, vérité*. ... The sound of *e* est rather open, as in our language before *r* and *s* as in these words, *perle, perte, beste*. ...
>
> 1670 (Oudin) 830: 308

Other grammars dealt with the "letters" in alphabetical order. Most often they were content to give the positive side of the question: The author of a German grammar published in Strasbourg at the beginning of the eighteenth century has: "A/a is pronounced as in French, whether it is single or double: *der Abt*, the abbot; *das Paar*, the pair. ..."[807:4] Cotgrave, among other authorities, gave a negative side as well, warning pupils what to avoid: "*A* is to be sounded fully, as in this English word *all;* not as we sound it in *stale, ale*."[275:1] This sort of prescriptive approach lasted through the nineteenth century, alphabetical phonetic guides being annexed to all grammars. Not unexpectedly, the most notable exceptions to this were books published by followers of the Natural Method, who regarded it as unnecessary.

Combinations and juncture were first treated by the phoneticians of the late nineteenth century: "Thus even initial [ts] may be difficult to English speakers, as well as such combinations as [ʃ+ʃ] in Russian because although [ts] is a familiar combination, it is unfamiliar when initial."[1054:61] But judging from the absence of the idea from the professional literature after this time, it did not have much effect on the individual teacher, in spite of the spread of phonetic techniques among teachers.

By an examination of the psychological processes of both teaching and language use, the psychologists of the early twentieth century arrived at a concept of phonetic teaching that implies the theory of the phoneme, as later developed by the Prague school in the 1930's. The formation of new sounds was regarded, not as a purely instrumental process, but as a psychological conforming to the "genius" of the foreign language. The psychologists of the Direct Method postulated the necessity of contrastive analyses on psychological grounds.[614:89] This "cultural" orientation of phonetic teaching fitted in with the importance given to cultural formation in other departments of language teaching.

During the 1930's the findings of experimental phoneticians began to find their way into the classroom. It was postulated that each language had its own peculiar motor habits which were not easily learned by foreigners.[984:353] The pendulum began to swing from the casual assumption that there were some sounds which were fairly close to those in other languages to the idea that no two sounds could ever be completely identified across language boundaries.[1054:512]. During the 1940's, owing to the development of phonology, language teachers began to rethink the business of differential phonetics in the classroom:

> The determining of the distinctive sounds that differ is only the first step in the scientific comparison of the language to be learned with that of the learner. Each language has not only its own set of distinctive sound features; it has also a limited number of consonants and vowels which make up the structural pattern of the syllables and words.
>
> 1945 (Fries) 431: 16

In practical terms this highlighted the problem of sensitization, which for Guberina was to become the first step. It also brought a change in emphasis: sound was not seen to clash with sound, but system with system. This led to a very important distinction between the two systems of phonetics and phonology:

> . . . both phonemics and phonetics play an important part in the teaching of pronounciation: phonemics in the realm of simplification, systematisation and guidance; and in the preparation of the groundwork for the interlinguistic comparison. But the comparison itself, the actual description

> of the speech sounds, and the articulatory exercises remain primarily in phonetics.
>
> 1954 (Politzer) 898: 27

One of the difficulties brought to light by the phonological research of the 1940's was the fact that sounds which are merely allophones in one language can be phonemes in another. This occasioned special difficulties:

> . . . if the allophonic variation in the target language is phonemic in the student's native tongue, these new allophones should be taught with care; the student must be taught not to carry over contrasts from his mother tongue which do not exist in the new language.
>
> 1954 (Weinstein) 1140: 30

For this reason it was commonly required that the teachers should know the language spoken by their pupils, in order to be able to understand almost intuitively why attempts to produce foreign sounds cause predictable types of phonetic deafness and interference. The only important dissenting voice was that of Guberina, who claimed that the teacher should merely be able to predict the pattern of his pupils' mistakes.[490:18]

Phonological approaches were implicit in the work of the International Phonetic Association, which, without adverting to it, used phonological criteria in analyzing the sounds of the languages it dealt with. This is especially noticeable in the work of Paul Passy in contrastive phonetics. Daniel Jones, therefore, had no difficulty in incorporating this approach in his own writings, welcoming the concept of the phoneme as a logical extension of his own work and of that of the Association.[600:171-174]

3.2.1.2 Philological Considerations. Though the practical teaching of pronunciation would seem to have little to do with the history of language, philology has played a most important part in teaching pronunciation, especially in the classical languages. Such considerations were not uncommon in the classical period, became usual during the Late Latin period, and formed one of the main preoccupations of the *orthographiae.* Scholars of the Carolingian Renaissance, for instance, often looked to the derivation of words to settle details of pronunciation: "Latin neutres in *el,* e.g., mel, fel, have a short *e.* Names borrowed from foreign languages, e.g., Daniel, Michael, Gabriel have a long *e.*"[948:635D]

Traditions of local pronunciations for classical languages go back for over a thousand years, attempts to revive or reconstruct the classical pronunciation being far from uncommon. Most pundits concentrated on intonation, as a correct idea of rhythm is essential to writing good verse. There was also some concern about relating pronunciation to spelling. (See pages 73-75, pages 76 ff.) As part of the Renaissance return to classical standards, attempts were made to reject the local pronunciations of Latin and Greek in favor of phonetic schemes based on philological reconstruction. But despite the efforts of men like Caius, Scaliger, and Erasmus, local pronunciations were not replaced by those derived from research results. The influence of native Greek scholars in Western Europe kept the modern pronunciation of Greek alive, while in Latin there were attempts to impose the contemporary Italian pronunciation:

> First they should begin with the necessary and chief rules of grammar . . . and while this is doing, their speech is to be fashioned to a clear and distinct pronunciation, as near as may be to Italian, especially in the vowels.
>
> 1644 (Milton) 758: 278

It was not until the end of the nineteenth century that a pronunciation based on philological research was accepted. It was a joint production of Oxford and Cambridge and was intended to obviate some of the inelegancies of pronunciations in use at the time. At least in the English-speaking world it was adopted very quickly.

Philology was largely ignored by modern-language teachers. Oudin (1670) did anticipate the neogrammarians of the nineteenth century with some of his remarks on Italian: "Almost every Italian *e* which is derived from Latin *i* is pronounced closed, as in the following words:

cenere, from *cinis*, ashes: . . ."[830:309] Several twentieth-century teachers reported good results for a similar approach using some elements of Romance philology. Apophonies like *dois/devons, veux/voulons* seemed easier to remember if the pupil knew that sounds usually diphthongized in the accented syllable of a Low Latin word, and not in the unaccented.[913:317] Yet those who used this idea saw pronunciation as only one of its goals, spelling and certainty of accidence holding equal importance.

3.2.2 Reproduction

Attempts to teach pronunciation by making the pupils conscious of analytical facts are easier to document. The oldest of all means of indicating the correct pronunciation is spelling. As spelling became uncertain, owing to linguistic change and the vagaries of printers, phonetic transcriptions were evolved. These date back to the Renaissance. Attempts at teaching by phonetic analysis can be inferred from the lists of phonetic directions given in the grammars of the classical period and the Middle Ages, but the periods where it was used most as a teaching technique were the Renaissance and the twentieth century.

3.2.2.1 Spelling. In all periods of teaching, teachers have tried to use written supports for teaching pronunciation, usually linking sound with the spelling. There are, of course, enough rigid conventions for this to be a fairly workable procedure.

The importance accorded to spelling as a guide to pronunciation has not been constant. The Roman position was that "unless there is an established custom to the contrary, we should write as we speak."[923:I.vii.30] This was the normal attitude in the late grammarians, even if Cassiodorus was to remark snappishly: "I find *fuisse, ivisse, esse,* and *causasse* written with two *s*. But in pronunciation I do not detect a double articulation."[195:1244] Attempts were made to keep the spelling up-to-date as far as pronunciation was concerned, but it was a losing battle.

Under the rather questionable theory that what was constant was right, Charlemagne ordered extant Latin texts restored to their classical spelling, and the pronunciation altered to suit.*[55:352] The results of the Carolingian Renaissance were not long-lived and the local pronunciations of Latin that rose through Europe were essentially spelling pronunciations using the phonology of the mother tongue. What was left was the important principle that in any conflict between spelling and pronunciation, the most constant member, spelling, was always right.

An important feature of classical spelling that did enter into pronunciation and composition teaching was the indication spelling gives of syllabic length, a critical element in classical poetics. In Latin and Greek the place of the accent depends on the length of the penultimate and antepenultimate syllables: apart from flexional rules which determine syllabic length, long syllables are generally followed by two consonants, short by one or none at all. This is one rule from the ancient grammarians that has been jealously preserved and transmitted to our time.

In modern languages one of the earliest guides to pronunciation was by a French student who is known only by the initials T. H. According to Mildred Pope, it was written some time in the early twelfth century. It establishes a procedure with which all language teachers are familiar: that of inferring pronunciation for collocations of letters within the word: "And you must know that *A* must sometimes be pronounced like *E*, e.g.: *Savez vous faire un chauncoun. Savez vous traire del ark. Savez vous raire la barbe* etc."[906:189] This carries on some of the tendencies of the *orthographiae*.

Some Renaissance teachers tried to find constants in the spelling customs of the language they were teaching. One such was Noel Barlement who wrote several polyglot dictionaries and grammars at the beginning of the seventeenth century. A feature of his *Colloquia* was the comparative table of spellings for the same sound in various languages:

C has various sounds, as noted below:

cha	xa	scia	sha	as in	charbonnier
che	xe	sce	she		chevalier

French	Spanish	Italian	English		
chi	xi	sci	shy		chiche
cho	xo	scio	sho	as in	chomeur
chu	xu	sciu	shu		chucas

1616 (Barlement) 78: §205b

Similar reliance on certain features of spelling was among the possibilities invoked by Cotgrave, who noted the phenomenon of diaeresis in words like *queuë* and *bouë*, which in his time were pronounced in two syllables. This sort of approach continued during the eighteenth century. Peyton's English grammar remarks: "*A* is long, when it is followed by a consonant and final *e*. Then it must be pronounced like the [French] diphthong *ai,* as in *place, table, plague, lame.* Pronounce *plaice, taible, plaigue, laime.*"[873:2]

The human liking for paradox has often turned the apparent lunacies of spelling to good account. For example, one eighteenth-century guide to French pronunciation makes great play with the silence of *l* in the third person pronouns—a characteristic which has disappeared from cultivated French but remains in the popular language:

> The liquid *l* is cut off in the pronoun before Verbs, if the Verb following begins with either a Consonant or a Liquid. Example, *il pleut*, it rains, Read *i pleut*. . . . But when the following Verb begins with a Vowel the Liquid *l* is pronounced. Example, *il a*, he hath. The Liquid *l* when joyn'd with *s* in pronouns is lost, if the following Verbe begins with a Vowel and the *s* is pronounced. Example, *ils ont*, they have. Read *is on*.

1720 (Blair) 120: 2

The seventeenth century saw an immense number of guides to pronunciation of various European languages, all based on spelling. The nineteenth century carried the idea on, without, however, accompanying it with the safeguards common during the Renaissance. During the twentieth century, spelling was largely replaced by some sort of phonetic script.

3.2.2.2 Phonetic Transcription. The purpose of a phonetic transcription is to represent in the least ambiguous way the pronunciation of a word. If alphabets were what most people believe them to be, phonetic transcriptions would not be needed. But most cultivated languages have alphabets and spelling systems in which the ancient pronunciations have become fossilized, and whose spelling is often some hundreds of years behind the times. The problem is compounded for the foreign learner by the clash between his own spelling system and that of the language he is learning. Two ways of dealing with the situation have been evolved. The first way is to distort the native alphabet and spelling to approximate the pronunciation of the new language. This technique, though still in use in the twentieth century, is almost as ancient as alphabets themselves. The other way, no older than the Renaissance, demands the invention of an entirely new sound-representation system.

Distortion of spelling, or "figured pronunciation" was a common procedure in Rome. Though Greek itself was written in the Greek alphabet, words borrowed into Latin were transliterated. The decline of Greek scholarship caused some confusion: in fifth-century Ireland, practically the only place in the West where Greek was studied at this time, texts were written in Latin characters. This custom continued through much of the medieval period. In the thirteenth century, probably owing to greater contacts between the Byzantine world and the West, there were attempts to reintroduce the Greek alphabet into the schoolroom. Thus in Roger Bacon's Greek Grammar we find attempts to establish equivalences based on contemporary, not classical, pronunciation:

e;	*au/af;*	*v;*	*eu/ef;*	*i;*	*u;*	*u;*	*iu/if;*	*y*
αι	*αυ*	*οι*	*ευ*	*ει*	*ου*	*ȣ*	*ηυ*	*υι*

1272 (Bacon) 69: 9

From this developed schemes for teaching reading by interlinear translation.

The oral orientation of living languages during the Renaissance gave full rein to those who wished to use figured pronunciation. In the grammar of Palsgrave we find:

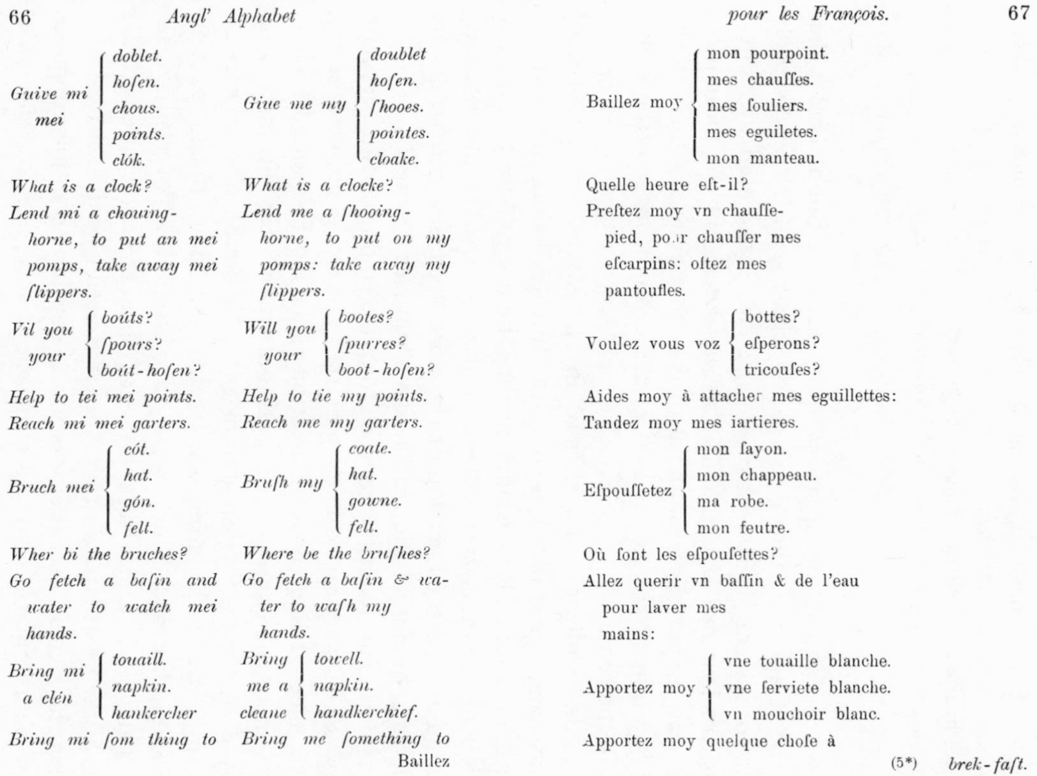

66 *Angl' Alphabet*		*pour les François.* 67
Guive mi mei { *doblet.* *hoſen.* *chous.* *points.* *clók.*	*Giue me my* { *doublet* *hoſen.* *ſhooes.* *pointes.* *cloake.*	Baillez moy { mon pourpoint. mes chauſſes. mes ſouliers. mes eguiletes. mon manteau.
What is a clock?	*What is a clocke?*	Quelle heure eſt-il?
Lend mi a chouing-horne, to put an mei pomps, take away mei ſlippers.	*Lend me a ſhooing-horne, to put on my pomps: take away my ſlippers.*	Preſtez moy vn chauſſe-pied, po.ır chauſſer mes eſcarpins: oſtez mes pantoufles.
Vil you your { *boúts?* *ſpours?* *boút-hoſen?*	*Will you your* { *bootes?* *ſpurres?* *boot-hoſen?*	Voulez vous voz { bottes? eſperons? tricouſes?
Help to tei mei points.	*Help to tie my points.*	Aides moy à attacher mes eguillettes:
Reach mi mei garters.	*Reach me my garters.*	Tandez moy mes iartieres.
Bruch mei { *cót.* *hat.* *gón.* *felt.*	*Bruſh my* { *coate.* *hat.* *gowne.* *felt.*	Eſpouſſetez { mon ſayon. mon chappeau. ma robe. mon feutre.
Wher bi the bruches?	*Where be the bruſhes?*	Où ſont les eſpouſettes?
Go fetch a baſin and water to watch mei hands.	*Go fetch a baſin & water to waſh my hands.*	Allez querir vn baſſin & de l'eau pour laver mes mains:
Bring mi a clén { *touaill.* *napkin.* *hankercher*	*Bring me a cleane* { *towell.* *napkin.* *handkerchief.*	Apportez moy { vne touaille blanche. vne ſerviete blanche. vn mouchoir blanc.
Bring mi ſom thing to	*Bring me ſomething to* Baillez	Apportez moy quelque choſe à (5*) *brek-faſt.*

Figure 6. Pages from G. Mason, *Grammaire angloise.*[722:66-67]

Example of how prose should be sounded by the beginning of the *Quadrilogue* of Alain Chartier:
A la tres haulte & excellente majeste des princes . . .
A la tre háuto e euzsellanto majesté de prinsos . . .

1530 (Palsgrave) 840: 56

Figured pronunciation appeared quite early in the dialogues that were the staple of the Renaissance classroom. No universally recognized system of transcription existed. Some used interlinear layouts, for instance Daniel Martin's *Colloquies*. But the more usual system was to put the pronunciation key in a third column. In the Mason "grammar" the key is in the first column; more often it was placed in the center.

Claude de Sainliens, the author of an immensely popular series of Romance language manuals, went a step further. Taking advantage of the unstable state of Renaissance spelling, he mingled normal spelling with figured pronunciation. Where he altered a spelling phonetically, he printed an accepted version of the word in the margin. To denote silent letters, he put a little cross under them (see Figure 7).

Though schemes like this are to be found even during the twentieth century, some language teachers preferred not to use phonetic script, but also rejected figured pronunciation as a danger to sound spelling habits. One of the consequences of this attitude was the transcription used by Berger in his English grammar (see Figure 8). Normal spelling was kept, but each letter was coded according to its possible phonetic realizations. There was some attempt at over-all consistency. Thus e^3, i^3, and u^3 all represent [3]; and a^2 and e^2 are varieties of [ε]. Some years later a similar idea was used by Michael West.

During the Renaissance the question of developing an unambiguous written representation of pronunciation was one of the chief preoccupations of scholars. It was not thought of as primarily an aid for teaching foreign languages, but as one of the aspects of spelling reform. The various ways evolved for dealing with the question are treated in §15.2.1.3; here we are concerned only with alphabets applied to language teaching. The first person to use an approximation to an alphabet in teaching was Jacques Dubois. His scheme

14 THE FRENCHE

though I ſhould teach him for a groate a moneth, it would be too deare for you and him.
Call me that boye which is there at the corner:
Gabriel, haue you bene long here?
how long haue you bene here?
About halfe a yeare Sir: a month:
a fourtnight: a ſeuennight: a yeare.
Can you ſpeake / *Do you ſpeake good* — *Frenche? Latine? Engliſh? Italian? Spaniſhe? highe Duche? Scotiſhe?*
Yea Sir: a litle Sir:
ſo, ſo: not verie good yet.
VVhat booke readeth your maiſter unto you?
As his ſhcolars are fit for:
vnto ſome he readeth Terence, Virgill, Horace, Tullies offices: vnto others, Cato, Pueriles, their Accidences, their Grammar: according to their capacitie:
as for me, I learne onely French, to read and write: and ſometime to cifer.
Maiſter Holyband,
looke ſomewhat narowly to my ſonne:
he is ſomwhat hard of — *witte, underſtanding, memorie:*
he is

LITTELTON. 15

encor' ke je l'enſegnaſſe pour vn gros le mois, ce ſeroit trop cher pour vous et luy. *que*
Appelez moé ce garçon ki eſt là au coin: *moy*
Gabriel, avez vous eſté long tans icy? *coing*
combien avez vous icy eſté? *temps*
Environ demy an Monſieur: vn mois:
kinze jours: huict jours: vn an. *quinze*
Sçavez vous parler / Parlez vous bon — François? Latin? Anglois? Italien? Eſpagnol? Aleman? Eſcoſſois?
Ouy Monſieur: vn peu Monſieur:
tellement kellemét: nó pas encor fort bon.
Kel livre vous lit voſtre maiſtre? *Quel*
Comme ſés eſcholiers ſont capables:
aux vns il lit Terence, Virgile, Horace, lés offices de Cicero: aux autres Cato, Pueriles, leurs Accidens, leur Grammaire: ſelon leur capacité:
kant à moé, j'apprens ſeulemét François, *moy*
à lire et eſcrire: et aucunefois à chiffrer.
Monſieur de Sainliens,
regardez vn peu de prés à mon filz:
il eſt vn peu dur — d'eſprit, d'entendement, de memoire:

Figure 7. Pages from C. de Sainliens, *The Frenche Littleton.*[312:14-15] Copy from Houghton Library, Harvard

partially preserved the spelling of the time, but he printed superscripts over some letters to show how they were pronounced. His method produced spellings like the following: *gambè* (jambe), *$\overset{h}{c}$eval* (cheval); *Alenćon* (Alençon), carité (charitê). The modern French accents are the sole remaining trace of his system; but one will notice that the cedilla is now a subscript and è now denotes [ɛ] not the *e muet*.

In England also, contemporary scholars tried to smooth out the intricacies of English pronunciation for the foreign learner:

> In pronunciation we see that the letters have different characteristics according to the people who used them. It is evident even to the least knowledgeable among men that the English have difficulty with French words, and Frenchmen and Italians have even more with English, because they are not used to such sounds being associated with the letters. For instance, *c̈ep*, to price; *c̈er* face; *uhït*, white; *huic*, which; *mic*, much; *θëf*,

13 CLÉ DE LA PRONONCIATION ANGLAISE. Voyelles.

	Anglais.	Français.	Anglais.	Français.	Français.
a	$\overset{1}{a}$	=* *é*	f$\overset{1}{a}$te,‡	*destin.*	*fée.*
	$\overset{2}{a}$	= *è*	f$\overset{2}{a}$re,	*prix, mets.*	*mère.*
	$\overset{3}{a}$	= *a* bref	f$\overset{3}{a}$t,	*gras.*	*patte.*
	$\overset{4}{a}$	= *â*	f$\overset{4}{a}$r,	*loin.*	*pâte.*
	$\overset{5}{a}$	= *au*	f$\overset{5}{a}$ll,	*chute.*	*épaule.*
e	$\overset{1}{e}$	= *î*	h$\overset{1}{e}$,	*il.*	*île.*
	$\overset{2}{e}$	= *e* bref	m$\overset{2}{e}$t,	*rencontra.*	*nette.*
	$\overset{3}{e}$	= *eu*	h$\overset{3}{e}$r,	*sa.*	*heure.*
i	$\overset{1}{i}$	= *aï*	n$\overset{1}{i}$ce,	*gentille.*	*naïf.*
	$\overset{2}{i}$	= *i* bref	l$\overset{2}{i}$ttle,	*petite.*	*liste.*
	$\overset{3}{i}$	= *eu*	g$\overset{3}{i}$rl,	*fille.*	*gueule*
o	$\overset{1}{o}$	= *ô*	n$\overset{1}{o}$,	*non.*	*le nôtre.*
	$\overset{2}{o}$	= *o* bref	n$\overset{2}{o}$t,	*pas.*	*notre.*
	$\overset{3}{o}$	= *o*	n$\overset{3}{o}$r,	*ni.*	*nord.*
	$\overset{4}{o}$	= *eu* bref	n$\overset{4}{o}$ne,	*aucun*	*neuf, 9.*
	$\overset{5}{o}$	= *ou* long	n$\overset{5}{o}$on,	*midi.*	*voûte.*
	$\overset{6}{o}$	= *ou* bref	n$\overset{6}{o}$ok,	*coin.*	*bouc.*
u	$\overset{1}{u}$	= *iou*	$\overset{1}{u}$se,	*usage.*	*pioupiou.*
	$\overset{2}{u}$	= *eu* bref	n$\overset{2}{u}$ts,	*noix.*	*neuf, 9.*
	$\overset{3}{u}$	= *eu* long	c$\overset{3}{u}$rd,	*gros lait.*	*cœur.*
	$\overset{4}{u}$	= *ou* long	fr$\overset{4}{u}$it,	*fruits.*	*goût.*
	$\overset{5}{u}$	= *ou* bref	f$\overset{5}{u}$ll,	*plein.*	*goutte.*
	oi	= *oï*	oil,	*huile.*	*Moïse.*
	ou	= *aou*	pound,	*livre.*	*caoutchouc.*

Les mots ci-après sont des modèles pour prononcer tout mot portant le même chiffre.

Les mots français, à droite, contiennent l'équivalent du son du mot-modèle anglais.

‡ Toute voyelle non numérotée est muette, excepté les diphtongues *oi* et *ou* qui n'auront pas de numéros et se prononceront comme dans les mots-modèles *oil* et *pound* de la CLÉ.

* Le signe = signifie : égale ou se prononce comme....en français.

SUITE DE LA CLÉ DE PRONONCIATION. 14

Consonnes et Diphtongues.

La 1re colonne se compose de consonnes et diphtongues anglaises.

Anglais.		Français.	Anglais.	Français.
c	=	*k*	c$\overset{3}{a}$t,	*chat.*
c̱*	=	*s*	r$\overset{1}{i}$c̱e,	*riz.*
ch	=	*tch*	ch$\overset{2}{a}$ir,	*chaise.*
g̃	=	*dj*	g$\overset{3}{o}$r'g̃e$\overset{4}{o}$us, 1	*pompeux.*
j	=	*dj*	j$\overset{1}{a}$il,	*prison.*
oy	=	*oï*	boy,	*garçon.*
ph	=	*f*	phr$\overset{1}{a}$s̱e,	*phrase.*
s̱	=	*z*	s$\overset{1}{e}$a's̱on,	*saison.*
sh	=	*ch*	sh$\overset{5}{o}$e,	*soulier.*
sion	=	*jeune*	v$\overset{2}{i}$'sion,	*vision.*
tion	=	*cheune*	n$\overset{1}{a}$'tion,	*nation.*
th	=	*z* ‡	th$\overset{1}{e}$, 2	*le, la, les.*
tȟ	=	*s* §	tȟ$\overset{2}{i}$ck,	*épais.*
w	=	*ou*	w$\overset{2}{e}$st,	*ouest.*
ow	=	*aou*	how, 3	*comment.*
x	=	*eks*	$\overset{2}{e}$xc$\overset{1}{u}$s̱e',	*excuse.*
x̱	=	*egs*	$\overset{2}{e}$x̱$\overset{3}{a}$ct',	*exact.*
y initial	=	*i*	y$\overset{2}{e}$s,	*oui.*
y final ¶	=	*i*	$\overset{1}{e}$a's̱y,	*facile.*
$\overset{1}{y}$	=	$\overset{1}{i}$	w*h*$\overset{1}{y}$. 4	*pourquoi.*
$\overset{2}{y}$	=	$\overset{2}{i}$	h$\overset{2}{y}$m*n*,	*hymne.*

se prononcent comme dans les mots anglais ci-après, à droite :

* Le signe ‒, sur ou sous une lettre, indique un son doux; le signe ‿ indique un son court, bref. — ‡ En pressant un peu la langue entre les dents. — § En pressant la langue fortement contre les dents. — ¶ Le son de *y* final tient de l'*i* et de l'*é* français.

Figure 8. Pronunciation Guide from F. Berger, *Methode d'anglais.*[102:13-14] Copy from le Petit Séminaire de Québec

thief; *θomb,* thumb; *uiþ,* with; *smyθ,* smith. These words are usually written thus: cheape, chere, white, which, mich, thef, thombe, with, smyth.

1568 (Smith) 1025: 5

Most of the other alphabets developed at the time had reference to only one language and thus, as far as language teachers were concerned, solved no problem.

The first truly international alphabet to be used in language teaching was that of the International Phonetic Association (that used in this book). The alphabet was used in many ways in the classroom. Besides symbolizing the sounds to be taught, it was found in phonetic readers to avoid contact with spellings which could be misleading. Phonetic spelling was never intended to be more than a temporary prop, to be set aside when the danger of interference between pronunciation and spelling was past.[1053:45] Jespersen used phonetic charts to teach both symbol and sound,[587:161] a procedure widely followed. At this stage transcriptions were exact, in Passy's words, "a photograph of the language studied."[850:5] This "narrow" transcription was later found to offer too much detail for easy assimilation and was abandoned for a "broad" transcription which gave only the major elements of the new sounds.[449:68]

There were abuses. In an attempt to appear modern, textbooks which followed the traditional Grammar-Translation style placed phonetic exercises at the beginning of the first volume, then, their duty done, they ignored phonetics completely. Another practice, especially prevalent in the 1950's, was requiring phonetic transcription from the pupils, even if they could not speak. The phonetic alphabet was treated as just another method of spelling.

Following some psychological research into the problem of visual perception of sounds, the phoneticians of the team that produces *Parlons français*[1019] devised a system of vowel symbolization based on the spectrum. Front vowels were thought of as warm, therefore at the red-yellow end, and back vowels were therefore in the green-violet area. Close vowels were lighter in color and open darker. Nasalization was symbolized by muddying the intense color of the primary vowel, and the front rounded vowels, [y], [ø] and [œ], were given pastel tonings based on the color of the appropriate unrounded vowel.[1019:III:104] In the later books of the part of the set designed for pupil use, vowels were printed in outline letters to allow the user to color them in, thus reinforcing kinesthetically the phonetic training from the teacher.

In general, phoneticians were not overly concerned with intonation and rhythm. These factors, however, had been one of the first preoccupations of the Greeks who set themselves to teaching their language to foreigners.

For instance, Aristophanes of Byzantium devised Greek accents during the second century B.C. to help foreigners cope with the tone system of classical Greek. Latin grammarians, not understanding their purpose, took them as showing where the ictus fell in a word, assimilating word accent to tone. In a modified form this was perpetuated until our own times. In the liturgical books of the Roman Catholic Church, texts of the services have intonation markings on them, while the prefaces and liturgical directions, which are in Latin also, but not meant to be read in public, are left unmarked.

As a language-teaching device the matter was taken up again by the early Direct Methodists. In 1909 Jones published a system representing the melody of English as a series of curves and accent points:

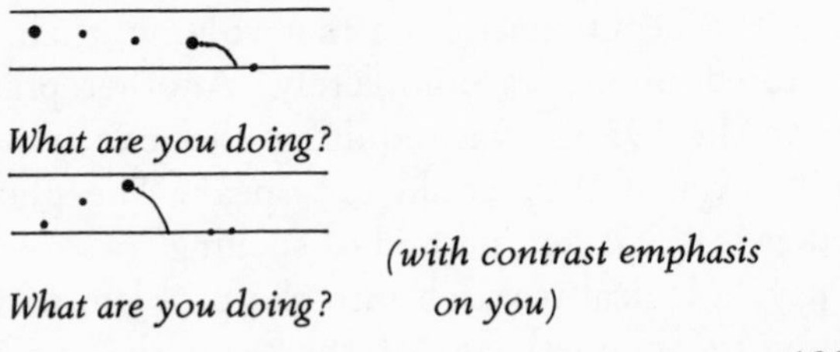

What are you doing?
What are you doing?
(with contrast emphasis
on you)

1909 (Jones) 600: 115

But owing to the difficulty of drawing these at speed his symbols did not become popular as either a scientific or a teaching tool. Later authorities often did not use phonetic script in intonation transcription either.

In the 1930's Jeanne Vidon-Varney adapted Fouché's intonation curves to teaching the intonation of French. As a necessary preliminary she here introduced pupils to the idea of intonation groups, then drew the curves on the blackboard to show pitch and intensity relationships both within the groups and outside them:

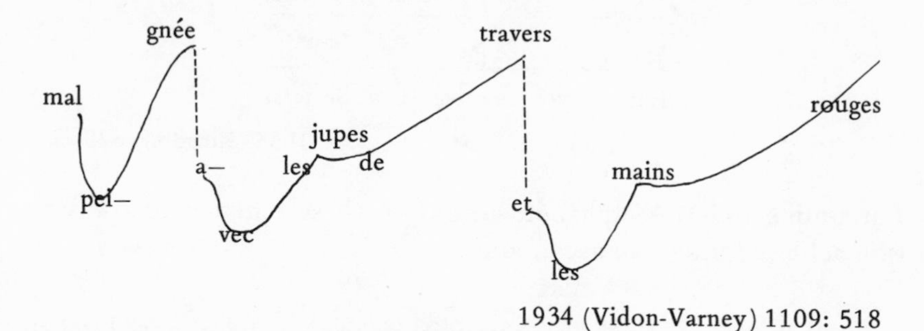

1934 (Vidon-Varney) 1109: 518

In the 1940's and 1950's, linguists used more diagrammatic means. Pike originated the system, later taken over by a large number of American linguists, of superimposing straight lines to show low, high, falling, and rising tones: e.g., What are you doing; Others, including Jones, experimented with musical staffs. From this developed yet another system which postulated four general pitch levels in the voice represented by lines drawn on the page:

4 Do-

-nnez

3 lui

l(e) dic-

2 -tio-

1 -nnaire, s'il vous plait.

Diagramme intonatif 18

1964 (Léon) 659: 81

In the books by Roger Kingdon two schemes are used. For exposition an adaptation of Jones's points and lines is used. But for fast transcription and general teaching purposes he developed the scheme of slanted and vertical accents shown in the text of the following examples:

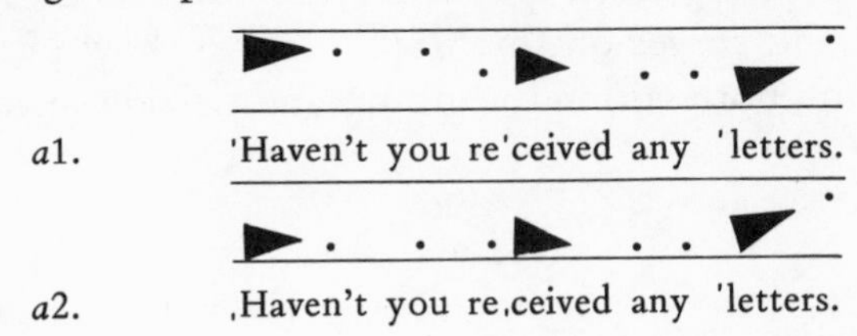

*a*1. 'Haven't you re'ceived any 'letters.

*a*2. ,Haven't you re,ceived any 'letters.

1958 (Kingdon) 625: 38

But unlike the IPA alphabet, no one of these schemes of transcription achieved universal acceptance.

3.2.2.3 Phonetic Analysis. The difference we have noted in the previous chapter between inductive and deductive approaches in grammar had its counterpart in the teaching of pronunciation. While some teachers were prepared to let the pupil arrive at a correct pronunciation by imitation and indirect use of phonetic analysis, others thought that imparting some knowledge of the anatomical processes involved was an easy short cut:

> Persons from 18-20 years old ought not to be expected to learn foreign sounds by the almost unconscious imitation, proper enough in the nursery. Sounds can be acquired without knowing the movements of the organs of speech . . . but by scientific instruction we can save time, and attain a degree of accuracy otherwise never reached by adults.
>
> 1885 (Brandt) 146: 63

An approach resembling this idea had been in use among the classical grammarians eighteen hundred years before; the most important aim seems to have been giving an ordered knowledge of phonetics as it was understood at the time:

> Let nobody scorn the elements of grammar as unimportant. Granted, it is no great achievement to distinguish consonants from vowels and semi-

vowels. But seeing that the immense subtlety of these matters will become obvious to those entering into this almost sacred discipline, boys, even with their limited capabilities, will be able to sharpen their minds and make use of the most esoteric disciplines of learning.

A.D. 100 (Quintillian) 923: I.iv.6

Throughout the classical and medieval periods phonetic analyses were common, but in the manner of the modern reference grammar, they were put at the beginning of the texts. In general, the Renaissance and seventeenth-century grammarians followed the same arrangement, but as we have seen, they tried to reinforce this by other means. As well as directions based on comparison between languages, there were analyses of the articulatory movements required. Petrus Ramus, for instance, grouped together [a] [ε] [i] as front vowels, commenting that the mouth was open and the tongue close to the palate. He added that the mouth was open wide (*magno rictu*) for [a], closed a little (*minore rictu*) for [ε], and that the smallest opening (*minimo rictu*) produced [i].[930:10] The grammars of the following century went into considerable detail. For instance, Oudin remarks of the bilabial fricative [β] in Spanish:

The first is *b* which is written indifferently for the consonant *v*. . . . They both have the same pronunciation, which is, however, unlike the French *b* or *v* which are noticeably different. But it resembles the German *w* or the Gascon *b*. To pronounce them properly, one must be careful not to allow the lips to close, but to leave a breathing space between them.

1660 (Oudin) 829: 2.601

Other grammars, like Cooper's *Grammatica linguae anglicanae*, provided tables from which the mouth movements necessary could be worked out by the pupil (see Figure 26).

The first application of the nineteenth-century science of phonetics was that of Trautmann, who used it in teaching French, English, and German in 1884, a move that was welcomed by the Direct Method movement. In his manifesto of the Direct Method, Vietor pointed out the absurdity of taking a word like *schwarz* and treating it as if it had seven phonemes instead of the five it really has, just because there are seven letters.[1110:4] The attitude of the movement is best summed up in the words of Rambeau:

> The instructor of French at school or college can not do without phonetics, if he really intends to teach modern French, and this he is generally expected to do, as far as I know, i.e., not alone to teach something or much about modern French.
>
> 1893 (Rambeau) 927: 321

Practice in the early twentieth century remained indefinite, but among those teachers who resorted to phonetics to teach pronunciation considerable emphasis was laid on visual demonstration. Jespersen, for example, used charts which depicted the way in which the speech organs worked, and the vowel trapezium of Daniel Jones became a familiar tool in many classrooms. By the late 1930's it was not unusual to accompany pronunciation teaching by an extremely thorough analysis of mouth and tongue movements and by exercises designed to give the pupils conscious command over their vocal organs.[910:3] This had already been endorsed by Palmer,[836:51] and had been recommended by the International Phonetic Association, which collaborated in preparing materials.

Matters remained thus until after the Second World War, when phonology began to play its part in the classroom. A similar division of opinion to that of fifty years before developed over the merits of introducing the formal jargon of phonology into the classroom. The idea of system became important, displacing the previous techniques of dealing with sounds in isolation. Politzer was one who approved of this new development, but in the same breath he pointed out that unless the units of the phonological system were accurately described, the teacher and pupil would settle for "a practical level of comprehension without ever attaining the pronunciation of a native speaker."[898:27] Thus, though phonetic analyses lost pride of place, they were still regarded as essential in learning the sounds themselves.

Phonologists also drew attention to the matter of juncture, i.e., clusters of sounds that are accepted in various languages. While some teachers tried to trick pupils into pronouncing these groups correctly (see §3.1.2), others preferred to discuss such problems with their pupils. This became especially important in teaching English, a language rich in consonant clusters, to Spanish speakers, for instance.[640:18] A parallel concern was the distribution of sounds in the word. It was found that sounds possible in one position of the word posed difficulties in others, e.g., the sound [5] is never initial in English but quite common in this position in Maori. Hence one has to combat the tendency to replace it by [n]. Similar problems occur with [3] in French.

In dealing with the above difficulties it was found that an explanation of the general articulation and distribution patterns of the second and first languages was useful. Palmer compared the science of phonetics to musical theory: phonetics was as essential to a student of language as musical theory was to a performer.[836:51] Many language teachers went into thorough discussions of physiology and anatomy as a preparation for the introduction of foreign speech sounds. Others, like Pierre Léon, tried to isolate key parts of the language system, for example articulatory force, speed of utterance, and vocalic tension, to forestall mistakes.

It will be obvious that pronunciation has been the Cinderella of language teaching, largely because the linguistic sciences on which its teaching rests did not achieve the sophistication of semantics, lexicology, and grammar until the nineteenth century. Now let us see how the knowledge of sounds, words, and structures has been transmuted into speech skills.

PART

II

MAKING THE LANGUAGE A HABIT

INTRODUCTION

The process of presentation is concerned with introducing the systems of the language, not with refining the skills of utilizing them. On the other hand, by repetition one builds on the knowledge imparted, trying to establish the four skills of listening, speaking, reading, and writing. It has been usual for teachers to group the first two together, under the heading of speech, and to treat reading and writing separately.

Techniques of repetition, like those of presentation, are chosen in accordance with the educational aims of the period. Thus, in periods when instinctive language behavior was the aim of teaching, inductive methods were used. But when language was treated as a sum of logical principles, it was taught and drilled through grammatical analyses. Thus, during the classical period, Renaissance, and modern period, languages were usually drilled so that, even if one could not repeat a grammar rule, one could use the language; and during the other periods, a learner could regurgitate grammar, in spite of his inability to use the language as a means of communication.

It is not, however, true to say that one approach excluded the other. Thus, during the Middle Ages, the conditions of life in the monasteries demanded the inculcation of speaking skills. During the Renaissance, deductive approaches persisted for two reasons. The first was a determined effort to stamp out medieval Latin and return to the stylistic conventions of the classics. The second was the increased importance of the vernaculars. They were coming of age, and by absorbing much of the point and exactness of the classical languages were being made into instruments subtle enough to displace Latin from scholarly literature. During the twentieth century, deductive approaches persisted even into the 1960's as a result of the ubiquitous book and the sudden pressure on the world's educational systems as the number of skilled teachers failed to keep pace with the expanding school population. In an effort to conceal their deficiencies, the teachers were forced to rely on the book and aim at a written command, which demanded less of them.

4

SPEECH

> Never be afraid to speak because you fear to express your ideas rather awkwardly. Every time you give utterance to strange sounds adds to your knowledge of pronunciation, and lessens your bashfulness, by giving you increased confidence in yourself.
>
> 1845 (Butler) in 180: 7

The primeval form of language is speech, a fact taken as first principle by the Direct Methodists who directed language-teaching research in the first half of the twentieth century. Though not enunciated as such, this same attitude guided modern-language teaching during the Renaissance and Greek teaching during the classical period.

Logically there are three steps in teaching speech: inculcating the phonological system; teaching the pupil how to manipulate structures; and conditioning a pupil to use his skills with ease.

4.1 PRONUNCIATION AND INTERPRETATION

It is only the rare teacher who has separated these two skills, as it is often impossible to deal with one without invoking the other. Exercises in use range from dictation to various forms of recitation and reading aloud.

4.1.1 Dictation

Dictation is one of the few exercises consistently employed throughout the history of language teaching. Until the end of the Middle Ages, it was the teacher's only resource to ensure retention, there being few textbooks from which pupils could rework their lessons. St. Cuthbert's account of the death of the Venerable Bede at Jarrow in 735 gives us an indication of how the exercise was used. At this stage it was not specialized to language teaching, but was merely a method of transmitting material from master to pupil. Bede, for instance, was dictating a commentary on Scripture at the time of his death. Spelling mistakes and orthographical variations in extant medieval manuscripts show that even outside the classroom, the accuracy of the exercise was not so good as one would have wished. Since the Middle Ages, however, the exercise has been specialized in teaching how to interpret and write the foreign language.[614:78] First, however, it became an important tool in the first-language classroom, and from there it seems to have passed into the second-language class.

Dictation seems to have been one of the key resources of the Direct Method. Passy, for instance, faced with the problem of teaching his pupils how to distinguish the sounds of the new language, replaced prose composition with dictation and was delighted with the results.[*57:62] Other Direct-Method pioneers added a refinement to the exercise: "Phonetic dictation is very stimulating to the pupils and serves as a useful test of their acoustic powers . . .," wrote Sweet in 1898.[1054:46] Later, however, it was considered that difficulties with the script and the stringent discipline it imposed on the normal pupil's ear made the exercise too difficult.[1002:54] Other teachers rejected it as its aim was too narrow: spelling was considered a legitimate aim of the dictation exercise, and it was this element that phonetic dictation removed.[998:35]

Dictation was not neglected in the classics classroom either. Some teachers added the refinement of marking all the long vowels so that later work with poetic language would be easier.[190:14] This impinged on later work in which dictation was directed towards teaching structure and morphology.[1142] The development of programed learning focused attention on dictation as a conditioning process in language learning. Here it was treated as a formal repertoire which conditioned sound discrimination,[644:283] becoming a transitional exercise that could lead to ability in both writing and listening.

4.1.2 Minimal Pair Drills

Phonetic pattern drills had a double purpose: they served to condition the receptive faculties of the pupil first, and then as material for conditioning production of phonemes.

During the 1950's and 1960's the commonest drill was the "minimal pair." This consisted of two words that differed in one phoneme only. By repeated listenings, the pupil was conditioned to perceive the differences; then by repetitions supervised by the teacher, he practised pronunciation of the sounds. In its simplest form, the drill consisted of juxtaposed sets of words: for instance, *heat, hit; beat, bit.* But in the advanced forms of the drill, which were necessary to ensure that the pupil could reproduce the contrast in normal speech, the contrasting words were put into sentences under different degrees of sentence stress and accent. In this way the pupil was accustomed to the various realizations of a foreign phoneme.

The idea of contrast developed further implications. It is not clear when teachers began introducing foreign sounds by contrasting them with related sounds in the mother tongue. Likewise the development of minimal-pair drills using native and foreign words is not easy to date. The technique was not popular, as on one hand it introduced the mother tongue where many authorities said the mother tongue had no business, and on the other it forced attention to the isolated sound, a tendency at variance with the modern preoccupation with structure. But some teachers saw it as a handy ancillary means of drawing attention to peculiarities of foreign sounds. Language laboratory drills, for instance, were constructed round pairs like *purr/peur*, being introduced after the pupil had been given some acquaintance with the foreign sound and the movements necessary to produce it.

Though made popular by the language laboratory, the idea had had a precursor in the seventeenth century. In his *Grammatica linguae anglicanae* Cooper hit on a technique of contrasting sounds by matching: "So if the short sounds are properly matched with the long, there will be no *mistake,* no *difficulty,* thus: wan/wasp; wen/wane; ween/wee."[601:8] But it is clear that Cooper had no inkling of the utility of his idea in constructing drills, as he uses it merely for illustration.

On a much less scientific plane, many modern language teachers borrowed tongue twisters from vernacular children's games. These are sentences which are deliberately difficult to pronounce: "She sells sea shells on the seashore," for instance. Introduced at a late stage, these were intended to ensure that both perception and production were well learned. Something of the sort existed during the classical period. As a stage in learning the alphabet, Greek and Roman schoolmasters used to have their pupils repeat strings of nonsense syllables as fast as possible in order to limber up their vocal organs. Then the same thing was done with strings of nonsense words.[129:213]

Drills embodying phonological patterns were not found until after the Second World War. While many teachers constructed drills using the same intonation pattern thoughout, others used a contrastive technique. The usual was to contrast different intonations possible in a given sentence (see the Jones and Kingdon examples on pages 82 and 84). A necessary part of the contrast was explanation of how different intonations created different meanings to the sentence. Kingdon made a special point of this, going into both the linguistic and social ramifications of given intonation patterns.[625:251] Others, Pierre Léon for example, contrasted the different intonation patterns of sentence units as they were integrated into the complex sentence.[659:84] Naturally, the emphasis placed on such drills varied according to the language in question.

4.1.3 Oral Reading

The ancients were suspicious of any "silent" use of language, be it musing, praying, or even reading. In the schoolroom, reading, though necessarily concerned with content, was directed to the skills of speech and delivery, as they were an important part of the skills of the orator. Punishment held a large place in such teaching. Plautus has one of his characters warn a pupil: "And when you read a book, if you trip over a single syllable, your hide will look as stained as a wet nurse's apron" (*Bacchides* 433-434). Even allowing for the comic writer's exaggeration, oral reading was an extremely important facet of literary production, and for poets the first public reading was equivalent to publication.[1057:22]

During the Low Latin period, reading kept its importance in the classroom. This was inevitable, as classical literature was never meant to be read silently. Thus it is that Ausonius prepares his nephew, Paulinus Pellaeus, for oral study of the Greek classics:

> You will have to pore over Homer and the delightful works of Menander. Bring life to innumerable verses with the subtle melody and skilled intonation of your voice. Feel the emotion as you read. The shape you give the sentence will show its meaning, and pauses will give vigor to limping verses.
>
> A.D. ?300 (Ausonius) 64: *Liber protrepicus* vv. 50-54

During the Middle Ages it seems that even Scripture was studied out loud, Bede remarking that it occupied both mind and tongue.[90:659]

By this time the classical pronunciation had long since been forgotten, and there were endless discussions over the rights and wrongs of Latin pronunciation, which the Carolingian Renaissance had done nothing to solve. Much of the disputed area was in the place of the word accent and its nature, some quite radical changes having been effected by Vulgar Latin. Many attempts were made to 'correct' the differences between the rulings of Priscian and the reading customs usual during the twelfth century.[711:399] Judging from similar complaints during the Renaissance, it seems that the efforts of medieval scholars had done little to stabilize reading customs.

From the Renaissance until the twentieth century, oral reading was usually taken as a propaedeutic to memorization work, an attitude which reached its zenith during the eighteenth century. Brinsley taught the skills of reading by imitation: he read the passage in question to his pupils, demanding exact reproduction of phonemes and melodic line. The melodic shape of the sentence was to be determined by the accent given the words which expressed the most important figure of rhetoric.[155a:213] Less discriminating teachers abused the technique: a hundred and fifty years later Fénélon rose up against the mannerisms of many teachers, claiming that this forced behavior destroyed the pupils' pleasure in reading.[401:256] To the Jesuits, too, enjoyment was one of the aims of the exercise, but they demanded that the pupils reflect on what they had read and memorize selected passages from it to help in later composition work.[613:19] Breul, like most of the early Direct Methodists, conceived reading as a means to teach sentence rhythm and intonation.[153:20] Other pundits were inclined to regard it as a test of comprehension. Rouse notes that "reading itself is generally a sufficient test. Neither Latin nor any other language can be properly read aloud, with due emphasis, unless it is understood."[975:107] Later experimentation tended to confirm this hypothesis. Gurrey added a caution that skill in foreign language reading often depended on first attaining fluency in the mother tongue, the abilities required being of the same order in both languages.[499:97] The only person to challenge the common opinion was West: "Reading aloud tends to establish a direct path between the eyes and the voice without disturbing the brain at all."[1149:76] Despite this dampening opinion, the position of oral reading was little modified during the twentieth century.

4.1.4 Poetry and Music

Recitation of pieces of poetry and prose is closely allied to oral reading. It is almost a prehistoric means of introducing pupils to the rhythm of their native language, but in the West, it was applied to second languages only when the Romans started learning Greek. The place of rhetoric in ancient society demanded that everything learned by heart should be tested orally. The primary purpose of poetry was to instill a sense of rhythm. Poetic rhythms were relevant to ancient prose rhetoric, as sentence cadences were composed according to certain well-defined metrical criteria and, in any case, the rules governing pronunciation had been rationalized on a metrical basis. Right through the history of Latin teaching Vergil was a favorite author for this exercise. The practice suffered eclipse during the late eighteenth century as Latin lost its oral dimension. Under the prompting of the Direct Method, Rouse and Ripman restored verse memorization and recitation, even to printing passages of Latin in phonetic script.[958:800]

In modern languages memorization and recitation never had the breadth of aim the Renaissance and Middle Ages had accorded the recitation of poetry. From a whole aesthetic experience it became an exercise with two main functions: teaching intonation, and providing a ready-made stock of expressions.[194:67] But as literary imitation was not envisaged, given the conversational bias of present-day language teaching, caution was strictly enjoined over what could be used in a piece of memorized verse.

Music and songs became an integral part of language teaching during the Middle Ages. The first introduction to Latin was given to most pupils in the "song school," or school of liturgical music. After the rhythm and flow of the language had been drilled by plain chant, which was based solidly on speech rhythms, the pupil began the formal study of Latin. From a rather ambiguous reference to *nenia* in the *Fecundia ratis*[359:2] it seems that songs were occasionally used in the secular classroom.

St. Jerome and Abelard both mention sacred music as an essential element in Latin teaching,[3:325] and many of the medieval tracts on music contain large sections on pronunciation. These detail matters like vowel quality, syllabic length, and intonation patterns. As it was taken for granted that spelling governed pronunciation, medieval scholars were faced with the problem of "silent letters." Liturgical music, it seems, was pressed into service to ensure that these letters were taken care of. Letters whose phonetic existence was threatened by the pronunciation habits of the new romance languages were strengthened by being sung on a "liquescent" note, i.e., separately from the vowel preceding them in the syllable, and in later centuries, this spread to all threatened consonants.[*102:12] Such pedantry had its own reward in producing a pronunciation that was more careful than that of Cicero himself, for many of the letters that were restored had been silent in classical times.

One of the most popular language teaching songs came out of Clenardus's school at Braga. According to his own account this song which dealt with greetings, was originally a dialogue taught as such in the school. The most probable explanation of its appearance in a musical guise is that it had been learned in a singsong fashion and the tune had developed of itself. Clenardus remarks with some amusement that even the muleteers of the city sang it and that its first words, *Heus puer,* became a normal form of greeting among all social classes.

Information on other uses of the idea before the twentieth century is scanty, and the formalistic turn language teaching took would lead one to suspect that such levities as music were not in favor. Owing to the cultural content of the twentieth-century modern-language course, interest in songs revived. Folk songs were especially common in the classroom, special arrangements even being made for school use. There was some question about the use of peculiarly national songs like "Bobby Shaftoe" or "Casey at the Bat," but it was agreed that if the course was to have a cultural content, such songs could hardly be avoided.[*44:71] Owing to the archaic tone of many folk songs, the popular song, despite raised eyebrows, found its way into the classroom and formed a large part of school broadcasts.

In teaching young children, to whom music and rhythm are extremely important as learning activities, song became quite important in the mid-twentieth century. Some authorities, such as R. M. Jones, linked music with mime and dance,[604:16] as both music and movement are natural ways in which children learn outside the classroom.

4.2 GRAMMAR DRILLS

Grammar drills fall into three types: pattern practice, which can appear either as a list of sentences with identical structure but different words, or as the substitution table; the cycle, based on describing a process; and the chria, a group of sentences in which one manipulates all the possible flexional forms of the paradigm to be practised. All three types can be found in Renaissance textbooks and the second two date back to classical times.

4.2.1 Pattern Practice

Pattern practice first appeared, not in the late 1940's, as was often claimed, but by the early 1500's. During the first half of the twentieth century it was the development of the language laboratory that focused attention on this group of techniques. It was clearly not realized that researchers were merely duplicating work that had been done before, and some rash statements were made by reputable authorities.[543:33]

An early use of this tool of the language laboratory was in the *Colloquia* of Erasmus with this passage on affectionate greetings to wife or sweetheart:

Salve {
mea Corneliola
mea vita
mea lux
meum delicium
meum suavium
mel meum
mea voluptas unica
meum decus
meum corculum
mea spes
meum solatium
}

1524 (Erasmus) 374: 629

Printers of the time did not set such tables in boxes, as became the custom in the twentieth century, preferring to reproduce the handdrawn bracket. As during the twentieth century, one of the aims of the substitution table was teaching vocabulary and its integration into the sentence. Thus in the Erasmian table, a pupil who knew *Ave* and *Vale* as well would have no difficulty in commuting them without mistaking their construction.

About the same period, substitution tables began to appear in modern-language texts. In the *Introductorie for to lerne French* of Gilles Duwes (1534?), a table of greetings is printed, with some unnecessary duplications which show he was not sure of his tool (see Figure 9). This particular table is a dialogue with a change of speaker at *Et.* The interlinear translation above the line is a peculiar feature of the Duwes table. Notice that *vo*^{9} (vous) is unnecessary in the second half of the dialogue, as the following column gives a full range of possible pronouns. In paradigm tables Duwes introduces the technique of guided choice. If one starts at the pointing hand in Figure 10, one can read right across the page. The colophon mark below the word *pourquoi* requires the pupil to omit it until it reappears on the last line.

Despite early isolated cases like that of Duwes, integration into the dialogue was to become one of the most striking features of the Renaissance table. By the end of the sixteenth century substitution tables were in very common use with some obvious structural awareness. De Sainliens, for instance, was one who used the Erasmian table as a matter of course. Among his innovations was introducing multiple choice on both sides of the bracket (see Figure 7). In his hands the device developed a notable freedom in structural terms, and the use of an English translation on the facing page served to introduce cases where a single item in one language may have a variety of translations in the other:

Andiamo	da lui la volta sua quella banda	Let us go	to him

1597 (de Sainliens) 315: 12-13

Salutatyons in frenche / whiche may be tourned two maner wayes / as whan ye saye in Englysshe / God gyue you good morowe / ye may saye / Good morowe gyue you god / as ye shall se here folowynge.

Good morowe
Bon iour
Good yere
Bon an
Good euenyng
Bon vespre
Good euyn
Bon soir
Good nyght
Bonne nuyt
Good metyng
Bon encontre
Good ioye
Bon ioie

	me	Good lyfe and longe	me	
	Me	Bōne vie et lōgue	Me	
	the	Good fortune	the	
	Te	Bōne fortune	Te	
God	hym gyue	Good prosperyte and to you	him	gyue god.
Dieu	Luy doit	Bōne psperite Et a vo⁹	Luy	doit dieu.
	vs	well to prospere	vs	
	Nous	Bien prosperer	Nous	
	you	Good lucke	you	
	Vous	Bon heur	Vous	
	them	Good begynnyng	them	
	Leurs	Bon cōmēcement	Leurs	

Good meane
Bon moien
Good ende / & well to fynisshe
Bon fin / ou bien acheuer
well to lyue / well to dye
Bien viure / bien mourir
Good helthe
Bonne sante
Paradyse at the ende
Paradis en la fin
The hole / or the fulfyllyng of your desyres.
Letier / ou lacomplissemēt de vos desirs.

God kepe / god blesse / god saue / god gyde you /
Dieu gart / dieu benie / dieu saulue / dieu vous cōduye / Dieu
god be within / god be your helpe / god be wyllynge to
Dieu soit ceans / dieu vous soit en aide / dieu vous veulle
helpe you / god kepe you from euell and trouble / I bydde you
aider / dieu vous garde de mal et dencombrier / Adieu vous
farwell / god be with you / I take my leaue of you / farwell tyll
dis / adieu soiez / adieu sans adieu / adieu iusques
we se agayne.
au reuoir.

The generation of colours / with the blason of them.

Colour is lyght incorporate in a
Coulleur est lumiere icorporee en vng
body visyble / pure & clene. There ben two dyf-
corps visible / pur et nect. Ilz sont deux dif
ference of perspectyues / the one is pure sepa-
ference de psppectifz / lung est pur sepa-
rate of erthlynesse / and the tother is spotted by the same /
re de terrestreite / et lautre est conquine par icelle
and myxed lyght is deuyded in four ptes / that is to say /
et mixtione lumiere est quadripartite / cest a dire /
clere: darke plentuous or scant / whiche is to vnderstāde
clere / obscure / habondāte et rare / qui est a entendre
great or small. wherfore it appereth that thre
grande ou petite. Pourquoy il appert que trois
thynges dothe cause the essence of whytnesse / that is to say /
choses causent lessence de blancheur / cest a scauoir /
clerenesse with habundaunce of the same / and a body visyble clene &
clarte auec multitude dicelle / et vng psspectif pur et
pure. And thre thynges lykewyse ben cause of
nect. Et trois choses semblablement sont cause de
blacke colour / it is to say / lyght / darke with
coulleur noir / cest a scauoir / lumiere / obscure / auec
scarsnesse of it / and perspectyue vnclene. And by this is
paucite dicelle / et perspectif impur. Et par ce est
open the sayeng of Arystotell / and of Auenrois / whiche haue
esclarcy le dict Daristote / et de Auenrois / qui ont
put blacknesse for priuation / and whytnesse for
mis noircheur pour priuacion / et blancheur port habi-

Figure 9. Table of greetings from G. Duwes, *Introductorie for to lerne French.*[356] Copy in the Houghton Library, Harvard

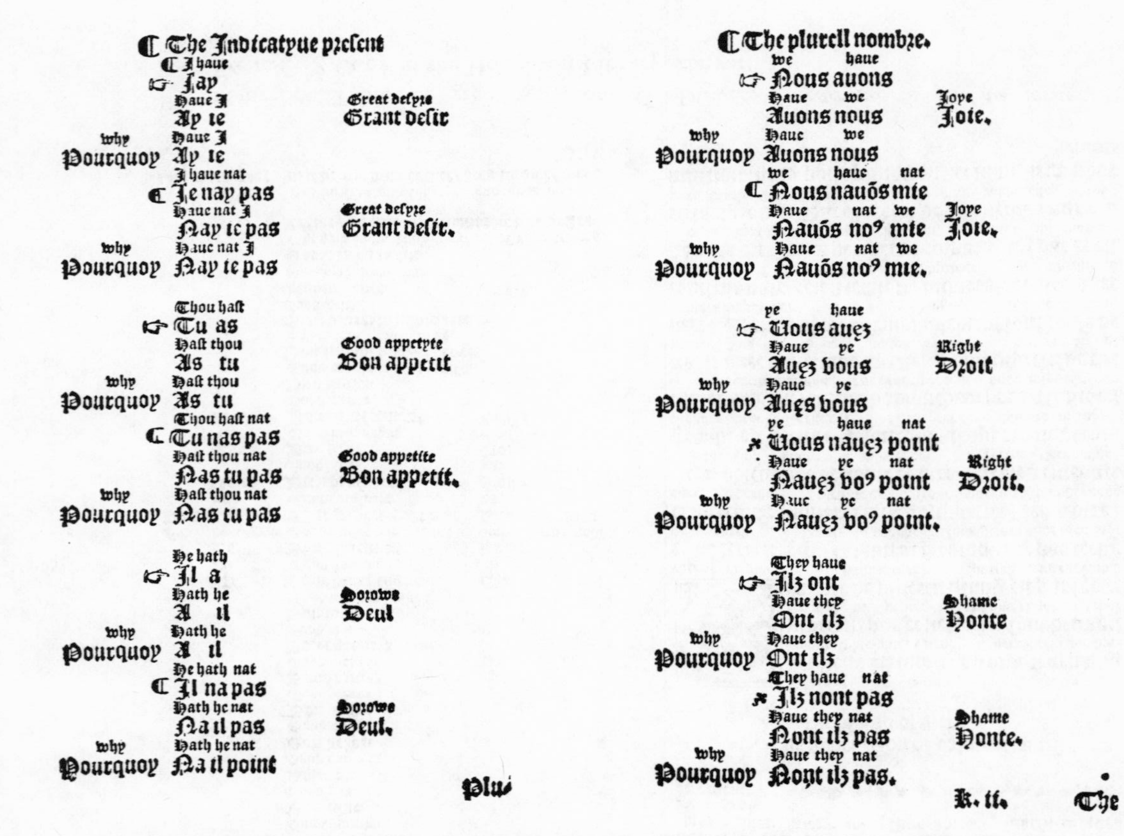
The Indicatyue present
I haue
Jay
haue I
Ay ie
Great desyre
Grant desir
why
haue I
Pourquoy Ay ie
I haue nat
Je nay pas
haue nat I
Nay ie pas
Great desyre
Grant desir.
why
haue nat I
Pourquoy Nay ie pas

Thou hast
Tu as
Hast thou
As tu
Good appetyte
Bon appetit
why
Hast thou
Pourquoy As tu
Thou hast nat
Tu nas pas
Hast thou nat
Nas tu pas
Good appetite
Bon appetit.
why
Hast thou nat
Pourquoy Nas tu pas

He hath
Il a
Hath he
A il
Sorowe
Deul
why
Hath he
Pourquoy A il
He hath nat
Il na pas
Hath he nat
Na il pas
Sorowe
Deul.
why
Hath he nat
Pourquoy Na il point

Plu

The plurell nombre.
we haue
Nous auons
Haue we
Auons nous
Joye
Joie.
why
Haue we
Pourquoy Auons nous
we haue nat
Nous nauõs mie
Haue nat we
Nauõs no⁹ mie
Joye
Joie.
why
Haue nat we
Pourquoy Nauõs no⁹ mie.

ye haue
Vous auez
Haue ye
Auez vous
Right
Droit
why
Haue ye
Pourquoy Auez vous
ye haue nat
Vous nauez point
Haue ye nat
Nauez vo⁹ point
Right
Droit.
why
Haue ye nat
Pourquoy Nauez vo⁹ point.

They haue
Ilz ont
Haue they
Ont ilz
Shame
Honte
why
Haue they
Pourquoy Ont ilz
They haue nat
Ilz nont pas
Haue they nat
Nont ilz pas
Shame
Honte.
why
Haue they nat
Pourquoy Nont ilz pas.

K. ii.
The

Figure 10. Paradigm from G. Duwes, *Introductorie for to lerne French.*[356] Copy in the Houghton Library, Harvard

Outside of dialogues, substitution tables were almost completely confined to the illustration of paradigms. It was the German humanists who applied it to adjectives:

So we say:

	gelerter	Man			
	gelerte	Fraw	der		Man
ein	gelertes (oder)		but die	gelert	Weib
	gelerts	Thier	das		Thier

1573 (Albertus) 21: 51

The logical development is illustrated by the page photographed from a Greek grammar by P. Gras (see Figure 11): the stems are printed once and the endings are under the bracket. This recalls the method Brinsley recommended of learning flexions by omitting the stem (see §2.2.2). It was this custom which probably gave rise to the curious tables in Alexander Gill's *Logonomia anglica,* in which Latin endings are separated from their stems and bracketed to translate English pronouns:

Ego ill{um / os}	accuso,	qu{em / os}	scio affine{m / s}	esse culpae.
	him	whum		
I akkuz	them	which	I know tu bi gilti.	
		that		

1621 (Gill) 460: 57

The pattern drill was first divorced from the substitution table by Samuel Hoadly, a contemporary of Locke. His Latin grammar, though published in 1683, has a nineteenth-century ring to the title: *The Natural Method of Teaching.* Hoadly distinguished ten "phrases" (in twentieth-century terms, "types of structure") in Latin, all of them based on the simple sentence. Though, at times, the English the pupil is asked to translate will seem to differ considerably from the model given him, he is required to stay within the structure dealt with in the chapter. Hoadly deliberately avoids the term "trans-

70

TABLE DES VERBES.

	Indicatif.	Subjonctif.	Optatif.
prés. έω	φιλ { έω, έεις, έει, ῶ, εῖς, εῖ. amo, as, at. έομεν, έετε, έουσι. οῦμεν, εῖτε, οῦσι.	ἐὰν φιλ { έω, έῃς, έῃ, ῶ, ῇς, ῇ. amem, es, et. έωμεν, έητε, έωσι. ῶμεν, ῆτε, ῶσι.	εἴθε φιλ { έοιμι, έοις, έοι, οῖμι, οῖς, οῖ, amem ou amarem. έοιμεν, έοιτε, έοιεν. οῖμεν, οῖτε, οῖεν.
imparf.	ἐφίλ { εον, εες, εε, ουν, εις, ει. amabam, as, at. έομεν, έετε, εον. οῦμεν, εῖτε, ουν.		
prés. άω	τιμ { άω, άεις, άει, ῶ, ᾷς, ᾷ. honoro, as, at. άομεν, άετε, άουσι. ῶμεν, ᾶτε, ῶσι.	ἐὰν τιμ { άω, άῃς, άῃ, ῶ, ᾷς, ᾷ. honorem, es, et. άωμεν, άητε, άωσι. ῶμεν, ᾶτε, ῶσι.	εἴθε τιμ { άοιμι, άοις, άοι. ῷμι, ῷς, ῷ, honorē, ou honorarē άοιμεν, άοιτε, άοιεν. ῷμεν, ῷτε, ῷεν.
imparf.	ἐτίμ { αον, αες, αε, ων, ας, α. honorabam, as, at. άομεν, άετε, αον. ῶμεν, ᾶτε, ων.		
prés. όω	δηλ { όω, όεις, όει. ῶ, οῖς, οῖ. manifesto, as, at. όομεν, όετε, όουσι. οῦμεν, οῦτε, οῦσι.	ἐὰν δηλ { όω, όῃς, όῃ. ῶ, οῖς, οῖ. manifestem, es, et. όωμεν, όητε, όωσι. ῶμεν, ῶτε, ῶσι.	εἴθε δηλ { όοιμι, όοις, όοι. οῖμι, οῖς, οῖ, manifestem, ou arē. όοιμεν, όοιτε, όοιεν. οῖμεν, οῖτε, οῖεν.
imparf.	ἐδήλ { οον, οες, οε. ουν, ους, ου. manifestabam, as, at. όομεν, όετε, οον, οῦμεν, οῦτε, ουν.		

Le Duel des verbes circonflexes se forme comme celui des Barytons, & se contracte à l'ordinaire.

Remarquez qu'il n'y a que le présent & l'imparfait de chaque mode & du participe qui reçoivent contraction.

71

CIRCONFLEXES ACTIFS.

Impératif.	Infinitif.	Participes.
φιλ { εε, εέτω, ει, είτω, ama, ato. έετε, εέτωσαν, εῖτε, είτωσαν.	φιλ { έειν. εῖν. amare.	φιλ amā { έων, έοντος. ῶν, οῦντος. έουσα, εούσης. οῦσα, ούσης. έον, έοντος. οῦν, οῦντος.
τιμ { αε, αέτω, α, άτω. honora, ato. άετε, αέτωσαν, ᾶτε, άτωσαν.	τιμ { άειν. ᾶν. honorare.	τιμ honorans. { άων, άοντος, ῶν, ῶντος. άουσα, αούσης, ῶσα, ώσης. άον, άοντος. ῶν, ῶντος.
δηλ { οε, οέτω, ου, ούτω. manifesta, ato. όετε, οέτωσαν, οῦτε, ούτωσαν.	δηλ { όειν οῦν manifestare.	δηλ { όων, όοντος, ῶν, οῦντος. όουσα, οούσης, οῦσα, ούσης. όον, όοντος, οῦν, οῦντος.

Figure 11. Paradigm from P. Gras, *Methode aisée pour apprendre la langue grecque.*[476:70] Copy in le Petit Séminaire de Québec

lation," preferring "imitation." His method of proceeding is best shown by the following example:

Ubi vos habitatis?	Where dwell the tribes?
Ego habito hic.	The tribes dwell here.
Familia habitat hic.	Families dwell here.

1683 (Hoadly) 541: 115

In accordance with twentieth-century practice, Hoadly assumes that the pupils will have a parallel reading program, but that they should know their accidence fairly well before beginning his course.

The substitution table seems to have disappeared for a century after Hoadly, to reappear in 1811 in a French grammar published in Montreal. It seems that the tables were merely for demonstration, as the textbook is meant to give a good enough knowledge of grammar to allow a start on Latin. One feature of the tables missing from their modern counterparts is the formal analysis of sequence of tenses that appears in the two columns on the right (see Figure 12).

Dissatisfaction with the results and methods of language teaching caused many to examine very closely the language learning of children in the hope of finding some feature on which to base a new approach. One of these, an Indian civil servant named Thomas Prendergast, noticed that young children usually drill a new structure which fascinates them by playing with it and forcing as much vocabulary into it as possible. Thus was pattern practice once again rediscovered. In 1870 Prendergast patented his "Mastery System." Like the Natural Method, it had no place for grammar rules; but it was a carefully graded method, easily adaptable to the pupil's rate of habit forming. Free enterprise was forbidden until response became quite automatic.[911:7] Speed was no object. He justified the almost endless repetition his system demanded by claiming the necessity of forming language reflexes and by reminding his readers that a language once learned is easily forgotten. Like Gouin, Prendergast required the pupil to operate with an easily expandable language system, claiming that one could learn a whole language by ringing the changes on a twenty-word sentence.[911:5] For him the substitution

de désir ; la phrase-sujet de narration, la phrase-sujet de désir.

La phrase-objet et la phrase-sujet de narration ont lieu, quand le verbe principal rapporte simplement la chose :.... *Je crois qu'il viendra : il est certain qu'il viendra.*

La phrase-objet et la phrase-sujet de désir ont lieu, quand le verbe principal marque le désir que la chose se fasse ou ne se fasse pas :....*Je veux qu'il vienne ; il est nécessaire qu'il vienne.*

Note. Tout ce qu'on dira de la phrase-objet, doit s'entendre de la phrase-sujet.

Phrase-objet de narration.

Regle I. La phrase-objet de narration se lie au verbe principal par la conjonction *que* mise immédiatement après : ....Je crois *que* votre père vient....Il est certain *que* votre père vient.

II. Si le verbe principal est sans négation, le verbe-objet se met à l'indicatif ou au conditionnel : mais il se met au subjonctif, si le verbe principal est accompagné d'une négation :....Je crois qu'*il vient*....Je croyois qu'*il viendroit*....Je ne crois pas qu'*il vienne*.

III. Si la phrase est interrogative, le verbe-objet se met à l'indicatif ou au conditionnel, si l'on s'informe simplement de la chose : mais il se met au subjonctif, si l'interrogation est mise pour marquer quelque mouvement de l'ame, comme de doute, de surprise, &c.

A quel temps du Subjonctif faut-il mettre le Verbe-objet, si la phrase est négative ?

Verbe principal.	*Temps du Verbe-objet.*	*Rapport au Verbe principal.*	*Rapport à une autre action.*
Je ne crois pas Je ne croirai pas	qu'il vienne actuellement.	présent.	
	qu'il vienne demain.	futur.	
	qu'il vînt hier, lorsque, &c.	passé.	présent.
	qu'il vînt demain, si	futur condit.	
	qu'il soit venu hier.	passé.	
	qu'il soit venu demain, avant, &c.	futur.	passé.
	qu'il fût venu hier avant moi.	passé.	passé.
	qu'il fût venu, quand même, &c.	passé.	futur.
Je ne croyois pas Je ne crus pas Je n'ai pas cru Je n'avois pas cru	qu'il vînt.	présent.	
	qu'il fût venu.	passé.	

A quel temps de l'indicatif ou du conditionnel faut-il mettre le Verbe-objet, quand la phrase est affirmative ?

Temps du Verbe principal.	*Temps du Verbe-objet.*	*Rapport au Verbe principal.*	*Rapport à une autre action ou à une période.*
Je crois Je croirai	qu'il arrive actuellement	présent.	
	qu'il arrivoit, lorsque, &c.	passé.	présent.
	qu'il arriva hier.	passé.	présent périod.
	qu'il est arrivé.	passé.	
	qu'il étoit arrivé avant moi.	passé.	passé.
	qu'il fut arrivé hier avant moi.	passé.	passé périod.
	qu'il arrivera.	futur.	
	qu'il sera arrivé, lorsque, &c.	futur.	passé.
	qu'il arriveroit actuellement, si	futur condit.	
	qu'il arriveroit demain, si	futur condit.	
	qu'il seroit arrivé, si	passé.	futur conditio.
Je croyois Je crus J'ai cru J'avois cru	qu'il arrivoit.	présent.	
	qu'il étoit arrivé.	passé.	
	qu'il arriveroit demain, hier.	futur.	
	qu'il arriveroit, si	futur condit.	
	qu'il seroit arrivé, si	passé.	futur conditio.
	qu'il seroit arrivé avant moi.	futur.	passé.

Rem. Après certains verbes, tels que *croire, espérer, s'attendre*, &c. le verbe-objet se met à l'infinitif, si le sujet en est le même que celui du verbe principal : alors au lieu de *que* on met ordinairement *de* :....Je crois *partir* demain...: Je me souviens *d'avoir lu*.

Phrase-objet de désir.

Regle. La phrase-objet de désir se lie au verbe principal par la conjonction *que* ; et le verbe-objet de désir se met toujours au subjonctif :....Je désire *qu'il vienne*....Je souhaite *qu'il* ne *vienne* pas.

A quel temps du Subjonctif faut-il mettre le Verbe-objet de désir ?

Regle I. Lorsque le verbe principal est au présent ou au futur : 1° Le verbe-objet se met au présent, pour marquer une action future par rapport au verbe principal :.... Je désire, je désirerai *qu'il vienne*. 2° Le verbe-objet se met au parfait, pour marquer une action passée par rapport au verbe principal :....Je desire, je désirerai *qu'il soit venu*.

Figure 12. Pages from *Grammaire françoise pour servir d'introduction. . . .* [473:46-47] Copy in le Petit Séminaire de Québec

table was merely a short way of putting down a drill. He explains at length the mathematical possibilities of such a table: the number of sentences possible can be found by multiplying the number of units in each column. Thus in Figure 13 there are 17,784 (18 X 19 X 4 X 13) possibilities.

Though Prendergast himself never became well known, his system attained some popularity in the work of Rosenthal, who, unlike many method makers, freely acknowledged the debt. In a series of grammars that appeared at the turn of the century, he made almost exclusive use of pattern drills worked into a dialogue format. A translation was printed on the facing page (see Figure 14). He also seems to have been one of the first to make systematic use of recordings: Edison cylinders recorded by native speakers were available with the text.

Pattern practice was slow in being accepted by the teaching profession. Its use in textbooks before the Second World War was rare, although it was taken up by some of the Direct Methodists. In an article which appeared in 1903, Charles Schweitzer (well known for his collaboration with Simmonot) recommended drilling oral patterns in class, following them with loaded questions which would force the pupil to use the patterns and vocabulary given.[1006:8] By now it was the structural use of pattern practice that was to the fore. Yet the ancient use to drill paradigms could still be found: Berger constructed the fan in Figure 15 to demonstrate the periphrastic tenses of the English verb, accompanying it with a full verb list on the facing page. After this it took its modern form with the ruled box and was definitely tied to more general structural questions.

After this it seems to have been rediscovered once again by Harold Palmer, this time as a derivation of his theory of ergonics, which bears some resemblance to the later theory of Transformational Grammar. It appears that Palmer believed that the pattern drill and substitution table were his own discovery. He makes no reference to anyone else who worked in the field. A large number of his tables were written in phonetic script, so that oral drill preceded written exercises.[836:182] Previous users of the table had not seen fit to specify whether their tables were for written or oral use, though one can

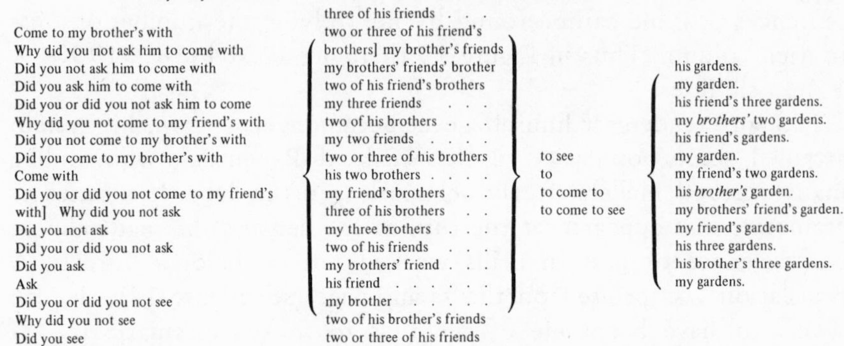

APPENDIX II.

Diagram showing how Variations may be formed from a single sentence–(Vide Paragraph 94.)

Why did you not ask him to come with two or three of his friends to see my brother's gardens?

	three of his friends . . .		
Come to my brother's with	two or three of his friend's		
Why did you not ask him to come with	brothers] my brother's friends		
Did you not ask him to come with	my brothers' friends' brother		his gardens.
Did you ask him to come with	two of his friend's brothers		my garden.
Did you or did you not ask him to come	my three friends . . .		his friend's three gardens.
Why did you not come to my friend's with	two of his brothers . . .		my *brothers'* two gardens.
Did you not come to my brother's with	my two friends		his friend's gardens.
Did you come to my brother's with	two or three of his brothers	to see	my garden.
Come with	his two brothers	to	my friend's two gardens.
Did you or did you not come to my friend's	my friend's brothers . .	to come to	his *brother's* garden.
with] Why did you not ask	three of his brothers . .	to come to see	my brothers' friend's garden.
Did you not ask	my three brothers . . .		my friend's gardens.
Did you or did you not ask	two of his friends . . .		his three gardens.
Did you ask	my brothers' friend . . .		his brother's three gardens.
Ask	his friend		my gardens.
Did you or did you not see	my brother		
Why did you not see	two of his brother's friends		
Did you see	two or three of his friends		

*These phrases apply to the second or fourth columns, but not to both of them collectively. By interchanging the words 'my' and 'his' we double the number of sentences producible by uniting any phrase of the first column with any one of the second. The third is designed to effect a combination between the phrases of the second and fourth columns.

Figure 13. Demonstration Table from T. Prendergast, *Handbook to the Mastery System.*[911:92] Copy in the Widener Library, Harvard

surmise from the early connection with the dialogue that it was treated as an element in conversation teaching.

Apparently Palmer himself was ignored in the development of pattern drills for the ASTP, but owing to the attention these Second World War language schools drew, pattern drills spread to civilian textbooks. Concentration on semantic problems inevitably brought about conflicts with the semantic aspect of language. At first the problem of synonyms was an annoyance to be ignored or shrugged off. But in the early 1950's Hornby suggested that the habitual structures in which words appear should govern patterns taught.[556:I:v]

Among the difficulties in using pattern drills was ensuring that the pupil knew what he was saying, and did not stop at parrot repetition. One way of preventing mindless manipulation of patterns was adopted by the Maori Language Advisory Committee of New Zealand. In the exercises in its textbook, entitled rather aggressively *Ka hao te rangatahi* (The new net goes out fishing) the pattern drill was consistently linked to illustration. In Figure 16, for instance, the

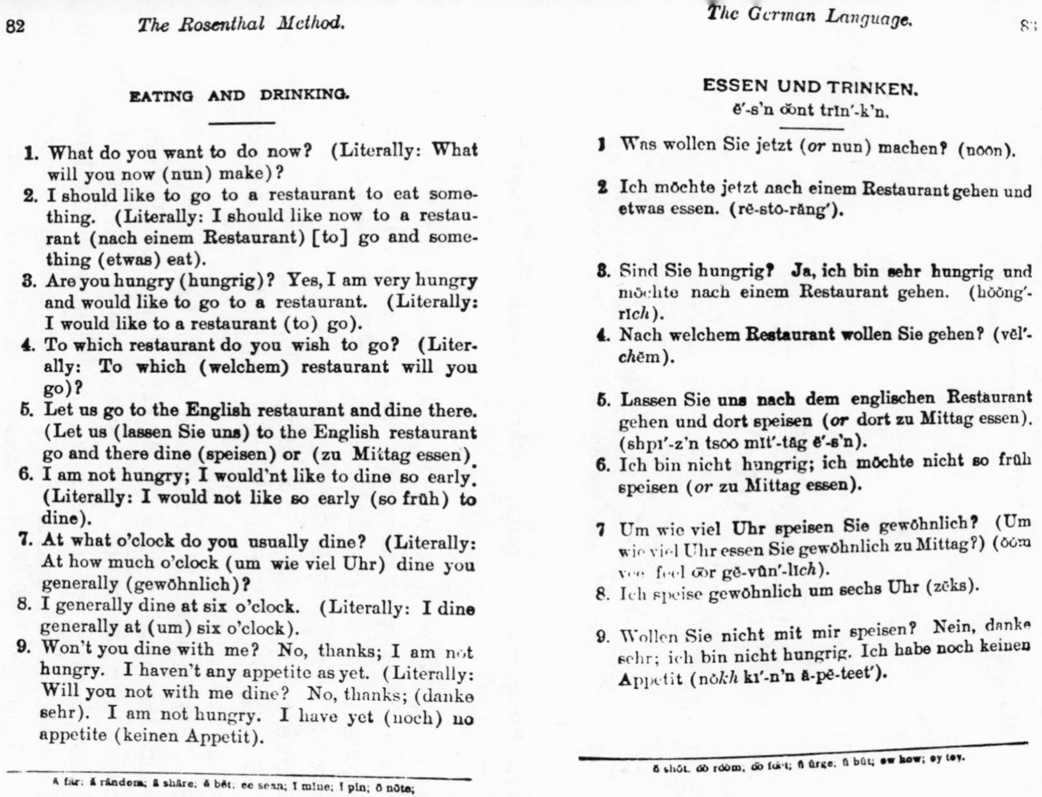

82 *The Rosenthal Method.*

EATING AND DRINKING.

1. What do you want to do now? (Literally: What will you now (nun) make)?
2. I should like to go to a restaurant to eat something. (Literally: I should like now to a restaurant (nach einem Restaurant) [to] go and something (etwas) eat).
3. Are you hungry (hungrig)? Yes, I am very hungry and would like to go to a restaurant. (Literally: I would like to a restaurant (to) go).
4. To which restaurant do you wish to go? (Literally: To which (welchem) restaurant will you go)?
5. Let us go to the English restaurant and dine there. (Let us (lassen Sie uns) to the English restaurant go and there dine (speisen) or (zu Mittag essen).
6. I am not hungry; I would'nt like to dine so early. (Literally: I would not like so early (so früh) to dine).
7. At what o'clock do you usually dine? (Literally: At how much o'clock (um wie viel Uhr) dine you generally (gewöhnlich)?
8. I generally dine at six o'clock. (Literally: I dine generally at (um) six o'clock).
9. Won't you dine with me? No, thanks; I am not hungry. I haven't any appetite as yet. (Literally: Will you not with me dine? No, thanks; (danke sehr). I am not hungry. I have yet (noch) no appetite (keinen Appetit).

ā fär; ă rändom; â shâre; ĕ bĕt; ee seen; ī mine; ĭ pĭn; ō nōte;

The German Language. 83

ESSEN UND TRINKEN.

ĕ'-s'n ŏŏnt trĭn'-k'n.

1 Was wollen Sie jetzt (*or* nun) machen? (noon).

2 Ich möchte jetzt nach einem Restaurant gehen und etwas essen. (rĕ-stō-răng').

3. Sind Sie hungrig? Ja, ich bin sehr hungrig und möchte nach einem Restaurant gehen. (hŏŏng'-rĭ*ch*).

4. Nach welchem Restaurant wollen Sie gehen? (vĕl'-*ch*ĕm).

5. Lassen Sie uns nach dem englischen Restaurant gehen und dort speisen (*or* dort zu Mittag essen). (shpī'-z'n tsoo mĭt'-tăg ĕ'-s'n).

6. Ich bin nicht hungrig; ich möchte nicht so früh speisen (*or* zu Mittag essen).

7 Um wie viel Uhr speisen Sie gewöhnlich? (Um wie viel Uhr essen Sie gewöhnlich zu Mittag?) (ŏŏm vee feel ŏŏr gĕ-vûn'-lĭ*ch*).

8. Ich speise gewöhnlich um sechs Uhr (zĕks).

9. Wollen Sie nicht mit mir speisen? Nein, danke sehr; ich bin nicht hungrig. Ich habe noch keinen Appetit (nŏ*kh* kī'-n'n ă-pĕ-teet').

ŏ shŏt. ŏŏ rōōm; ŏŏ fŏŏt; û ûrge. ŭ bŭt; ow how; oy toy.

Figure 14. Drill from R. S. Rosenthal, *The German Language.*[971:82-83] Copy in le Petit Séminaire de Québec

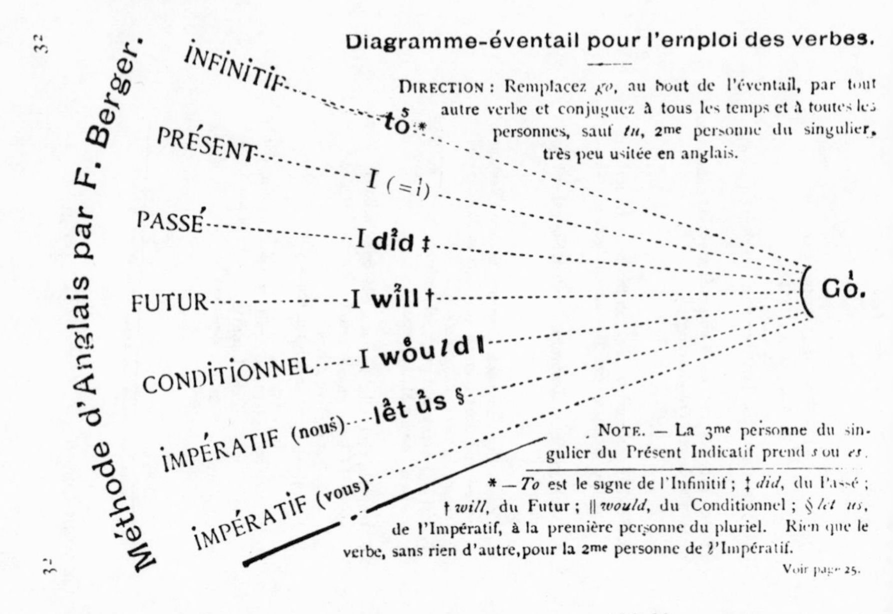

Figure 15. Paradigm from F. Berger, *Méthode d'anglais*.[102:32] Copy from le Petit Séminaire de Québec

pattern to be followed is given in full under the first picture. It will be obvious that the answer to each question is arrived at by rearranging the words and including, as the object of the new sentence, a word whose cue is given by the picture. Thus the completion for B1 reads: "Kei te to a Rewi aua ko Tamahae i te *tepu*." For C2 it is: "Kei runga *poti* a Rewi." The content element is *underlined* in each case.

In the 1960's, pattern drills came under fire from psychologists. The following opinion of Wilga Rivers is typical: "Unremitting and intensive drill is seen to be much less desirable as a way of learning foreign languages. Instead of increasing learning, in the hands of all but the most adept teachers, it can cause boredom by sheer quantity of reinforced acts."[959:39] The work on satiation of W. E. Lambert and L. Jacobovits at McGill University, Montreal, tended to confirm this opinion, but as usual, the results took a long time to reach the general teaching body.

B.

Kei te tō a Rewi rāua ko Tamahae i te aha?

Kei te tō a Rewi rāua ko Tamahae i te poti.

Kei te tō a Rewi rāua ko Tamahae i te aha?

1. Kei te tō _ _ _ _ _ i te _.

Kei te horoi a Rewi rāua ko Mere i te aha?

2. Kei te _ _ _ _ _ _ _ _ _.

Kei te mahi a Mere rāua ko Pani i ngā aha?

3. Kei te _ _ _ _ _ _ _ _ _ _.

Kei te tiki a Hata rāua ko Rewi i ngā aha?

4. Kei te _ _ _ _ _ _ _ _ _.

Kei te karanga a Hata rāua ko Pani i ngā aha?

5. Kei _ _ _ _ _ _ _ _ _ _ _.

C.

Kei runga aha a Hata?
Kei runga hōiho a Hata.

Kei runga aha a Mere?
1. Kei _ _ _ _.

Kei runga aha a Rewi?
2. Kei _ _ _ _.

Kei runga aha a Rewi rāua ko Tamahae?

3. Kei _ _ a _ rāua ko _.

Kei runga aha a Mere rāua ko Mārama?

4. Kei _ _ _ _ _ _ _ _ _.

Kei runga aha a Rewi rāua ko Tamahae?

5. Kei _ _ _ _ _ _ _.

Figure 16. Exercise from H. Waititi, *Te Rangatahi* I.[1129:44-45] (Reproduced by permission of the New Zealand Government Printer)

4.2.2 Cycles

In essence the cycle is the description of a series of actions taking place. It is commonly referred to as either "cycle," the name used here, or "action chain." Like many promising developments it was the work of one man, who based his ideas on the observation of language learning among children.

Prendergast and Gouin, though contemporaries, were poles apart in their approach. Where Prendergast demanded the drilling of a limited number of self-expanding structures, Gouin based his approach on a limited number of topics that could be endlessly subdivided to arrive at the fineness of language command required of the pupil. The process that was the subject of the exercise was mimed to the class, who imitated both the mime and the commentary. Where miming was not possible, the lesson was translated to the class before they tried to imitate the teacher. During the imitative phase of the lesson, the teacher commented in the foreign language and gave encouragement. In Gouin's terms, the lesson taught the *objective language* of information, and the teacher's comments taught the *subjective language* of emotion, both being a necessary part of expression. He tried to help recall by providing a pivotal point in the sentence. As he considered that the verb was the kernel of the sentence, he listed it separately on the right of the page to assist the pupil to cue repetition. The importance of minute steps in the miming and description of each part is amply illustrated by the number of sentences used to describe each simple operation.

Gouin's experiences as a child watcher had directed him to another facet of language learning: the eagerness with which a child comments to himself on his own actions. The encouraging comments from the teacher were meant to parallel the affectionate language of the parents to a child who has succeeded in learning something new. Whereas Prendergast hit on the child's fascination with language as a toy, Gouin perceived the child's desire to express everything he does and coupled it with the human liking for praise. But like many teaching methods, the emphasis on acting and mimicry demanded a lack of self-consciousness and a willingness to repeat rare among teachers; the method gained few followers.

The cycle, however, appears very early in language teaching. In third-century Alexandria we find this description of a boy getting out of bed and being dressed:

Dies; sol ortus est; solis ortus; lux; lumen
ἡμέρα· ἥλιος ἀνέτειλεν. ἡλίου ἀνατολή. φῶς. φάος

iam lucet; aurora; ante lucem mane surgo; surrexit
ἤδη φωτίζει. ἠώς. πρὸ φάως πρωΐ ἐργόμαι. ἠγέρθη

de lecto lectum; vigilavit heri diu;
ἐκ τῆς κλίνης. κλίνη. ἐγρηγορήσεν ἐχθὲς ἐπι πολύ.

vesti me; da mihi calciamenta et udones et
ἔνδυσον με. δὸς ἐμοὶ ὑποδήματα καὶ τοὺς πιλούς καὶ

bracas; i am calciatus sum.
ἀναξυρίδας, ἤδη ὑπεδέθην.

(Day; the sun is up; sunrise; light; the sun is shining; dawn; I get up in the morning before sunrise; he got out of bed; bed; he went to bed late last night; dress me; give me my shoes, my slippers and trousers; now I have something on my feet; . . .)

A.D. 250 (Pseudo-Dositheus) 916: 637

In the original the Greek glosses are intercalated in the Latin text. The exercise is part of a vocabulary intended for the use of Greek boys learning Latin. But the survival of these vocabularies in an eighth-century German manuscript would lead us to believe that the idea lasted in isolated places until well into the Middle Ages, and that it was turned into a Greek text, rather than a Latin one. But the process of transmission poses a fascinating problem for both the historian of language teaching and the palaeographer.

The idea seems to have been taken up in colloquies, such as those of Aelfric and Alexander of Neckham, but with its absorption into the reading lesson this form of drill disappeared until the Renaissance. Cordier's *Colloquia* (1556) bring us back to such sequences as getting out of bed and going to school. The cycle pattern is much clearer than before, but once again it seems to have been an accidental discovery.

Gouin had other uses for his cycle than trips to the bedroom; but the theme is common enough in twentieth-century cycles (which were considered sufficiently original to be written up in articles). Some modern authorities recommend them as a preparation for free composition. Gurrey discusses this topic, referring to them as "action chains."[499:38] Nevertheless the predominance of pattern practice kept them in the background.

4.2.3 Chria

The chria is the most ancient form of grammar drill, and one peculiarly suitable to inflected languages. It is an exercise in varying the flexions of nouns and verbs. Along with all else that the founders of Greek rhetoric had developed during the fourth and fifth centuries B.C., it was adopted by the Romans and adapted to their own use. Originally an exercise to drill in a moral saying, it became a method of teaching students how to achieve a rhetorical balance in spite of having to handle cumbersome case forms. The following example comes from the fourth-century grammarian, Diomede:

<table>
<tr><td>Marcus Porcius Cato
dixit

Marci Porci Catonis
dictum fertur

Marco Porcio Catoni
placuit dicere

Marcum Porcium Catonem
dixisse fertur

A Marco Porcio Catone
dictum accepimus

O tu Marce Porci Cato
egregie dixisti</td><td>literarum radices amaras,
sed fructus dulciores.</td></tr>
</table>

A.D. 350 in *Keil* I: 310

In the drill version of the exercise the learner then went through the plural of the italicised words. There was a set way of using the chria in a display of rhetoric which compelled the student to use every one of the cases, but for many pupils the very conditions of language teaching forced it to teach the language itself, Latin being a foreign language in a large part of the Empire. Priscian's *Praeexercitamina* mentions the exercise as being particularly important, and it must be remembered that he was teaching Latin in Constantinople, the capital of the Greek East.

The late Renaissance use of the chria was divorced from rhetoric and seems to be purely an aid to the learning of flexions and patterns. Lubinus suggests basing the chria on a picture:

> This example being bothe in the picture and in the sentence exposed to the eyes of the children, the Master may in the noune, & in the verbe go through the cases, numbers, moods, tenses and persons. As in the nominative of First Case: *Hic, Aquila devorat cor Promethei*. In the genitive or Second Case: *Pictura Aquilae qui devorat cor Promethei*. In the verbe *devorat* one may passe over through numbers, moods, persons, etc.
>
> 1550? (translated Hartlib) 519: 32

Here we see that the ancient rhetorical purpose had given way to grammatical teaching. It is odd that none of the attestations of the chria from this time are otherwise.

After almost two centuries, the chria appeared in an altered form in Lemare's *Cours de la langue latine*. Though he credits the schools of Pestalozzi with the use of the chria he complains that the examples used were synthetic Latin, i.e., sentences composed for the purpose. In contrast he builds his paradigms from classical quotations (see Figure 17). The control over the pupil was extremely tight indeed. First he was not to deviate from the structural patterns in the exercises; second, the vocabulary he used was to be limited to the words in the textbook, all of which had excellent classical authority. The old aim of teaching style as well as structure was almost ferociously respected, a return to the teaching philosophy of the sixteenth-century humanists.

Déclinaisons régulières. 93

2e *MODÈLE*, ou *MODÈLE DES NEUTRES.*

VINUM, *vin.*

GÉN.	Vin-*i* vitio feci[a], ...	j'ai fait cela par le vice du *vin.*
DAT.	Vin-*o* indulgent[b], ...	ils se livrent *au vin.*
ABL.	Vin-*o* forma perit[c], ...	la beauté périt *par le vin.*
ACC.	Vin-*um* potas? album an nigrum[d]?	bois-tu *du vin* blanc ou du vin noir, (c.-à-d. du vin rouge)?
NOM.	Vin-*um* sublimia pectora fregit[e],	*le vin* a énervé des cœurs sublimes.

Le vocatif singulier des neutres est toujours semblable au nominatif du même nombre; l'acc. est aussi toujours semblable au nominatif.

Pluriel.

GÉN. Vin-*orum* diversa genera[f], | il y a divers genres *de vins.*

DAT. Vin-*is*. NOTA. Cette forme et celle de l'abl. sont semblables dans les cinq déclinaisons.

ABL.	Vin-*is* oculi natabant[g], ..	les yeux nageaient dans *les vins.*
ACC.	Vin-*a* liques[h], ...	coule tes *vins.*
NOM.	Vin-*a* repertori nocuêre[i],	*les vins* ont nui à leur inventeur.

Ainsi se déclinent

Tous les substantifs neutres et tous les adjectifs neutres (positifs et superlatifs), qui ont le génitif singulier en I, ou le génitif pluriel en ORUM.

1°. *Substantifs neutres.*		2°. *Adjectifs.*	
Fanum,	temple.	*Bonum*,	ce qui est bon.
Mancipium,	esclave.	*Malum*,	ce qui est mauvais.
Jussum,	ordre.	*Æquum*,	ce qui est juste.
Mandatum,	commission.	*Optimum*,	ce qui est très-bon.
Vinculum,	lien.	*Pessimum*,	ce qui est très-mauvais.
Damnum,	perte.	*Æquissimum*,	ce qui est très-juste.
Malum,	pomme.		

Une remarque bien importante, c'est que tous les neutres, de quelque déclinaison qu'ils soient, ont toujours les trois derniers cas semblables, et que ces trois cas sont toujours en A, au pluriel (22).

a PLAUT. *Aul.* 4, 10.
b VIRG. etc.
c OVID. *Metam.*
d PLAUT. *Men.* 5, 5.
e OVID. *l.* 1, *Fast.*
f CELS.
g OVID. *Fast. l.* 6.
h HOR. 1, 10.
i PROPERT

Figure 17. Page from P. A. Lemare, *Cours de la langue latine.*655:93 Copy in le Petit Séminaire de Québec

The chria again disappeared until the beginning of the twentieth century. It was used sporadically in teaching German during the 1920's; and was dubbed "the paradigm in narrative form" by a teacher writing in the 1950's. The example he gives is the following:

> *Der alte Mann* geht zum Artz.
> Die Gesundheit *des alten Mannes* ist schlecht.
> Der Artz gibt *dem alten Mann* Medizin.
> Die Medizin heilt *den alten Mann.*
>
> 1954 (Chamberlain) 205: 336

In this example, like the classical chrias, all the cases are accounted for. What is new here is an elementary story line, all previous authorities either ringing the changes on the one sentence to give occasion to use all the possible cases and tenses or assembling a heterogeneous collection of sentences which happened to use the same noun in a variety of cases.

4.3 DIRECTED CONVERSATION

Confident handling of phonological and structural drills is only the first step in acquiring conversational ability. Ways of changing the one into the other all rest on some sort of dialoguing. The dialogue itself (or "colloquy," as it was known prior to the eighteenth century) has been in constant use since the early Middle Ages. Drama, because of the classical prejudice against actors, is not mentioned until the eleventh century, reaching the height of its popularity during the Renaissance. Games involving language seem to have been a Renaissance development, although references in Quintillian would indicate that such means were used in Roman schools.

4.3.1 Dialogues or Colloquia

In a sense, all teaching is dialogue, it being understood that the pupil questions and the teacher answers. But as a teaching tool the dialogue first appeared among the Greeks, philosophical texts often being couched in the dialogue form in order to make it easier for the reader to visualize the discussion as an argument that actually took place. This form of treatise continued in Rome, and until at least the eleventh century, it was the accepted form for a teaching manual. The Middle Ages made a distinction between this sort of text and one specifically oriented towards language teaching, calling the second "colloquium." As catechetical ways of teaching lost favor, the first term ousted the second, taking over both meanings.

Though the word "dialogue" immediately conjures up the traveler's bilingual phrase book, the dialogue was in constant use in the language classroom right through the history of language teaching. Usually it was introduced by question and answer methods, following the learning of vocabulary and structure. In both traveler's pocket and school, the dialogue, as it concerns us here, appears with a translation in a parallel column, though dialogues expressly for the school market often dispensed with the translation. Twentieth-century teachers tended to regard free dialoguing with caution, as the temptation for both teacher and pupil was to go outside the narrow range of the pupil's knowledge in both structure and vocabulary.[331:48]

The colloquium appeared in the Middle Ages, the two most famous examples being those of Aelfric and Alexander of Neckham. Both deal with the life of their periods. In both the dialogue element is, however, minimized, as they take the form of set expositions on a topic punctuated by questions. In this they resemble the classical dialogues on philosophical subjects. It is not certain who added the glosses to these works, the translation appended to Aelfric almost certainly being the work of one of his pupils. The mixed English and Norman-French gloss in Alexander of Neckham was probably also added by frustrated pupils.

In the evolution of colloquia we must not assume an uninterrupted line of development from the Middle Ages.[*133:51] Like so many techniques of teaching, it was forgotten and its rediscovery was prompted by related techniques. The impetus came from the dramas of Terence and those of his Renaissance imitators. It seems that the Renaissance colloquium first appeared in Germany. In its new form the sentences were shorter and it represented real conversation, not merely question-answer sequences.

In the classical languages, the colloquium rarely went outside the pupil's immediate interests, but in modern languages it treated all phrases of social life. The best of them, for instance, John Florio's *First Fruits* and *Second Fruits*, tried to school the pupils in social behavior and in graceful conformity to the genius of the language. Hence there are passages dealing with social calls, courting, and quarreling as well as the usual shopping and traveling. Certain scenes from Shakespeare that satirized the contemporary gallant are clearly modeled on lessons from Florio.*194:84-85 The colloquia of *Erasmus* follow the same lines. Renaissance teachers soon realized that the colloquium could teach rudeness as well as courtesy, and sought to liven their teaching by drilling the well-turned insult:

> Good day, you traveller's nightmare. R. And good day to you, you glutton, epitome of greed, gobbler of good cooking. V. My deepest respects, you enemy of all virtue. R. Pleased to meet you, you shining example of uprightness. V. Good morning, you fifteen-year-old hag. R. Delighted, you eighty-year-old schoolgirl. . . .
>
> 1524 (Erasmus) 374: 629E

Little wonder that the dialogue soon fell under suspicion from more squeamish teachers. But the Renaissance colloquium had a very long life: Erasmus was still being published in 1750 (and was never expurgated); the colloquia of Mathurin Cordier, first edition 1556, were reprinted until 1786.

In their original form there was no vernacular translation consistently annexed, the custom apparently beginning with Cordier. As his book was widely pirated, the original French translations were replaced by versions in the language of the intended market. Occasional Latin-Greek dialogues appeared as well, like those of Posselius (see Figure 18). Teachers using these parallel versions took full advantage of both languages:

> As they learne these dialogues, when they have construed and parsed, cause them to talke together; uttering every sentence pathetically . . . and first to utter every sentence in English, as neede is, then in Latine.
>
> 1627 (Brinsley) 155a: 217

Imitations of the idea were extremely common, and writers of the beginning of the seventeenth century added a third column in which the target language was represented in phonetic notation. The bilingual dialogue gradually became standard, there being only one note of revolt: a set of Italian dialogues published in England during the eighteenth century omits the customary translation, inviting users of the book to make their own if they need it.[19:ii] One other amusing note is the persistence of the same set of dialogues in a large number of French-English textbooks of the eighteenth century. Their light character was attacked, as unfitting to the serious business of teaching:

> Besides some of their [i.e., Miège, Boyer, etc.] discourses are too familiar, not fit to be put into a young gentleman's hands, much less a young lady's, having likewise deviated very much in their Dialogues from the idiom of the English tongue.
>
> 1788 (Berry) 108: xii

In the nineteenth century the fact that dialogues taught speech skills was enough to exclude them from the language classroom. But even some of these who opposed the current grammatical trend distrusted the dialogue. In the words of Marcel, "dialogues, like extracts learned by rote, teach to recite, not to converse."[718:219] But in the thinking of most Natural Methodists, dialogues did not have this disadvantage. During the twentieth century they became part of the classroom routine, often being used to consolidate what was learned in the language laboratory.

4.3.2 Drama

Plays have been employed to teach skill in language only since the Middle Ages.

In Greece and Rome performing on stage was beneath the dignity of the class whose children could afford to go to school and a social ban remained on this activity until the tenth century, when a German abbess, Hroswitha, composed Latin plays for her novices. The expressed aim was to replace the plays of Plautus and Terence, then considered too saucy for use in the cloister. Owing to the now usual way of acting out the Bible stories in mystery plays, stage work was not an unusual recreation among clerics. Latin plays, written in the classical manner, were often played in the monasteries by the troupes of monks who staged the mystery plays in the churchyard.

Taking their cue from these mystery plays, the Jesuits developed another approach. Many of their plays were in a classical style, but the characters were abstractions drawn from grammar and literary criticism. The plays were meant both to drill pupils in speaking Latin and Greek and to teach formal grammar. It is not unlikely that the characters were modeled on the personifications of the *De nuptiis Philologiae et Mercurii* of Martianus Capella, which was still known during the Renaissance. This type of allegory had been a favorite device among medieval poets, and Martianus Capella had had many medieval imitators in vernacular languages.

One of the last sets of this type of play was the dramatized version of the *Ianua linguarum*, published in 1664.[255] The adaptation was made by D. Sebastianus Macer for the use of the school of Patakina, at which he had taught, and which was regarded, even by the master himself, as a model school. Though the book followed all the allegorical conventions of the Jesuit play, there were several important differences. First, the Comenius plays were in prose, while the others had been in verse. Second, the exact classical format was not followed, the plays being of varying length and shape. But as the taste for allegory waned, so too did interest in this sort of play.

Classical drama formed an integral part of the Renaissance classics curriculum. In England several who founded grammar schools specified that a classical play should be performed every year; and on the continent, where Catholics were teaching in Protestant schools and vice versa, the religious climate excluded contemporary religious plays, so the classical repertoire was used exclusively. But medieval scruple hung on grimly, even into the eighteenth century, drawing the approval of Rollin:

> . . . this principal, prompted by laudable zeal for the progress of youth in piety as well as in culture, composed several plays in the style of Terence, but on subjects drawn from Sacred Scripture.
>
> 1740 (Rollin) 965: I: 172

In England especially, the custom of an annual performance of a classical play was still vigorously flourishing at the end of the nineteenth century, school editions being prepared with staging in mind. Owing to the activities of the great German classicists, the basic texts were now solidly established, but for school use they were carefully expurgated, a difficult task considering the exigencies of meter. Many editors normalized the preclassical spelling and even added stage directions.[1064:6] The place of such presentations was strengthened by the advent of the Direct Method, and they spread to the teaching of modern languages. Though it was considered most desirable to use plays written for native audiences, this means of instilling confidence was made available to younger pupils by providing them with plays in simplified language and style. As far as modern plays were concerned, teachers were inclined to choose those which reflected the culture of the country.

In modern schools and universities the modern-language play came to be a special show put on for the delectation of students' parents and staff wives, but it also had the serious purpose of having pupils exercise their oral skills under some difficulty. In Russia, some schools encouraged the pupils to run puppet theaters in the foreign language, a natural outcome of the general interest in this art form.[*106:121]

4.3.3 Free Conversation and *Comédie Spontanée*

The step from parrot memory to free conversation is a difficult one, and the ways of forcing pupils to make the change rest on improvisation of some kind. It is not certain when conversation was recognized as a separate teachable skill. But for the Natural Method it was a self-sufficient procedure: According to Marcel, "conversation is more than an agreeable pass-time: it is a very active agent in circulating opinions and information, in forming the taste and character."[717:I:235] But in his essay on the Direct Method, Laudenbach advised caution, "Artifical conversation as a means of studying a language of which one knows almost nothing, certainly gives less return than the indirect method. The error is the same; a beginning is made where one should finish."[648:15] During the twentieth century conversation was often taken as an advanced stage growing out of the dialogue.

The beginnings of *comédie spontanée* are equally difficult to trace. Its first clear description is that of Gouin, who used elements of the *comédie spontanée* in his cycle. The most sophisticated scheme of the sort was that of Rouse, who elaborated it in the early years of the twentieth century. To make the speeches of Cicero come alive to his pupils he restaged the trials in which Cicero had pleaded. His pupils prepared themselves for the part they were to play by reading and rereading the appropriate speech, and then studying the circumstances of the case. Then with all the solemnity of the Roman forum they tried the case, improvising every part, witnesses, defendant, jury, prosecutor, and defender.[977:30] Forty years later in the language schools of the American army such improvisation was one of the most valued ways of teaching. The men were made to place themselves in situations they would expect to meet on active service and act them out. Thus they learned how to interrogate prisoners, buy supplies, and question local people.[*5:92] Such improvisation was used in civilian classrooms after the war as a development of dialogue practice.

4.3.4 Games and Projects

Attempts to enliven the classroom atmosphere are not common, and, when they appear, not well documented. Having met with a mixed reception, games do not seem to have been used often to teach languages. Quintillian and St. Jerome both mention using appropriately shaped blocks to teach letters, a suggestion taken up during the Renaissance. Montaigne[767:I:xxv] and Erasmus[377:512A] speak of learning flexions by playing games resembling draughts and dominoes. But while Montaigne does not make it clear whether he approves or not, Erasmus is definitely against the idea. Games did not receive unqualified approval in the classroom until Comenius used them in his own schools. He saw seven essential elements in all games: movement, spontaneity, social mixing, combined effort, order, ease, and relaxation.[255:iii]

Games were not revived in the classroom until the days of the Natural Method, and their use then was far from systematic. Several uses of games were arrived at almost in desperation. Lord Frederick Hamilton, a British diplomat who spent some time teaching French in a service hospital in 1917, recounts how he taught numbers by having the men number off in good parade-ground style, but in French. In the ordinary classroom language games were adaptations of vernacular children's games, many combining movement and mime with speech. Games could be directed at any of the four skills and were usually worked into the recapitulation stage of the normal lesson.

The precise relationship between learning and games caught the attention of child psychologists during the early years of this century. When educational authorities began experimenting with foreign languages in primary schools, the aspect of learning was recognized as important. For the very young child classroom games are just another extension of his daily learning experience into the classroom.[380:120] Modern educators have hardly improved on Comenius's requirements for language games, although they know much more about their theoretical justification. In his paper for the Moncton Conference, R. M. Jones underlined the element of activity and make-believe in such games. A child will become totally involved in them, and unless a classroom game encourages this, it is of little use. In her comment on his paper, W. Rivers agreed and pointed out that a game patterned on the familiar life of the child was by far the most effective.

Similar needs for active participation were filled by expedients like the Unit Method, developed during the Second World War. This was based on the Dalton Plan, but made some concessions to the rigidity of timetabling in the ordinary school. A unit of work was limited according to the topic it would deal with, the work that would naturally follow in the next unit, and the activities and ancillary interests it would present to the pupils.[1066:85] The method placed much importance on a definitive objective for each unit and, like the Dalton Plan, tried to assure that the pupil knew as well as the teacher what the aim was.[951:2] Private research was directed more closely than in the Dalton Plan. Teamwork by pupils was encouraged, and though individual work was not frowned on, it was regarded as not essential to the method.[679:12] The work was linked with games like charades,[1066:97] and the class was expected to take an active part in the discussion and criticism of the work of every pupil.[679:14]

This research approach was used extensively in the ASTP and in the postwar "Language and Area Programs." It became especially important in learning the culture of the second language and connected areas like philology. The type of research required, like the type of game, was fitted to the age of the pupil to allow for variations in both ability and range of interest.

It is clear that crystallizing language skills through speech was most usual during the modern period, the Renaissance, and the classical age. Though not entirely neglected during the intervening centuries, oral skills were subordinated to written. The first of these, reading, is considered in the next chapter.

5

READING

> Now who has acquired any facility in reading unless he has looked at the poets and conned over the historians and orators?
>
> 1450 (Piccolomini) in 878: 70

Throughout the history of language teaching, reading has been approached as part of the other skills teachers were to impart. In the late classical and medieval periods, it was often absorbed into literary and Biblical exegesis; from the Renaissance on, it was usually conflated with the art of translation, achieving complete independence only during the twentieth century. For our purposes we divide it into the skills of interpretation of symbols and the fluent handling of the matter to be read.

5.1 TEACHING INTERPRETATION

Reading is a matter of interpreting a system of symbolization which follows a complicated series of rules proper to each language. Teaching interpretation begins with the alphabets used by the language in question and the customs which govern their use. The second stage of interpretation is taught in three complementary ways: intensive reading, comprehension exercises, and translation into a more familiar language. Alphabet teaching, as an indispensable stage, has always been part of the procedure; intensive reading goes back to the Greeks, as does the comprehension exercise, and translation is a Roman innovation which went out of use only during the Middle Ages.

5.1.1 Alphabets and Spelling

The Western world has generally taken it for granted that alphabets represent sound. Sergius in his commentary on Donatus puts this idea in its most extreme form: "A letter is an element of sound articulated by the voice."[1014:486] Before the nineteenth-century development of phonetics there were few to dispute this statement. For this reason the teaching of writing and pronunciation tended to be thought of as one process, despite some sound research into the question during the Renaissance (see Chapter 15).

The traditional manner of presenting foreign alphabets was by printing them in a table alongside the native equivalents. Usually one added transcriptions which indicated the functional pronunciations and the name of the letters in the foreign language. Part of the task was learning the order of the alphabet, so that one could usefully refer to a dictionary. Accents, if any, were learned separately and then immediately applied in spelling. Ways of enlivening the teaching of letter recognition pop in and out of literature. During the fourth century St. Jerome recommended that pupils should play with wooden blocks shaped like letters,[586:107] an example followed 800 years later by Abelard. Renaissance teachers sometimes followed the recommendation of Erasmus, that a child should be rewarded for the knowlege of a letter with a cake of the appropriate shape.[377:511E]

During the twentieth century, other approaches were attempted. One Greek course began by having the pupils read a story in English, but every word of Greek derivation was printed in Greek characters. The same etymological approach was worked out for Russian. A not dissimilar idea had been in use during the Middle Ages, but had backfired on occasions: Abbo of Fleury protested that the Greek ἀρχή was *arche* not *arxe*,[1:§11] and silent letters became and remained a constant source of trouble. The proliferation of different styles of script according to the tradition of the scriptoria was another element of confusion. Piccolomini comments on the difficulties of the old and new scripts, the one simpler than the other.[878:190] And it was not until the standardization of type face caused by the invention of printing that this particular difficulty was minimized.

The twentieth century sought to regulate the matter by frequency counts. In 1923 Dewey established the relative frequency of letters in English, building on the amateur interest of authors like Edgar Allan Poe (see "The Gold Bug") and the research of cryptographers. I. A. Richards welcomed this development, but added the important rider that the first letters introduced should be those "least liable to be mistaken one for the other."[954:94] This approach was used in the Richards and Gibson *First Steps in Reading English* and by West's *New Method English Course.*

Some teachers preferred to use transliterations and to leave teaching the alphabet itself until near the end of the course. In defence of this practice Sweet claimed that language learning was difficult enough without distracting the pupil with another alphabet.[1054:30] In addition, once the language itself was known, learning the alphabet would be much easier. Palmer heartily agreed.[836:197] From medieval courses still extant, we know that this was the normal medieval approach to the problem. Insistence on authentic alphabets was a peculiarity of the Humanists which was transmitted to our time. In deference to these authorities and to tradition, Sweet was willing to modify his position enough to admit that if reading knowledge was all that was required, the pupil could be introduced immediately to the new alphabet, and he even countenanced using the native phonetic habits to fix spelling in the pupil's head.[1054:33]

The teaching of spelling was a vexed question, complicated by difficulties in making up one's mind about the claims of etymology, tradition, and sound. Medieval treatises show that teachers were trying to combat the influence of popular pronunciations on spelling. Renaissance teachers faced a similar problem. Some were inclined to allow medieval spelling if it had some sort of authority behind it, others went right to sources and admitted no other spelling at all. Thus the Harvard copy of Aldus Manutius's *Orthographia* was glossed by an anonymous critic who based his differing opinions on Priscian and Quintillian. The manner of the hand-written marginal glosses suggests the outraged schoolmaster:

> *Paricida,* spelt with a single *r* in ancient books. [Gloss: *Parricida,* spelt with a double *r,* see Priscian Book I.]
>
> 1561 (Manutius) 712: 36

Similar struggles were going on in modern languages.

Fluency in handling foreign alphabets was assured by reading aloud and by transcription. Though the main purpose was learning to spell, recognition was an essential part of the process. Indeed, in all periods, many pupils learned their alphabets, or the new customs of using a familiar one, as a by-product of spelling. This means was not supplanted even in the most iconoclastic period of the twentieth century. In classical languages spelling had been fairly well standardized during the Middle Ages, even if the Renaissance was to alter some important details. In modern languages, owing to the interference of etymology and the technical difficulties of justifying lines in the printeries, spelling was a fluid affair until the eighteenth century. Even now, in languages like English with two cultural traditions, spelling can be confusing. In general, however, recognition is taught as a preparation for active use, the most important means being dictation, transcription, and free composition.

5.1.2 Intensive Reading

The modern distinction between intensive and extensive reading was first spelled out, it seems, by Palmer: "Reading may be intensive or intensive. In the first, each sentence is subjected to a careful scrutiny–in the latter book after book will be read through without giving more than a superficial and passing attention to the lexicological units of which it is composed."[837:205] Extensive reading is not primarily concerned with the skills of reading itself, but takes in grammar, stylistic analysis, and even translation.

Intensive reading, and its French equivalent, *lecture expliquée*, are derived from the classical exercise of *praelectio*, which was still in use at the beginning of the nineteenth century. During the late Middle Ages, this was linked with translation by the development of "construing," which consisted in dismembering the sentence, describing the grammatical function of each of its parts, and linking them with vernacular equivalents. The exercise had relevance in teaching the cultural facts of the foreign language, as some of the comment dealt with literary and social topics.

Classical *praelectio* was an exercise based on intensive grammar analysis:

> At the stage of *praelectio* the teacher will have to analyze even the most minor details of the passage in order to arrive at the parts of speech and the properties of the metrical verse feet. In verse these must be so analyzed that the knowledge will also be applicable to prose. In addition, the teacher must censure writing that is barbarous, unfitting, and ungrammatical.
>
> A.D. 100 (Quintillian) 923: I.viii.3

The technique of *praelectio* was widened in scope by the early scholiasts, who commented on literary content and the social relevance of the works they treated. Even before the Carolingian Renaissance, a balance had been achieved between the literary and grammatical aspects of the exercise.[*100:79] Its aim remained prescriptive, however, and until the end of the Renaissance, it was both an introduction to stylistic niceties and the final stage of learning grammar.

Essentially the same method was used in studying Scripture. Indeed, many comments on the Bible, especially during the Carolingian Renaissance, could be made to serve either purpose. Owing to its manifold purposes, *praelectio* began to develop specialized branches and a jargon of its own:

> *Commentum* is an explanation of the words, leaving aside their relationship to each other, and just considering their meaning. *Glosa* is an explanation of the sentence and the manner of writing it, taking in the meanings of the individual words as well.
>
> *fl.* 1200 (Huguccio) *158: 118

The rigid formality of *praelectio* encouraged pedantry, a tendency played up by many teachers, especially during the Renaissance. Erasmus found it necessary to warn the profession not to go searching after every grammatical quibble in the passage under discussion. But his warnings had little effect.

During the Renaissance one school of thought updated the medieval form of *praelectio;* the other, to which Ratke and the Jesuits belonged, deemphasized grammar as much as possible:

> The method of handling Cicero's speeches will be: (a) a discussion of the subject; (b) an analysis by the teacher of the first period [i.e., sentence] including any points of rhetoric that are worth noting; (c) then, leaving aside what pertains to effective use of words, the teacher will give some attention to commonplaces, anecdotes and stories used.
>
> 1560 (*Ratio Studiorum*) 832: II: 163

Ratke, according to contemporary sources, taught his texts in small doses, going over each gobbet thoroughly until any literary or grammatical peculiarity was quite clear.[*58:200] At this time the technique was rarely used in living languages, being introduced to them near the end of the eighteenth century.

Eighteenth-century teachers reverted to the medieval form, introducing construing and placing grammatical above literary analysis:

> The next subject is the explanation of Cicero, Vergil, or any other author suitable for the schools. This falls into five or six parts, which are briefly summarized in the next few lines. The first is a review of the technique of *praelectio;* the second, explanation and thorough analysis of each sentence, whether it be short, difficult or complex; the third deals with anything of scholarly interest . . .; the fourth, peculiar to advanced classes, seeks out those features peculiar to rhetoric or poetics; the fifth weighs up the quality of the Latin.
>
> 1764 (Juvencus) 613: 133

Construing brought with it translation. The link seems to have been formed in the fourteenth century and strengthened by the formal type of "vulgar." In its strictest form, one began by parsing all the words in the sentence, i.e., giving a full grammatical analysis and stating their function. The next step was to set out the sentence in the vernacular order and to translate each word literally.

Renaissance teachers were inclined to see it as an invention of their own time, ascribing it to Leech and Crusius.[155:50] But many of its rules can be traced back to the *grammatical speculative* of the fourteenth century, as in the following from Crusius, for instance: "A word which governs another is placed before it; one which qualifies is placed after."[155:94] Construing also had its roots in classical rhetoric; the best teachers trained their pupils to view the sentence as a whole before analyzing it:

> *quis, cui, causa, locus, quo tempore, prima sequela* [who, to whom, why, where, when, immediate result] This verse I would have every scholler to have readily; and always to think of it in his construing. It is a very principall rule for the understanding of any author or matter whatsoever.
>
> 1627 (Brinsley) 155: 123

But in practice it is difficult to see how a pupil was to reconcile this philosophical overview with the clinical dissection of the sentence that was laid down elsewhere:

> If there be a vocative case, I must take that first: then I must seek out the principall verb and his nominative case; & if there be an Adjective or a Participle with him, then I must English them next, and such words as they governe; then the Verbe: & if there follow an infinitive mood, I must take that next; then the Adverbe; then the case which the Verb properly governeth; & lastly all the other cases in their order.
>
> 1525 (Leech) 155: 93

Such construing was considered to be so important that it is specifically mentioned in the statutes of several English grammar schools.

Though during the Renaissance it was assumed that construing was a technique of universal application, it was not applied to modern languages until the advent of the Grammar-Translation Method. By the end of the eighteenth century it had come to pervade the whole spectrum of language teaching, even the advanced stages which it had never entered during the sixteenth century. Protests were few, but trenchant. On the continent Lemare attacked it as doing irreparable harm to the pupils' sense of style.[655:xxxiii] In England Thomas Arnold castigated it as absurd, and refused to use it.[*64:214] Seventy years later in the climate created by the Direct Method, such attacks received better hearing and were renewed. Rouse was one who claimed that construing "is a danger to English because it encourages the misuse of words and idiom and fosters the habit of writing nonsense."[975:110] Despite the growing chorus of such attacks, the "construe" was not dislodged from the classics classroom until over forty years later. In Soviet Russia it was to survive in modern-language teaching as part of the "Conscious-Comparative Method."[*106:62]

Whereas the "construe" continued the grammatical tradition of the Middle Ages, its techniques of literary comment were perpetuated in countries of French tradition by *lecture expliquée*. This exercise, while not neglecting grammatical and lexical knowledge, concentrated on the literary values of *praelectio*. It assumed ability to translate and a good knowledge of grammar. It was intended to instill sensitivity to the stylistic and literary conventions of the foreign language, and in the hands of most teachers it became a rigorous introduction to the life and thought of the other culture.[599:14]

5.1.3 Exercising Reading Comprehension

It would be rash to trust to the primary sources consulted and to state that comprehension exercises did not appear before the twentieth century. They are such a natural tool in teaching that it is unthinkable that they were ever absent from the classroom.

Comprehension questions were probably taken for granted in *praelectio*. This can be read into the quotations from Huguccio on page 132, from the *Ratio Studiorum* on page 133 and from Brinsley on page 134. But one cannot argue from silence that this technique was never used on its own. It is true, however, that the first mentions of comprehension exercises as such seem to date from the nineteenth century.

The usual form of the exercise is the obvious one: questions are asked after the pupil has read and digested the passage. West, however, saw the question as a possible teaching aid as well as a test of comprehension, and gave his pupils "before questions." These covered important details of the passage, the pupil being directed to read with the questions in mind. Cited in Cole.[242:91] Once these were satisfactorily answered the pupil was faced with "after questions" in the usual manner. This is reminiscent of the advice of many teachers to examination candidates: read the questions over first to get a clue as to what the passage is about. It is important to note that moderns took this process as a necessary preliminary to all translation work.

5.1.4 Translation in Reading Comprehension

It may seem odd to class translation as merely a device to exercise comprehension, as if one were ignoring its importance as a stylistic exercise. But one of the chief obstacles to the twentieth-century restriction of translation to senior classes was the conviction of many both inside and outside the teaching profession that translation was the one way of checking that the pupil had understood the passage he had just read. Under the influence of construing, translation was indeed judged by its textual faithfulness to the original, and not by the pupil's skill both in understanding the meaning and spirit of the passage and in writing his own language.

For the Romans only one type of translation was of any real value: translation into Latin. It was a rhetorical exercise that was first attempted near the end of one's studies and continued throughout one's oratorical career: As such, it demanded all one's skill as a stylist: transference of meaning was taken for granted, the most exacting part of the exercise being the preservation of the flavor of the original without going counter to the genius of Latin. Consonant with the Roman theory of literary imitation, a translation must convey the spirit of the original by avoiding the literal and the obvious, and yet preserve the author's intentions so well that the translation is worthy to stand beside its source.

It seems to have been the schoolmasters of the Greek communities of Egypt and Gaul who introduced translation into elementary teaching.[*144:317] Greek was the first language of Alexandria, and even in Gaul it seems to have been spoken by many in Aquitaine and Marseilles as late as the third century of the Christian era.[*100:80] Editions glossed in Greek and accompanied by parallel translation were often used to teach Latin in these communities. Translation and construing was encouraged by the teachers, as such methods were not taxing for them, and because it was felt that Latin style could only gain by interference from Greek. By the time of Priscian, translation was an established procedure in the Latin classrooms of the East, where Latin still retained some of its old imperial prestige.

We hear little about translation in the early Middle Ages until King Alfred ordered certain religious books to be translated into Anglo-Saxon. These were certainly not teaching tools, and in spite of the importance of such translation to the layman, the scholar's patronizing attitude to the vernaculars kept them out of the classroom. Hence, as far as we can judge, the classical revival of Charlemagne made no use of translation as a teaching method. There was some dilettante interest in the vernaculars shown by the compilation of glossaries like those of Kassel and Reichenau but what this implied in the classroom is hard to say.

The first clear indication that translation was used as a teaching method comes from fourteenth-century England. At the beginning of the century the University of Oxford had outlawed the growing vogue of translating into English, insisting that teachers should keep to the traditional use of Norman-French. Final victory for the supporters of English came in 1362 with the legalization of English in the law courts and in public life outside the universities. Parallel developments on the continent are not so easily documented, but it seems that vernaculars entered the classroom, bringing translation with them, at about the beginning of the thirteenth century.[*96:70] Doubtless the appearance of translation as a teaching technique was partly due to the growing popularity of vernacular translations of the classics, which first appeared in large numbers about the middle of the fourteenth century. However isolated examples go back to the twelfth century. Those who used translation techniques were probably aiming as much at teaching the art of translation as at teaching Latin, there being a ready market for good translation.

Most of our information about the Renaissance use of translation comes from early seventeenth-century England. The first step was always construing (see §5.1.2); then, after the "construe" had been judged perfect, it was worked over until the English was acceptable. It must be emphasized that this approach was practically confined to classical languages, modern languages being taught by "direct" methods.

Port-Royal completed the downfall of direct methodology, being the first school of any importance to aim its teaching at the native language. Latin and Greek were no longer the center of the curriculum, it being considered that a sound training in classical languages would cause an improvement in the handling of the mother tongue.[45:29] This was merely the logical outcome of the movement in favor of the vernaculars that had been gathering momentum since the thirteenth century. Translation began to enter modern languages, some impetus coming from its existence in the literary and commercial worlds. But until the adoption of the Grammar-Translation Method, it remained on the fringe of modern-language teaching.

During the next two centuries translating and construing into Latin were gradually abandoned. In France, Rollin suggested translating Greek into French, following the theory current at the Renaissance that French had more affinities with Greek than with Latin,[965:I:140] but the reform was not definitively adopted until the nineteenth century. In England schoolmasters were inclined to mourn the passing of the Latin version, suspecting that what was replacing it was less valuable.[*37:15]

By this time the procedure was being justified by the training it gave in exactness of thought, but except in Latin, perception of stylistic differences between languages was not regarded as important. Indeed the first treatises on the art of translation were written for the use of Latin pupils. At the end of the century the modern-language and classical camps revolted simultaneously: Laudenbach denied that translation was of any use in acquiring the foreign language,[648:10] while Rouse distinguished two types of translation: the art form and the test. For him ability in translation followed skill in interpreting documents and composing in the two languages in question.[975:105]

The French inspector, Emile Hovelaque, a strong supporter of the Direct Method, concurred in this judgment, noting that translation shows the pupil where the genius of the two languages differs. For this reason, seeing that it presupposes a certain maturity, all translation exercises were to be left until the end of the course.[560:297]

Apart from a temporary eclipse of translation in progressive circles, the situation did not change after the beginning of the twentieth century. The persistence of Grammar-Translation methods among orthodox teachers maintained a running polemic, in which the ideas of Laudenbach and Rouse have been quoted, and even discovered, again and again. But the armor of most teachers has remained unscratched, protected as they are by the circumstances of their profession against any fortuitous awareness of a side opposed to their own.

5.2 ACHIEVING FLUENCY

Each of the means already treated demands that the pupil should proceed slowly and carefully, checking what he is doing and deliberately analyzing his actions. This is not the way we read our own language, but a means we adopt if we are not sure of the import of an isolated passage. Three ways have been developed of teaching a pupil to read with the fluency of a native. Simplified readers and supports first appeared in ancient Greece, extensive reading during the Renaissance.

5.2.1 Simplified Readers

One problem in exercising the skill of reading is making sure that the pupil practices within the limits of his knowledge. Traditionally, this has been done by giving him authors that are considered to be simple. Editing works especially for beginners is likewise an ancient proceeding, though usually it has been simplification of concept that was aimed at, rather than simplification of language.

It has always been usual practice to introduce a pupil to reading skills through the simplest authors. In Latin Caesar and Phaedrus have usually held this distinction, and in Greek Aesop and Herodotus. Because of the purist tendencies of the post-Renaissance discipline of classics, Hellenistic Greek and Late Latin were rejected in spite of their greater simplicity. Not until the twentieth century did some classics teachers experiment with literature from these periods. Owing to the importance of Hellenistic Greek to Biblical studies this approach was more acceptable in Greek than in Latin.[808:iii] Its application to modern languages was difficult, as their literatures evolve with the language, and what is easy for one generation can be made quite difficult for succeeding ones owing to linguistic and social change.

Abridgment of standard works is a very ancient procedure, going back to the golden age of Greece, and continuing through Roman times until the end of the Middle Ages. Thus the later decades of Livy's history of Rome are known only in *periochae,* and the famous Greek grammar of Dionysius Thrax, which set the tone for most of the grammars to follow it, has survived in both the original and in several abridged Latin versions. Cassiodorus and Isidore of Seville introduced a new type of textbook into the school, the collectanea: by the time of the Carolingian Renaissance these were standard texts. They were collections of selected passages, some abridged and some in their original form. The choice of authors was truly eclectic: extracts from the Vulgate and the Fathers appeared cheek by jowl with classical authors and medieval secular literature; indeed, all seven of the liberal arts were represented.[*199:190] It is doubtful whether these books aimed at simplification of language, their aim being more to condense the material to bring it within the range of the pupil's understanding. It may well be that in a language book, grammatical simplification came about by accident, abridgments not being given the additional quality of grammatical simplicity until the turn of the twentieth century. In classics and modern languages the many abridgments turned out were mediocre in both linguistic and literary quality. Michael West pointed out the harm this could do to both the pupil's grasp of the foreign language and his interest in its literature. He demanded that abridgment should be interesting and worth reading, and above all should inspire the pupil to read the real thing when he had sufficient command of the language.[1149:54]

Simplification divorced from abridgment was an invention, it seems, of Guarino, whose recension of Caesar appeared in the late fifteenth century. This type of book, current during the Renaissance, was the beginning of a long line of original readers in simplified language. Until the end of the nineteenth century the writers of such texts invariably followed their own instincts of what was simple and difficult. It was notable that although there were wide variations, a norm was arrived at by consensus of opinion. The idea of a quantitative measure was found as early as Henry Sweet, who discussed it as a theoretical possibility, and with the development of vocabulary lists based on statistical measures, it became feasible during the 1920's.

Two types of reader were developed: the progressive reader which took the pupil by easy stages from one level of vocabulary to another; and the plateau reader which exercised vocabulary at a certain level, without aiming at expansion. The most serious fault in these books was noted by Michael West: they tended to control vocabulary without controlling grammar.[1152:49] Another difficulty with this sort of reader was maintaining the interest of the reader. Simplification of grammar often brought with it dilution of the intellectual worth of the book, and many teachers felt that it was not worth the candle to ask mature people to read childish matter just because it was written in simple language.[1156:23]

Simplification changed its emphasis at the beginning of the twentieth century. Until then, it was usually the grammatical structure of the passage that was simplified, even if it was merely arranging the sentence to accord with the order of words in the mother tongue. This practice did not go uncriticized, especially during the eighteenth century, and though an integral part of the construing technique, it was slowly abandoned during the nineteenth century. With the development of statistical linguistics, vocabulary and phonology came under consideration during the twentieth century. As vocabulary is the most obvious fact of language to the layman, and most of the early work was done in this field, this was the aspect that became most important.

5.2.2 Reading with Supports

The traditional kind of support is the interlinear or parallel translation; the modern world has added the pictorial support and the recording.

The first detailed specification for interlinear translation seems to be that of Roger Bacon:

> Then the pupil is to learn the *Our Father, Hail Mary, Creed, Magnificat, Nunc Dimittis* and *Benedictus* which are the foundation of the faith, so that in reading these few things he may more easily progress to more difficult things. They are to be set out in the following way. On the first line the teacher writes the Latin, below it the Greek in Latin characters, and on the third, the Greek in Greek letters. Then, by looking at the Latin, one will be able to read the Greek in its turn. This will be easy to do without mistakes by the help of the Greek transcribed in the Latin alphabet.
>
> 1272 (R. Bacon) 69: 13

The interlinear gloss had already been used in the colloquies of Aelfric, occasioning a comment from Thorpe, whose edition appeared in 1858: "In this colloquy the Anglo-Saxon is only an interlinear gloss to the Latin; the design of the author being, by means of a Hamiltonian version, to facilitate to children the acquirement of Latin. (There is nothing new under the sun.)"[12:vi] Another common layout at the time was intercalating the translation of each sense group into the running text.[*96:87]

Interlinear layouts, or something approaching them, were common all over Europe during the tenth and eleventh centuries, and many of these glossed books furnish philologists with the earliest texts in the Romance languages. In Spain, for instance, service books and books used for spiritual reading, like the sermons of St. Augustine, occur in glossed "editions." The best known are the *glossae emilianenses* and *glossae silenses* from the north of Spain near the Basque country. Indeed, as well as glosses in Spanish, the first contains some in Basque. Most of the glosses are interlinear, but where the disposition of the page does not allow this, they are wrtitten in the margin.

Judging by the handwriting of the extant manuscripts it seems that they were copied, Spanish commentary and all, from a manuscript now lost.[*55:408] This would indicate that classroom use was one of the possibilities envisaged.

Parallel translation dates back to the schools of third-century Alexandria and Gaul. Apart from bilingual exercises like the *Hermeneumata Pseudo-dositheana* (which was taken over to teach Greek in the monastery of St. Gall), parallel versions of the Aeneid are still extant from the classical schools.[*140:317] The verse forms would have facilitated using a parallel format, as would the contemporary method of making a *volumen* by gluing finished pages together to form a roll. It is possible that the *Hexapla* and other polyglot editions of the Bible that appeared in the following centuries served their turn in the classroom. These were in the form of codices, books with a sewn spine like the modern book. The text was laid out in parallel columns across the full opening of the page, a necessary format when six languages were involved. During the twelfth and thirteenth centuries, it became common to enter vernacular translations around the ample margins of Latin manuscripts. It is in this way that Adam de Suel's version of the *Disticha Catonis* was preserved. From the manuscript it appears that the Old French was added later, probably by some harassed pupil.

Renaissance teachers were deeply divided over the merits of the interlinear and parallel translations. The first grammars use interlinear supports: that of Gilles Duwes printed the English translation in a smaller but identical type above the French (see Figures 9 and 10); John Holt's *Lac puerorum* and the fragments we have of John Anwykyll both use interlinear Latin-English sentences to illustrate grammar rules.

Colloquies, however, favoured the parallel translation. The fashion seems to have been set by modern-language dialogues, which were designed as conversation manuals and could be used without a teacher. But it was not until the end of the sixteenth century that Latin colloquia appeared with a parallel version, the first to be so treated being those of Mathurin Cordier, whose early editions appeared with a French version. There was a short vogue for parallel colloquies in Latin and Greek, owing, no doubt, to the employment of Greeks to teach their own language in Western schools (see Figure 18).

Yet another possibility was exploited at the beginning of the seventeenth century by John Brinsley: his edition of Vergil, for instance, does not give the original Latin, but a literal translation with a scholarly introduction to each poem, explanations of the subject matter, elucidations of difficulties in translation, and glosses on individual Latin words. These are printed in four columns disposed across the whole opening of the book. In this way he solved the problem of removing the translation once its usefulness was finished. He was against interlinear translation on principle:

> When both are joyned together, as in the interlineall translation, the eie is as soone upon the one as the other: I meane, as soone upon the Latine as upon the Greeke; and so likewise upon the Greeke as upon the Latine, because they are so close joyned one to another. So that the boke, instead of being a master to helpe onely where it should, where the mind can not study it, it becometh a continuall prompter, & maketh the mind a truant, that it will not take pains which it should.
>
> 1627 (Brinsley) 155: 237

Colloquia familiaria.

Πατήρ / Κύριός { μου περιμένει τὴν φιλανθρωπίαν σου αὐτὴν, ὅταν ἐθέλῃ, ἐπὶ τὸ { ἄριστον / δεῖπνον } ἐλθέτω.
Διδάσκαλε λαμπρότατε, πάντες οἱ κεκλημένοι ἤδη πάρεισι, μόνον σε ἀναμένοντες, καὶ ἐὰν μή σε προσδοκῶσι, νῦν ἂν ἀνέκειντο.
Διὰ τοῦτο δέονταί σου, ἐπὶ τὸ { ἄριστον / δεῖπνον } ἐλθεῖν.
Ἐπίκειται / Ἐπικρέμαται { ὥρα { πέμπτη. / ἕκτη. / δεκάτη. / ἑνδεκάτη.
Ὁ τοῦ { ἀριστᾶν / δειπνεῖν } χρόνος πάρεστι.
Πάρεισιν οἱ κεκλημένοι ἐπὶ τὴν θύραν.
Εἴσαγε τοὺς κεκλημένους.
Ὑποδέχου τοὺς συνδείπνους.

Υἱός.

Χαῖρε διδάσκαλε αἰδέσιμε.
Κεχαρισμένως ἡμῖν ποιεῖς, ἀξιώσας ἡμέτερος εἶναι συμπότης.

Πατήρ.

Ἑτοίμασον τὸ { ἄριστον / δεῖπνον } παιδάριον.
Παρασκεύαζε / Στρῶσον { τὴν τράπεζαν.
Παράτιθει { ἄρτον / κοχλιάρια } { ἀργυρᾶ. / ξυλικά.
Φέρε { κάρδοπον. / ὀθόνην. / ποτήρια.
Ἔκλυε { τὴν κύλικα. / τὸ ἀργυροῦν ποτήριον.

Τὸν

Colloquia familiaria.

Pater / Herus { meus expectat humanitatem tuam, ea, ubi volet, ad { prandium / cœnam } veniat.
Eximie Domine Doctor omnes convivæ jam ad sunt, unum te expectant; & nisi te expectarent, jam accumberent.
Ideo te rogant ut ad { prandium / cœnam } accedas.
Imminet / Instat { hora { quinta. / sexta. / decima. / undecima.
Prandendi / Cœnandi { tempus adest.
Adsunt invitati pro foribus.
Duc intro convivas,
Excipito convivas.

Filius.

Salve Præceptor observande.
Gratam rem nobis facis, quòd non dedignaris noster esse conviva.

Pater.

Para { prandium / cœnam } puer.
Adorna / Sterna { mensam
Appone { panem. / cochlearia } { argentea. / lignea.
Adfer { panarium. / mappam. / pocula.
Elue { calicem. / argenteum poculum.

Cir-

Figure 18. Page from Posselius *Colloquia familiaria.*[908] Copy in the Houghton Library, Harvard

From this time, though interlinear translations were common in self-teaching books, and continued as illustrative material in reference grammars until the twentieth century, they were never fully accepted by the teaching profession. The parallel disposition was much preferred. In France, Lemare attacked interlinear translations as contrary to nature, as harmful to any teaching aim, and as typographically grotesque. The need to jump alternate lines was a serious disadvantage, as it slowed up reading and caused fatigue. There is ample evidence to show that by the end of the seventeenth century, parallel editions in classical languages were common, both for the schoolboy and adult reader. It also became common for modern language textbooks to include parallel versions of literary extracts and models for formal composition, a custom that lasted until early in the twentieth century. One might add that parallel editions are still being published in the classical languages, the Loeb Classics from Harvard University Press and *Les Classiques de la Société Guillaume Budé,* for instance. In the United States especially, various publishing houses have adapted the idea to modern languages.

Interlinear props, without being interlinear translation proper, were part of the resources of the programed approach to language teaching. Certain readers printed translations of new words between the lines in a running text. Several such readers provided a movable grid which blacked these props out unless the pupil was either stumped or wished to confirm a guess. The selection of words to be translated was governed by frequency statistics and by occurrence in the text. The authors of such readers tried to work on a principle of gradually withdrawing the prop. The virtues claimed for this method included continuous enrichment of vocabulary, awareness of the difference between structure and lexicon, and continuous reinforcement of learning.[379:ii] A germ of this technique can be found in some manuals published at the beginning of the nineteenth century; but there the aim was composition rather than reading (see page 175).

Usually the accompanying translation aims merely at teaching a pupil how to read, but several who have used the idea taught the whole language through it. The late eighteenth century expressed uneasiness about grammar in many ways. The most commercially successful method was the Hamiltonian system, which was based on the interlinear translation. Its inventor, James Hamilton (1769-1831), was a Scottish businessman turned teacher, who had learned his German from a French *émigré.* His teacher had worked from literary texts which he interpreted orally, then immediately reread in German, while the impression of the translation was quite fresh. In his version of the idea, Hamilton substituted interlinear translation. In order to prevent the pupil from getting a distorted impression of the foreign language, he made his English as literal as possible, even to the point of being grotesque. It was an inductive method of sorts, as the pupil was expected to make the connection himself between the translation and the original. Though claimed as a new invention, Hamilton's system was developed from the widespread use of interlinear translation in eighteenth-century France. The father of the method was César du Marsais, whose Latin course appeared in 1722. He assumed at least a smattering of grammar, teaching the art of reading Latin by printing a literal translation below the line in smaller type. This was followed by drilling the points that rose from the text. Thirty years later de Launay adopted the idea, but demanded that the proprieties of neither language should be offended. To this end he proceeded from a selected vocabulary to the original and a good translation through versions in the "natural order" (cf. Figure 19).

There were a few writers who combined simplified versions and reading by supports. This was especially common during the eighteenth century, though some moderns, like W. E. Sweet, have experimented with the practice. A typical series of texts was that prepared for the dauphin of France by Crispinus during the 1730's. This was a set of scholarly editions of standard classical authors complete with the usual footnotes and *apparatus criticus.* However, in the wide margins of the early editions there was printed in smaller type a version in simpler Latin. Poetic works were rewritten in prose. The footnotes were in Latin too and acted as a link between the authentic and simple texts.

Editors of nineteenth-century readers in classical languages introduced another type of support based on the précis. The book was divided into short sections which were prefaced by a summary written in the language of the pupil. Usually this summary was enough to give the gist of the matter, an invaluable service in a language which became treated more and more as a crossword puzzle. Certain authors of the twentieth century who wrote Latin readers for beginners used such summaries, but wrote them so that the pupils' curiosity was roused, the only way to satisfy it being to read the section in its entirety. [see 206]

Though the written support remained the most common, technol-

2 *EXPLICATION.*

Liber . . . Libĕr, bri. *m.* Un livre, un volume.

primus. . . Primùs, ă, ūm. Premiér, principal.

fabularum . Fābŭlă, æ. *f.* Une fable, un conte, une hiſtoire.

Æſopiarum. Æſōpĭŭs, ă, ūm. *ou* Æſōpicŭs, ă, ūm. Eſopien, d'Eſope, *ou* fait à l'imitation d'Eſope.

Phædri . . Phædrŭs, ī. *m.* Phédre, *affranchi d'Auguſte, èxcèllent Poëte latin, & Auteur de beaucoup de fables.*

liberti . . . Lībertŭs, ī. *m.* Un affranchi, un éſclave mis en libèrté. *Les affranchis rèvèroient comme des Dieux, ceux qui les avoient mis en libèrté.*

Auguſti . . **Aūgŭſtŭs, ī. *m.* Auguste,** *Empereur Romain.* Le mois **d'Août.**

Prologus. . **Prŏlŏgŭs, ī. *m.* Un Prologue**, un avant-propos.

Ego . . . . **Ĕgŏ, mĕī. Moi, *ou* je.** *Pronom de la première pèrſonne.*

polivi . . . **Pŏlĭŏ, is, īvī, ītūm, īrĕ.** Polir, ornér, embélir.

verſibus . . **Vērsŭs, ūs. *m.* Un vèrs, une Poëſie,** un Poëme. Une **rangée, une ligne.**

ſenariis . . **Sĕnārĭŭs, ă, ūm. Sénaire,** *ou* iambique, qui a ſix piés.

hanc . . . **Hĭc, hæc, hōc. Celui-ci,** cèlle-ci. *Pronom.*

materiam . Mātĕrĭă, æ, *ou* mātĕrĭēs, ēī. *f.* La matière, la cauſe, **le ſujet.**

quam . . . Quī, quæ, quŏd, *ou* quĭd. Lequèl, laquèlle, qui, que. *Pronom.*

Æſopus . . Æſōpŭs, ī. *m.* Eſope, *né Phrigien & èſclave. Il ètoit tout contrefait de corps, boſſu, tortu, petit, laid de viſage, & bègue, ayant une grande difficulté de parlér; mais d'un éſprit ſupérieur & admirable. Il èſt l'inventeur des fables.*

Autor . . . Aūtŏr, ōris; *ou* Aūctŏr, ōris. *m.* Un Auteur, un inventeur.

reperit . . . Rĕpĕrĭŏ, is, rĕpĕrī, rĕpĕrtūm, rīrĕ. Trouvér, inventér, imaginér.

EXPLICATION. 3

Livre	premiér	des fables	Eſopiénnes *ou* faites à l'imitation d'Eſope
Liber	primus	fabularum	æſopiarum

de Phédre	affranchi	d'Auguſte.	Prologue.
Phædri	liberti	Auguſti.	Prologus.

moi	j'ai poli *ou* ai poli	*en* vèrs	ſénaires *ou* de ſix piés iambiques	cétte *ou* la	matière
Ego	polivi	verſibus	ſenariis	hanc	materiam

que	Eſope	l'Auteur	a trouvé *le premiér.*
quam	Æſopus	Autor	reperit.

Phædri Auguſti liberti fabularum Æſopiarum Liber primus.

PROLOGUS.

Æſopus Autor quam materiam reperit,
Hanc ego polivi verſibus ſenariis.

Livre premiér des fables de Phédre, affranchi d'Auguſte.

PROLOGUE.

J'ai poli la matière qu'Eſope a trouvé le premiér, & l'ai miſe en vèrs iambiques.

A ij

Figure 19. First Lesson from de Launay, *Nouvelle Méthode pour apprendre la*

ogy produced two other types. Improved techniques of printing resulted in the pictorial support, the first such book being the *Orbis pictus* of Comenius. This was primarily a vocabulary written in complete sentences, but it could also be used as a reading book. There was little change in the technique until the twentieth century, the relevant parts of the text being linked to the picture by reference numbers. The Berger English grammar used basically the same technique, but modified it to allow for a continuous story line. In one exercise, for instance, based on folk tales about a fox, he uses a picture of the English countryside. The various exploits of the fox are all depicted and linked with a dotted line which indicates his route. Each episode is numbered to correspond with the different depictions of the fox in the picture. When comic strips appeared, they were pressed into service in the classroom, being more convenient than a composite picture of the type used by Comenius and Berger. Where one could get hold of them, comic strips produced for the home market were used, but there were many textbooks, especially the *Méthodes audio-visuelles* of CREDIF, that adopted the idea and included picture stories designed for language teaching. Here, though, it must be remembered, the pupil was supposed to be listening to the taped text as well as looking at the pictures and text. One minor development of the pictorial support deserves mention: one Latin reader of the 1930's used pictures strategically placed. The pictures depicted the main point of the relevant section and their English caption was a translation of the key sentence.[206]

Some experimentation was carried out with tapes of vernacular translations of reading texts. This kind of aid was especially important in programed courses. The technique of letting the pupil hear a passage in his own language while he reads the original is quite old: it inspired the Hamiltonian method and can be traced at least as far back as the Renaissance. There the application was indirect: while one pupil read his translation aloud, the others followed through in their books. Sturm's approach to translation implies that he used this approach as part of his repertoire. It is merely an adaptation of the less formal parts of the construing technique.

5.2.3 Extensive Reading

Only in this century has the skill of reading been divided into intensive and extensive types. Extensive reading is aimed at ideas rather than grammatical structure and is definitely distinguished from translation. In extenisve reading one approaches a book in the same way as a native speaker.[544:44] This aspect of the matter was put very clearly by de Brisay, a teacher in the Hamiltonian tradition:

> The Latin sentence does not need to be dissected; it is more beautiful and more logical as it stands. If it seems awkward and unintelligible to the young student in its natural form, that is because his modern mind has only been accustomed to think in the narrow and inflexible English mould. What he must do is to free himself from his fixed habits.
>
> 1897 (de Brisay) 293: 14

This quotation illustrates one constant that can be found in discussions of extensive reading from the medieval scholiasts: that it should be part of the introduction to the foreign culture.[134:6] Another theme is the idea that reading should be enjoyable, otherwise the exercise would not be worth teaching.[153:26] The third point of emphasis is that reading is not translating.[610:43]

While most teachers relied on a saturation technique, Peter Hagboldt, professor of German at Northwestern University, based his teaching of extensive reading on reading material that was already familiar in one's own language. Without realizing that his principle dated back to the late Renaissance, he made reading exercises out of German translations of stories known to his pupils, the aim being to help them develop the facility with which native speakers group written structures and link them with their meaning. He was aware that the process he was demanding from his pupils was actually the reverse of real reading.[501:345] The next step from this was to let the students try themselves out on new material, so that they could exercise the motor skills and reflexes they had learned.

Hagboldt had been anticipated by Otto Bond, the editor of the first Oxford progressive readers. These books used simplified English versions of European folk tales. Among others who established the procedure was Henry Sweet, who makes the point that what is familiar to the native adult is not necessarily so to the foreigner.[1054:174] He himself carefully controlled the selection of reading passages to avoid placing extraneous cultural difficulties in the way of the beginner. The germ of the idea had already appeared during the Renaissance, without, it seems, being widely accepted. Ratke believed in introducing pupils to the classics through translations.[*54:68] This was part of an integral approach to Latin through reading, but it was so unorthodox that it was rejected by contemporaries as unsound.

The normal approach to reading was through grammatical analysis, an approach roundly criticized by the Natural and Direct Methods. Marcel, for instance claimed that this was not real reading.[717:I:393] Marcel's position was amplified by teachers of both classical and modern languages who suggested some sort of conditioning process:

> The Latin sentence is constructed on a plan entirely different from that of the English sentence. Until that plan is just as familiar to the student as the English plan, until, for page after page, he takes in ideas as readily and naturally on the one plan as the other, until, in short, a single steady reading of the sentence carries his mind through the very same development of thought that took place in the mind of the writer, he cannot read Latin otherwise than slowly and painfully.
>
> 1887 (Hale) 503: 8

This line of inquiry was taken up again by the twentieth-century structuralists.

Independent reading outside the classroom has always been strongly recommended, and various means have been used to encourage, or even force, pupils to do it. Apart from books which come to the pupil through class collections and lending libraries, magazines and newspapers have been used. They drifted into language teaching at the end of the eighteenth century judging from a reference in Wiseman's English grammar.[1163:xv] Newspapers and magazines for the native market were originally used, but as the idea spread, publishers began to find that magazines directed specifically at the learner were a commercial affair. One of the first languages in which such newspapers were printed was Latin, *Hermes romanus* being published in France from 1816 to 1819.[753:273] The custom became quite widespread, and by the end of the nineteenth century Latin magazines were being published in most European countries and the United States.[752:197] A similar type of publication continued during the twentieth century, ranging in sophistication from *Latinitas* (Vatican Press), which began publication in 1954, to *Acta Diurna,* published in London for the school market. Modern languages shared in this development too, but because magazines for the vernacular market were accessible, sales of learner material in this market were relatively small.

Until the twentieth century there is hardly a mention of silent reading. We do not even know when it became common, let alone usual. The only reference to it in Roman times shows what a rare ability it was. Speaking of St. Ambrose, St. Augustine says: "When he read, his eyes were drawn down the page and his mind was sifting the material, but his voice and tongue were silent. . . . I saw him reading silently, and to my knowledge, he never read any other way."[62:I:272] It is possible that eighteenth-century teachers knew about silent reading: Juvencus in his commentary on the *Ratio Studiorum* recommends that pupils should read new material *submissa voce.*[613:19] As a liturgical direction this means "in a low voice," but in this passage we are inclined to believe from what follows that it means "silently." But we do not have enough other evidence to resolve the question. Palmer's sections on extensive reading leave no doubt that silent reading is meant. What happened in the centuries between Juvencus and Palmer on this matter we cannot say.

One of the functions of reading has been exposing the pupil to the foreign language as a preliminary to training him to write it. It is this aspect of language teaching we shall treat next.

6

WRITING THE FOREIGN LANGUAGE

The art of writing is neither simple nor straightforward enough to be learnt by formulas: reflection and reasoning are necessary.

1841 (Burnouf) in 175: xi

In the ancient world, the peak of education was the art of rhetoric, which combined artistry in word use, logical reasoning, and, usually, the techniques of public speaking. Though its descendant, free composition, is no longer the sole goal of an education, enough of its original purpose has been carried over for teachers to demand more than correct manipulation of linguistic units and structures from their pupils. For just as in learning a foreign language one aims at a native command of speech skills, one's goal in composition is acquiring the native sense of proprieties, style, and grace.

Ancient and medieval rhetoric included all forms of composition, verse as well as prose; and as it was assumed that the results would always be read aloud, elocution played an important part in the discipline. Though Renaissance scholars tried to restore rhetoric to the classical state of excellence, they were unsuccessful, and, indeed, any speaking that went on in the language classroom in the following two hundred years was usually accidental. During the twentieth century, classroom composition normally concentrated on prose, and was relegated to the advanced stages of learning.

Learning the art of writing another language falls into three parts. First, there is the mechanical process of learning the written symbols and the conventions of their use. Second, one has to learn composition itself. Third, complementary to this, but not absolutely essential, is the most difficult art of all: translation into a foreign language.

6.1 PENMANSHIP AND SPELLING

As a language skill, writing has an ambivalent place: "The art of using a pen or a Chinese brush forms no part of language study proper, but is certainly a necessary preliminary to it" (Palmer).[836:52] Formation of letters and diacritics is an instrumental process which can be learned outside the context of a foreign language; the use of Greek symbols in mathematics is a case in point. Linguistic skills enter only when the pupil learns to use the alphabet to express thought.

The modern age is less careful in teaching penmanship than the Renaissance was. Few textbooks of languages with alphabets different from that familiar to the learner took much trouble to detail the way they are to be formed. By placing an asterisk at the relevant part of the letter, some Greek courses showed where the pen strokes were to begin, but this is as far as many twentieth-century texts were prepared to go. During the Renaissance, however, copybooks were used for both Greek and Hebrew:

> For fair writing in our own, and all the chief learned tongues Copie books, prepared of purpose for the Grammar schools, as in Secretarie for our English, so for the Latine, Greek and Hebrew, together with directions for writing in the beginning of them . . .; whereby all Scholars, well entered and practiced from their beginning, every day a little, may come to write commendably and many of them very faire every of these hands, without hindering their learning as is proved by experience.
>
> 1622 (Brinsley) 157: 79

There is no information about teaching the skill of writing in the Middle Ages, except that wall charts were in use, the pupils tracing the outlines on sheets as the master ran a pointer around the letters drawn on the charts.*12:11 This aspect of language teaching was especially important during the Carolingian Renaissance, as one of its aims was the reform of handwriting, and the improvement of the penmanship of contemporary scribes.

The exposure method so far described was occasionally refined by calling on the pupils' knowledge of the alphabet of his own language. The early nineteenth century interest in comparative linguistics, as well as affecting grammar teaching prompted a new way of learning alphabets:

> This new method is based on a system of transcription founded on the identity (though details are different) of three alphabets of the ancient world: the primitive alphabet of the Hebrews, the alphabet of the first Greeks, and that of the first Romans.
>
> 1826 (Beuzelin) 112: iii

During the twentieth century a similar method was developed for teaching the Russian alphabet: cognates in Russian and in the pupil's own language were compared and the equivalences pointed out. The approach of West and Richards was also applied to the active learning of alphabets, the pupils learning to write after they could read (see § 5.1).

Learning writing and spelling were not separable. After the first introduction to penmanship, letter formation was practiced by writing words and sentences: both dictation and transcription were used to teach punctuation, spelling, and letter formation. Spelling drill seems to have been uniformly rejected by the most creative teachers at all times. The final fixing of spelling seems to have been done by composition and translation exercises. Thus, in the classical and medieval *orthographiae,* spelling is taken as a facet of the possible use to which a word is going to be put, being treated incidentally with semantic and structural possibilities. Spelling seems to have been deemed worthy of exclusive attention only after the seventeenth century, but few special drills to teach it on its own were devised.

6.2 COMPOSITION

Any educated man who tries to compose in a foreign language is expected to write at a level corresponding to that habitual in his own. This implies several things: as it is the finished product by which he is judged, he must eliminate any sense of foreignness in his choice of register, words, idioms, or structures; his handling of any kind of writing on which he embarks must be faultless; and in the interests of efficiency, his speed of output must approximate that of the native. Both prose and verse composition find their place here. Prose composition is still in vogue in modern languages; in classical languages it is a dying art. Verse composition still has a precarious existence in classical languages, but except for a brief flowering between the thirteenth and seventeenth centuries, it has not been considered relevant to modern languages.

Four types of exercise have been used in teaching composition: transcription and consequent rote learning of models, structural variation of models, imitation, and original writing, each leading on to the other.

6.2.1 Transcription

Transcription of set passages has served two functions: it has been used as an end in itself and as a means of compiling a permanent record of passages worthy to memorize and imitate.

Until the beginning of the nineteenth century, exact transcription was considered an exercise of inestimable value:

> And so that he will better remember what he learns, his teacher must have him write out the lesson he has done, just as he find it in the book, warning him to copy exactly as he finds it in his book. Care must be taken with accents, punctuation and distinctions, and there must be as many words to the line, neither more nor less, as in the book.
>
> 1612 (Anon.) 297: 86

The cardinal point of this exercise was the aid it gave memorization, the practice of the time clearly demanding transcription as both an aid and a test. The value of committing passages to memory was unquestioned, providing that what was memorized was of high literary worth.[289:43] However, despite its importance it was never taken as a self-sufficient method or goal. Erasmus, for instance, did not regard a thing as memorized unless it was understood.[366:522C] In this he was at one with medieval teachers, for whom transcription was part of the exercise of *praelectio* (see § 5.1.2).

The most common Renaissance application of transcription was the commonplace book, which, according to Ascham, "be very necessary to induce into an orderly general knowledge, how to refer orderly all that he readeth *ad certa rerum capita,* and not to wander in study."[53:124] Its main purpose was to furnish the pupil with striking passages from his reading for imitation. The effort of compilation was regarded as important in forming habits of reading and a sense of style. It is probable that the practice of jotting down interesting passages was inspired by the preface of Aulus Gellius' *Noctes atticae,* a very popular book during the Renaissance.[63:I:xxvi] Though first utilized by Guarino in teaching Greek,[*96:108] the form and use of the commonplace book were laid down by Vivès:

> He is to have a largish notebook in which he is to note by his own hand any words he comes across in his reading. They are to be taken from good authors and are to be of daily use, rare, or especially graceful. He must also look for turns of phrase that are subtle, lovely, well-turned, and learned. In choosing sentences he must seek out the serious, humorous, witty, courteous, and false. He should also pay attention to anecdotes as examples for his own behavior.
>
> 1523 (Vivès) 1119: 266

It was given special attention in England, even appearing as "paper book" in the required book lists of English grammar schools.[*96:433] But the degree of judgment and maturity required in their compilation caused John Brinsley to have misgivings about their value for beginners:

> I do account them a great help where the schollers have leisure and judgment to gather them; I meane to gleane out all the choise sentences and matter in the most authors. Or, because it is over-greate a toyle, and requires more judgment than can be looked for in so yong yeares; if they had only bookes of references, it would be exceedingly profitable.
>
> 1627 (Brinsley) 155: 188

The decline of the commonplace book into the grubby little vocabulary notebook was hastened by the appearance of such reference books and by the decreasing importance of style as an aim in composition.

It was Erasmus who accorded the commonplace or *exemplum* its fullest treatment.[368] The other authors who treat commonplaces seem to assume that almost their sole use will be as models for intelligent imitation, but Erasmus expects his pupils to go beyond mere variation of models to sifting out the techniques which formed the models themselves. He begins his treatment with detailed instructions of where to look for *exempla* and what to have in mind when looking. This could have occasioned Brinsley's uneasiness about the maturity required by the pupil in order to gain profit. Then he hurdles textual imitation as if it were too obvious to discuss and writes what is almost a résumé of the whole work on how the pupil should sift the examples he gathers to fashion a style that is at once personal and reminiscent of that of the great classical authors.

With the more grammatical orientation of language teaching after this time, transcription lost much of its importance. After the nineteenth-century neglect of the exercise it was used extensively by Rouse[974:131] and although the element of exact memorization was not so important during the twentieth century as it had been,[1070:45] reproduction of material read or heard was regarded by many teachers as an important first step.[507:51] Though the decline of this aid was directly due to the importance of translation during the nineteenth century, this neglect would have rejoiced the heart of John Locke, who remarked that a man who had his head full of somebody else's thoughts could only be a pedant.[684:III: § 7]

6.2.2 Variation

The next step in teaching composition is, traditionally, variation of a source passage. In modern times language teachers have only played with the idea, being impatient to get on with the real business of writing, but after a tentative proposal made during the heyday of the Direct Method, variation was used by some:

> To prevent them from going outside their proper role, such exercises will have to be merely imitation or retranslation. They must not force the pupil to create new expressions—which will certainly be dangerous, but must force him to use expressions which are already familiar to him.
>
> 1905 (Varenne) 1100: 24

Under the name of *periphrasis* it had been known in Rome, but condemned, as it consisted of taking a finished piece of oratory and trying to put its meaning in other words: the result was never so polished as the original.[53:101] It had a very slight vogue in the early Middle Ages, and reached a peak in the fourteenth century with the *ars dictaminis.* As this type of composition aimed purely at communication rather than style, such variation of models did not come under the classicists' ban. From the textbooks which survive, it is certain that variation of model letters and documents in both Latin and the vernacular was of crucial importance in imparting the skill of writing. As most of the writing dealt with legal formulas, this was only to be expected.[*219:382]

This first step of sentence variation was not at all removed from the manipulation of pattern drills, the only difference being that the sentences concerned were longer:

> Whereas they reade in Latine *Gallus gallinaceus dum vertit stercorarium ostendit gemmam; quid, inquiens rem sic nitidam reperio?* they might imitate it by this or the like expression: *Mendicus, dum vertit stercorarium, ostendit talentum: quid, inquiens tantum argenti hic reperio?*
>
> 1660 (Hoole) 551: II: 64

The next step after this was sentence expansion. This was the normal way of beginning verse composition. In the following example from seventeenth-century France, which is typical of Renaissance practice, pentameter verses are made by expanding short sentences:

Matière de vers: Procella agitat solum. Carmen effugit rogos. Terra fructus dedit.

Vers: Exagitat totum saeva procella solum.
Effugiunt avidos carmina sola rogos.
Innumeros fructus prodiga terra dedit.

1673 (Mercier) 745: 259

The examples given in this section of Mercier are remarkable in that they are all "golden lines," which were considered the peak of perfection by Roman and Greek theorists: they are made up of verbs whose subject and object are qualified by adjectives.

The medieval *orthographiae* and Renaissance *copiae* furnished the raw material for the exercise and for later steps in composition. As did his medieval and Renaissance colleagues, Erasmus distinguished two levels at which a pupil could vary a sentence submitted to him: those of structure and style. Structural methods were classed under eleven heads, most of them fairly mechanical: one could replace words by synonyms; vary their number, person, gender, or case; alter the relationship of adjective and noun (*altitudines maris* [the depths of the sea] for *mare altum* [the deep sea]); substitute simple for compound expressions and vice versa; alter the tense or mood of verbs, or substitute words of different declensions or conjugations. He then devotes a chapter each to semistylistic ways of variation: use of patronymics (*Pelides* for *Achilles*), periphrasis, figures of speech, and allegory.[368:§§ viii-xv] This was largely a codification of medieval practice.

It is hard to escape the impression that Erasmus leaves the question of structural variation with some relief and attacks stylistic variation with relish. As a teaching book *De Copia* is not very good. It teaches mainly by example, the progression is somewhat unsystematic, and there are no exercises. But the pupil is meant to draw two lessons from it: that in all things restraint is necessary,[368:3-6] but that this does not mean an impoverished, or even an Attic style. The most important difference between Erasmus and his medieval predecessors was that every element he discusses is related to the frame of an oration.

The *De copia* is the central work in Renaissance language teaching, affecting vernacular teaching as well as classics. Like many of the classical masterpieces it was published in summary form, reworked as a school text, and often translated. Editions appear in Latin and other languages as late as the early nineteenth century. Thus it is that the methods evolved by Hoadly, Hoole, and Lemare looked past mere structural skill; and while style remained clear as an aim in the minds of teachers, manuals like the *copiae* and the synonym dictionaries, of which *Gradus ad Parnassum* is a good example, kept their importance.

In classical languages variation methods survived, despite the Grammar-Translation Method, until the middle of the nineteenth century. The traditional application is clearly demonstrated by a composition manual which appeared in 1831 (see Figure 20). This is a series of models of various types of free composition. Before each model appears the raw material to be used, a mass of truncated sentences that give some idea of the tenor of the finished piece. Sentence links, a factor of prime importance in Latin, were also indicated. Then were given in italics short directions on what is to be done with the raw material: in the case before us in Figure 20, the middle style (see page 409) is to be adopted. As always, the pupil's critical sense of style was to be trained along with facility in composition.

In modern languages this type of composition was slow in taking root, the eighteenth and nineteenth-century preoccupation with grammar effectively countering any move in this direction. Both the Natural and Direct methods paid some attention to it, but its main use seems to have been remedial. Belyayev writes: "One may ask a student to copy out five times a sentence in which he has made a mistake, but it is better if the student himself invents three new sentences of similar form and content."[97:11] Other twentieth-century teachers seem to have made similar use of sentence variation, at least as an idea to put forward to teacher trainees.[1142] But in modern languages it never attained the importance it had had in classics teaching.

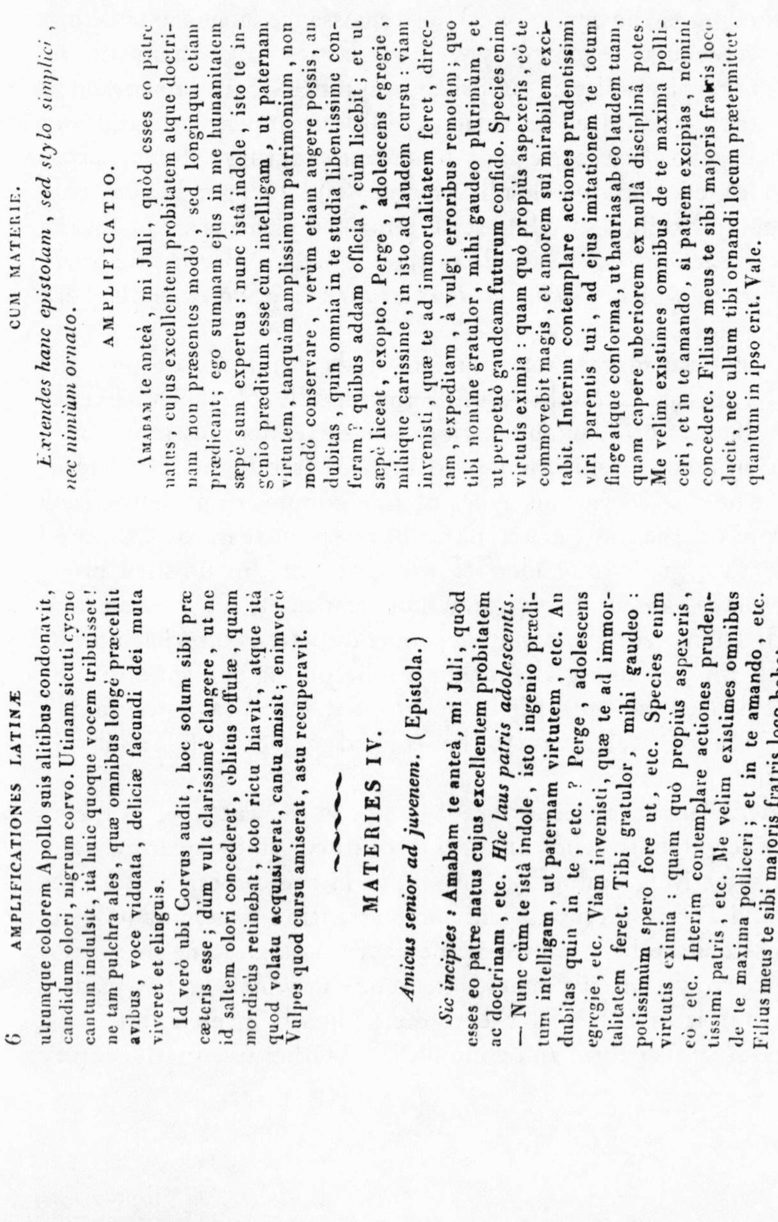

6 AMPLIFICATIONES LATINÆ

utrumque colorem Apollo suis alitibus condonavit, candidum olori, nigrum corvo. Utinam sicuti cycno cantum indulsit, ità huic quoque vocem tribuisset! ne tam pulchra ales, quæ omnibus longè præcellit avibus, voce viduata, deliciæ facundi dei muta viveret et elinguis.

Id verò ubi Corvus audit, hoc solum sibi præ cæteris esse; dùm vult clarissimè clangere, ut ne id saltem olori concederet, oblitus offulæ, quam mordicùs retinebat, toto rictu hiavit, atque ità quod volatu acquisiverat, cantu amisit; enimverò Vulpes quod cursu amiserat, astu recuperavit.

MATERIES IV.

Amicus senior ad juvenem. (Epistola.)

Sic incipies : **Amabam te anteà, mi Juli, quòd esses eo patre natus cujus excellentem probitatem ac doctrinam, etc.** ***Hìc laus patris adolescentis.*** — Nunc cùm te istâ indole, isto ingenio præditum intelligam, ut paternam virtutem, etc. An dubitas quin in te, etc. ? Perge, adolescens egregie, etc. Viam invenisti, quæ te ad immortalitatem feret. Tibi gratulor, mihi gaudeo : potissimùm spero fore ut, etc. Species enim virtutis eximia : quam quò propiùs aspexeris, eò, etc. Interim contemplare actiones prudentissimi patris, etc. Me velim existimes omnibus de te maxima polliceri; et in te amando, etc. Filius meus te sibi majoris fratris loco habet, nec, etc. Vale.

CUM MATERIE.

Extendes hanc epistolam, sed stylo simplici, nec nimiùm ornato.

AMPLIFICATIO.

Amabam te anteà, mi Juli, quòd esses eo patre natus, cujus excellentem probitatem atque doctrinam non præsentes modò, sed longinqui etiam prædicant; ego summam ejus in me humanitatem sæpè sum expertus : nunc istâ indole, isto te ingenio præditum esse cùm intelligam, ut paternam virtutem, tanquàm amplissimum patrimonium, non modò conservare, verùm etiam augere possis, an dubitas, quin omnia in te studia libentissime conferam? quibus addam officia, cùm licebit; et ut sæpè liceat, exopto. Perge, adolescens egregie, mihique carissime, in isto ad laudem cursu : viam invenisti, quæ te ad immortalitatem feret, directam, expeditam, à vulgi erroribus remotam; quo tibi nomine gratulor, mihi gaudeo plurimùm, et ut perpetuò gaudeam futurum confido. Species enim virtutis eximia : quam quò propiùs aspexeris, eò te commovebit magis, et amorem suî mirabilem excitabit. Interim contemplare actiones prudentissimi viri parentis tui, ad ejus imitationem te totum finge atque conforma, ut haurias ab eo laudem tuam, quam capere uberiorem ex nullâ disciplinâ potes. Me velim existimes omnibus de te maxima polliceri, et in te amando, si patrem excipias, nemini concedere. Filius meus te sibi majoris fratris loco ducit, nec ullum tibi ornandi locum prætermittet, quantùm in ipso erit. Vale.

Figure 20. Model Exercise from *Amplifications latines.*[34:6-7] Copy in le Petit Séminaire de Québec

6.2.3 Imitation

In the classrooms of the twentieth century, imitation of foreign models was a rather vague idea with no clearly defined goals. In modern languages its utility has never been clear: the multiplicity of possible models has prevented any precision of techniques and aims. In the classical languages, however, the universal recognition of certain authors as ranking above all others gave a point and direction to the exercise.

Though literary imitation is often thought of as a Renaissance peculiarity, it flourished during the Middle Ages. Speaking of his master, Bernard of Chartres, John of Salisbury says: "He used to put before us poets and orators to direct the pupils' early exercises in prose and poetic imitation. He would order us to imitate their characteristics, analyzing their ways of using words in sentences and their oratorical cadences."[593: §56] This exercise developed a keen sense of style, but little sympathy for the aims of authors. The results can be seen in the flourishing art of parody: some genuine imitation as in St. Thomas Aquinas's *Pange lingua,* the hymn for the feast of Corpus Christi, based on Sedulius hymn for Good Friday, and some quite blasphemous like the many drinking songs based on the Ambrosian hymns from the Divine Office.

During the Renaissance, imitation was not merely an introduction to stylistic niceties, but also a training in literary technique:

> There be three kindes of imitation in matters of learning:
> 1. The whole doctrine of comedies and tragedies is a perfect imitation, or fair lively painted picture of the life of every degree of man. . . . The second kind of imitation is to follow for the learning of tongues and sciences the best authors. The third kind of imitation belongeth to the second; as when you be determined, whether ye will follow one or more, to know perfectly and which way to follow that one. . . .
>
> 1570 (Ascham) 53: 136

The effects of the last approach are manifest in all European literatures of the period. In treating the subject of Renaissance imitation in relation to Latin teaching it is essential to underline that Latin, despite its status as a second language, was so much a part of scholarly life that it was not really a foreign language.[*195:360] Indeed, what the Renaissance teacher added to the technique of imitation was a deep admiration for his models, an element often lacking in the centuries before.

The first step was sentence imitation and variation (see §6.2.2). The next was careful analysis of the literary technique according to which the piece to be imitated was conceived. Where a Greek inspiration was extant, it was compared with its literary descendants and the lessons applied to free composition. According to Cardinal Bembo, consciously echoing Cicero, an imitator aimed at producing something as good as his original without hiding his individuality.[98:25] While most of the Renaissance pundits looked to Cicero and the classical poets to provide models, Justus Lipsius saw the technique of imitation as a means of breaking the hold Cicero had over scholars of the time. Thus he demanded that writers should be free to choose their own models: he himself chose Tacitus, an action which then as now was an act of rebellion.[*47:210] But, as we have already seen he was on the losing side.

Books of models were written to ease the pupil's introduction to imitation of great authors. The exercises were written in such a way that the bones of the prose or poetry showed to guide pupils through the technique. One suspects that the great writers of the past were to be preserved from bumbling and unskilled imitation as long as possible, so that the pupil's respect for great writing would not be harmed by his own clumsy attempts at a Ciceronian oration:

> For furnishing with matter and substance, besides Reusner's *Symbola* mentioned, Erasmus *Adages* of the largest and last Edition is a rich storehouse. Also Lycosthenes his Apothegmata, printed by G. Bishoppe at London 1596 is of good use. Lycosthenes of the last edition (as I heare) is dangerously corrupted with Popery and ragling [railing] against King Henry VIII and King Edward, and our late Blessed Queene; and therefore not to be permitted unto children.
>
> 1612 (Brinsley) 155a: 182

The passages chosen for imitation were complete in themselves: a full poem, or a section of a speech delineated according to the rules of rhetorical structure, for by this exercise pupils were learning not merely prose composition, but also the arts of authorship.

Despite obvious demands on the maturity of the pupil, this idea seems to have been used very early in a child's school career. Opinions differed over just how much one could learn through imitation. Some claimed to be able to teach the whole language; others fought the idea bitterly: "Imitacyon of autours without preceptes and rules is but a longe betynge about the bushe and a losse of tyme to a yonge beginner," was Whittinton's attitude.[*95:35] The quarrel gained in virulence during the sixteenth century until the whole principle of imitation was questioned even for teaching style:

> And coming to make school exercises the pupils can partly steale unreasonably: and partly immitate their authours making little or no use of grammar or any part thereof but doing all by apish imitation, and grose theft, being sure of this only, that their Authour writes true Latin, and good matter and so by guessing what he speaks, tye it to some other matter, stollen out of some other place, wherebye it comes in the end to some misshapen body with never a sound ioynt in it, knit together with sinews of sand.
>
> 1616 (Granger) 475: Preface

Two hundred and fifty years later Gouin tried to integrate imitation into his cyclic style of teaching. He was sure that any literary work could be broken down into cycles without doing violence to it. Once the teacher and the pupils had worked on it in the usual way, the pupil was asked to write it down from memory. Gouin, however, wanted the pupil's script to be more than a memory exercise: "The pupil has not learnt the fable by heart–he has created it with his judgment–he has made it his own by conceiving it in his mind. The work before him is really his own work . . . and because it is his own work he has not the power to forget it."[468:330]

Contemporary classics teachers were also toying with the idea of imitation. Latin textbooks in which the principle was embodied were published, and theorists, jolted by the success of the Direct Method, began to look into their own resources. In Jesuit schools, some tried to link intensive reading to prose composition, reviving part of the Renaissance approach.[74:176]

But as the popular orientation of language teaching during the early part of the twentieth century was oral, the importance of literary imitation has not been reestablished. In classical languages it proved almost impossible, as few twentieth-century classicists ever got their pupils past the deciphering stage, or themselves had, one suspects, a reasonable command of the languages. To teach by imitation one needs almost a native command of the language.

6.2.4 Free Composition

In classroom composition the twentieth century has tended to restrict itself to prose writing, though the practice of verse composition held an important place in Latin and Greek during the centuries before. Verse still remains on the fringe of classics teaching as an extremely advanced activity and as a hobby of the inveterate classicist. In modern languages it has never been fully accepted as a reasonable and feasible goal.

During the early twentieth century, free prose composition held an ambivalent place. As it does not involve translation, Grammar-Translation teachers reserved it until the end of the course, sometimes omitting it altogether. As it involved writing, audio-lingualists would have preferred to do the same thing. But for both types of teacher, syllabuses and examination requirements usually forced them to yield a fair amount on principles.

Though Palmer was never acknowledged, most teachers solved their difficulties by adopting what he called "the multiple line of approach."[837:113] This meant refusing to be bound by any one theory or method, but choosing means to fit an end. As far as free composition was concerned, this brought about a widening of techniques. Since the rise of the Grammar-Translation Method composition had been largely identified with translation. The old rhetorical orientation of the exercise had not been reintroduced.

Preparation for composition was usually based on reading or on retelling experiences. Thus several authors recommended that students should write an account of simple experiences like the trip to school, or rewrite simple stories heard in class. Others used pictorial cues. For example, by taking commercially available comic strips, Werner Neuse evolved a system of language teaching by reconstructing the anecdote. The strip was given on the right-hand page and appropriate vocabulary was printed on the facing page. The pupil was then cued by a series of questions. Though published in 1938 the book was reissued in 1958, a rare commentary on its appeal in a century when the life of any method is so short.

Over fifty years earlier W. H. D. Rouse had perfected a technique of introducing the skills of Latin composition through stories. He advocated telling, not reading, a story to the class and following it up by question and answer in Latin with, perhaps, some chorus work on difficult points of grammar. Then the pupils were to write the story out, if necessary staying within a restricted vocabulary and grammar list. It seems that at times Rouse used something like the Werner Neuse technique, drawing pictures on the board to illustrate as he went along.[976:7]

From the little that was said about free composition during the nineteenth century, we can assume that its place had been taken by translation, a displacement partly due to the vehemence with which it had been attacked during the eighteenth century. It seems that living languages followed the classics in this regard. The rejection of composition was approved by Rollin, at the time rector of the Sorbonne. In its place he recommended more exegesis of authors.[965:141] Interest in the well-rounded Latinity of the Renaissance was on the wane.

The best index to the priorities of the Renaissance "theme" is the following description of the ruling method of correction:

> In examining exercises in the highest forms (as in Theames, Declamations, Verses, Orations and the like) besides the faults against Grammar the diligent master should note, first all barbarous phrases, or poeticall Phrase in Prose, or contrary: secondly, tautologies or oft repetitions of the same thing or words; thirdly want of transitions; that is of fit bonds or phrases

> whereby to pass elegantly from one point to another, so that they might be more easily understood; fourthly, harsh composition; fifthly, lack of matter; sixthly, want of elegancy in tropes and figures; and so like elegancies noted in Grammar.
>
> 1627 (Brinsley) 155: 200

All of this, of course, was inferred from Quintillian. Brinsley saw the necessity of following up his written corrections by making his pupils turn in a version with all its faults emended. As the Renaissance "theme" followed the Roman rhetorical syllabus, it was an exercise in reasoning as well as in prose composition; declamation in a Roman court was never far from the mind of either pupil or teacher. Elyot even suggests that the first Latin book a pupil should see after he has learnt his rudiments should be Cicero's *Topica,* a treatment of logic as applied to oratory.[364:173] It is probable that the logical orientation of the "theme" and the essentially medieval concept of logical reasoning that it kept even during the Renaissance accounts for the monopoly of translation, which demanded neither of these qualities, from the late seventeenth century on.

There was no period during the Middle Ages in which rhetoric was not cultivated. Free composition was only one aspect of the discipline, which was treated as part of the philosophical and theological corpus of knowledge. Its range included Biblical criticism as well as love poetry. As during the classical period, it had two important dimensions: the inculcation of virtue and the development of logical expression of thought. It is interesting to note that Remigius of Auxerre regarded the three subjects of the trivium, grammar, rhetoric, and logic, as an indivisible whole.[940:23]

Unlike classical rhetoric, which had accorded equal value and attention to the spoken element, medieval rhetoric concentrated on written composition, without, however, neglecting the spoken component of the discipline. Students were expected to defend orally with the same intellectual vigor as they wrote. At times of stress, as during the Western Schism, skilled oratory was valued by both sides in their efforts to confound their opponents. Despite the loss of most of the important documents, like Quintillian and the

Rhetorica of Cicero, the medieval tradition of rhetoric followed the classical comparatively closely. The tradition was transmitted by copies of *Ad Herrenium,* a work ascribed to Cicero, and by manuals such as that of Adrianus de But, which were reminiscent of Quintillian. But despite the classical norms in all other departments of the art, both lexicon and structure deviated from the classical standard.

Prose was only part of the discipline of rhetoric; until comparatively recently verse was also part of the discipline, and at times was considered to be of equal importance to prose. It is significant that the first grammars of Romance languages were written to guide foreigners through the verse conventions of the troubadour courts of Southern France. During the high Renaissance, Rabelais demanded verse-writing skills from the members of the Abbey of Thélème, which was the archetype of the scholarly community. Milton was typical of a large number of Renaissance poets who wrote fine poetry in languages other than their own. But as the vernaculars became surer of themselves, and men less cosmopolitan, poets preferred to keep to their own language, and verse lost its precarious hold in the modern-language classroom.

In Rome, verse writing in both Latin and Greek had been valued as a rhetorical exercise. Owing to the importance of metrical structures in prose rhythms, ability in verse composition was considered essential to an orator. Cicero played a leading part in the development of the Latin hexameter, his translation of Arator inspiring, it is said, Lucretius. Verse writing in Greek was considered a polite accomplishment, and remained so until the end of the second century. The Roman Empire transmitted two Latin verse traditions to the Middle Ages, both being productive even until our own times: the classical tradition of quantitative verse and the accentual verse of popular poetry and Christian hymnody. Owing to the erotic content of much of Rome's lyric verse, the classical meter most common during the Middle Ages was the hexameter, as used in epic and satire. Models for the others were not considered fit reading for a celibate scholar.

Except for ignoring the classical canons of vocabulary, medieval scholars taught versification with all the rigor of the classical pundit. Verse composition became a favorite recreation, as the extant corpus of excellent medieval verse shows. The medieval hexameter, in spite of its slightly artificial air, is as polished as the classical. But it is the medieval accentual hymns that are the finest examples of the poetry of the time. Both types of verse were taught at school, but accentual verse was always an appendage to classical versification. Indeed verse composition was so important that in medieval England nobody could be granted a teaching certificate unless he was competent in Latin composition, both prose and verse.

In the return to classical standards which followed the rise of Humanism, the classical approach to sound rhetoric through verse composition was continued: apart from assuring a good sense of rhythm, the strict requirements of good verse sharpened the pupil's feeling for language.[41:71] The school approach left nothing to chance: Brinsley demands that pupils should be able to make a passable attempt at prose, should have already read a lot of poetry, and should be able to scan a verse in any of the classical meters. Only then were they guided through verse composition by the exercises used for prose.

Scholars of the later Renaissance became more critical of verse composition and of the supposed benefits it conferred. Milton remarks: "And that which casts our proficiency so much behind, is our time lost in . . . forcing the empty wits of children to compose themes, verses and orations, which are the acts of ripest judgment and the final work of a head filled by long reading and observing with elegant maxims and copious invention."[758:278] Nevertheless, verse composition remained an important part of the curriculum, being reserved for the middle and senior stages of the classics course. In England especially, verse composition was considered essential, and extempore improvisation in a given meter was an accomplishment expected of every schoolboy in the grammar schools.

Much of the teaching of prose and verse composition was mechanical, and some techniques were not designed to do more than teach manipulation of structure. Thus pupils were often set to re-editing verse as prose and vice versa, an exercise which kept its vogue until almost the end of the nineteenth century. Among exercises used by the more original to develop sensitivity to Latin styles was editing the Aeneid, which had been left unfinished by Vergil's death. The "revision" consisted of finishing the half lines that Vergil had not had time to round out.

By the beginning of the twentieth century criticism of verse composition was increasing, occasioning a cry of alarm from Rouse: "How an ordinary person can understand the rhythm of prose if he cannot understand the rhythm of verse passes my comprehension; on the other hand, verse once understood, it is a shorter step to the teaching of prose rhythm."[973:vii] But though twentieth-century teachers paid lip service to this statement by fairly rigorous teaching of scansion, practice in verse composition slowly slipped out of most classrooms.

6.3 TRANSLATION INTO THE FOREIGN LANGUAGE

The history of language teaching is dominated by translation, which, at certain times, has even driven reading and composition from the classroom. Translation into the second language is regarded as complementary to composition, its two special virtues being formation of a sense of style, and a rigorous training in perceiving the immense differences between resources of different languages. The only period from which it is largely absent is the Middle Ages. Simple translation has existed during most periods of language teaching. But during the Renaissance, it was supplemented by "double translation," which combined translation in both directions with intensive reading.

6.3.1 Simple Translation

Translation did not originate as a school exercise, but as an administrative necessity in the multilingual empires of 3,000 years ago. As a scholarly exercise, it was developed during the third and second centuries B.C. by the first Roman poets, Livius Andronicus, Naevius, and Ennius, who adapted the Greek conventions. It was clear to the Romans that the difficulties entailed fitted this exercise for the mature scholar, rather than the schoolboy, the work of manipulating the two languages together requiring intimate acquaintance with both. It made its first appearances in the elementary class in the Greek communities of the Roman Empire in the third century. The need was simple: to fully participate in the life of the Roman community one had to know Latin, and as those who needed Latin were relatively mature and were literate, this seemed the most obvious way. But its life in the early stages of teaching Latin was short. Relatively soon after, the political separation of the Empire, the lack of status of the vernaculars outside Romania, and the conviction that Romance languages were merely a local variety of Latin effectively disposed of its *raison d'être.*

Alfred the Great's efforts to make Anglo-Saxon a literary language and the appearance of Aelfric's bilingual glossary would lead us to suspect that translation methods were used during the Middle Ages in some places. But we have little clear evidence of it until the fourteenth century: masters in the grammar school at Troyes dictated French sentences to their pupils for translation into Latin, the result being checked the next day.[*35:20] Judging from later casual appearances of translation and its denunciation as a common and pernicious exercise, its use was not confined to Troyes.

For the Renaissance translation became the basic exercise in forming stylistic consciousness. In his rather offhand way Pace defined the contemporary idea: ". . . many things escape a person when he is reading, but absolutely nothing if he is doing a thorough translation."[831:136] Out of such statements of principle Lilly erected practical teaching policy:

> A great help to further this readiness of making and speaking shall be, if the Master give him an Englishe booke, and cause him ordinarily to turn every day some part into Latin. This exercise can not be done without his rules and therefore doth establish them, and ground them surely in his mind for readinesse, and maketh him more able to speak suddenly. . . . And it doth

help his learning more a great deal, to turn out of English into Latin, than on the contrary.

1574 (Lilly) 673: i

In the schools of Renaissance England translation appeared in the form of the "vulgar," which was a group of English sentences describing the daily life of the period. The English is natural, but obviously written with an eye to translation. It seems to derive from the grammar by John Anwykyll, a Latin teacher at fifteenth-century Oxford.[797:xi]

The routine of tackling a "vulgar" has hardly changed since then: Stanbridge gives a long list of instructions whose familiarity is obvious from the first sentence: "What shalt thou do when thou hast an Englishe to make into Latine? I shal rehearse myn Englishe ones, twyes or thryes, and loke out my principle verbe, and aske the question *who* or *what*. . . ."[1034:1] An inverted form of construing was recommended as the surest and easiest way of embarking on a piece of translation. The sentence was treated just like a Latin one, each word being parsed according to its function in order to arrive at the Latin case required. From this "construe" the pupil then built a Latin version in the "natural order"; when it was grammatically faultless, a piece of respectable prose was then made out of it by rearranging the units. Then the pupil learned his own Latin by heart, reciting it in class.[*38:13]

In England the "vulgars" sparked a quarrel paralleled by similar disagreements on the continent. Some teachers, headed by Whittinton, thought of the "vulgar" as an aid to learning grammar, while the opposite camp under Horman used it as the first introduction to classical authors. The School of Whittinton built their sentences around grammar points, even quoting the rule at the head of the page: Horman based his on selected passages from Livy and Cicero. It was a counterpart of the differences already noted between partisans of the direct and indirect approaches within the Erasmian circle (see §2.1). Whittinton's ideas fitted in better with the prevailing fashion, and Horman had to wait a century before his approach was vindicated by Joseph Webbe.

Though good style in Latin was a Renaissance preoccupation, the "vulgar" took little cognizance of anything but the elementary skills of translation. The basic points of style were not ignored; the main purpose of the "vulgar" was correctness in the elementary skills of putting a language together. It is worthy to note that, as yet, such translation was not a regular part of the modern language course.

During the seventeenth century the pattern was continued. One can gauge the importance of translation from the flood of books published on it: apart from formal grammars like that of Lily, which survived into the nineteenth century as the *Westminster Grammar,* there were phrase books, compiled to forestall error on the part of the pupil. A typical example is *Les Particules reformés,* by the Oratorian, F. Pomey, which consists of an alphabetical list of French idioms with various translations annexed:

> A escient:
> Sponte data vel dedita opera, de industria, ultro conscio animo, mente ac voluntate consciis.
> A bon escient, tout de bon:
> sevio, ex animo, extra omnem iocum, plane atque ex animo, remoto ioco.
>
> 1699 (Pomey) 903: 203

Such books were accompanied by a large number of excellent bilingual dictionaries. As a further guide there appeared works on the art of translation into Latin, which are really the first incursions into the field of comparative stylistics.[402] As yet, such books were not common for modern languages.

Partly because modern languages were unusual as school subjects, information on translation in their teaching is rare before the nineteenth century. They were usually learned in private, either under a tutor or by self-instruction from books, the oral aim not admitting translation. But as universal grammar came to dominate all approaches to language, translation and its dismembered relative, the "vulgar," crept into modern languages in the form developed by Seidenstücker and Meidinger, eventually to permeate all language teaching well into the twentieth century.

Eighteenth-century authorities had little new to say about translation. During the first half of the century it was abandoned by many teachers for literary study, as in the hands of all but the best pupils it proved unsatisfactory. So little is said about preparation of a passage for translation that it is probable that the elaborate Renaissance methods of preparation were either taken for granted or no longer in use at this time. All authorities, however, discuss very thoroughly the way in which the teacher should analyze the pupil's shortcomings. Translation teaching was beginning to take a strong negative cast.

Some of the early nineteenth-century teachers tried to introduce an interlinear layout into the grammars that taught composition through translation. The English editions of de Lévizac and the English grammar of John Jump printed complete sentences in the first language, translating only the content words interlinearly, the pupil being left to fill in the structure words in the lesson. As the matter became more advanced, there were fewer and fewer props, until by the end of the course, interlinear helps were entirely withdrawn. This technique lasted until the 1830's.

As late as Dr. Arnold's tenure of the headmastership of Rugby, the traditional "vulgar" was still in use in Latin, coupled with reading and free composition. The aim of the exercise was not merely translation, but imaginative imitation: a very free translation in which the pupil expressed some of his own personality and literary skill. As described in *Tom Brown's School Days,* the ideal form of the exercise approached Milton's idea of imitation.[*92:248] It was accompanied by free composition, usually in verse. But by the last years of the century, translation had ousted composition from the classics curriculum of most schools, and in the few where composition was still taught, even in modern languages, it was approached through translation.

The Rugby approach was an anachronism even in its time. In its place under the impetus of the Grammar-Translation Method there developed an approach heavily biased towards grammar:

> The pupil must study the lesson beforehand so that he can reply to all the questions with ease. First the master will read the sentences and words contained in the vocabulary and he will require the pupil to give him the

> English from memory. At the same time he will make sure by his questions that the pupil has a good understanding of the rules and comments on them. Then the teacher will put his questions in English. . . .
>
> 1852 (Badois) 71: 15

Where the emphasis had once been on ideas and grace of expression, it was now on structure and linguistic equivalence.

Twentieth-century theorists who treated the use of translation gradually forced the schools back to Renaissance theory and practice. In the first enthusiasm for the Direct Method many had abandoned translation for free composition, mistakenly interpreting the recommendations of the pioneers of the method. Nothing in Viëtor endorsed such a drastic stand, and other theorists, like Sweet and Jespersen, stated that in the advanced stages of the course, translation definitely had its uses. As during the Renaissance, two streams of practice and thought developed: the traditionalists clung to translation as their only resource for teaching all aspects of language, while the minority refused to use it. It was not until quite late in the century that the middle view received any hearing at all.

One of the factors in the survival of translation was its importance in examination syllabuses. Various expedients were evolved to close the gap between Direct-Method practice and official examination requirements: Hovelaque, for example, suggested that teachers should prepare translation assignments by Direct-Method lessons.[560:366] This was the beginning of a reaction against the nineteenth-century emphasis on grammar. Within fifty years, the ruling method of preparing a translation assignment had swung back toward content, so that a teacher could be expected to discuss the ideas of a passage and not merely its grammar.[54:46]

After the Second World War the so-called "Bilingual Method" was developed. This was a fusion of direct methodology with translation. All the appurtenances of the Direct Method were used, but the original cue was given in the first language after the patterns had been introduced to the pupils.[332:10]

Further clarification of the utility of translation in modern-language teaching resulted in a rethinking of aims and methods. Its most important function was seen to be sharpening the pupil's linguistic sense in both languages: "The value of translation, which is hardly recognized in the modern educational climate, is that it serves to clarify knowledge which would probably remain hazy without it."[283:351] As previous inductive teaching will have accustomed the pupil to handle groups rather than single words, this approach will be easier to inculcate in teaching translation. The pupil would have the opportunity to remain on known ground while learning the arts of translation and improving his sensitivity to the differences between his vernacular and foreign languages. Greater attention to differential analyses of languages refined the exercise, making it more useful and effective.[1112:1] Owing to this development, the twentieth-century return to the Renaissance view of this exercise was accelerated and translation was made more meaningful to both teacher and pupil.

6.3.2 Double Translation

Renaissance pedagogues felt that translation and the composition techniques described in §6.2 were relatively unsure. They supplied no clear basis for comparison of the pupils' individual styles with those accepted in the second language, even if their grammar and vocabulary were quite faultless. Renaissance teachers had their pupils translate vernacular versions of Latin and Greek texts back into the original, and then, under close supervision, compare results. Usually the vernacular version was the pupil's own which had already been approved by the teacher. Much was expected: in Ascham's view, "here his wit shall now be set to work: his judgment for right choice truly tried; his memory for sure retaining better exercised."[53:94]

Although typical of the Renaissance, double translation was first recommended by Pierre Dubois in 1306 in his book, *De recuperatione terrae sanctae.*[344] He suggested undertaking the conquest of the Holy Land by military measures and infiltration. As preparation for the second means, he suggested setting up a group of schools like the Second World War language schools of the Allied armies to train elite cadres to spearhead the retaking and holding of territory. Boys were to be taught Latin and Oriental languages to fit them for administrative posts; girls, hand-picked for their beauty and religious fidelity, were to learn the same languages and then marry Moslem nobles in order to convert them to Christianity. Double translation of religious texts is prescribed as an alternative to free composition.[344:xlv:71] Even at this early stage construing seems to have been taken as an integral part of the exercise. There is no evidence, however, that any part of this scheme was ever put into practice; it seems that the earliest use of the technique was in the school of Guarino during the late fifteenth century.[*96:109]

Though double translation was very common in the schools of the sixteenth century,[*36:7] the name habitually associated with it is that of Roger Ascham:

> First let him teach the child cheerfully and plainly the cause and matter of the letter [of Cicero], then let him construe it into English so oft as the child may easily carry away the understanding of it; lastly parse it over perfectly. This done, let the child both construe it and parse it over again so that it may appear that the child doubteth in nothing that his master taught him before. After this the child must take a paper book, and sitting down in some place where no man shall prompt him, by himself let him translate into English his former lesson. Then, showing it to his master take from him his latin booke, and pausing an hour at least, then let the child translate his own English into latin again in another paper book. When the child bringeth it turned into latin, the master must compare it with Tully's latin, and lay them both together, and where the child doth well in either the choosing or true placing of Tully's words, let the master praise him and say here do ye well.
>
> 1570 (Ascham) 53: 13

This was the definitive statement of principle, refinements being added by other pedagogues. Brinsley broke the retranslation stage down into construing and stylistic exercises. Like all schoolmasters, he tried to make his teaching as pupil-proof as possible:

> 1. When they have made it in the naturall order, onely reade unto them how Tully, or the Authour, whom their sentence is taken of it, doth place

> it, & some reason of his varying, and cause them to repeat both wayes, first as they have written, after in composition. 2. After that they have practised in the former plaine manner, you may make them doe this: cause their bookes to be ruled in 3 columnes; in the first to write the English, in the Second the Latin verbatim, in the third to write in composition, to try who can come nearest to the authour.
>
> 1612 (Brinsley) 155a: 153

John Cleland suggested that the second stage of the exercise should be delayed till the next day,[230:80] and proposed introducing other languages, especially French, into the cycle.[230:79] That this suggestion took root is clear from the testimony from schools in Milton's time, a couple of generations later, when Greek, Hebrew, and modern languages all had their place in the retranslation cycle.

All through the life of double translation stylistic nicety was the important aim, and this came to overshadow teaching of structure:

> In the matter of imitation, which is of the greatest utility in forming style, it is useful to take some passage, from Cicero, for example, and turn it into the vernacular. Then after some time, you will turn it back into Latin. The next step is to compare your version with the original and to correct it. In this way your own style will acquire the elegance of Cicero's.
>
> 1764 (Juvencus) 613: 21

As construing conflicted with the formation of a good style, it was increasingly relegated to the "vulgar." But though other writers mention double translation with approval,[229:41] by this time it was going out of fashion, being replaced by grammar learning and simple translation.

Languages other than Latin entered the cycle where it was considered important to teach the art of rhetorical composition. It was in this way that Milton learned to handle all his languages.[*66:318] But in Greek and Hebrew the choice of texts was limited, especially as they often appeared together in the chain of languages used. Thus the Bible was the key text; the Vulgate, being written in unclassical Latin, was not in favor, its place being taken by the Renaissance version of Junius and Tremellius. When Greek alone was being taught, one could use Renaissance and classical translations of Greek works, thus exercising both languages at once. The range for modern languages was somewhat wider, especially for Italian, a favorite language during the Renaissance, boasting a large corpus of texts with classical inspiration.

During the eighteenth century the philosophical orientation of language teaching probably caused the demise of double translation. Stylistic considerations declined in relevance, as Latin and Greek lost their practical value as languages of scholarship. Since then, sporadic revivals of the technique have been attempted, always in classical languages, but without being accepted by the profession at large.

Though it is natural to begin all discussions of teaching by detailing how one teaches, what is taught is an equally important question and often limits the choice of techniques. Now we shall look at the ways in which material for the language course has been selected.

PART

III

WHAT IS TO BE TAUGHT?

INTRODUCTION

The choice of linguistic units to make up a given language course is governed by two considerations: the aim of the course and teaching conditions.

The purposes for which foreign languages are taught fall into three groups: literary, scholarly, and social or practical. In linguistic terms, this determines the language skills which will receive the most emphasis and the registers in which one's pupils will operate. It also demands that the items chosen should be in harmony—one cannot risk producing a class of Eliza Doolittles. By selection of phonological items one determines the accent one's pupils will speak with. The balance between the three aims governs the tolerances the pupils are allowed in grammar, the vocabulary they learn, and the way they are expected to use it. The solution to these questions has varied according to the preoccupations of each period of teaching.

Though mainly a linguistic process, selection cannot be entirely divorced from teaching. The time available will necessarily affect the amount the pupil can absorb and retain. Questions of environment can also determine word selection: for example, if one is to use one's English in North America it is necessary to know "elevator" instead of "lift"; in French Canada one will soon learn that "char" can equal "voiture." Though gradation is not part of selection, the later process of ordering the material for teaching will have to be kept in mind, so that one does not introduce needless difficulties.

In this part, we pay more attention to the linguistic aspects of selection, as they are the more important and better documented.

7

SELECTION

> Then, in compiling vocabularies, my next concern was to select the words in most frequent use, and to order the lists in such a way as to leave out nothing necessary to express concepts, which, once identified and put to use, had to be given a precise definition.
>
> 1631 (Comenius) in 250: i

The twentieth century views as its own the scientific approach to selection. At the beginning of this century statistical measures were applied to vocabulary and during the 1920's grammatical structures were assessed according to their frequency. The process of refining the rather gross measure of frequency began at the same time by reference to the concept of range, to which, twenty years later, were added the dimensions of availability and coverage. Men like Michael West, more teachers than linguists, insisted on further refining this statistical approach by taking into account aspects of learning and of classroom practice.

But in reality, all the twentieth century added to known principles were accurate mathematical procedures, the computer, and a revised set of technical terms. Frequency, though the best known of the four statistical measures, was actually the last to be discovered, consideration of range being inherent in the literary studies of classical times, and treatments of both availability and coverage being foreshadowed in some detail in philosophy. The other selection procedures began as a matter of professional instinct and largely remained so.

7.1 FREQUENCY

In a discussion of frequency counts it is usually their application to vocabulary selection that first comes to mind. This is natural owing to the popular idea that learning a language is primarily learning words. Grammar, however, has had its share of statistical analysis, and some attention has been paid to statistical treatment of phonology. Moderns at first tended to take it for granted that frequency equaled relevance, an attitude at the root of Michéa's rationalization that frequency was a balance between the contradictory needs of economy and diversity in language.[750:191] But frequency counts are not always regarded in this light.

Their first recorded use was selecting rare words fit for the noble style of elevated prose and poetry. This guided the research of the Alexandrian school of literary critics and scholars that flourished in the first century B.C. Following the canons of Aristotle's *Poetics,* they sought out rare words (γλῶσσαι) whose judicious use would add a remote and noble atmosphere to their verse. In Rome the tenets of the school were adopted by a circle of young scholars, one of whom was the poet Catullus. The cult of the γλῶσσαι was not without influence in the Roman literary world of the first and second centuries of the Christian era, and finally ran riot. A balance was restored by the grammarians of the fourth century, and it was largely respected by medieval scholars who were, it seems, not at all concerned with playing the numbers game in language. Besides, by now the artistic uses of Latin were subordinated to the needs imposed by civil and religious administration and scholarship. Except for the peculiarities of the *Hisperica famina* and the like, and the satire of parodists, Latin style remained the property of the sober.

In Hebrew, however, the ninth-century religious movement which led to the production of the Masoretic text of the Old Testament, the recension of the Talmud, and the subsequent destruction of all other editions of the Hebrew sacred books, turned to frequency statistics as an aid to textual criticism. The result was a list of *hapax legomena,* and a general frequency list according to which the divergent texts extant at the time were harmonized. The accuracy of their work was unexpectedly confirmed during the 1950's by the discovery of the Dead Sea scrolls, containing some books of the prophets which compared almost word for word with the received text.

Due to the appearance of shorthand during the sixteenth century, some interest was shown in frequency, but the lists were usually drawn up according to the instinct of the writer. The pioneer in the field seems to have been John Bright, the author of *Characterie, an Arte of Shorte, Swifte and Secrete Writing by Character* (1588). He included 6,000 words, arranged in lists of relative frequency. The first specific application to foreign-language teaching seems to have been made by Winckler and Leusden (1649), who independently compiled frequency lists for the Greek New Testament. Given the polemical nature of the times, it is probable that any utility in language teaching rose out of the usefulness of such lists in textual criticism.

But the predominant activity was still collecting rare words, drawing a testy comment from a Jesuit editor of Clenardus: "Now, what in the world is the use of sniffing out words for which we have little or no use?"[769:iii] Comenius tried to refine the role of frequency in vocabulary limitation by trying to impose some statistical limit: "I have chosen the more usual words out of a short list of a thousand. These I have used in sentences, some simple, some of two members."[251:303] But this lead was not widely followed: indeed the Port-Royal grammar could claim that, in contrast with its competitors, it did not "fill the rules with words so useless, so rare, and so unusual, that the pupil's memory is loaded down rather than aided."[48:ii]

Teachers of the following centuries were not concerned with frequency counts, vocabulary being selected on its suitability for demonstrating the grammatical concepts in the course. There were, however, some teachers, like those of the Pestalozzian schools, who used their own instinct in selecting frequent vocabulary. They were imitated by both the Natural and Direct Methods. The American Committee of Twelve (1901) laid down that what was to be memorized "should consist of nothing but natural, oft-recurring forms of expression."[1074:53] But they did not go into how this material was to be gathered.

In modern times the laborious statistical technique was first used by Kaeding, a German civil servant, who analyzed texts totalling 11,000,000 running words, all of which were counted by hand. This was designed to help government stenographers to spell, the idea not being applied to foreign-language teaching until the 1920's. Though Thorndike's *Teachers' Word List* (1921) was directed primarily at teaching English as a first language, it was not long before his word lists were applied to teaching English to foreigners, his results being refined by Palmer's group in Tokyo. For French, the first frequency list was drawn up by Henmon in 1924, elaborated by Vanderbeke, and further improved by Cheydleur as part of the American Modern Language Study (1929). Similar lists were worked out for both words and structures in Spanish and German. At first these lists were used to check the value of existing textbooks by seeing whether what they taught appeared in the frequency lists. But soon the value of the lists themselves was being questioned because they were compiled from written documents: it was postulated that their greatest use was in reading courses, not in general language courses.[242:154] Until the invention of a convenient and portable method of recording, the dilemma could not be resolved.

It was the tape recorder that provided a satisfactory method of freezing language so that its units could be counted. This was pressed into service by CREDIF in compiling its *français fondamental* and in Australia by Schonnel, who applied his results to teaching English to both Australians and foreigners. It seems that CREDIF was one of the first research organizations to attempt to find out what frequency really represented. By now it was common knowledge that structure words outnumbered other lexical units and that the frequency curve rose sharply for the first hundred or so words to flatten out after the first two or three thousand. Some difficulty had been found in applying the raw results to the classroom, a difficulty largely resolved by the invention of availability as a scientific dimension of words and structures.

The inventors of Basic English had paid only cautious homage to frequency. Their mild skepticism was followed during the Second World War by the rejection of current frequency statistics in the forces' language schools for lists compiled by linguists and teachers based on the spoken language. Frequency itself came under attack in England after the war:

> The language class is not for producing bilinguals, but for giving access to a new channel of thought and action. Failure to realise this is responsible for the belief that the right words to teach a beginner can be discovered by the statistical analysis of the words used by the native.
>
> 1958 (Abercrombie) 4: 24

Five years later Lee postulated that frequency statistics could actually work against sound language teaching owing to the diversity of social conditions between the country and period in which the count was made and the country and period in which the language was being taught.[651:110] By the 1960's, frequency was no longer the sole statistical criterion in use, but was giving place to the finer measures of range, availability, and coverage.

7.2 RANGE

Frequency counts are necessarily bound by range, for no one count can possibly be exhaustive. It was for this reason that Henmon isolated the range factor in his counts to show whether a frequent word was an idiosyncracy of a few or was common property. When lexicologists began to deal with spoken language, range became the number of speakers who used the word.

All consideration of range implies selection of certain registers in which to work. By deciding to base a vocabulary or grammar on a certain group of books or speakers, the course designer accepts the bounds his sources have put on themselves. As well as the grosser limits of subject and correctness, language users conform to the subtler controls of taste, both literary and social, imposed on them. These controls can be brought about by restricting attention to certain authors, the normal classical practice. The modern approach to this matter tends to suppress the written language on the theory that language is primarily spoken, and that writing tends to be unduly formal. Thus range has two contradictory purposes: the older practice was to restrict intake according to the norms of a select few; modern authorities tend to take wide use of a linguistic unit as evidence that it must be taught.

7.2.1 Range and Register

The first linguists to concern themselves with questions of range were the Alexandrian scholars. In comparing the golden age of Greece with the times in which they lived, they were struck by the immense degeneration of the Greek world. This they attributed to the decay of the arts of literature, for the orator, as the good man par excellence (καλοκἀγαθὸς), was considered to be the stabilizing influence of Greek society during the golden age. In a sense this was true, power lay with the persuasive speaker. To bring about a rebirth of the old Greek world they tried to recreate its literature, beginning by analyzing the great orators and poets.

Rome took this to heart. The Roman poets of the early Empire were recruited by Augustus in his efforts to remake the ethos of the Saturnian Age, as the legendary past was known. This in part accounts for their preoccupation with the Alexandrian school and its methods. Later writers were aware of this aspect in the poetry of the early Empire, and identified Cicero with the forces that were trying to reverse the decline of the late Republic. Thus they drew on both periods, bringing together the canon on which selection of linguistic material for the classics course is based.

This literary approach to the problem coexisted with a social snobbery towards language, the constant search for *urbanitas*. It seems to have begun in the Scipionic circle (140 B.C.) and reached its height with Cicero. It was a consistent reaction of the cultured city man against the country, of the hardheaded modern against the archaist, of the fastidious artist in language against the common herd.

It tempered the excesses of Alexandrianism until oratory became an unreal amusement under the early emperors. But during the last years of the Republic, in which was formed the Latin style still taught, the Alexandrian and cultured aristocratic attitudes to Latin style remained in balance. It was this that, in spite of the archaists of the second century, was discovered by the fourth century and kept alive during the next sixteen centuries.

One of the basic features of Roman literary practice was the separation of poetical and prose language, in essence a distinction based on register. The language of poetry, like the popular language itself, drew on wider sources and was a more expressive instrument than the chastened language of prose. One of the features of the archaic style mentioned above was the destruction of this difference, which was restored by the grammarians of the fourth century. This essential part of Roman linguistic consciousness was to dominate Latin teaching until after the Renaissance.

Following Renaissance scholars it is usual to deplore the medieval abandonment of the classical canon. But this was merely a response to the changed registers in which Latin was now used. The classical canon was not so much ignored as amplified by the addition of the Vulgate and the Fathers. The more licentious poets and prose writers were left to oblivion, or so the moralists hoped. What had really happened as Latin became the lingua franca of Western Christendom was a sudden increase in the number of registers used. Classical Latin had descended from the philosopher's classroom, the scholar's study, and the courtroom, to the common people in the works of Christian apologists like Tertullian and St. Augustine. The popular translations of the Bible, which, as sacred books, were read by cultured Christians as well, brought the popular language to writing, a thing which had not happened apart from bawdy graffiti in public places. Owing to the need to present Christianity in vigorous terms, Christian writings were placed beside the others.

This was how matters stood when Latin began to be taught as a foreign language. As Latin became a normal means of communication for all scholars in all things, it developed colloquial registers which were perforce not the same as those of the classical period;

and these were committed to writing in satire, in erotic poetry that would make a modern pulp novelist blush, and in administrative language. It was no wonder that the classical canon was overlaid by other registers that fitted the needs of an intensely vital and earthly society. In their reverence for the classics, men of the Renaissance overlooked this to a large extent.

Renaissance scholars quarreled bitterly over selection. Some kept to the medieval attitude, being prepared to welcome vocabulary from anywhere, provided it filled a need. Yet, as in the medieval period, the final stamp of approval was not given a word unless it appeared in a good author. Henri Estienne laid down as a principle that words were to be coined to fit needs, but that their adoption was assured only if a recognized author used them.[389:12] On the other hand the old reverence for Cicero appeared and developed into a mania. Latin was already retreating from the market place. Renaissance versions of the Bible in classical Latin were legion, and the Humanists even went so far as to rewrite the medieval hymns of the breviary, at the order of Pope Urban VIII, to bring them into line with classical norms. The importance of the rolling periodic style of the courtroom even caused some to abandon the use of Latin in the classroom for fear that in spontaneous speech the "barbarisms" of medieval Latin would remain. It is from this time that concordances of classical authors began to appear to guard against corruptions in style.

Vivès was not impressed by this development: "There are some who fear that they will be contaminated if they use any word not found in Cicero. I consider this touchiness ridiculous and a sign of ignorant superstition."[1119:81] One of the most vociferous of the *anticiceroniani* was Henri Estienne, who, between trenchant attacks on Cicero and his sycophants, commented shrewdly on the foundation of the Ciceronian style:

> . . . many things are ascribed to Livy. But if Cicero had seen fit to use these words and expressions, they would be not only Livian but also Ciceronian. But there is not a trace of them in Cicero's extant works.
>
> 1576 (Estienne) 389: ii

Estienne and another rebel, Justus Lipsius, were willing to recognize that some Latin authors stood out above all others, but they demanded that each Latinist be left free to choose his model according to affinity of temperament, purpose of writing, and subject.[389:iii]

Erasmus stood between the opposing schools. While recognizing the preeminence of Cicero, he demanded that one should be allowed to incorporate in one's style the features of the best authors of all periods. The table of terms of affection quoted on page 101 is an excellent expression of the catholicity of his sources. Authorities in whom these words can be found range from Plautus and Terence to Cicero's letters and the elegaic poets of the Silver Age. The same breadth of vision can be seen in his *Copiae,* which are what his *Colloquia* are not, the product of a man of exquisite taste. His guiding principle was simple: "We do not think it absurd, if we are to begin this book with advice, to recommend that the stylistic sense of a pupil should be fostered, so that his writing should become truly Latin, elegant and polished."[368:I:x] He distinguishes between good Latin words (which may or may not appear in Cicero), barbarisms (such as *compilare* for *colligere*), and turns of phrase that are otherwise unfitting. He classes these last under nine heads:[368:14]

derogatory (as *congerro* for *amicus*); ["crony" for "friend"]
unusual (*vagor* for *vagitus*); ["puling" for "crying"]
poetic (*clarare* for *illustrare*); [to "illumine" for to "light"]
ancient (*temetum* for *vinum*); ["the grape" for "wine"]
obsolete (*hostem* for *hospitem*); ["host" for "guest"]
harsh (e.g., *castrata est respublica morte Camilli*); [The state has been castrated by the death of Camillus]
foreign
obscene
neologisms

By the time a student was advanced enough to profit from the *copiae,* he was expected to be well enough trained in scholarship to be able to check the *bona fides* of any word he wished to use.

Though Latin prose was bound down to Cicero and Caesar after the Renaissance, poetic models were more varied. The French *Gradus ad Parnassum* (seventeenth century) quotes about 130 sources ranging from the dramatist Plautus to the Jesuit Latinists of the late seventeenth century. It was constantly revised to keep it up to date. What is more surprising is the respect paid to the great religious poets of the Middle Ages. The metrical schemes analyzed for the pupil's imitation are not the strict Horatian meters but their more permissive medieval and Renaissance counterparts. But in spite of the relative freedom accorded the users of this book, every syllable still had to have the authority of a recognized Latin poet behind it.

The classical reliance on authority was well illustrated from the twentieth century by the *Vocabulaire de base du latin* of Mathy. This is a frequency list, but it is based on a list of eleven authors, the earliest being Cicero and the most recent Cornelius Nepos (first century of the Christian era). Admittedly this list was compiled with examination purposes in mind, but it shows a narrowness of selection that would delight the hearts of the Renaissance *ciceroniani.*

In modern languages very little of this development took place. Not much was done beyond emphasizing that the pupil's style and usage must be based on that of good authors. Considerations of register proved to be of capital importance, especially as the dialogues in common use were based on cultivated use, one of the aims being, as we have seen, the teaching of etiquette (see §4.3.1). This remained important during the Renaissance and the two following centuries, so that the dialogues of these periods used words and expressions drawn from the conversation of polite society. During the nineteenth and twentieth centuries the norm became more literary, and the register taught was usually that of formal discourse and writing. Hence the choice of words and structures tended to be governed by literary considerations, as if every student of French were to be made into a Victor Hugo. Though this approach remained in classical languages, the frequency research of the early twentieth century caused its disappearance in modern languages.

Though the preoccupation of most people has been selection of words, selection of phonetic features is also an inescapable part of the process. In general, a cultivated society is one in which pronunciation is a social marker, and this outlook is imposed on the foreign learner. Cicero goes to some length to describe the cultured accent in Rome, and this has remained an ideal throughout the last two thousand years. However, this ideal has not prevented the rise of local accents, nor has it guaranteed that the various attempts at restoring Roman Latin (those of the Carolingian scholars, Renaissance scholars, and modern linguists) were entirely successful.

This same linguistic snobbery operated in modern languages. With the emergence of standardized versions of Romance dialects, some pronunciations were excluded on the grounds of register. De Bèze (1583) advises the learner of French against certain popular pronunciations, castigating the pronunciation /io/ for /əo/ or /o/ in words like *beau.*[288:58] This attitude continued until the twentieth century. In line with the less normative orientation of modern linguistics and the less aristocratic cast of twentieth century society, teachers were inclined to review the traditional thinking, recognizing a whole range of pronunciations as possible, provided they were intelligible. The practice over a "received pronunciation" varied: in French, a heavily centralized language, only one norm is recognized; but in English, owing to a diversity of cultural traditions, the teacher may choose the accent he wishes to teach. Thus it sometimes happens that a British teacher in an American milieu can find difficulty with features strange to him. But the constant of conformity to the language customs of cultivated society remained to discipline the variations taught in the foreign-language classroom.

7.2.2 Range and Common Use

The ruling aim of the selection technique discussed in the previous section was artistry in language. It was the utilitarian aspect of language that dominated the thought of twentieth-century experts, and so attention was focused on the spoken standard, as being the most often used and the most obviously useful in communication. Thus conformity with the spoken norm became a modern article of faith, and linked to this was the idea that the larger the range number of a linguistic unit, the more necessary it was to the natural uses of language. In a sense this was the attitude of the *anticiceroniani* of the sixteenth century, but the full application of this principle was possible only in spoken languages.

We have seen how the usage of popular Latin influenced medieval Latin by invading the written language. This will be referred to again in the section on availability. As far as modern languages were concerned, the question did not rise until the Renaissance. Since modern languages were taught then as spoken languages rather than as written, it was taken for granted that the usage of the majority would be taught; nobody saw fit to analyze scientifically what was evident. Modern language texts of this time have a breezy lack of solemnity and reflect very well the spoken standard of the age group toward which they are directed. In them there is no whiff of the gutter, as appears in the Latin colloquies of Erasmus; the raw good humor of these books excited the horror of the inhibited seventeenth and eighteenth-century teachers.

It is hard to judge how much of the spoken register was covered. Sixteenth-century texts rarely go into the elevated or extremely colloquial registers of language, but they are obviously not aristocratic in standard either. This popular tone among even cultivated people was offensive to the professional pedants of the following century, who imposed their views on European languages through the academies and salons. In no language was this movement stronger or more long-lived than in French. Malherbe and Vaugelas, though ostensibly appealing to majority rule in their judgments on usage, were really basing their decisions on the usage of the restricted circle in which they moved. While regulating language at home, they were also dictating to the second-language teacher what he was to teach.

Thus, while during the Renaissance the material taught in the modern-language class conformed more or less to the spoken language, during the centuries which followed written texts were normally taken as guides. No authors were accorded the eminence of

Cicero in Latin, so that the material selected was usually the property of a large number. In dialogues, however, teachers were not unaware of the importance of following the norms of conversation. An Italian author of the early nineteenth century writes in his preface:

> The phrases are those of the most common occurence and indispensable use in conversation; and the dialogues represent the various occasions of social intercourse, and the ordinary proceedings of a day from its beginning to its close; particular reference being had to the customs and manners of Italy.
>
> 1835 (Bachi) 67: viii

This attitude was far from normal at the time; the literary language was at the center of classroom attention. It is clear from the early lack of unanimity in the Natural Method that they were not sure whether it was right to teach the spoken language: teaching through reading implies selecting a written standard in language (see §8.1.3). But by the end of the century the oral standard was becoming respectable. Rosenthal divided "the whole language into the languages of literature and the language of everyday life. . . . Which do our children speak when they enter school? The language of everyday life!"[971:15]

Conformity to spoken standards, and therefore to colloquial registers, became an important part of the twentieth-century doctrine. The *français fondamental* of CREDIF was the very embodiment of the attitude which regarded the spoken language as primary in both time and importance, and the written language as an outgrowth. The basic material of the list was based on tape recordings of children and ordinary people carefully chosen to reflect the full socioeconomic range of French society. On this count alone the linguists concerned drew the fire of those who accused them of neglecting

> . . . the written language, the French of books, the French of reasoning and abstract thought. Now, the language of conversation cannot represent the entire language: it is only a momentary shape, generally impoverished,

often transformed, of an instrument of communication that is infinitely richer and more complex in its lexical resources and its structure.

1955 (Cohen) 241: 68

But though this attitude received some scattered support, the intellectual climate was against it.

7.3 AVAILABILITY

Whereas frequency judges the worth of a linguistic unit according to how often it is used, range refines the measure by showing who uses it. Availability is a further refinement detailing in what circumstances speakers use units. This important measure was not fully developed until the twentieth century, appearing in the work of the St-Cloud team who developed *le français fondamental.* Availability is essentially the resolution of a paradox: a person tends to think of many infrequent terms as frequent because his daily activities keep them before his mind. St-Cloud invented the concept of the center of interest to channel this human peculiarity and to elaborate a meaningful language course. Both the investigations and the lessons that were made from them were based on focuses of daily experience like the home, the family, work, and school. It is around concepts of this sort that lessons are built.

This criterion of social need had already been working during the Middle Ages. Many vocabularies, including that of Aelfric, were listed according to subject, but selection was made by instinct. The classical restraints were so modified that nobody took it on himself to legislate on linguistic selection until the fourteenth-century proponents of the *ars dictaminis* violently impugned the traditional philosophical and literary approaches as unrelated to the reality of document writing for the legal and business world. These men exalted the principle of need above all others, taking to extremes the already noncommittal attitude to stylistic questions. The normal medieval attitude, of which the *ars dictaminis* was a cancerous development, was clearly summed up by Sadoleto, who "woul rather have the pupil led openly and simply to learn those things tha are useful and necessary."[988:106] This attitude later humanists set ou to modify by their insistence on style.

But despite the publication of *copiae* and other books on style there were many who kept to availability, one being Robert Cardina Bellarmine, who arranged the vocabulary lists of his Hebrew gramma according to subject headings, which are very like the *centre d'intérêt* of St-Cloud. In modern languages, however, the mai Renaissance application seems to have been in grammar: "to restric myself to the things necessary to come easily and directly to knowledge of the English language," as an anonymous seventeenth century manual put it.[470:iii] Though the principle of availability an that of range clearly entered into conflict, yet there were meetin points in modern languages. Florio, whose preoccupation wa teaching foreign-language learners to act like gentlemen at all times seized on the Renaissance love of the conceit, seeing it as part of th available resources of the society which his pupils were to enter:

> Proverbs are the pith, the proprieties, the proofes, the purities, the elegancies as the commonest so the commendablest phrases of a language. To use them is a grace, to understand them a good. . . .
>
> 1591 (Florio) 417: 5

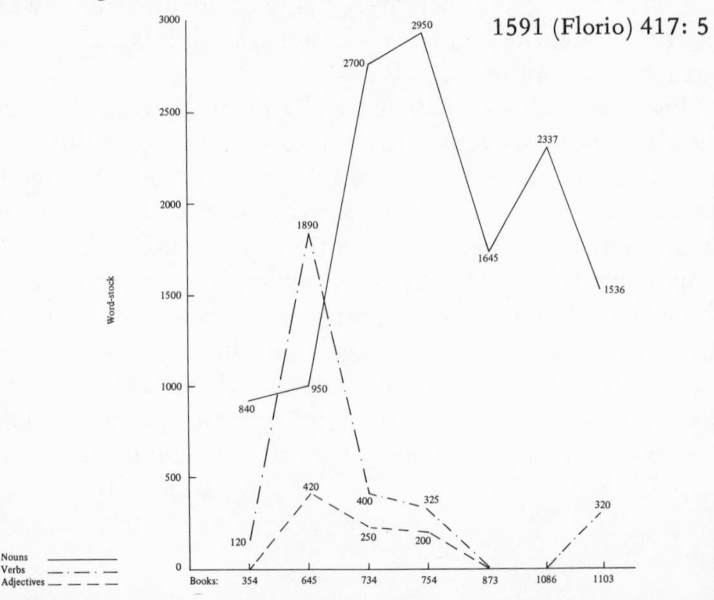

Figure 21. Word lists in Seven Seventeenth-century Textbooks. (Numbers refe to bibliography)

During the seventeenth century, vocabularies were arranged under subject headings according to the necessities of daily life. The idea was elaborated by Comenius, whose *Ianua linguarum reserata* was the first actual teaching book to be arranged around this principle, if one excepts the vocabulary of Aelfric (ninth century). The appearances of multilingual versions of his textbooks implied that the availability statistics for all European languages were more or less the same. In a sense, with Europe culturally dominated by France, his editors were right.

In the grammars of the eighteenth century, utility or necessity was the overriding criterion of selection for the vocabulary lists included. The layout, according to centers of interest, shows that the criterion of availability was still the ruling principle. But there is little agreement over what is necessary and what is not. The centers of interest are all more or less the same, ranging from religion to the minutest details of dress, but the total number of words in the lists varies between 1,000 and 3,000 according to the author's preoccupation. It is rare for these lists to include every content word that appears in the body of the work.

During the nineteenth century, progressive teachers tended to return to the Comenian idea of words and things. L'abbé Gaultier distinguishes two types of availability: active and passive:

> First, I observed that the Latin language could give rise to two different grammars. One had as its only purpose to facilitate understanding in the pupils, the other to allow them to compose. So, I have searched the most classical and comprehensive grammars for rules . . . which will lead directly to understanding, and I have left out those which were particularly directed towards composition.
>
> 1839 (Gaultier) 448: 6

The evolution of the world away from the stock of ideas and things covered by the available repertoire of words in Latin forced classical scholars into an unenviable position, not without some soul searching:

> New discoveries in art or science, new offices, new inventions, . . . new coins, new weights and measures, frequently require new names. In such cases, it is often impossible to avoid a barbarism without descending to a tedious and languid circumlocution, more offensive than the evil it is intended to avoid.
>
> 1846 (Crombie) 277: 3

During the next 120 years there were many who welcomed th challenge of bringing Latin up to date, probably spurred on by th possibility of having it as a world language. A group of enthusiast even went so far as to modernize the *Orbis pictus* of Comenius creating a whole new vocabulary to adapt it to the world of the lat nineteenth century (see § 1.2). It is important that organizations tha had a vested interest in the vitality of Latin paid most attention t vocabulary selection by availability criteria based on modern life Thus the Roman Catholic Church diligently kept the vocabulary o Latin from falling behind the evolution of modern society. In magazine directed at advanced learners and dedicated Latinist (*Latinitas*), the Vatican Press spread the latest coinages. A few o these were based on borrowings, but most were derived fron authentic Latin roots. The zeal with which this was done and the fac that a modern dictionary was published in the 1950's by Antoni Bacci, one of the foremost Latinists of the Vatican, were due to th feeling that the very life of the discipline was at stake.

In modern languages there was little of this sense of urgency Availability was a natural consequence of the new cultural orienta tion of language teaching. One of the less desirable results of earl appeals to frequency had been neglect of the cultural dimension o language courses, and this in spite of the cultural preoccupations o the late nineteenth century: Gouin had rather aggressively stated tha he taught what was useful,[468:72] while Huebner demanded tha material presented in the language course should provide a natura introduction to the culture.[564:48] But frequency or no frequency, i was noted that less useful words were easily forgotten.

Though it is clear that CREDIF merely put a label on the idea their importance lies in putting availability on a statistical founda tion. Their insistence on the cultural value of such a process of selection was a much-needed reminder that language was largely a social reality. For the first time a list based on a calculated refining of instinct was related to a fully described principle. And, most important from a teaching point of view, this selection provided a basis for gradation.

Morris took a similarly refined view of vocabulary control.[778] In the skills the student was to be given he envisaged a range of possiblities going from mere communication to complete command of the language. In his thought, range and frequency were more fitted for linguistic analysis than for application in teaching, and the distinction between active and passive vocabulary that had been applied by Gaultier at the beginning of the nineteenth century was one of the key issues in his approach. His analysis was not unlike that of Michael West. He postulated three classes: concrete vocabulary, abstract words, and structural words, classing them according to ease of translation, of identification with reference, and of synonymy. It will be obvious that in so doing he was weakening the rather artificial distinction between availability and coverage.

7.4 COVERAGE

Availability deals largely with the utility of a unit in a social situation, coverage is rather a linguistic issue. It arises from two properties of a unit: its extension and its ability to enter into combination.

7.4.1 Extension

The concept of a word's extension is an outgrowth of Aristotle's theory of predication: in general, what is predicable of a subject cannot logically be contrary to its nature. Thus predication spells out a quality that is already present in the subject. This concept was translated into terms suitable for language teaching by giving close attention to synonymy and definition. Both of these techniques appeared in the classical and medieval *orthographiae* and their successors, the Renaissance *copiae*. But their aim was not vocabulary limitation, but controlled expansion or the clarification of knowledge already gained. This aim was continued during the eighteenth and nineteenth centuries by books such as the *Gradus ad Parnassum* and Roget's *Thesaurus*.

Gouin seems to have been the first to realize that extent and diversity of use could justify the inclusion of a word in the language course. In discussing the verbs in his series he says: "Open any good dictionary at these words and from the length of the columns devoted to them, judge whether these are the idle words in a language. We can then appreciate at their true value the expressions which form so large a part of the ordinary language."[468:76] With nouns, however, he regards those of a general meaning as less useful, as they do not appear very often in the normal language of people.[468:77]

Until Max Müller came to his famous conclusion that the educated man's vocabulary contained about 4,000 words, few hazarded a guess in this matter, but the figure was seized on by teachers.[467:iii] The important question for which there was no satisfactory answer at that time was which 4,000 words were to be chosen. The founders of Basic English sought to answer this and similar questions by refining the science of semantics. As they approached language from the discipline of philosophy, they were concerned with exactness of meaning, and the first step in selection was finding "the central, pivotal, or key meaning" of each unit.[953:25] This naturally led them to definition as a means of expanding vocabulary along sound, sure, and salutary lines:

> In our joint work we came to the theory and practice of definition. In comparing definitions . . . we were struck by the fact that whatever you are defining, certain words keep coming back into your definitions. Define them, and with them you can define anything.
>
> 1943 (Richards) 953: 26

The practical implementation of this theory was Basic English, which was designed both as a lingua franca and as a base for controlled expansion. The vocabulary of 850 words was general enough to define every new concept likely to come within the purview of the learner, and more complicated structures could be defined with the limits of the grammatical resources of the language.[952:74]

Michael West was deeply influenced by these theories. He claimed that a person who enters a foreign community needs, not to be able to refer to specific objects and concepts, but to be able to ask questions and to define what he is talking about. His *Definition Vocabulary* and *New Method Dictionary* use a vocabulary of about 1,490 words, in which a large range of sophisticated concepts were defined. This stock of words he called the "minimum adequate vocabulary." It was made up of structure words and content words, that were usually of quite general meaning. Definition was done by juxtaposing these words so that they limited each other. A little of West's idea was behind the compiling of *le français fondamental,* which was aimed at a bare command, rather than the rich mastery of the language. The cultural orientation of the courses that grew from it, however, had a strong influence on perception of meaning and semantic coverage:

> Too often the pupil tends to believe that every word has a sole, fixed meaning which is given in a totally adequate way by the first dictionary he comes across, and that, as languages are constructed on the same logical model, the words and constructions of one always correspond to something exactly equivalent in the other.
>
> 1951 (Michéa) 751: 192

Unlike Basic, *le français fondamental* did not aim at becoming a franca, but solely at providing a base for further expansion.

7.4.2 Combinability and Generative Power

Combinability, as a factor, received greatest attention during the twentieth century; the power to generate other words was especially important before the eighteenth century.

Combinability is the case with which an item of language enters into a structure. Thus it is a factor of considerable importance in selecting phonological items like junctures and combinatory variants. In choosing grammatical items, combinability has two faces: the power of absorption of smaller units and the ability to enter into larger structures. Words are more difficult to select on these criteria: one can look either to their power of combining with other words to form new semantic units, a trait especially important in the Germanic languages, or their ability to enter into grammatical structures. In general it is rare that meaning has much role in determining combinability; there is some link with specificity and generality, but questions of register enter as well. Educated prose registers tend to restrict the combinability of units, and these are the normal registers taught in the classroom.

In the *copiae* and *orthographiae* progression there was from words with maximum combinability to those with minimum. But no formal selection of semantic or grammatical resources was ever made with this in mind. The first definite hint of a possible connection was in the book by Samuel Hoadly, whose ten "phrases" were carefully chosen and ordered for the opportunity they gave for structural expansion and absorption of vocabulary. An example followed, at least in spirit, by Sears a hundred and fifty years later.[1010:14]

The principle of combinability is at the root of the substitution table, the first to perceive it in these terms being Prendergast. Palmer stated the principle in more general terms recommending "ringing changes on a small number of words on the basis of previously memorised models."[837:126]

The most far-reaching application of this aspect of coverage is in Basic English. Richards characterized it as "a system of English words and the way they are used together."[596:11] This was a very apt description. It exploited the characteristic ease with which English words concatenate with much more daring than modern English does. Compound nouns, each of whose members restricted the extension of the other, were allowed, and the simple verbs in the basic list combined freely with any preposition to eliminate the need for complicated verbs, e.g., "go in" replaced "enter." The basic list was chosen for its high combinability, with the result that though Basic did look slightly strange, it did not have the outlandish aspect that certain "artificial languages" had.

The aspect of coverage that has traditionally received the most attention is the power to form derivatives or to suggest cognates. Twentieth-century lists tended to ignore this possibility, while during the sixteenth and seventeenth century there were entire vocabulary lists which allowed no other. As we have seen, this aspect predominated in teaching vocabulary from classical times until the mid-nineteenth century (see §1.4.3).

7.5 FACILITY

The criterion of facility has had little effect, because in language, facility and utility do not often coincide.[699:188] Good teaching includes trying to ease the lot of the pupil, but rarely can this be done in the selection process without falsifying the language. Attempts to do so can be traced back to the beginning of teaching. Most of them are confined to efforts to eliminate irregularities or to work on some sort of resemblance to units of either the target language or the pupils' own language. The principles that have been invoked in this type of selection were classified during the twentieth century as follows: similarity, regularity, clarity, brevity, and learning load.[699:187-189]

Before the twentieth century theorists were inclined to treat all these questions together. Quintillian remarked that one of the most important things a teacher should know is that there are sections of the grammar that do not deserve to be learned.[923:I.c.8] This remark was taken to heart sixteen hundred years later by Port-Royal and the Jesuits.[*164:21] Comenius, however, summed it up in the pithiest fashion: "The teacher should teach not as much as he himself can teach, but as much as the learner can grasp."[256:159]

One of the important reasons for the emphasis on etymology

during the first eighteen hundred years after Christ was the help such resemblances afforded the memory of the pupil. After its rejection in the late nineteenth century, Sweet pointed out that as long as the teacher was careful to emphasize the pitfalls, this means had its uses, and that even false etymologies were of some utility in teaching.[1054:89] Later in the same book he remarked that "the first and strongest associations of the learner ought to be with those elements of the language which are the common foundation."[1054:173] This idea was still recognized as valid in the 1950's,[639:6] but it was taken up as a principle in the selection of phonological features.

The principle of regularity is implicit in the work of Port-Royal, but in the writings of those who used this criterion it is difficult to decide whether they were using it as a selection or a gradation device. The same remark can be made about the criteria of brevity and clarity of meaning. Selection according to learning load in the ninth century was practiced by Aelfric, who taught the commonest meaning for each word to avoid confusing his pupils,[11:2] a custom rare after his time. It does not seem to have been taken up again until the late seventeenth century by Gaultier. Lemare's comment on him was most uncharitable: he did not see how this approach could do anything but amuse the pupils.[655:xxxiv] Several twentieth-century teachers took this as the only sensible approach to teaching pronunciation: "The wiser course, therefore, is to aim at teaching an intelligible, rather than a correct, pronunciation."[742:129]

West tried to put the matter on a scientific footing by applying the methods of cost accounting to language teaching. He asked two questions:

What does a word cost in learning effort?

Is it worth it?[1145:121]

On this basis he divided useless words into three classes: those of little cost and little use (e.g., inaction); those of high cost and little use (e.g., lassitude); and those that were useless, no matter their cost, because of register and the pupil's age. The ideal for him was low cost and high usefulness. He separated vocabulary into "heavy" and "light" words: the first class is made up of words of many uses and meaning–in fact the framework of language; the others are words of very specific meaning of application, which are not in everybody's vocabulary. The first had priority, whether they were easy or not. Of the others, the easiest among those needed should be learned first. West's work showed that facility was of restricted value in selection, as it had to give way to the linguistic qualities of the material.

The criteria of selection have been largely dominated by range, as even in applying the other criteria, it is humanly impossible to work from a complete sample of the language. But before selected material can be taught it must be arranged in a suitable order. We examine the ways of dealing with this problem in the next two chapters.

PART

IV

HOW IS THE COURSE ORDERED?

INTRODUCTION

In teaching a complex of skills, it is inevitable that it should be presented in a certain order. The problem of establishing such a progression has two dimensions: staging and gradation. The first deals with the constituent skills and the relationship in time between skills and theoretical knowledge. The second has to do with steps in each skill.

In language teaching, staging deals primarily with the order in which the skills of language are presented to the pupil. The question is complicated at times by the widespread teaching of translation as a substitute or supplement for reading and composition. The other facet of staging concerns the relationship between the practical use of language and knowledge of grammar. In general the two elements are interrelated: where written skills are given priority in time, grammar usually precedes the functional teaching of language. Gradation abstracts from skills, being concerned with the items of a language. Once it has been decided what to teach, it is up to the teacher to arrange the material in its order of teaching, with due regard to the aims of the course. The role of gradation is to keep the balance between easy introduction and the ability to use what one has. Thus, as well as questions of sequence, gradation takes in the questions of rate and type of intake, and the over-all time necessary to learn a language.

8

STAGING

Everything must be learned step by step in an orderly fashion. Therefore those who, for example, introduce children to languages by means of definitions and other obscure and difficult things, act contrary to reason.

1556 (Cordier) in 273: Introduction

The question of staging has been one of the most controverted in the history of language teaching. Practice has swung from introduction through oral skills, practiced during the classical period, the Renaissance, and the twentieth century, to the opposite approach through written skills, which was in vogue during the Middle Ages and the nineteenth century.

8.1 SEQUENCE OF SKILLS

The four basic language skills may be classed thus:

	Written	*Oral*
Receptive	Reading	Listening
Reproductive	Writing	Speaking

Translation is a fifth skill that holds an important place in the history of language teaching, but as it is secondary, it has no place on the above table. In many periods of language teaching it has taken the place of written skills, either forcing them out of the curriculum entirely or postponing them until a very late stage. During the history of language teaching, all possible orders and combinations of language skills have been used, with or without the added complication of translation. There are three principles that have been applied in determining staging: passive before active; ear before eye; written before oral. The place of translation is another problem and will be treated separately.

8.1.1 Passive before Active

The separation and staging of the skills in this order is at the root of twentieth-century methodology. The widespread opinion that this was an invention of certain twentieth-century theorists is probably due to the fact that though the distinction between reading and writing was clear, the other two skills were traditionally summed up in the one skill of speech. Yet the necessary separation of these two was clear at least as early as Vivès: "Now, many understand spoken languages, even when they do not speak them themselves. We seek information by speaking: let it be offered to the hearing and we absorb it."[1123:56] The broader application of the principle to textual and translation skills was standard Renaissance practice. During the eighteenth century, predominance of formalized approaches to grammar caused teachers to insist on the reproductive aspects of language to the detriment of the others, drawing a strong protest from Lemare:

> If there existed in the world a single enlightened man who believed that it is easier to write or speak a language than to understand it, in our opinion, he would be a wonder. We would like to see him to find out how darkness could coexist with the light.
>
> 1819 (Lemare) 655:xxxviii

Such protests had so little effect that the Natural and Direct Methodists had to fight the battle all over again during the late nineteenth century.

One of the most extreme positions was that of Harold Palmer, who recommended a long incubation period in which pupils learned to understand the foreign language. It seems that both listening and reading were taught during this stage: "It is an undoubted fact that the active use of language under natural conditions is invariably preceded by a period during which a certain proficiency is attained in its passive aspect."[836:76] The Tan-Gau method picked up the idea without any acknowledgment to Palmer, making this "incubation period" a central part of its methodology.

8.1.2 Ear before Eye

Twentieth-century authorities agreed in principle that passive should precede active, but accorded primacy to the view that oral skills should precede written: "The scientifically valid procedure in language-learning involves listening first, to be followed by speaking. Then comes reading, and finally the writing of the language."[800:21] Scientifically valid or not, the introduction to language through oral skills is really much older than many modern educators would care to admit, being found at least as early as the beginning of the Middle Ages.

Though medieval schools acquired a reputation for an extremely formal approach, the pupils arrived able at least to pronounce Latin. In the song schools, which were really schools of liturgical practice, pupils were introduced to the skills of pronunciation, without, however, understanding anything except the general drift of what they were saying. These were the descendants of the *scholae cantorum,* founded by Gregory the Great during the sixth century. In the Latin rites of the Roman Catholic Church this type of introduction to Latin lasted until 1965, becoming redundant as the part of the liturgy that concerned the layman was put into the vernacular. In Protestant Europe, of course, this development took place as early as the late sixteenth century, as the Roman liturgy was replaced in the churches, though in parts of Germany the Lutheran church worshiped in Latin until the mid-eighteenth century. The early humanists, Guarino for instance, adopted the medieval order of presentation, with the difference that oral skills were integrated into classroom work.

The attitude of those who began with oral skills was remarkably like that of many twentieth-century teachers—in the natural order speech came first. Justification for this stand rested on various concepts of human nature, including a rather cynical comment from Sturm: "Men are more eager to speak than to think and to ponder. So in acquiring an education, we should start from what is most natural to each of us."[1048:4] There is every reason to believe that in many schools Latin kept its oral dimension up till the end of the eighteenth century, though the tide of opposition rose higher and higher.

In the field of modern languages our evidence is not so precise. Granted, during the sixteenth century the oral approach held the field, but the evidence points in contradictory directions: judging from the existence of dialogues reading seems to have been the first step for many, but the *Polyhistor* of Morhof assumed that there is an ordered progression from oral comprehension, to reading aloud, to speaking and writing.[776:429] This position is akin to that of Comenius, a century before (see page 216).

Certain of the early nineteenth-century authorities disagreed: George Ticknor claimed that "the easiest and best method, therefore, for persons of all ages and classes to learn a living language is undoubtedly to learn it as a spoken one."[1079:429] Forty years later Prendergast translated this theoretical statement into a demand for the complete exclusion of reading and writing at the early stages, a position that had been held by some Natural Methodists. Gouin's attitude was more positive, in that he invoked a reasoned progression of skills from listening, to speaking, to reading, to writing.[468:133] Thus, Lado's advice, given eighty years later, though by now typical, was far from new: "Teach listening and speaking first, reading and writing next. . . . from linguistics we know that language is most completely expressed in speech."[640:51]

8.1.3 Eye before Ear

Lado and his school were not allowed to go unchallenged.

> That the 'living' speech consists of sounds, no-one would dispute, nor that the written language consists of signs-but what of it: Are sounds more important than symbols? An overwhelming part of all communication in the world is in the form of books, newspapers, magazines, letters . . .
>
> 1945 (Huse) 567:65

Psychologists were worried about the difficulty of comprehending new oral-aural material in a classroom situation: Rivers was inclined to think that "a lengthy period in which material is presented in an aural form can only arouse tensions in the pupil which may prevent him from organizing and retaining what he has heard."[959:160] Without appealing to psychology West was just as forthright in claiming that owing to the greater ease of learning the skills of reading, it was wrong to slow reading skill to keep pace with speech and writing.[1147:3] In one sense this vindicated the nineteenth-century conviction that skill in speaking was a step beyond knowledge of other aspects of language.

Even in the Naturalist school there were some who held this same opinion. In 1869 Marcel claimed that starting from hearing instead of reading was a confusion of the order of learning the mother tongue with that of learning a second language.[718:17] He also questioned the primacy of speaking, pointing out that many pupils would never need it. The order he recommended was reading, hearing, speaking, and writing. In classical languages, Sauveur followed the same idea: "From the first day we place before our pupils a Latin or a Greek author: that author is our teacher."[996:17] His writings on modern languages do not make it obvious whether he considered the same procedure valid for them or not.

The position of Comenius on this question is likewise not clear: he seems to consider listening and reading as two facets of the same skill of understanding: "The study of a new language should proceed gradually. The pupil must first learn to understand (this is the easiest skill), then to write (in this skill time is given for thought), and finally to speak (which is difficult because this demands immediate reactions)."*210:48 From the introductions to his *Orbis pictus* and *Ianua linguarum*, it seems that by the device of reading aloud, reading and oral comprehension were drilled together. His placing of speech as the last of the four basic skills was a reflection of the doubts of quite an important group of Renaissance teachers who feared for the standard of Latin speech, if Latin was to be the language of the classroom:

> . . . for wordes right choice is smallie regarded, true proprietie whollie neglected, confusion is brought in, barbariousness is bred up so in yong wittes, as afterward they be, no onlie marde for speaking, but also corrupted in judgment.
>
> 1570 (Ascham) *38: 14

Ascham's German contemporaries, Melancthon and Ratke, used reading as an introduction to linguistic skills, but for different reasons. Melancthon saw in this a ready source of examples for crystallizing grammatical knowledge, while Ratke thought of it as a true first step.

In Latin, primacy of written over oral skills was mainly the result of two things: the prevailing distrust of medieval standards of Latinity, which forced scholars to rely heavily on texts for all grammatical and stylistic guidance, and the widespread use of dialogues as means for teaching oneself. The weight and authority of the printed word was invoked to counter the standards of the Middle Ages, and the religious upheavals of the times destroyed the song schools in which pupils had had their first introduction to Latin.

8.1.4 The Place of Translation

The mid-twentieth century is probably the only period since the Middle Ages in which translation was relegated to an advanced stage in language learning. Translation was used in the initial stages of the foreign language by the schools of Bordeaux and Alexandria in the third century of the Christian era. But the first precise mention of translation as an introduction to language occurs in the Renaissance discussions of double translation, in which it is shown how modern languages could be introduced into the cycle. During the following centuries reading came to be identified with translation into the first language and composition with translation in the opposite direction. This was one abuse the Direct Method tried to correct: "Yet it is essential to put each thing in its place; and the place of translation is not at the beginning, but at the end," wrote Passy.[848:27] This position the twentieth century adopted as its own.

The only period in which the priorities of the various skills were clear-cut was the eighteenth and nineteenth centuries, where written skills, in the form of translation, dominated the classroom. In every other period teachers have adopted contradictory approaches, each group finding valid arguments to defend its position.

8.2 THE PLACE OF FORMAL GRAMMAR

Whether the pupils are to be given the formal analysis of the language depends partly on the purpose of the course, partly on the theory of learning current at the time. In general, there is a direct correlation between the importance of formal grammar and the priority of written aims. During the Middle Ages and the nineteenth century, the increased rigor demanded in the written language drew, attention to grammar, while ages like the twentieth century, which aimed at a functional command of the language, relegated grammar to a late stage in the learning sequence.

8.2.1 Grammar First

Though the Latin teaching of the Middle Ages was extremely formal, grammar was not really introduced until some apparent foundation for the spoken language had been laid by the song schools. But one can discount this as unimportant, because only the skills of pronunciation were taught, the skills of use being introduced through a formal course in which grammar played an essential part. During the first part of the Middle Ages (i.e., until the tenth century) grammar was the inevitable preparation for rhetoric: pupils began with morphology, went on to syntax, and finally to stylistics, a progression taken directly from Roman and Greek practice. After the tenth century, as a philosophical approach had become more important than a rhetorical, language was envisaged as resting on a set of principles which provided much of the groundwork for philosophy and logic. In the classroom, this produced little real change in technique.

Thus it was that the Renaissance tended to have elements of both approaches. The rhetorical was much more important: memories of the "barbarous" Latin of the Middle Ages made an introduction through the elements of grammar seem necessary, so that the pupil would have a constant reasoned check on himself. Erasmus put the orthodox position in his usual pithy style: "Consequently, after the first elements have been imparted, I should like the pupil to pass immediately to speech."[366:524A] In this he was following the classical tradition of Quintillian, for whom intimate acquaintance with classical authors was the basis of grammar. At the same time, the philosophical idea of a grammatical principle was far from dead. This approach seemed to have lasted longest in England, where the Renaissance was in good measure the flowering of the best elements of the Middle Ages rather than a reaction against them. Thus, one highly respected teacher could write: "First, there must be principles, or the light of nature in the scholler, otherwise light is not comprehended out of darknesse."[475:ii]

The seventeenth century returned to the philosophical ideal of grammar in teaching. Analogy was considered to be the natural basis of language learning and teaching, so that the inductive methods of Ramus and Ratke provoked counterattacks of surprising bitterness:

> The idea of those who will have no truck with grammar is the product of a lazy mind which wishes to conceal the fact. And far from being a help to

> children, it loads them infinitely more than rules, because it deprives them of an aid which would facilitate the understanding of books.
>
> 1670 (Nicole) 289: 42

Nicole's attitude was typical of that which was prevalent two hundred years following; with the introduction of the Grammar-Translation Method, opinions hardened even more. But despite the position of Plötz as the High Priest of the Grammar-Translation movement, he showed the moderation which is often an attribute of the leader, but absent in the disciples:

> It is important that grammar should be the most important part of a linguistic training and all language course should begin with this basic teaching. But it is dangerous to believe that everything is done once grammar is learned.
>
> 1865 (Plötz) 892: iv

It was inevitable that the success of the Direct Method should be greeted with outraged alarm by traditionalists: prefaces of grammars published round the turn of the century provided some excellent pieces of polemical writing:

> We state the result of our long and undivided attention to this branch of education when we say, that every endeavour to teach or learn German in which Grammar does not hold the principal place, must necessarily prove an unsatisfactory, if not unsuccessful, attempt.
>
> 1901 (Aue) 56: v

Grammar, complete with its initial capital letter, survived well into the twentieth century.

8.2.2 Language Skills First

Despite the twentieth-century insistence on inductive methods there were many respected figures who gave grammar a place in the language course. Morris for instance writes, "we ought to concede that there is a stage in language learning beyond which only formal grammar is conducive to language mastery."[779:55] In sum, this had been the position of those Direct Methodists who had kept their sense of proportion, including many of the young psychologists.[614:67] Following the usual pattern, however, the rank and file of the movement roundly condemned grammar, forgetting that their mentors had taken grammar as a valuable method of "establishing relationships, comparing, fixing categories," and "giving the pupils frames of reference."[1100:21]

In the century before, Prendergast had rejected grammar as an introduction to language, pointing out that many whose grammatical knowledge was excellent could not operate in the language at all.[911:65] But he, like the Natural Methodists, was counted as a theorist outside the main stream and little notice was taken of him. Likewise, during the preceding century there had been a small group of dissenters. Among "the blunders of common teaching" had been listed "the beginning with Grammar, and that a Latin one so ill-contrived as Lily's is."[226:13] In France l'Abbé Pluche was as cutting: "During the first stages of study, may childhood be ignorant, and that for a long time, that there are grammars in this world."[289:13] Such men were a remnant of the seventeenth-century group that had tried to put Comenius's teachings into practice, but who were submerged as the impetus toward grammar and linguistic analysis became stronger. The Jesuits too were an influential group swimming against the current: grammar was based on and subordinated to authors.[*60:415]

Grammar had not been regarded with unswerving devotion during the Renaissance either. In modern languages it was, at best, an afterthought: ". . .as the occasion requireth," ruled Desainliens, "he shall examine the rules."[312:9] Even from within the Erasmian circle protest and language was blunt: "Grammar is not a help, but a grave hindrance. It is not the basis of the Latin language, but a stumbling block."[*184:573] The most interesting Renaissance experiment in dispensing with grammar was that of Clenardus, who, in teaching Latin to illiterates, was forced to "instill a taste for grammar" into his pupils after they had a fair command of the spoken language.

Rebellion against grammar occurred during the Middle Ages too. A fourteenth-century bishop of Exeter, Grandisson, warned against the folly of those who tried an approach like that used by Marcel in the early nineteenth century:

> They . . . observe a form and order of teaching which are preposterous and useless . . . in that, as soon as their scholars have learnt to read or say even imperfectly the Lord's Prayer with the Hail Mary and the Credo, also Matins and the Hours of the Blessed Virgin Mary and the like . . ., although they do not know how to construe or understand any of the things before mentioned, or to decline or parse any of the words in them, they make them pass on prematurely to learn other schoolbooks of poetry or in metre.
>
> 1357 (Grandisson) *124: 103

But the approach castigated did not receive encouragement until the early Humanists tried to establish it fifty years later.

The place of grammar in the learning process has never been really clear, for even when the tide has been running in a certain direction, some teachers have always tried the opposite.

Questions of staging are intimately linked with the order in which the actual items of the foreign language are presented to the pupil, since the effective use of certain types of item depends on the pupil's grasp of a certain skill. For example, one can hardly apply phonology unless one can speak. In the next chapter we trace the ways in which problems of gradation have been met in language teaching.

9

GRADATION

> The more condescention is made to a childes capacity, by proceeding orderly and plainly from what he knoweth already, to what doth naturally and necessarily follow thereupon, the more easily he will learn.
>
> 1660 (Hoole) in 551: II: 9

Gradation deals with two problems: sequence and grouping, and the rate of intake. In general, the periods most concerned with gradation were in the twentieth century and the Renaissance. During the Middle Ages and the eighteenth and nineteenth centuries, gradation was an accidental result of the order of analysis rather than the deliberately calculated procedure it became during the other periods of teaching.

9.1 SEQUENCE AND GROUPING

The most delicate problem in teaching any subject is deciding on the order to follow, for this, in its turn, determines methods of presentation and repetition. In language teaching an item may be a unit or a structure, or in a formal course, a rule. The basic questions to be put can be presented thus:

	Sequence	*Grouping*
Units	Which units come before which?	What goes with what?
Structures	Which structures come before which?	What goes into what?
Grammar Rules	Which rules come before which?	What leads to what?

In the classroom these six questions have been approached in three different ways. In using the first approach, the teacher looks at them from the pupil's point of view, aiming at the easiest arrangement possible. The second is purely formal, taking the order of analysis as the order of teaching. The third is pragmatic, establishing what can be done with a given stock of knowledge and arranging the course to give the maximum yield at each stage.

9.1.1 Facility

This is the aspect of gradation that has attracted the most attention, as it is the easiest for the teacher himself to control, and, indeed, it has more to do with the teacher than the linguist.[651:88] In general terms this was the medieval position. During the sixth century Cassiodorus had suggested that matter to be taught should be suited to the pupil's abilities,[195:§7] an idea that Alcuin paid at least lip service to two hundred years later.[23:268] During the Renaissance the principle was loudly preached by scholars such as Maturin Cordier,[273:vii] but the implications of gradation were not properly studied until Comenius, whose treatment of it has hardly been bettered since.

Comenius proceeded from two basic principles: that matter was to be suited to the maturity of the pupil; and that introduction to each new difficulty was to be based on successful resolution of the last. He summed up the whole of his theory and practice thus:

> Let us teach and learn: the few before the many; the short before the long; the simple before the complex; the general before the particular; the nearer before the more remote; the regular before the irregular.
>
> 1648 (Comenius) 256: 123

Though Comenius was gradually absorbed by the formal approach of the eighteenth century and he repudiated his more liberal early thought, some elements of his ideas on gradation remained. Teachers were now conscious that some elements were more difficult than others, so that in the grammars of the time, notably those of Port-Royal, exceptions and other difficulties were printed in small type to allow teachers with more than the usual regard for their pupils' problems to pass them over. The selection of such items was made by instinct, and it is probable that no two grammars agreed on all points on what was easy or difficult. Beauzée revived Cassiodorus' idea that presentation and gradation should be governed by the sophistication of the pupil:

> The teaching of these elements must be clear and one must avoid all abstract and metaphysical reasoning, because only mature and vigorous minds can master its full complexity.
>
> 1782 (Beauzée) 286: 693

During the nineteenth century, except for a few teachers who were not satisfied with the ruling order of teaching, facility was the last concern. Gouin was one who sought to suit the teaching to the child instead of, as was usual, the other way round: "It is by the ordinary duration of a child's game that the duration of a series, and so the extent of its development, should be regulated."[468:87] This idea was taken up by the Direct Method psychologists at the beginning of the twentieth century.

The most exhaustive contemporary treatment of the problem was that of Harold Palmer. He was inclined to qualify the principle of easy before difficult, even to contradicting it.[837:70] His most concise statement was in his earlier book:

> What we can do, however, to ensure gradation on sound and salutary lines is to regulate the quantity of units in accordance with the capacities of the average student, to work from the easier to the more difficult forms of expression, to select the more used in preference to the less used ergons, and to avoid abrupt transitions.
>
> 1917 (Palmer) 836: 121

The distinctions here are subtle: Palmer is rejecting the idea of starting with ideas simple in themselves, and putting forward that of beginning with easier skills and making difficult items easier by readily comprehensible forms of presentation. In this he was not far from Comenius.

Other twentieth-century schemes of gradation rested on changed methods of presentation. It became commonplace that words easily demonstrated should appear in the course before others.[434:61] American authorities, with their emphasis on structure, advocated lightening the student's load by teaching phonological and grammatical structures with a minimum vocabulary, and then expanding vocabulary once the bases of the language were well known.[640:52]

In practice, however, this kind of gradation proved to be the least important; and where it entered into conflict with other criteria it was allowed to slip.

9.1.2 Gradation according to Grammatical Analysis

In teaching a language, there is a temptation to follow the order of analysis. By according some importance to the principle of teaching the regular before the irregular, Comenius shows the influence of this approach. It has been usual practice ever since, losing ground only during this century.

It was, of course, the normal procedure during the classical and medieval periods, as the aim was precisely that of teaching the skills of grammatical analysis. But during the Middle Ages the perception of purpose subtly changed, and the idea grew that one was actually teaching the language by this method. By the Renaissance it was a recognized way of approaching a classical language: "After the child hath learned perfectly the eight parts of speech," wrote Ascham, "let him then learn the right joyning together of substantives with adjectives, the noun with the verb, the relative with the antecedent . . ."[53:11] This, of course, is straight out of Quintillian. In the centuries which followed the order of grammatical analysis pervaded the teaching of modern languages as well, as is quite obvious from the textbooks.

The progress of the idea can be traced from attacks on it, one of the first being that of Comenius, who restates very clearly the earlier objections of G. H. Cominius and Petrus Ramus:

> And the second grave error is that right from the very beginning of the course, youngsters are driven to the thorny complexities of language; I mean the entanglements of grammar. It is now the accepted method of the schools to begin from the form instead of the matter, i.e., from grammar, rather than from authors and dictionaries.
>
> 1648 (Comenius) 250: 73

Such statements are not uncommon during the next two centuries, but they do not represent the official voice. Far more in keeping is this statement from Burnouf:

> Grammar takes the place of logic for children. This logic they learn, so to speak, without adverting to it, because the application keeps pace with the precept. The art is showing them concepts one by one, passing from the known to the unknown always, simple to complex, easy to less easy.
>
> 1841 (Burnouf) 174: vi

The growing power of the Natural Methodists can be seen in their own invasion of the field of analysis, the most original invasion being that of Gouin. In rejecting the Latinate analysis of the current grammars, he proposed dividing the language along psychological lines into objective, subjective, and figurative. The objective language gives reason for the use of the subjective; and after these two are mastered, one can begin the language of metaphor and poetry. Gouin's analysis was forgotten along with the rest of his method.

In spite of the success of Direct Methods, especially after the Second World War, gradation along grammatical lines was still common enough to provoke bitter attacks: "Scientific gradation means gradation from more to less common features," stated Gauntlett. "Unscientific gradation, on the other hand, means gradation from more to less regular grammatical elements."[449:52] And even in the early 1960's, especially in classical languages, there were still textbooks written which used this kind of gradation.

9.1.3 Productivity

In its simplest terms, productivity is a statistical measure showing what one can do with what one has. It is determined by the compatibility of the structures and units known, one with the other. In this form the principle is an outcome of method analysis which rose out of discussions between British linguists and methodologists on approaches to judge the value of language texts.

Overt statements of the principle of productivity are not found before Samuel Hoadly's *The Natural Method of Teaching* (1683). His scheme was based on a series of expanding structures or "phrases" (see §4.2.1). Though the deliberate gradation is from simple to complex, the side effect is a progression from the most immediately productive to the least, the vocabulary being introduced in a similar fashion. The two criteria for selection and staging are ease of integration into structures taught, and the facility with which each item generates new vocabulary by derivation, or by semantic processes like synonymy or antonymy.

Apart from Prendergast, those who used pattern practice before the twentieth century were not concerned about the mathematical aspects of the question. Yet they certainly realized the possibilities of playing with words and structures:

> If, for example, a pupil knows only the sentences in which the various forms of *dominus* and *do* are used, he can, by beginning from one of these sentences, like *dabis improbe poenas,* construct the following:
>
> | | |
> |---|---|
> | Scoundrel, you are punished | *Das, improbe, poenas* |
> | The culprit is being punished | *Dat improbus poenas* |
> | The culprits are being punished | *Dant improbi poenas* |
> | The culprits will be punished | *Dabunt improbi poenas.* |
>
> 1819 (Lemare) 655: xxix

Whereas modern authorities tend to approach the problem of productivity to justify including material, Lemare used it as a flail with which to belabor teachers of former ages. One of these unfortunates was Comenius:

In my opinion this method is vitiated by the following four defects:
1. it is beyond human capabilities;
2. it teaches a large number of useless things;
3. it gives modern Latin, which does not differ from lists of isolated words;
4. it is immensely vague, not being a 'prenotional' method which relates everything to fixed points.

1819 (Lemare) 655: 1j

He makes it clear that his main quarrel with Comenius is the material which has little productivity when judged by the classical canon, pointing in contrast to his own selection of 3,000 words which are carefully arranged to be of maximum usefulness at all stages of the course.

Prendergast was convinced that a whole language could be taught by controlled expansion of a basic sentence "if changes are made *one by one* for the practice of oral translation."[911:46] The tool he used to guide and control expansion was the substitution table, whose mathematical bases he was probably the first to work out (see §4.2.1).

During the twentieth century the question of productivity was treated by Palmer, who divided the material of a language into primary and secondary matter. The first was material that was unanalyzable; the second could be broken up into primary matter without doing violence to the language as it was at the precise stage of historical development at which the learner was assimilating it. The elements with the greatest possibilities of combination were to be learned first.[836:96]

In the form envisaged by Mackey, productivity is a mathematical measure arrived at by multiplying together the number of words or units that will fit together in a given number of structures, and then adding together the productivities of all the structures accessible in a course. This is merely a refinement of the method Prendergast used to justify his "mastery system" (see §4.2.1), and a mathematical dimension added to Palmer's concept of "ergonics".[836:74] In its later elaboration, this mathematical approach proved useful in criticizing the content and gradation of methods on the market. But the length of the calculations and the tedium of the counting demanded the use of computers in establishing the characteristics of methods.[700:160]

9.2 RATE OF INTAKE

There are three factors involved in this part of gradation: regulating the intake of material; assigning an amount of time; and regulating the amount of repetition and testing.

Regulating intake has never taken much of the teacher's attention. It has been done by instinct, the principle being rarely adverted to. Likewise it is only during the twentieth century that much attention has been paid to the question of the time necessary to learn a language, though the question did cross the minds of some Renaissance theorists.

9.2.1 Regulating Intake

In any learning process, for efficiency the intake must be regulated fairly strictly, if possible according to the learning rate of the pupil. West stated the principle in two different ways. He specified that new words should follow a certain rhythm of introduction,[1149:22] and that grammar should be introduced in short bursts, followed by long periods of assimilation.[1149:94] This manner of regulating intake was, of course, not new, being a natural part of language teaching. The first clear statement of principle was by Comenius. He decreed that one should attempt only one thing at a time, while being reluctant to define what "one thing" was. He was insistent that no topic should be abandoned until it was thoroughly mastered. This meant that he did not demand a rigidly regular progression from his pupils, but allowed the class to dictate the pace, within limits.

Despite his disagreement with Comenius, Lemare, as well, held to the principle of one thing at a time: "Ten other considerations demanded ten other sentences, so that there is only one thing to be studied at a time."[655:xv] There seems to be a strong correlation between this opinion and structural principles in teaching. For Prendergast, Gouin, Rosenthal, and Viëtor all held this view, and it was one of the basic ideas behind programed instruction, which began to flourish in all fields during the 1950's. Yet it is noticeable that followers of the idea were careful not to be too rigid in its application. De Sauzé's practice was to introduce grammar in very small units, preferably only one major rule in each lesson with the possible addition of one or two minor points.[320:ix]

9.2.2 Allotment of Time

In considering the time necessary to learn a language there are two ways in which it can be envisaged. By the first one determines the over-all allowance for the whole course, expressed in years, months, days, or contact hours. The second aspect of the problem is the amount of time to be devoted per lesson and the frequency of exposure.

Pronouncements on the amount of time necessary are rare before the twentieth century. But from our knowledge of school systems in ancient civilizations, we can guess the amount of time considered necessary. In Rome, a large portion of the last five years at school was taken up by the formal study of Greek, which then continued for an indeterminate period in the "universities" of Athens. During the Middle Ages, most of the ten years or so spent at school was taken up by the study of Latin, and the course continued at the universities. This system was passed on to the Renaissance, and began to suffer a gradual erosion during the eighteenth century. We can get some idea of expected rates of progress from Scioppius, whose course was supposed to enable a pupil to read a Cicero letter at the end of the first year and to write at the end of the second, a rate of progress one gathers to be exceptional:

> *Paedia grammaticae* or *Mystagogus latinitatis,* whose purpose is to bring one who has an understanding at all of Latin, more certainly and quickly to a reading knowledge, than another who spends thirty years toiling through

ordinary methods. In only another year, the pupil will be taught to write Latin, not only without faults of grammar and style, but also with considerable elegance.

1636 (Scioppius) 1008: 10

Little was said about spacing the course over time: Erpenius followed the Comenian idea of one thing at a time, adding the dimension of one rule a day.[383:iv] Juvencus, in his commentary on the Jesuit *Ratio Studiorum,*[613:5] expects two hours a day to be devoted to Greek–but does not expand on how long this is to last. Estimates of the total time necessary to learn a language tended to be utopian: "Whoever can and will give up five hours a day to the study of a language, will with certainty have assimilated the language at the end of six months," was Gouin's estimate.[468:294] The amount of time necessary to attain tangible results had already made the Natural Method the target of some extremely unsympathetic comment. Its position in America was not made any better by the refusal of Sauveur to take up a challenge to have his method tested in a control group in a Boston secondary school.[665:15] The traditionalists took this as an admission of defeat, instead of realizing that the method as Sauveur used it, though effective, was inherently unsuitable for a school. One of the triumphs of the Direct Method was adapting the Natural Method to a school situation.

The ASTP programme used the principle of saturation, deliberately concentrating the pupils in an environment from which the home language was excluded, and giving them eight or more hours a day of lessons. This regime gave a tolerable mastery of the most elementary parts of the language in six to twelve months, depending on the relative difficulty of the language studied. After the Second World War, the same principles were applied in teaching immigrants and displaced persons the language of the country in which they had been resettled. One of the most important factors in the development of saturation courses in modern languages was the founding of the European Economic Community. The consequent freedom of movement of skilled and unskilled labor across Europe prompted the writing of various audio-visual courses to help these migrant workers adapt to their new environment. For their proper functioning, these courses required concentrated dosage—at least four hours a day—over five months to a year. It was found that the efficacy of one of the most popular of these courses, *Voix et Images de France* in particular, varied according to the milieu outside the school: according to its director, in the civil service language school in Ottawa, Canada, which is predominantly English, the course took twice as long to teach as in France, even with the same teachers.

Palmer's analysis of the problem tried to take into account the ordinary school situation, in which foreign languages have to share a limited amount of time with other subjects of totally different types. He envisaged a course which can be flexible enough to last three years at the minimum and seven at the maximum. His first stage is purely assimilatory, lasting at least a term. In his second stage, he continues comprehension exercises, but adds simple reproductive and catenation exercises. The third stage is meant to end in complete mastery of the language, including the ability to translate at sight.

As one of the important aspects of course planning, those who developed programed instruction tried to fix the time devoted to learning a language. The lists of such courses compiled by Lane for 1963 stated the time necessary to complete the course under normal conditions.[644:292-295] This was dependent on the frequency and efficacy of the repetition provided for in the course.

The emergence of programed learning brought about almost a complete reassessment of the nature of repetition. The manner of advance was so gradual that each question supplied review as well as directing the pupil a step further. Early programed learning worked on the frustration principle: the student proceeded by trial and error, the number of unsuccessful tries at attaining an answer being a negative sort of repetition. Until means were found of harnessing digital computers to help the student judge his performance, or to judge it for him, this situation was inevitable. With the digital computer, two methods of approaching the problem (or "teaching logics") were worked out. The first, "tutorial logic," was based on the inductive principle, the other, "inquiry logic," was based on the deductive. In both, a student having difficulty could, either involuntarily or at will, be phased back to an earlier stage he had already mastered. However, the same steps were not repeated, the computer being programed to prevent this. Repetition was effected without the risk of boredom.

It should be pointed out that languages were only one of the areas in which programed learning was applied, and indeed the early experimental work in the most sophisticated system was not carried out in language teaching at all. Its importance lay in the perfecting of certain types of repetition, which allowed the student to proceed at his own pace without holding up the class or trying the patience of the teacher. Variation when the need arose was its most attractive feature: it was easier for the machine to improvise ways of repetition, and thus control the rate of intake, without seeming to do so, than for a teacher.

"Miracle" methods of language teaching have not neglected the advertising value of exaggerated claims about the amount of time in which one can learn a language. Charlatans are common in language teaching, as in every field, and it is difficult at times to separate them from genuine teachers with unusual ideas. The twentieth century seems to have suffered most from this plague of methods which promise an adequate knowledge of language in a matter of weeks, but it is impossible, owing to the lack of efficient mass media before 1900, to gauge the extent of such pretentions.

Teachers have known for centuries that the over-all time necessary to learn a language is proportionate to the frequency of repetition in the course; but as has been pointed out in this section, it is only during this century that one has been controlled to conform with the other.

With the discussion of the history of gradation, we have finished with the principles of method. It is now appropriate to consider the media through which they are put into practice.

PART

THE MEANS OF TRANSMISSION

INTRODUCTION

Teaching is, in essence, communication, an act shaped by the available means of transmission. In terms of communications media, cultures of the period covered by this book have passed from the oral-aural, to the written and typographic, and finally to the electronic, each successive change overlaying, not replacing, the one preceding.[*156:17] *Our modern age has at its disposal the machine, the book, the teacher, and the environment.*

The teacher is central to them all. At first he was a philosopher who sought to introduce his pupils to the speculative sciences through rigorous language training. In the classical world language in its formal registers was an oral instrument with strong social implications. The teacher and his voice were the center of the teaching process and the environment was a live force in a way it is not today. The link with environment was essentially an oral one, and language learners were subjected to pressures from a bilingual environment that was fostered to a degree since unknown in the West.

The book began as a memory aid subordinated to the needs of oral composition. While it remained a manuscript it had little relevance other than as a prop. Not until printing brought mass production did the balance between teacher and book begin to shift. The shift was accelerated by the imposition of the old classical standards, which could only be transmitted through the printed page, so that the teacher became an interpreter of the book, rather than a scholar who used the book to amplify the positions he took in class.[*156:61] *From here it was but a short step to dispensing with the teacher altogether. In any case the next two hundred years saw a sudden increase in the importance of the written word. It even came to be assumed that speech was derived from writing, and that oral-aural* *skills could be derived from written. Language teaching became book-centered and reduced the teacher almost to a cipher and isolated the pupil from the society of which the language could have made him a part.*

Machines dominate communications in the modern world, and hence are well established in teaching. By electronic means oral-aural skills have come to the fore again and the antisocial behavior inherent in book-centered learning has been modified, but not completely eliminated, by techniques like the recorded lesson. The language environment has been re-created artificially, while the teacher and the book have been forced to integrate themselves to these new tools of transmission.

Much of what has already been described in this book takes shape only when details of the media of teaching are discussed, as the influence teaching ideas and transmission tools have on each other is reciprocal.

10

MECHANICAL MEDIA

It is this monotonous, unnatural and 'inhuman' drill which the machine can do tirelessly—hence more efficiently than the teacher.

1961 (Parker) in *163: 70

Perhaps the most crucial problems in teaching languages are effective demonstration of meaning, semantic or grammatical, and ensuring that repetition is efficacious. The commercial development of machines which reproduced sound and added sound to pictures brought certain types of drill to the attention of the teaching profession.

The influence of machines and teaching on each other was reciprocal. Experts developed repetition methods that made use of the particular virtues of the machines in question without realizing that what they had discovered had been in common use three hundred years before. In their turn, teaching needs forced manufacturers to make certain modifications in the design concept of machines like tape recorders, film projectors, and TV sets. By the 1960's method writers were assuming that language teachers would have machines of various sorts at their disposal, and machine teaching was becoming an integral part of the approach.

As with all new developments, problems arose, many of them needless. Not the least was the impression that the machine would work miracles, and the later balanced thinking on machine teaching was often the result of exploded hopes and theories. At first, many teachers tended to fear that they would be replaced, causing the comment that a teacher who is afraid he will be replaced by a machine should be. In releasing the teacher from much of the mechanical drudgery of the classroom, machines placed new strains on his qualifications and ingenuity, resulting in either rejection of the principle of machine teaching, or in adaptation of the teacher's art to turn the challenge to good use.

For the teaching profession, its industrial revolution began with Edison's invention of the phonograph in 1878. As machines have become more sophisticated and versatile, teachers have reacted with the same suspicion as the craftsmen of the early nineteenth century. During the first half of the twentieth century, teachers used machines developed for the commercial market, making them extensions to their own classroom schemes. It was not until after the Second World War that mechanical classrooms were designed and used. When machines effectively combined both dimensions of sound and image, teachers began to see threats to their jobs and professional status.

The earliest machines commonly employed were those which reproduced sound. They were followed by machines which projected images and could often reproduce sound as well. The teaching machine proper was the last development.

10.1 SOUND RECORDING AND BROADCASTING

Recording machines were introduced into teaching near the turn of the century, their first use being the obvious one of teaching pronunciation. Structural teaching by this means did not begin in earnest until after the Second World War, although experiments go back to the 1900's. Radio was first utilized in teaching background material, schools' broadcasts dating from the early thirties.

10.1.1 Phonograph and Tape

Experimentation with recording and reproduction machines as teaching tools followed close on their first commercial exploitation.

From the first, exaggeratedly high hopes were held. Sweet castigated those who thought that the new phonograph would remove the need for sound training in phonetics,[1054:45] for the new machines had been seized on as the answer to the problem of giving the pupil consistent models to imitate. But apart from being unable to control imitation, the machine of the time presented a defective model. No phonograph was able to record sounds outside a very narrow band of the sound spectrum, and consequently most speech sounds were presented with their upper partials missing and their formants badly distorted. In addition, the model itself was often faulty: it was not yet considered necessary to use native speakers as recording artists.

This last was one defect corrected by the International Correspondence Schools of Scranton, Pennsylvania. In 1902 and 1903 they issued courses in English (for French speakers), German, and French (for English speakers). The conversation books were accompanied by Edison cylinders on which the entire text of the book was recorded by native speakers. Even at this early stage it was realized that a student would advance more quickly if he could repeat at will some of the especially difficult parts of the recording. So ICS supplied a specially adapted machine: it was a standard Edison phonograph fitted with an attachment that allowed the student to repeat passages without risking damage to the cylinder. Patent rights and later development of the disc ensured that the idea was not imitated.

Until the First World War few followed the example of ICS, but it slowly became clear that for effective demonstration of sounds and intonation, native speakers had to be used as recording artists.[224:117] Phonograph teaching became, of course, a common Direct-Method activity, but if one is to believe some of the bitter complaints of the time, enthusiasm was often coupled with lack of knowledge of how to use it.[810:16] The first group to exploit language teaching discs commercially was probably Linguaphone, which began operations in the early 1920's.

Technical improvements in recording equipment increased the efficiency of the phonograph as a teaching instrument: the background noise common on early discs lessened; more important still, the change to electric recording in 1926 increased the frequency response of the average disc to the range between 40 c.p.s. and 5,500 c.p.s. However, this was still far short of the range of human hearing, which has an upper limit of about 13,000 c.p.s. Unless these high frequencies are present, certain fricatives and plosives may be difficult to distinguish and easily confused. The next step was the development of high-fidelity recording in which most of the frequencies are present. This came on the market in the early 1950's. By the thirties the phonograph had become a common item of classroom equipment, not only in the foreign-language class, but also in the literature and music classes. There was, of course a cross-fertilization, all three, language, literature, and music, being part of the cultural heritage of any nation. Despite the warnings by many teachers the early magical aura of the phonograph to which Sweet had objected still clung to it.[205:333]

The need for the pupil to hear himself was recognized early, but no effective way of meeting the problem was found until the tape recorder was invented. ICS had attempted to meet the difficulty by supplying blank cylinders with their machine: the pupil recorded his own efforts and then sent the recorded cylinders to the school for evaluation. During the twenties, some attempt was made to keep track of students' progress in pronunciation by recording them on professional equipment. As recording equipment became more sophisticated and expensive the idea was dropped. In 1931 R. E. Monroe, of Ohio State University, suggested using the dictaphone, which was in common use in business offices.[766:212] Yet the aim envisaged still did not go beyond teaching pronunciation.

During the 1940's, teachers experimented with two new recording machines: the Mirrophone and the magnetic recorder: both recorded sound by inducing a magnetic field of varying intensity in a strip of sensitive material. The Mirrophone was developed in 1939 to train pilots in the techniques of transmitting into oxygen masks. When it fell into the hands of civilians later during the Second World War, it was taken up by teachers to drill children in pronunciation skills. In 1944, for instance, it was used at the University High School of the University of Illinois as an aid in teaching reading. The pupils read a short passage into the machine and then analyzed their performance with the help of the teacher. It was found that the best results were obtained if the pupil had a permanent record of his progress on discs that had been made at various times during the course.

However, the Mirrophone had a very short life: on the one hand, its recording time was no more than two minutes; on the other, long-playing tape recorders came hard on its heels. The replacement of the fragile paper tape by plastic tape, and the comparative simplicity of the tape recorder, prevented any further work on the Mirrophone. In addition, the development of recorders that provided two recording tracks instead of one made it a much more versatile instrument and paved the way for the language laboratory. The wire recorder was another casualty in the adoption of the tape recorder. This operated by inducing a magnetic field in a coil of iron wire, but it was awkward to use, and the quality of reproduction was far from good.

Few tried to teach grammar and vocabulary with the recording machine. One exception was Rosenthal in 1901, whose course could be accompanied by Edison cylinders if the pupil so wished. This lead was not followed by commercial courses until the 1950's. Firms like Linguaphone relied on books to teach most of the grammar and vocabulary, and on the record for pronunciation and fluency.

We get a glimpse of the possibilities of the tape recorder, as they were seen at the end of the 1950's, from notes issued to teacher trainees in a New Zealand Training College. There is the passive aspect of training the students' ear by exposure. On tape recorders with variable speeds features like diphthongization can be demonstrated by slowing the tape. It was used also for giving models for repetition drills, the teacher circulating in the classroom and checking by ear. Rare discs and broadcasts could be recorded for use at the teacher's convenience, and students could record plays and conversations. One of the most interesting uses was recording tapes for exchange with overseas schools. It will be seen that many of these ideas were later taken over by the language laboratory.[1142]

However, in all but the smallest and the largest schools, class size made individualization of teaching with the phonograph and tape recorder difficult. It was not easy to single out one person to perform or to give attention to a small number of pupils without leaving the others unattended and idle. Owing to the availability of discs and the expense of good tape recorders, the phonograph was not replaced, and the two usually coexisted in the classroom.

10.1.2 Language Laboratories

The language laboratory was developed to ensure that even if pupils were being taught together in one room, they could at the same time receive individual treatment and be kept working for the duration of the class. Two forms developed: the more usual was a battery of double-track recorders linked to one or more consoles. The pupil had the choice of working either independently or from a master program that was fed to all the machines from the console. In either case the pupil was expected to listen to his own attempts, judge them, and correct deficiencies. The simpler type had merely headsets and microphones connected to the console; the pupils listened to a taped program and instructors monitored their responses, switching from pupil to pupil. In both types, pupils were often isolated from their fellows by acoustically treated booths which damped the sound from the rest of the laboratory.

The germ of the language laboratory goes back to the 1920's. As part of a scheme to teach phonetics, several American universities built "phonetic laboratories." In 1924, Ohio State University built one that consisted of sixteen sets of headphones linked to a single output. The teacher circulated among the students as they repeated the program, checking them by ear. As an examination and a permanent check on their progress, each student made a disc at stated intervals in the course. Experiments of this sort continued over the next twenty years. It is almost impossible to trace the early history of the device with certainty because of the immense differences in terms applied to it.

The present term has been current since the end of the Second World War, but it was not universally applied. Hence some of the most interesting experiments in laboratory teaching remained unrecorded, because the experimenters did not know what was going on elsewhere. For instance, a primitive laboratory was installed in 1946 at Université Laval, Quebec. It used the Mirrophone and spaced discs. The model was on the disc, and the Mirrophone recorded the pupil's imitation. Both were then compared.[1063:27] Many other similar experiments must have been going on at the time, but we know only of those whose authors had the time and the energy to write articles about them.

In other areas as well developments not unlike the language laboratory were in use. For instance, signalmen in the New Zealand Army learned their Morse code in a training device which was not unlike a language laboratory without recorders. The instructor used a console equipped with a Morse key, a set of earphones, and an elaborate series of switches which allowed him to send to the whole room, to an individual student, or to a selected group. In addition he could link students so that they could send to each other or to the whole room. At the student positions there was a headset and a Morse key. All the monitoring and calling functions of the modern laboratory were possible. It was in a room like this at the military camp at Papakura that the author learned his Morse code in 1949.

The advent of magnetic recording and the American confiscation of German patents on magnetic tape in 1945 brought about a sudden development of the tape recorder on the American continent. In the late 1940's, the double-track recorder was first put on sale: with the addition of extra recording and erasing heads the laboratory machine was born. As plastic tape was now out of the experimental stage, it was possible to allow pupils to use the machine with less risk of breaking the tape. The invention of unbreakable tape in the mid-1960's removed the last vestiges of an annoyance that had seemed until then to be unavoidable. For a while makers of magnetic disc recorders competed for this lucrative market. The fidelity of recording was not so good as the tape, and the machine was not capable of double-track recording. Models had to be fed into the booth from a master recording, and the learner imitated them in the usual way.

The language laboratory idea had some odd extensions: from 1964 commercial firms in both Canada and the United States experimented with teaching languages over the telephone. With a special head and chest set, the telephone became the equivalent of a simple laboratory booth: the pupil's hands were free to write, and the teacher operated from a normal switchboard through which he fed the taped lesson and monitored the class in the usual way. But because the frequency response of an ordinary commercial line did not go past 3,500 c.p.s., phonetic teaching was not certain.

As part of their study of language acquisition, the Center for Research in Language and Language Behavior at the University of Michigan developed a device whose essential component was a computer programed to pass only a restricted range of phonological tolerances for each sound. By this time teachers had realized that a pupil's own judgment could not be trusted, as he was a prisoner of his own phonology, and hence he tended to misinterpret what he had heard. Thus, if the student's imitation was faulty the machine would stop and rewind to the last point where the answers were faultless.

Among the various typologies of laboratory exercise, the most inclusive was that of Mathieu, who distinguished four types of exercise: the audio-evaluatory, the audio-passive, the audio-active, and the audio-creative.[725:123] The author recommends that the first should be used sparingly: if the pupil's imitation is too inexact and remains so too long, it can lead to discouragement. The second is merely listening and analyzing the characteristics to be imitated or remembered. The third depends on exact mimicry. The fourth required variation of patterns within the limits set down for the lesson. For the fourth technique two types of drill were developed: the three-phase, in which the pupil gives his answer once only, and then listens to a correcting response from the tape; and the four-phase in which the pupil repeats the correcting response as a reinforcement. The two sequences then are summarized as follows: *master-pupil-master;* and *master-pupil-master-pupil.*

One of the difficulties with the language laboratory was its inflexibility. Installations were usually permanent, demanding special wiring for the room and expensive acoustic treatment. Some teachers also found that it was difficult to keep up the personal contact with the pupils that is one of the aspects of good teaching. To obviate this defect, some firms produced laboratories with all the booths, machines, and consoles on castors. In another effort to combine the flexibility of the classroom with the advantages of the laboratory, some schools adopted "electronic notebooks." These were portable tape recorders with built-in, low-powered radio transmitters, whose range was limited and frequency fixed. The teacher had a receiver whose frequency could be varied, and thus he was able to monitor everybody in the room without interference between pupil machines.

As with all new aids, once the language laboratory left the hands of careful experimenters, too much was asked of it and it seemed not to live up to its promise. Part of the difficulty rose from the selling tactics of the firms manufacturing the machines, who themselves were more interested in sales than in education. The teaching profession was not guiltless either, for those who had no conception of the problems involved in using the laboratory expected miracles from it. It soon became clear that to use a laboratory, one had to be either well trained or well supervised, for it was a complicated tool. Thus the laboratory, which was feared by many teachers as a possible replacement, sparked a new interest in teacher qualifications.

However, attacks on the laboratory came from informed quarters as well. The verbal satiation studies of Jacobovits and Lambert which were carried out in the 1950's and 1960's cast doubt on the value of repetition as a learning procedure. Phoneticians, bearing in mind the concept of the phoneme, were not sure of the utility of allowing the pupil to judge his own efforts.[1099:81] But instead of killing the idea, this brought about more attention to the types of repetition involved and greater care in the use of the laboratory as a teaching medium.

10.1.3 Radio

Radio came under discussion as a possible teaching aid for all subjects early in the 1930's. Before this time, its technical state was as primitive as that of the phonograph, and its expense precluded its purchase by educational authorities. In some countries, it drifted into teaching as an adjunct to correspondence courses. But the immense hold radio gained over the minds of the general public prompted consideration of its educational possibilities:

> . . . have not some few million people learned the grammar and vocabulary of Amos and Andy? If, for commercial purposes, a great network can be spread over the nation, is it not conceivable that the great universities of this country may be hooked up in an educational network by means of which high school classes everywhere may learn French, German, or Spanish given by a native speaking his own language?
>
> 1931 (Monroe) 766: 213

Monroe's dream was realized in many countries by the formation of educational networks in both radio and television, but it was still usual for educational programs to be handled on commercial stations.

The BBC provides an interesting example of what is possible for a big network in the matter of teaching languages. By the mid-1960's, the Overseas Service of the BBC was broadcasting English lessons in thirty languages to most of the world. This immense service began in 1943, when five-minute English lessons were produced as part of the barrage of propaganda that was being broadcast by short wave into occupied Europe. In 1945, the BBC began to expand its facilities, setting up its English by Radio Department, which broadcast English lessons covering all stages from elementary to advanced. The dialogue remained the basic form, but vernacular commentaries were added. For effective learning, support material and activities were found to be necessary. As the world returned to normal after the war, the BBC found retail outlets for books and broadcast scripts. In addition, they encouraged the formation of listening groups and provided a clearinghouse through which those who wanted it had the opportunity to make personal contact with English speakers. The success of these lessons was due partly to the fact that they adapted many features of the popular "soap opera." In the manner of a radio series, the dialogues revolved round incidents in the life of a limited number of stock characters, who soon attained an individuality of their own, thus making sure that the radio audience developed a loyalty to the series that went beyond their desire to learn English.

The Americans entered the field of language teaching by short-wave radio during the mid-1950's. The United States Information Service and the Voice of America worked together, the VOA broadcasting, and the Information Service helping with publicity and the distribution of written material. Judging from the material kindly furnished by the USIS, the courses were a good deal more formalized than the British ones. Teaching method rested on an extended application of pattern drills of various sorts. A quarterly, *English Teaching Forum,* began publication in the spring of 1963, replacing the earlier *English Teaching Newsletter,* whose first issue appeared in 1961. In its pages teachers were invited to exchange information; regular contributors included Lado, Fries, Marckwardt, and other well-known American linguists, who wrote on theoretical problems as well as those more directly related to the classroom. Book reviews were a regular feature, as were articles on American culture.

Educational radio faced several difficulties: first, creation of interest is difficult and often beyond the powers of teachers who are not used to working under such conditions; second, the difficulty of fitting the broadcasting timetable into school timetables was enormous; third, nobody really knew what was wanted from the medium. Content programs were not easy to broadcast, as they needed frequent programing and put a drain on producing facilities that few networks were willing to afford; enrichment programs were passed over by "no-nonsense" teachers as frills. Many schools deliberately upset their timetables to make use of the broadcasts; others infringed copyright regulations by copying them, using the school tape recorder.

Radio did not go under to the challenge of television. Part of the reason is undoubtedly the technical limitations of television: carrier waves could not be transmitted over the long distances open to radio, and interference was more pronounced. The lack of a visual component, while limiting its means of demonstration, gives radio a flexibility denied television; indeed the extra possibilities of television constituted an embarrassment for many who were quite capable of handling the difficulties of radio teaching.

10.2 SOUND AND IMAGE

Language teaching has also tried to utilize films and television, the extra dimension of sight giving them some advantages over radio and phonograph, especially in presenting cultural material. However, this extra dimension brought problems that proved difficult to solve.

10.2.1 Films

For various reasons, films met with little success in language teaching. This was more obvious with moving pictures, as they fit in less easily with the cadre of an ordinary lesson. But even the filmstrip and the slide met with more acceptance outside language teaching than within it.

For much of their efficiency, audio-visual methods depended on projected images: the filmstrip proved to be the most useful tool, as by this method the sequence of the pictures was automatically taken care of, but the speed and rhythm of presentation stayed in the hands of the teacher. Audio-visual methods prided themselves on their linkage of sound and object, as if this were a new principle. The formalism of the rigid audio-visualist was, likewise, no new phenomenon: "Until the acoustic ensemble is mastered, the picture should precede the sound signal by two or three seconds and disappear two or three seconds after. Such a rhythm is very important for understanding and memorizing the meaning as well as the pronunciation" (Guberina).[490:20] Though the association of filmstrips with tapes is a postwar development, filmstrips of cultural material have long been competing with charts and pictures in the school. Despite certain difficulties associated with their use in the classroom, ease of storing and convenient manipulation recommend their use. Slides also share these advantages and, in addition, are not fixed in a rigid order if needed in lessons on cultural material.

The motion picture was applied to language teaching in the 1930's. Normal practice was to take films made for the home market and show them to pupils in the hope that exposure would result in learning. Except with the advanced learner, this procedure often had the opposite effect, incomprehension leading to discouragement. The requirements for effective teaching films were quite rigid:

> Films, unless specially made for first year work, are likely to have a highly discouraging effect. The only films that can conceivably be of value at this stage are: a. silent background films; b. talkies, slowly pronounced, whose script has been seen, and perhaps memorised in advance.
>
> 1955 (Thimann) 1070: 46

More recent authorities would prefer not to slow the stream of speech, and require instead much repetition with very clear demonstration techniques, for by slowing down, one risks distorting the rhythm of speech.

The development of special films for language teaching was begun during the 1930's by the Walt Disney studios, which produced a series of cartoons to teach Basic English. These films were probably the first in which animated cartoons were used in teaching. In 1943 the *March of Time* series produced a film to teach Basic English using live actors. From that time films were made with the limitations of learners in mind, but the expense and technical knowledge required, added to the difficulties of utilization under normal classroom conditions, did not encourage widespread experimentation. Later teaching films include those of CREDIF, which produced short films aimed at teaching a single structure or a small part of the grammatical system within a limited vocabulary. The script involved a considerable amount of repetition, and the speed of delivery approximated that of educated native speakers.

While many researchers went ahead with live actors, others developed the cartoon. This form was chosen for various reasons. Gerald Fleming felt that a film photographed from reality would have too familiar an atmosphere to awaken preception and retention in the pupils. With the cartoon the creator could eliminate all extraneous detail and achieve an air of novelty that would be both amusing and instructive.[412] The question of artistic standard caused some controversy. Certain people, whose theories were exemplified by *Le français international,*[967] preferred a very neutral style of drawing, so that art would not detract from language. The opposite school of thought claimed that unattractive drawing would harm motivation and demanded cartoon lessons that were a joy to look at.[412]

At first the sound track of films was presented normally. Later teachers experimented with presenting short films without sound to advanced pupils to allow them to create their own commentary and then check it against what was actually said. All were agreed on the advantages of cutting the sound track on repeat presentations to allow the pupils to reconstruct the dialogue themselves, once the pupils knew what was coming. It is interesting to note that language-teaching films became shorter as time went on, some actually going as low as four minutes to allow for careful development of entertainment into learning.

10.2.2 Television Teaching

Television was invented in 1926 by the Scotsman, John Baird. By 1948 it was being commercially exploited in two countries, Britain and the United States, and by 1959 it had spread to forty-eight countries. As far as educational television is concerned, it seems that the United States was first in the field, experiments having been carried on over closed circuit at Creighton University, Omaha, Nebraska, in 1947. The first language teaching over a commercial station began in Atlanta in April, 1951.[*163:65] Since then, interest in educational television has spread all over the world. In most parts of the world where there was no prospect of training enough teachers, teaching by television received serious attention.

As a teaching medium, television has several advantages. It is one of the most accessible of all the mechanical visual aids: in affluent countries it has become cheap enough to permit ownership by a large number of households; in poorer countries many communities own sets which the local people can watch. It can bring to viewers an event as it happens, and owing to its technical resources, it has a vividness lacking in both radio and classroom teaching. Its main utility proved to be its ability to show its viewers things and places to which they would not normally have access. By reason of its command of both human and technical resources, it can give pupils access to outstanding teachers, striking visual aids, and films.[196:4-7]

The most valuable aspect of television, and one it shared with the film, was its power of linking linguistic behavior with the environment and cultural context which occasions it.[196:59] (It was always difficult to do this in a classroom, as no situation there was really a natural one.) It also widened the possible applications of the film. Under normal conditions, it did not prove easy to use selected passages from a film, but as Corder put it, "TV can use film for long or short sequences, or as a single item in a sequence of demonstration processes."[271:7]

Part of the early experimentation with TV concerned program length. It was found that most teachers used either five-minute, fifteen-minute, or thirty-minute sequences. Whether this was merely acceptance of normal programing policy is hard to say. In order to avoid fatigue, it was suggested that language programs should be limited to five minutes in length and repeated. By this stage one was well aware of the hypnotic effect of the repeated advertisement; could not linguistic items be learned as easily as advertising jingles?[271:68] But this suggestion was not taken up.

In adapting television to the classroom, the most urgent problem was assuring that the pupil took an active part in the lesson. Various expedients were tried to meet the lack. In programs where there was a teacher on the screen, the class teachers were asked to assign a number or foreign name to their pupils so that they could respond when questions were asked on the screen.[196:120] For the proper functioning of a television course, co-operation from the classroom teacher was necessary and his part in the lesson was carefully laid out. This was all the more essential as, especially in the primary classroom, the teacher was often unskilled, and had to learn along with his pupils.

However, this lack of feedback had its advantages too. As teaching skills were not necessary to the same degree as in a real classroom, some networks employed actors instead of teachers, with a considerable improvement in the standard of diction and on-camera skill. As a further development, language programs were put in a normal language setting. The French, for instance, used this format in 1962.[491:216] They also used a dubbing technique whereby the most difficult concepts were translated into the language of the viewers.

Television teaching took over many techniques from the entertainment world that had never been applied in the classroom itself. One American French course depended for a large part of its effect on puppetry, the length of the puppet sequences matching the average attention span of a child of eight or nine.[1019] Many programmers used very elaborate settings against which characters acted out sketches; others incorporated animated cartoons. Like the BBC language courses, there was a whole battery of books and discs as support material, with sets designed for the differing needs of teachers and students.

The problem of putting this comprehensive medium to the best use was not easy to solve. Teachers could not decide whether to create another classroom in the studio, or to attempt to teach from real situations; both alternatives offered disadvantages affecting the whole gamut of problems ranging from dovetailing into the uncertain training of the classroom teacher, to arousing and keeping the interest of the pupils. From the technical angle, arranging the normal classroom so that everybody could see the screen was difficult. Ways were found around this by placing the set at a determined height and by a careful seating plan in the classroom. To enlarge the image, some schools and universities experimented with "telebeam," a device which projects a TV image on a screen.

Despite its expressed aim of replacing the teacher in the classroom, like the other mechanical aims, TV actually made him more necessary. There is a definite skill in assisting the TV teacher to communicate with his class. And those who design the programs had to be expert teachers to be able to utilize all the possibilities of the medium.

10.3 TEACHING MACHINES

After the Second World War, there was much talk of "programed instruction." Though machines were in no way essential to its functioning, the teaching machine was identified with it.

The original machines were those of Pressey, appearing in 1924. These were essentially boxes with a small window cut in the side. Questions and multiple choice answers appeared there, and by a system of rachets, the pupil was prevented from passing on until he had found the correct answer. As the teacher shortage that plagued the world after the Second World War had not yet begun, the idea of general application of the device received little attention.

The grave shortage of teachers that developed after the Second World War caused a revival of interest in the idea, and under the twin influences of behavioral psychology and modern electronics, the machine was revived. These ranged from very complicated contrivances to devices as simple as Pressey's original model. They were capable of presenting both visual and auditory stimuli to the pupil. On his signaling the correct answer to the stage presented, the machine moved on to the next problem. Until the 1960's, programed instruction was not considered a self-sufficient method for several reasons: the progression was fixed, so that both fast and slow pupils were frustrated by being constrained to a mode of progression that suited neither.[640:11] It was true that each type of pupil could work at its own pace, but the slow pupil needed more stages and the fast, fewer. In addition, the teacher was necessary to give live practice for the neatly ordered knowledge required. The machine was an individual device for self-instruction and was meant to free the teacher for more demanding tasks in the classroom.

Attempts were made to meet this problem by the development of "Programmed Logic for Automatic Teaching Operation" (PLATO) under the auspices of the American armed forces at the University of Illinois in 1960.[118] The core of the system was a digital computer programed with all the information and possible procedures for learning certain subjects. Various degrees of fineness of programing were attempted, even to the rejection of faulty spelling and punctuation. The importance of the project can be realized from two developments it made possible. First, several pupils could work at the same time in a laboratory with all machines connected to the same computer; second, if the pupil needed help, he could switch to supplementary circuits by simply pressing a button, and could regulate his own progress by skipping unnecesary circuits at will. Language programing was one of the later developments: PLATO was first used to teach mathematical subjects.

As well as the headset and TV screen usual with the electronic machines of the time, each booth in the PLATO system contained a typewriter keyboard through which each pupil could "converse" with the computer. In the experimental laboratory, there were twenty such booths linked to the computer, which was programed so that in the event of a pupil requesting information another pupil was using, it was also made available to him. It is paradoxical that, by making programed instruction a mass aid, the computer individualized teaching.

As Lado points out, programed instruction does not automatically get rid of the teacher. It may remove him from the classroom for most of the time, but it requires him to tell the machine what to do. So programed instruction went only halfway to relieving the shortage it was meant to combat. The utility of machines lay in their ability to bring the new language to the pupil in a way often beyond the teacher's capabilities. In the centuries before this function had belonged to books and other visual aids. It is to these that we now turn our attention.

11

WRITTEN AND PRINTED MEDIA

We be moche bounden to them that brought in ye crafte of printinge. It concludeth many things in shorter space than ye written hande doeth and more ornately showeth. It hyndreth not so moche ye scryveners, but profeteth moche more poore scholers.

1519 (Whittinton) in 1158: 106

Though language teachers have always had access to books, the same cannot be said for their pupils. Over the history of teaching the importance of textbooks has varied, not so much according to current theory, but according to the cost, availability, and layout of the book. Apart from classical times, when the rich alone could afford books—and they were the only ones who received an education—textbooks became important to the pupil only after the sixteenth-century development of printing. They became essential during the eighteenth and nineteenth centuries, only to have their value questioned during the late nineteenth and early twentieth. Part of the importance of the book is also traceable to the growth of self-instruction in languages. This development dates from the sixteenth century, being made possible solely by the existence of books and their relative cheapness.

The use to which textbooks have been put has never depended entirely on teaching theory, but also on their availability to the pupil and on their format. In this one department, teaching is partially governed by the printing trade, and, indeed, many developments in book use have followed far-reaching changes in the art of book making. It is only recently that teachers, realizing the importance of books, have ceased to take them for granted and have tried to influence their format for educational ends.

The same can be said about auxiliaries to teaching, such as the various types of poster and chart. The blackboard is in a class of its own. Though its beginnings are shadowy, the uses to which it has been put have received almost as careful attention as those of the book.

11.1 THE USE OF TEXTBOOKS

In the ancient world, books were scarce, cumbersome, and difficult to produce. Booksellers had them copied by slaves, one reader dictating to a roomful of scribes; but the expense of books produced in this way meant that very few could afford them. Nevertheless, as it was only the sons of the well-to-do who could afford to go to school or have a private tutor, some textbooks did find their way into the classroom. Horace indicates this in his rueful comment on the probable fate of his Epistles: "This too will be your fate. Your doddering old age will be spent in teaching the elements of Latin to boys in the remote corners of the world" (Epp. I.xx.17-18). The teacher, of course, taught from a book; where boys were taught in private, both teacher and book belonged to the pupil. The rarity of books is indicated by the similarity in meaning of *lego* and *doceo,* and by the strong emphasis on oral goals in teaching. St. Augustine's invention of catechetical methods is another indication that books were not common in the Roman classroom.

Though our evidence for the classical world is scanty, there is no doubt that the only text in the medieval classroom was in the hands of the teacher, the pupils taking down both the text and commentary from dictation. Several extant book lists give the books a teacher might own, without implying that they were to be found in the hands of the pupils. Haskins produces evidence that in university circles books were bought and sold,[*84:72] but his information seems to exclude purchase and sale by students—though some of the model letters of the *ars dictaminis* do ask for money to buy books. As in classical times, dialogue and dictation methods persisted because of the scarcity of books, though in the monasteries there was no shortage of blank sheets to make up student's notebooks and to supply the scriptoria. In the universities there was a thriving trade in blank sheets for use in lectures, some of them new, some of them old sheets carefully scraped to remove the old writing.

Improved methods of production and a gradual increase in the number of paper mills in Europe gradually brought the price of books down until during the high Renaissance a teacher could count on a limited amount of book ownership: Cordier believed that few books were necessary in the classroom, "but they should be good."[273:vii] Clenardus took the opposite view, forbidding books in school until his pupils could speak Latin.[*58:102] The limits imposed on the book trade by the Stationers' Company of London give an indication of the demand for textbooks during the sixteenth century: editions were to be limited to 1,250 or 1,500 copies unless they were schoolbooks or religious books. Regular book lists for pupils date from the beginning of the next century.[551:I:et passim] It is interesting to note Hoole's regrets that the *Orbis pictus* by Comenius was too expensive for school use owing to the cost of printing the illustrations.[551:II:6]

One of the indexes to the ready availability of books was the recognition that pupils were capable of teaching themselves, given the right materials. Guarino was one of the first to realize this, but his recommendations were of little use, as books were still scarce. However, the situation changed rapidly: the layout and the preface of John Colet's books for St Paul's School (1613) point to pupil ownership; modern-language textbooks were definitely intended for individual use, modern languages not yet being a regular part of the school curriculum. One of the first unequivocal statements about self-teaching occurs in the preface to Cardinal Bellarmine's Hebrew grammar (1578): "I have tried to design this text with the following purpose in mind: so that the individual pupil, without the help of a teacher, can of himself acquire the rudiments of Hebrew, if not a perfect command of the language."[96:iii] Half a century later, Milton, in referring to Italian, took self-teaching for granted, again assuming a ready availability of books.[758:280]

During the seventeenth and eighteenth centuries, book ownership became common and almost obligatory. Yet one can sense a note of caution in Moquotus, who wrote in 1656: "There is scarcely anybody who does not possess a dictionary."[769:iii] as if one might expect gaps elsewhere. Copies of textbooks from this period held in the libraries of the Petit Séminaire de Québec and the Collège des Jésuites (Quebec), both of which trace their history back to the French regime in Canada, show by their annotations and other marks of misuse that they were pupils' copies. Another important piece of evidence is the constant appearance of new editions and abridgements of standard texts, especially of Despauterius, Port-Royal, and Clenardus; these were usually cheap and shoddy jobs. The long publishing life of standard texts also points to pupil ownership; the competition in the printing trade was cutthroat, popular books being pirated continually, and the cost of unofficial versions was as low as consistent with minimum legibility. Notwithstanding, these early texts had a publishing life of over a century—even if sales were small by our standards, they absorbed each printing. It seems from Comenius that few besides himself realized how necessary it was to have the same textbook in the hands of every pupil in the class: evidence from United States shows that even at the end of the eighteenth century, a teacher could face a class in which every pupil had a different textbook.[*213:30] By the early nineteenth century, this situation was, it seems, rectified, it being no longer doubtful that every pupil would have his own books. In the competition for sales, several texts of the time pointed to the price of their competitors as a justification of their existence.[737:i]

The easy availability of books was also one factor in the prevalence of translation methods, which require a text in front of the student for constant reference. While this was not necessarily in book form, lack of books would have seriously hampered the application of the method. Translation did not become a popular method of teaching until the book was readily available. And with the flood of books coming off the powered presses of the nineteenth and twentieth centuries, translation methods became more firmly entrenched.

Yet a dislike of translation methods did not necessarily mean rejection of books. Marcel preferred books to conversation, remarking, "Books as models of expression, are preferable to conversation. They exhibit more especially the right usage, the only guide for speaking and writing in conformity with the genius of the language."[718:16] The first real revolt, of course, came from the other Natural Methodists. According to them, reliance on the book during the first stages of language learning prevented the formation of sound linguistic reflexes and good pronunciation habits. Lambert Sauveur expressed the less extreme attitude to the book: "Give your pupils the book to read at home, as a preparation for your teaching, but forbid them to open it in the class; their ears alone must be occupied there."[994:26] However, this did not stop the naturalist movement from being identified with a ferocious and almost religious opposition to books in the classroom, the zealots of any movement being better targets for malicious opponents. The Direct Methodists who followed inherited this cautious attitude towards the use of books as teaching aids, adopting, in the main, the idea of Sauveur that the book could be introduced into teaching at a certain point in the cycle.[993:10] But later, certain members of the Direct Method movement and the structuralists after them developed a positive antipathy to books. As usual, there were protests, for instance, that of Michael West: "A textbook is necessary: the pupil keenly feels the need of one . . . even with a lesson every day, much of today's teaching has faded by tomorrow."[1146:64] During the 1950's, the textbook fell out of favor in the elementary levels, and was linked to the teaching of formal grammar and used as reading material after the basic skills had been formed.

11.2 TYPES OF TEXTBOOKS

Teachers in general were slow to realize the importance of book layout as a teaching aid, and truths that should have been self-evident after four hundred years of textbook printing were still being put to teachers as late as 1939: The British Board of Education, in a manual addressed to language teachers, laid down the following specifications: "The print should be good, the layout clear and emphatic . . . pictures accurate and well-produced . . . ; the price should be low and the weight not too great for the daily journey to and from school."[478:27] It is only during the twentieth century, however, that these qualities have ceased to be self-contradictory.

The ancients had two types of book: the *volumen,* a roll of parchment or papyrus, which could contain about 850 hexameter lines; and the *codex,* which resembled our modern books with the sewn spine. Difficulties of production made the second even rarer than the first. The dictation method of mass-producing such books was consecrated by Cassiodorus during the sixth century, and the tradition of such scriptoria lasted until after the invention of printing. Both types of book were produced until the Renaissance, but the *codex* gradually superseded the *volumen,* probably owing to the growing necessity of books in religious services, the *volumen* being unthinkably clumsy for this purpose.

It is far from odd that the earliest printers were also humanist scholars. Printing was an important factor in the spread of the "new learning," and as such was taken to be one of the many-sided activities of the scholar, who brought an artistic consciousness to his task that set guidelines which are still being followed. The first printed books (incunabula) looked just like manuscripts: the type face was modeled on the handwriting of the time, and in order to save paper, the niceties of spacing were not observed. These early books were too precious to be entrusted to schoolboys, but by the beginning of the sixteenth century, textbooks were being produced a little less expensively, and were within the reach, it seems, of a large part of the school population.

The gradual change from the rather illegible blackface of the incunabula to the roman and italic faces was a matter of internal policy of the printing trade. But what had been developed as an artistic procedure soon became tacitly accepted as a teaching tool. Text came to be printed in roman type, and notes in italic, a procedure dating from the earliest years of the sixteenth century.

Equally ancient is the use of type faces to distinguish languages: the foreign language was usually in roman and its translation in italic (see §4.2). This was, of course, subject to variation: owing probably to the influence of German, *Fraktur* is sometimes found for English; the size of these other types was usually different from the ordinary type used (see Figures 6, 7, 9, 10, 22).

The most important function of type size was showing the layout of the course: unimportant points were often set in small face, rules in a large face, and commentaries in an intermediate face. This seems to have been more a matter of instinct and common sense than of rule.

Teachers were slow to realize that the uncrowded pages produced by masters of the craft were more effective as teaching instruments than the solid blocks of type to which they had been conditioned by manuscripts, incunabula, and pirated editions. The factor of cost prevented wide acceptance of good layout in textbooks for some time, this being aggravated by the prevalence of pirating: quality was often sacrificed to speed and cheapness of production. Perhaps the first protest against this state of affairs as far as teaching was concerned was that of Rollin, who demanded that the student should have in his hands "a well-designed volume which pleases the eye, holds attention, and by these innocent means invites study."[965: I:137] Some progress towards this goal had already been made: mnemonic aids like columnar listing of paradigms on uncrowded pages appeared for the first time in the grammars of Lonicer and Macropedius.[*108:15] Though this innovation was widely imitated, it was several centuries before the profession and the printing trade managed to agree that an artistically composed page was one of the best teaching aids possible.

Color appears fairly late on page layouts. Although red ink was used on title pages, difficulties of register obviated its use in text. Eighteenth-century printers experimented with its use, prompted by resourceful teachers. An edition of the Port-Royal grammar, published in Paris by Florentin Delaulne (1714), printed flexions in red, while one edition at least of Shickard's Hebrew grammar[1001] printed the root in red. but these experiments were never widely imitated. Not the least of the troubles seems to have been difficulty with the ink–red was never so successful as black, and the secret of mixing fast colors was not found until relatively late in the nineteenth century.

It was not until Port-Royal that the use of printing layout as a teaching aid became at all common. The preface to the Latin grammar analyzes the author's use of capitals and type size to indicate grammatical relationships and the relative importance of parts of the text:

> I have printed the flexions, e.g., VEO, BO, LO, in capitals, Latin words in other type faces different from that used for French, and the notes in smaller letters to distinguish various parts of the text and avoid all possibility of confusion.
>
> 1656 (Arnauld and Lancelot) 45: 28

Other authors did much the same thing: John Clarke's edition of Corderius has an interesting use of italics: the Latin is arranged in the English order and alternate sense groups are set in italic. The English is set in the same way, type face corresponding to type face (Figure 22). But in the years that followed these developments were abandoned. With the gradual extinction of artistic sensitivity that was the hallmark of nineteenth-century tradesmen and schools, the textbook became a monster, symbolizing the aridity of its contents.

Gouin was one for whom layout was of grave importance. The ruling idea was to hinge the exercise on the verb, which he considered the most important element in the sentence. As each clause or sentence was to remain within easy memory span, repetition units were kept to one line. He claimed that "in this manner the book itself aids us in distinguishing and analyzing the thoughts, brings out the unity of the sentences, isolates them in order to better manifest them."[468:71] Modern courses were seldom as original in this matter, but they did, at least, preserve the best practice of the preceding four hundred years.

The first illustrated books in language teaching were medieval psalters, vocabularies, and editions of classical authors, which, however, show little systematic purpose in illustration. The pictures

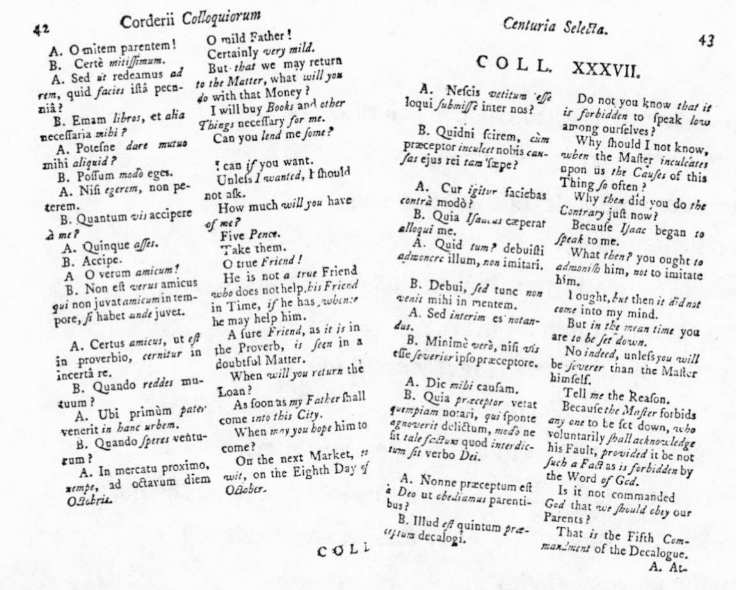

42 Corderii Colloquiorum

A. O mitem parentem!
B. Certè mitiſſimum.
A. Sed ut redeamus ad rem, quid facies iſtâ pecuniâ?
B. Emam libros, et alia neceſſaria mihi?
A. Poteſne dare mutuo mihi aliquid?
B. Poſſum modò eges.
A. Niſi egerem, non peterem.
B. Quantum vis accipere à me?
A. Quinque aſſes.
B. Accipe.
A. O verum amicum!
B. Non eſt verus amicus qui non juvat amicum in tempore, ſi habet unde juvet.
A. Certus amicus, ut eſt in proverbio, cernitur in incertâ re.
B. Quando reddes mutuum?
A. Ubi primùm pater venerit in hanc urbem.
B. Quando ſperes venturum?
A. In mercatu proximo, nempe, ad octavum diem Octobris.

O mild Father!
Certainly very mild.
But that we may return to the Matter, what will you do with that Money?
I will buy Books and other Things neceſſary for me.
Can you lend me ſome?
I can if you want.
Unleſs I wanted, I ſhould not aſk.
How much will you have of me?
Five Pence.
Take them.
O true Friend!
He is not a true Friend who does not help his Friend in Time, if he has whence he may help him.
A ſure Friend, as it is in the Proverb, is ſeen in a doubtful Matter.
When will you return the Loan?
As ſoon as my Father ſhall come into this City.
When may you hope him to come?
On the next Market, to wit, on the Eighth Day of October.

COLL.

Centuria Selecta. 43

COLL. XXXVII.

A. Neſcis vetitum eſſe loqui ſubmiſſe inter nos?
B. Quidni ſcirem, cùm præceptor inculcet nobis cauſas ejus rei tam ſæpe?
A. Cur igitur faciebas contrà modò?
B. Quia Iſaacus cæperat alloqui me.
A. Quid tum? debuiſti admonere illum, non imitari.
B. Debui, ſed tunc non venit mihi in mentem.
A. Sed interim es notandus.
B. Minimè verò, niſi vis eſſe ſeverior ipſo præceptore.
A. Dic mihi cauſam.
B. Quia præceptor vetat quempiam notari, qui ſponte agnoverit delictum, modò ne ſit tale factum quod interdictum ſit verbo Dei.
A. Nonne præceptum eſt à Deo ut obediamus parentibus?
B. Illud eſt quintum præceptum decalogi.

Do not you know that it is forbidden to ſpeak low among ourſelves?
Why ſhould I not know, when the Maſter inculcates upon us the Cauſes of this Thing ſo often?
Why then did you do the Contrary juſt now?
Becauſe Iſaac began to ſpeak to me.
What then? you ought to admoniſh him, not to imitate him.
I ought, but then it did not come into my mind.
But in the mean time you are to be ſet down.
No indeed, unleſs you will be ſeverer than the Maſter himſelf.
Tell me the Reaſon.
Becauſe the Maſter forbids any one to be ſet down, who voluntarily ſhall acknowledge his Fault, provided it be not ſuch a Fact as is forbidden by the Word of God.
Is it not commanded God that we ſhould obey our Parents?
That is the Fifth Commandment of the Decalogue.
A. At-

Figure 22. Pages from *Corderii colloquiorum centuria selecta* (ed John Clarke 1786).[228:42-43] Copy from le Petit Séminaire de Québec

were drawn by hand either in the margin or directly in the text at an appropriate place. Except in specific cases like vocabularies and encyclopedias, i.e., bestiaries and lapidaries, the drawings were meant only as a hint to the content of the text (see Figure 23). The illustrations were usually labeled to relate them to their text. The Aldine editions of classical authors, which appeared in Venice during the sixteenth century, used full-page illustrations with a commentary (cf. Figure 24). These were wood blocks, whose style was exactly the same as those used by Comenius, almost a century later (cf. Figure 2). Unlike their medieval prototypes, these illustrations are relegated to an introductory section, linked to their text by a page reference, and accompanied by an explanatory commentary. Manutius seems to have introduced the technique of numbering critical parts of the illustration to link it to its commentary. His edition of Caesar also seems to have introduced maps. Those in Figure 25 were on a foldout, making for easy reference. Apart from names of rivers, mountains, and a few administrative divisions, the names on the maps designate Gallic and Spanish tribes.

Non maior. Thais. quam ego sum maiuscula est.
Misit porro orare ut uenirem serio.
Aut dicat quid uult. aut molesta ne siet.
Non hercle ueniam tercio. heus heus. et quid hic est?
Ego sum Chremes. PYT O capitulum lepidissimum.
CHR Dico ego michi insidias fieri. PYT Thais maximo
Te orabat opere. ut cras redires. CHR Rus eo.
PYT Fac amabo. CHR Non possum inquam. PYT At tu apud nos hic mane.
Et quis cum ea una. quid habuisset cum periit.
Dum redeat ipsa. CHR Nichil minus. PYT Cur mi Chremes?
CHR Malam rem hinc ibis. PYT Si istuc ita certum est tibi.
Amabo ut illuc transeas ubi illa est. CHR Eo.
PYT Abi Dorias. cito hunc deduc ad militem.

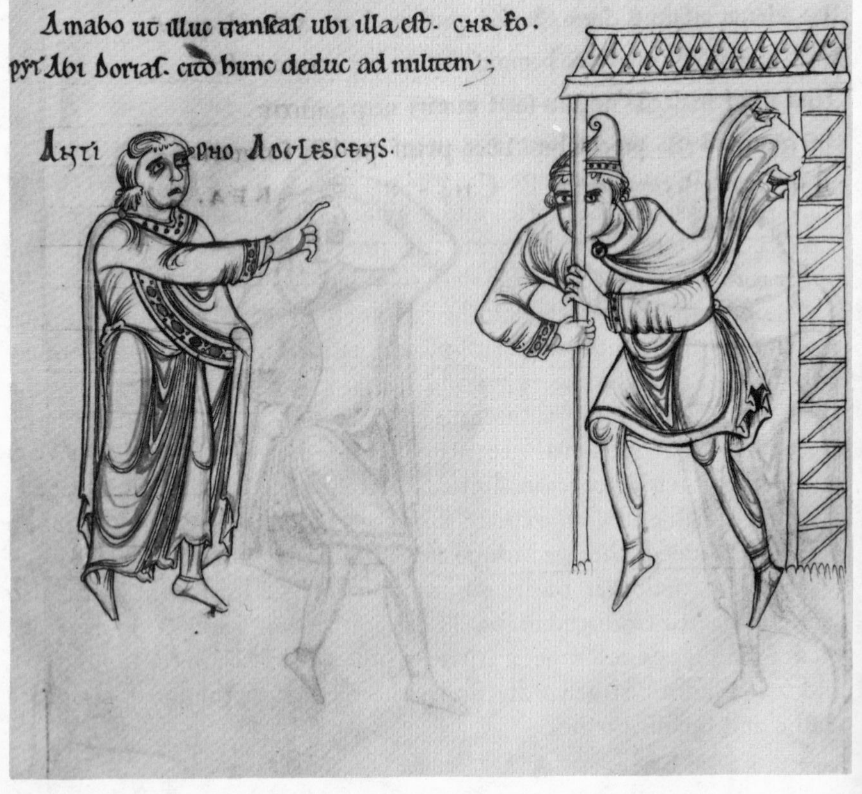

Figure 23. Illustration from Terence (Bodl. MS. Auct. F.2.13) *Eunuchus* III.3.31 (from T. S. R. Boase, *English Art 1100-1216*, Clarendon, Oxford, 1953).

The first consistently and purposefully illustrated text seems to be the *Orbis pictus* of Comenius, which was really an illustrated vocabulary, each object illustrated being numbered to link it unmistakably with the corresponding word in the text. The nineteenth-century reissues of Comenius adopted contradictory policies about the illustrations. That of Bardeen used the original copper engravings; while the modernized edition published in Prague a few years earlier substituted water colors whose content was changed to suit the taste and realities of the nineteenth century (see Figure 4).

In the seventeenth and eighteenth centuries, the ruling emphasis on indirect methods effectively blocked this line of development, until some interesting attempts were made by the Natural Methodists. In Sauveur's *Causeries,* for example, the illustration has only a general connection with the text. But in a grammar of Blackfoot published about the middle of the nineteenth century, a return is made to the Comenian style by placing the picture actually in the sentence structure in English and giving the Blackfoot word.[407] The illustration from Sadler's English grammar (see Figure 3) is actually a water color and is the first of many such schemes for representing prepositional relationships in languages as diverse as German and Greek. But the illustration was either a tour de force or an incidental: it was not really until the first years of this century that it came into wide use as a teaching aid and not only an ornament. Breul recommended the use of maps and national emblems in language textbooks, advice followed quite widely before the First World War.[153:45] By 1923 illustrations were so taken for granted that it could be remarked that "the unillustrated method is doomed; and in a few years we shall be as critical of the pictures as we are of the grammar or of the phonetic transcription."[492:261]

The early illustrations were detailed etchings in the manner of ordinary book illustrations of the time: fussiness of detail was a common feature. Line drawings and photographs were not common in the textbook until after the First World War, and even then the tradition of excessive detail lingered. It was not until the thirties that the simple line drawing became standard. This can be traced partly to

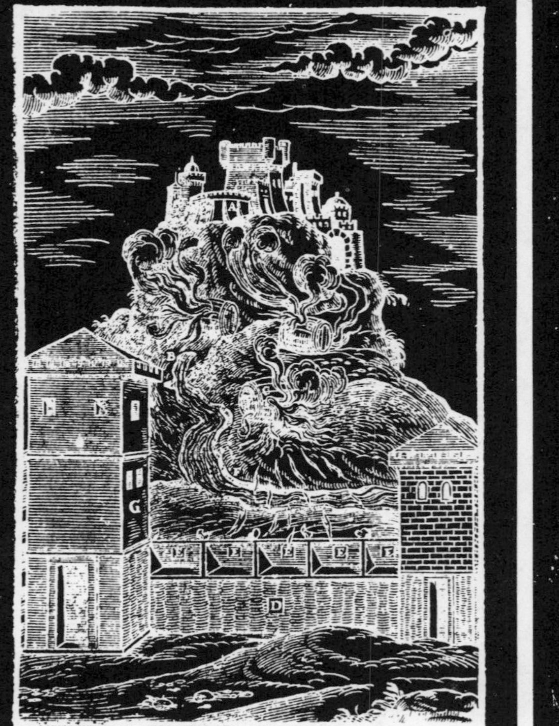

LIB . IIX . DE . BELLO . GALL.
pag. 257. & 261.

A VXELLODVNVM, opidum egregie natura loci munitũ, in finibus Cadurcorum, inter Celtas, non longe a prouincia Romanorum.
B Fons, quem Caesar, cuniculis actis, & uenis eius intercisis, auertit.
C Cupae, seuo, pice, scandulisque, completae, & ardentes, ad comburenda Caesariana operà ab opidanis demissae.
D Vallum.
E Plutei.
F Flumen, quod infimam uallẽ diuidebat, & paene totũ montem cingebat, atq; ita imis eius radicibus ferebatur, ut nullam in partem depressis fossis deriuari posset.
G Turris decem tabulatorũ, quae fontis fastigium superabat, ex qua cum tela tormentis iacerentur, ab aquatione opidanos prohibebat. IVCVND.
Cadenac, communi lingua.

LIB . II . DE . BELLO . CIV.
pag. 229.

MASSILIAE descriptio, quae ex tribus fere opidi partibus mari alluitur.
A Massiliae moenia, & turres.
B Turris ex opere latericio tabulatorum sex, ab legionarijs exstructa contra Massiliensium eruptiones.
C Storiae, ex funibus anchorarijs contextae, praepẽdentes contra hostium tela, atque tormenta, quibus tecti milites turrim construebant.
D Summa contabulatio, laterculis, & luto, & centonibus tecta, ne quid ignis hostium nocere posset.
E Musculus, ab ipsò Caesare descriptus, a turri lateritia, ad suffodiendum, & disiiciendum, hostium turrem, & murum.
F Mare, alluens fere ex tribus partibus urbem.
G Vallum.
H Plutei.
I Cerui.
K Pinnae. IVCVN
Marsiglia, communi lingua. b

Figure 24. Illustration of Puy d'Issolu (Lot et Garonne)? Manutius Edition of Caesar.[714] Copy in the Houghton Library, Harvard

a linguistic emphasis on unambiguity in association made possible by a clear picture, partly to the use of such drawings in the children's books of the time. The impetus given direct methods and comic strips during the Second World War produced courses based on a series of pictures with texts attached, often accompanied by recordings.

In the history of the language textbook, we can see a reflection of the history of language teaching, its changes of emphasis and method. The number of texts required and their content is especially revealing. During the classical, medieval, and Renaissance periods, one usually had recourse to a multiplicity of books; until the twentieth century one book usually sufficed. But the modern range of textbooks shows the confusion of the methods in use, ranging from formal grammar to informal dialogue. The most striking characteristic of the modern text is its short publishing life. The great Renaissance grammars were still being published in 1780; but as the old was successfully challenged, and the new not given time to take root, the life of a modern text is not much more than twenty years.

11.3 AUXILIARIES TO BOOK AND TEACHER

The book is intended for use of the individual in the classroom, but for efficient class handling teachers often need to focus the attention of everybody on one point in the room. This can be attained by the use of blackboards, wall charts, or flash cards.

The blackboard is such a ubiquitous feature of the classroom that very few people have seen fit to do more than just mention it. We can not even argue from silence that it did not exist at a given time. It seems that something of the sort existed during the third century of the Christian era, but details are quite vague.[*132:369] Children in medieval monasteries learned their letters by watching them traced on large wall charts.[*13:36] There are likewise hints that something of the sort existed during the Renaissance, but details are again quite vague. For the rest, we have to rely on articles and quotations that take the blackboard for granted. All we can comfortably say is that

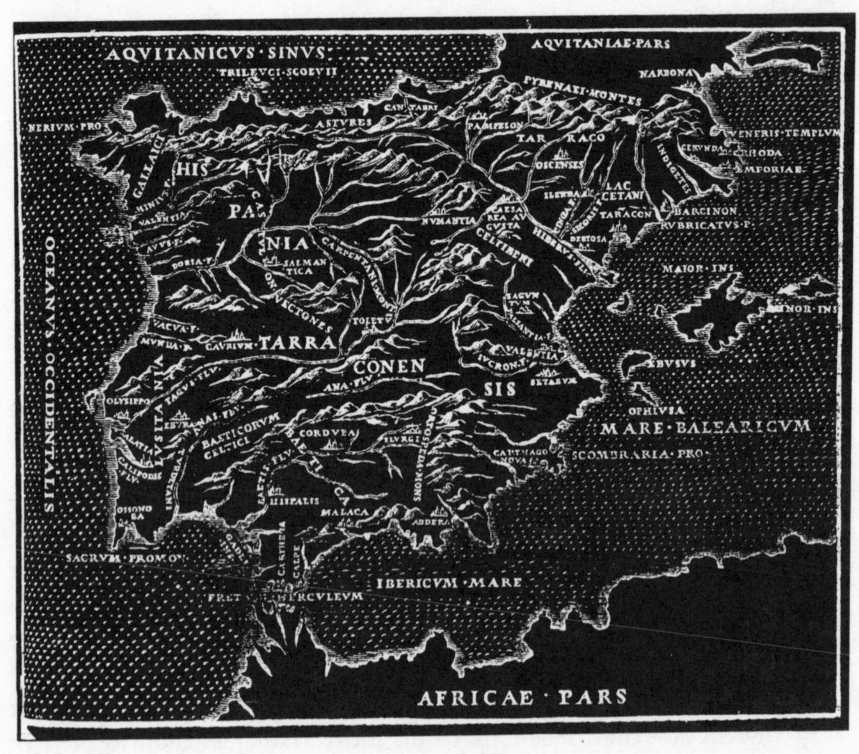

Figure 25. Maps of France and Spain from Manutius Edition of Caesar.[714] Copy from Houghton Library, Harvard

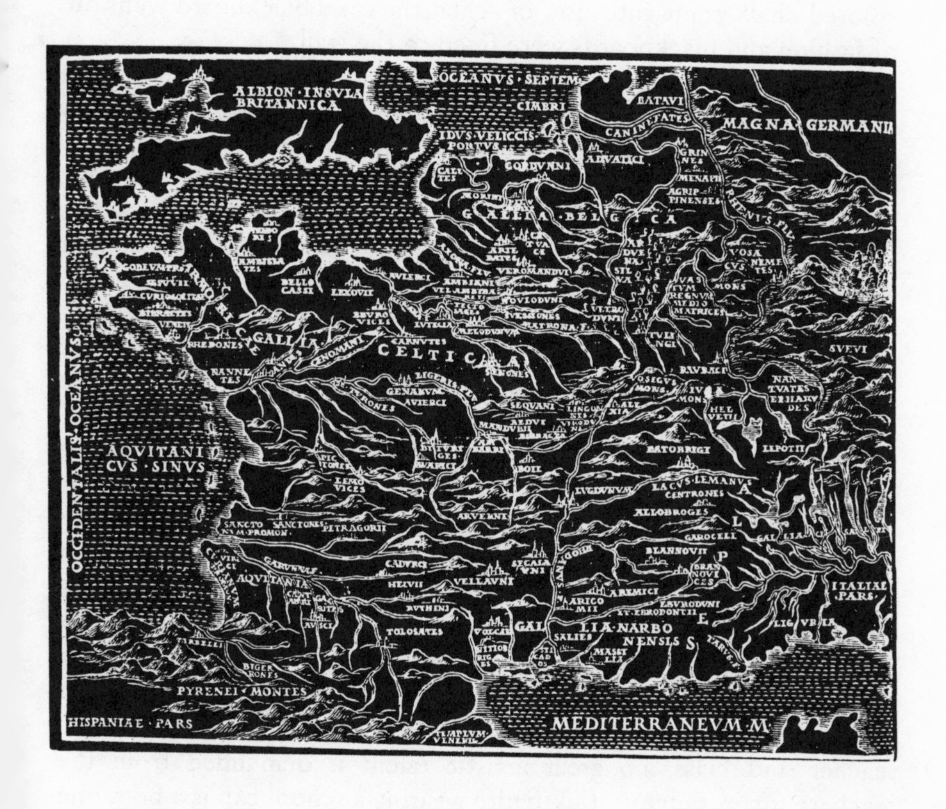
ALBION · INSVLA
BRITANNICA
OCEANVS · SEPTEM
CIMBRI
BATAVI
CANINEFATES
MAGNA GERMANIA
GALLIA · BELGICA
RHENVS · FLV
CELTICA
GALLIA
SVEVI
AQVITANICVS · SINVS
OCCIDENTALIS · OCEANVS
LACVS · LEMANVS
ALLOBROGES
AQVITANIA
GALLIA · NARBONENSIS
ITALIAE PARS
PYRENEI · MONTES
HISPANIAE · PARS
MEDITERRANEVM · M

by the end of the seventeenth century blackboards were in common use. Basedow speaks of cartooning on the board to teach Phaedrus: de Bigault-d'Harcourt, professor at the *Collège militaire royal de France* in 1819, recommends that pupils should take down teaching material from the blackboard.[289:187] It is not even known when colored chalk came into use, or when the easel blackboard went out of fashion and blackboards were fixed to the wall.

Blackboards, though very flexible in their possibilities, proved dirty in actual use. This, coupled with the poor handwriting and drawing of many teachers, was one factor introducing in the flannelboard from the primary classroom. This is a piece of flannel or another type of rough material hung or mounted on a frame. Cutouts with a flannel or sandpaper backing will then stick to it. It had the advantage of speed and legibility, even if some flexibility is lost. There were also attempts to replace this with a polythene sheet to which smooth-backed figures will stick by air pressure. The dust in the ordinary classroom atmosphere made this very difficult to use effectively.

Before the twentieth century, there was very little discussion of the blackboard as a pictorial medium. Certain of the early writers on the Direct Method suggested that teachers should be able to draw, but the most exhaustive treatment of blackboard technique is that of Riégel which appeared in 1961. He codifies existing practice, drawing indifferently from primary school and secondary school techniques. The greatest advantage of a blackboard sketch is that it can be easily changed; indeed, it is the most adaptable of any visual aid yet invented. As long as a code of representation is agreed on between teacher and class, no great artistic talent is demanded from the teacher: for instance a stick figure wearing a school cap is a boy, one with plaits and a skirt, a girl. To be effective, a sketch should be large, quickly drawn, easily recognizable, and, if possible, amusing.[955:260] Figures for the flannel board could be more detailed because they did not have to be created in front of the class. This also allowed for careful planning of possible layout and sequences of use.

Wall charts were found during the Renaissance[519:30] and the Middle

Ages. Colored wall charts were first mentioned by the Oratorians, a French teaching order of priests, in the early seventeenth century,[*57:177] but their example was not followed by the profession at large. They were reintroduced by the Natural and Direct Methodists, becoming more important as time went on. The advent of four-color printing brought the price down, while increasing their sophistication and effectiveness. Some teachers, again copying the techniques of the primary classroom combined them with cardboard cutouts in order to make them less static as visual aids.

By the middle of the First World War, flash cards were in use to teach various aspects of language.[459] They were as versatile in their early as in their later uses. As well as giving practice in matching word and picture, even at this early stage they were used to drill phonetics, vocabulary, and grammar. For some time, it was left to individual teachers to produce them, but after the Second World War, publishers entered the field, marketing sets of flash cards independently of established courses. They were also part of the resources of the complicated courses that proliferated in the twenty years after the war. Their advantage was flexibility. Whereas with blackboards and wall charts it is difficult to remove the support to memory and still keep it conveniently in reserve, flash cards can be shown to pupils, and, if necessary, shown again if the pupil shows that he needs the support. They do not have to be remade, like a blackboard picture that has been rubbed off. Flash cards lend themselves to extempore games and to adaptations of children's card games as well. Their versatility is limited only by the teacher's resourcefulness. In the next chapter we shall examine the qualities required of him.

12

HUMAN MEDIA

> A student can become proficient only by degrees. Therefore a student needs someone to guide him, admonish him, and correct him.
>
> 1648 (Comenius) in 256: 101

An idea finds expression only through men, an art through practitioners. Hence in language teaching, the human factor is essential, for teachers have shaped the application of ideas, conceived new ones, and rejected old. For our purposes, those who have taught languages fall into two groups: the professional teacher and those he calls on to assist him in the classroom.

Though it has long been the dream of language learners to do without a teacher and to substitute self-teaching aids for him, books and machines often had the opposite effect. In freeing a teacher from much of the routine work in teaching, they enabled him to concentrate on the more delicate aspects of the subject. Thus, teachers had to be better qualified in order to stand the competition from aids and put them to best use. What happened with books during the early Renaissance was repeated with machines during the twentieth century. Thus, paradoxically, while the teacher was being replaced in drill aspects of his subject, he was made to call on much more sophisticated skills to deal with those students who were prepared to go beyond what the aids could give them.

Though the first grammarians were such because they wished to teach languages, language teachers before the eighteenth century were primarily scholars in language and literature. The decline of the discipline of the classics and the increase in the numbers of children being educated brought more emphasis on the narrowly professional qualities of a teacher, and the scholarly qualities considered necessary for a teacher declined in importance until it was generally considered that anybody could teach anything. The situation described in the first chapters of Evelyn Waugh's *Decline and Fall* at the school of Llanaba, though exaggerated for the purposes of satire, is not so far from the truth as it existed in the schools of the time. After the 1940's, the necessity of specialization slowly gained acceptance, but its full application was subject to teacher supply and demand.

12.1 THE PROFESSIONAL TEACHER

Few societies have taken the teacher seriously enough to ask more from him than the ability to talk, walk, and punish. But they have accorded education itself sufficient importance to regulate it either through religious or secular agencies. The qualities necessary to a teacher can be grouped under three heads: personal gifts of probity, kindness, and firmness; skill in teaching; and a good knowledge of his subject. Unfortunately for the reputation of the profession, there has never been an age when all three have consistently appeared together.

12.1.1 Personal Qualities

In Rome the first language teachers were Greek slaves and freedmen, a group with a questionable reputation: "Your empty-bellied little Greek will try his hand at anything: elementary or senior teaching, geometry, painting, massage, augury, rope-dancing, medicine, magic," as Juvenal remarked in his third satire.[612:III:76-78] Part of the bad reputation of the profession was undoubtedly due to its fondness for punishment, a constant in all Roman references to teaching.

Quintillian, taking his cue from the founders of Greek rhetoric, saw the teacher as the epitome of the orator: "An upright man, skilled in speaking." In both the teacher and private tutor he demanded a balanced personality, teaching skill, and a cultivation of spirit quite out of the ordinary. Quintillian was probably guided by the group to which he himself belonged, the select few who were chosen as tutors to the imperial house. From contemporary literature, we might suspect that it was rare to find in the ordinary schools teachers who came up to his requirements. As teaching became a function of the imperial civil service, Quintillian's ideas had, in theory at least, wide currency. The Christian principle of charity and brotherly love also found echoes in the works of Quintillian, and with the growing interest in education in the Christian Church, his ideas received the homage of plagiarism, especially from St. Jerome and St. Augustine. But the passing of the classical standards of rhetoric heralded a long decline in language teaching. Despite the great teachers of the medieval schools and monasteries, there is a murky current of cruelty and ignorance which filters through in dialogues and satirical verse. This brought down the wrath of the fifteenth-century Humanists, and coupled with the notorious corruption of many monasteries, resulted in renewed emphasis on the moral qualities necessary in a teacher.

Ethical requirements led to religious, medieval moralists tending to identify moral probity with religious orthodoxy. Hence the medieval church councils passed regulation after regulation requiring a letter from a bishop before a person could teach, so that as the Council of Rouen (1074) put it, one would "avoid the manifold and detestable errors taught by the unlearned."[162:66] The Renaissance followed suit, and a denominational dimension was added to the purely ethical one: bishops who indulged in the favorite Renaissance form of philanthropy, founding schools, produced some delightful sets of requirements, like the following from the statutes of Chigwell School:

> Item. I constitute and appoint that the Latin schoolmaster be a graduate of one of the Universities not under seven and twenty years of Age, a man skilful in the Greek and Latin tongues, neither a Papist nor a Puritan, of a grave Behaviour, of a sober and honest Conversation, no Tipler or Haunter

of Alehouses, no Puffer of Tobacco; and above all that he be apt to teach and severe in his Government.

1550? (Bishop Harsnet) 1159: xv

Erasmus was quite clear that a teacher's probity should be verified before he was employed in either school or private home.[375:714] But at the same time authorities were beginning to realize that teachers should be human beings, conscious of the weaknesses and strengths of their pupils and sympathetic to them.[551:10] Comenius added the qualities of stamina and energy to the already formidable list of requirements.[256:103]

To a large extent the purely ethical requirements remained. With the development of religiously pluralistic societies in Europe, religious requirements quietly slipped out of consideration, while the human qualities of a teacher lost ground during the eighteenth and nineteenth centuries, except among exceptional teachers like Dr. Arnold of Rugby, to come back into focus in this century.

12.1.2 Teaching Skills

It must be emphasized that until the late nineteenth century, teaching was hardly a professional business: teacher training was almost unheard of and educated people who found their way into teaching felt their own way in the classroom.

Until the end of the Renaissance, it was considered that any educated man was capable of teaching. Teaching ability was an honored part of scholarship, passing on knowledge to others being considered an essential duty of scholars. The last of the great Renaissance teachers in this tradition was Comenius, but he had had some sort of teacher training in the Moravian training college of Alsted. He sums up his specifications for a teacher in three sentences from the *Didactica analytica:*

XVII. A teacher should be competent to teach.
(a skillful teacher)

XVIII. A teacher should be skillful in teaching.
(a capable teacher)

XIX. A teacher should be zealous in teaching.
(one to whom indolence and distaste are unknown)

1648 (Comenius) 256: 103

Absorbing interest in both subject and pupil are the two most important teaching qualities Comenius demands. Scholastic competence does not loom large in his thought, as it was still unusual to find an incompetent scholar in the classroom. Yet, in spite of the fulminations of his predecessors about inhuman teachers, the profession as a whole was still not concerned about their pupils as people.

The invention of the Grammar-Translation Method deeply affected professional standards. Those with no teaching skill found their way eased by the control the method exercised over pupil activity: it required little ingenuity to devise assignments, as they were laid down syllable by syllable in the book. Thus, despite the impressive quality of many teachers, the profession became a refuge for the incompetent, a situation which lasted well into the twentieth century. The Direct and Natural Methods tested to the full the teaching skills of their practitioners, and proved to be beyond the capacities of the unskilled. This development coincided with a new awareness among educational administrators and the public that teaching was a professional activity demanding a professional training.

One of the earliest attempts to look to teacher training, apart from issuing a license that entailed no professional training whatsoever, was the French *agrégation,* established in 1810, an example followed in several European countries. This was more a test of scholarship than of teaching skill, but it did ensure that teachers knew what they were teaching. Professional training in the narrower sense, except for isolated experiments like J. H. Alsted's training college in Moravia, which had been attended by Comenius, hardly dates before the mid-nineteenth century.

In a very large number of countries, teacher training devolved upon the universities, in some others training colleges handled it, in others still teachers were trained on the job. Indeed, it is the rare country that does not show all three of these patterns at some time in the history of its educational system. State training colleges date back to the late nineteenth century in Europe and to the beginning of this century in America. Retraining of language teachers was first undertaken in the United States by Lambert Sauveur in the 1870's. He instituted a series of summer schools at which teachers were taught to handle the Natural Method. In official teacher-training establishments little specialization was evident, so that a teacher with general training was put into the language classroom and expected to survive.[921:38] Special treatment of language-teaching trainees did not become common until the 1940's.

Serious deficiencies in the competence of those detailed to teach languages caused a complete rethinking of training. Many countries, e.g., Great Britain (1944), demanded that their teachers should take series of in-service courses or spend some time abroad. As a stopgap measure, general teachers who were saddled with language classes were supported by radio and television programs and itinerant specialists. But few countries were willing to thin out the talent available in the classroom by training specialists, or by assigning the specialists they had to the one subject they were trained to teach.

Twentieth-century theorists and policy makers focussed attention on the necessity for training specialist teachers, but in this, as in other aspects of education, little unanimity was evident. The training through which most teachers who held certificates passed consisted of a university degree concentrating on the literature and history of the language, followed by a short course in education. While this was not condemned outright, it was felt that a teacher's training should be biased more towards the language side of the discipline and that he should have some grasp of linguistics. The Direct Method singled out phonetics as the key area, while Palmer left the question open, requiring a good knowledge of all branches of linguistics.[836:27] This idea remained a counsel of perfection until events forced the control of new developments in language teaching into the hands of linguists. The development of crash language courses during the Second World War and the "invention" of Basic English brought to the attention of both public and educational authorities the relevance of linguistics and the importance it should have in developing teaching awareness.

The effects of this were not altogether desirable. The structural school of linguistics succeeded in convincing a large part of the profession that every productive idea flowed from linguistics. Outside the ranks of linguists, this misconception produced another: that linguistics is concerned solely with language teaching. These legends are slowly being eroded during the late 1960's. The most extreme result of this exaggerated devotion to linguistics is the development of certain commercially successful methods which are accompanied by special training courses for teachers. The disadvantage is that the exponents of these methods are comfortable only in what they have been trained and, to a large extent, they lacked the essential virtue of versatility and open-mindedness toward other effective ideas not provided for in their method.

12.1.3 Teachers' Language Skills

From the beginning of language teaching until almost this century, it was considered that learning a subject was equivalent to learning how to teach it. With the institution of degrees by the universities of the Middle Ages, the granting of higher degrees of Master and Doctor conferred the privilege and obligation of teaching, and this attitude remained until the nineteenth century. During the last part of the century, as training in pedagogy became more common, the teacher was expected to be able to go into any classroom and pick up knowledge of his subjects as he taught his pupils. In languages this meant the employment of teachers who could not really speak the language they taught. The swing to oral-aural methodology in the twentieth-century schools produced a generation of teachers who had at least a limited command of the language they taught, and many countries demanded that their language specialists should have studied in the appropriate country. Indeed, speaking ability had been taken for granted in the universities for some time.

One of the most controverted questions in language teaching is the use of native speakers as teachers. In Rome, the first teachers of

Greek were Greeks, but their social position had an adverse effect on their status. The native teacher was later a Renaissance commonplace: the exodus of scholars from Constantinople flooded the school systems of the West with Greeks, who made an excellent name for themselves as both scholars and teachers. The Norman courts of southern Italy had already employed some Greek teachers during the Middle Ages, but not to any great extent. Religious persecutions occasioned by the Reformation caused wholesale migrations: many educated men found employment teaching their own language in their new country. Several of these teachers, like Claude de Sainliens and John Florio for instance, became famous.

Yet most of these men perpetuated the amateur tradition in teaching. As an eighteenth-century French teacher, L. Chamband, put it; "Teaching French is to become the profession of Foreigners of all sorts, who know not how to shift for a living and often have no qualification at all."[203:vii] This complaint is echoed with more detail and bitterness by Lichtenberger in 1898, who claims that because of the glut of jobless foreigners on the English labor market, no headmaster was ever short of incompetent French teachers.[670:30] Those who know the "public school stories" will be familiar with the French master, a figure characterized by his defective English, slow wits, and quick temper. Properly qualified foreign teachers did not escape censure either. Lichtenberger condemned the foreign teacher outright, claiming that a person who had had to go through the same difficulties as his pupils was more efficient as a teacher.[670:30] This was the opinion of the American Committee of Twelve (1901),[1074:34] and it was shared by Palmer: "The least competent person to teach English is an Englishman who does not possess the students' language."[839:20] Similar complaints were voiced during the 1950's, teachers looking with a jaundiced eye on the missionary zeal of foreign-born experts and of those trained abroad. The usual accusation was that they lacked both a sense of proportion and sympathy with the difficulties of their pupils.[1164:475]

Of all the opinions on the teacher, this has been the most hotly argued, especially as there was no clear indication from language classrooms that either type was superior.

12.2 ASSISTANCE IN THE CLASSROOM

In one of his more cynical moods, G. B. Shaw observed that the most efficient way of learning a subject was to teach it. While teachers have educated themselves by practical observation, they have also applied Shaw's principle to the teaching of others. Thus there are few teachers who have not asked pupils to help them in the day-to-day running of the classroom, including some of the less skilled aspects of teaching. Help has also been asked from people outside the classroom.

12.2.1 Assistance from Pupils

Comenius was convinced that "every pupil should acquire the habit of acting as a teacher,"[256:193] but he was merely stating what had been implicit in Renaissance practice. At its worst, the Renaissance use of pupils as assistants in class was crude and inhuman. Emphasis on speaking Latin, while the main methods used rested on texts, demanded efficient policing of the class. Certain pupils, termed *asini* (asses), were designated to report on those who spoke the vernacular in class. In his colloquies, Brinsley has a vivid picture of a pupils' quarrel over this custom:

a. Who hath the note for speaking English?
b. I.
a. Whom have you noted?
b. Servatius.
a. Have you noted me?
b. Yea.
a. For what cause?
b. Because you have spoken English.
a. To whom have I spoken?
b. To me.
a. To the most notable lier? . . .

1617 (Brinsley) 156: 19

The quarrel continues for the next two pages. In general these *asini* were the weaker pupils who passed on this unwelcome and degrading task to those they "noted" most often. Ascham and Brinsley urged its abolition, noting the effect on the popularity of the stool pigeons and pointing out the conflict between the attention needed to identify culprits and concentration on schoolwork.[156:219]

In Jesuit schools of the time their place was taken by *decuriones,* for whom the post was recognition of work well done. It entailed a fair amount of responsibility: they helped with class supervision, assisting in both teaching and discipline.[*206:35] These boys gained their status from the importance of *aemulatio* (rivalry). The immense classes of the Jesuit schools were divided into teams of ten, each headed by a *decurio* who was responsible for the good performance of his section. The element of competition inherent in the Jesuit scheme of teaching was heightened by team contests in all departments of classroom life: the amount of correct work handed in, the soundness of knowledge of the subject, and the tone of each section were the responsibility of the *decurio.* Through the reputation of his team, each boy realized his own strengths and shortcomings. Clenardus used a similar approach in his own school at Braga.[232:302] The system survives in the house system of schools in the English tradition. But who invented it is an open question. There is an extension of this approach in a more sophisticated modern scheme evolved to deal with large groups of immigrants. The teacher trains a small group of the more receptive pupils in both the matter and the way of imparting it. These pupils go on to handling groups of their fellows, while the teacher goes round the classrooms, checking on the teaching and the progress of the classes.[697] A similar scheme, known as the "Madras snowball," was used in teacher training in India.[1023] The first batch of trainees trained subsequent batches, the number of teachers trained increasing by a geometric progression.

Apart from organised schemes of these types, it has always been recognized that being able to impart knowledge enhances both understanding and retention.[256:193] One cardinal feature of the modern FLES programme of the United States is the role of learners in drilling their classmates, for in many cases, the class teacher is as ignorant as his pupils, and he learns along with them.

12.2.2 Help from outside the Classroom

Other help came to the teacher from outside his class of learners. The American ASTP popularised the "informant," a native speaker who acted as drillmaster in the classroom, and whose function was not teaching, but making sure that each step in a previously laid-out course was reached and absorbed.[123:2] They were not trained teachers: indeed there are reports of school children filling this function in some of the lesser-known languages. The concept was a development of an old technique in scholarly analysis of unwritten languages. It was perfected by the American anthropologist Boas, and the linguist, Bloomfield, for the recording and analysis of Amerindian languages during the 1920's and 1930's.

Long before this, the principle had been applied in Rome by the employment of *paedagogi,* educated slaves who were charged with the formal education of the children of the Roman nobility. As the name implies, they were originally Greeks, and Greek coaching was their most important duty. But when Latin-speaking slaves of the same level of education gradually took over later in the Republic, their duties did not change very much. During the golden and silver ages, they escorted their charges to school, carrying their books and protecting them against the dangers of the early morning Roman street. In school, they often sat behind the boys to ensure that the teacher was able to carry on the lesson without interruption. Their duties included home tutoring. The importance of this institution can be gauged from the fact that the father of the poet, Horace, who could not afford the luxury of such a slave, performed all these three functions for him, earning an affectionate tribute (*Satires* I.vi.71-75).

Rabelais's account of the education of Pantagruel would lead us to believe that in rich families this same custom was followed during the Renaissance,[924:75] but the rousing accounts of indiscipline in the classroom from the colloquia and *vulgaria* of the period show that such *paedagogi* were not common. The most enterprising use of help in the classroom was that of Clenardus, who used his three Negro slaves. He spoke only Latin to them, and in his school they acted as demonstrators and drillmasters.[232:303]

It has never been forgotten that language exists in an environment, as do all facets of human activity, including teaching. Our next concern is the role of environment in language teaching.

13

ENVIRONMENTAL MEANS

> Hit shall be expedient that a noble mannes sonne, in his infancie, may have with him continually onely suche as may accustome him by little & little to speak pure and elegant latine.
>
> 1531 (Elyot) in 364: 35

As language is a social phenomenon, the environment in which it is used can be a most important means of transmission. As the best schools aim at being a microcosm of society, teaching a language by using it as a means of communication with the pupil is an ancient method indeed. For this reason, language learners have always aimed at spending some time living in a society in which their second language is spoken. This is probably the most ancient method of language learning, as it was the only method possible of learning living languages until the first grammars started appearing in the fifteenth century.

13.1 FOREIGN LANGUAGES IN SCHOOL

Using foreign languages as vehicles of instruction is not the revolutionary means many moderns would like to think. It dates at least from the seventh and the eighth centuries in Western Europe. By that time it is probable that the Romance vernaculars were different enough from Latin to make it a foreign language, and anyway Latin had been taught in Ireland from the fifth century. Modern languages are first recorded during the Renaissance, but we know little of what went on before then. In school, the use of foreign languages as teaching media falls into two divisions, the use of the language to teach itself, and the use of the language in other classes.

13.1.1 Running the Language Lesson in the Foreign Language

One of the hottest debates raging in modern foreign-language teaching concerns the use of the language itself as a teaching vehicle. As far as the twentieth century is concerned, the idea was restored by the Natural Method. Given the importance of behavioral ideas in language teaching during this century, excluding the mother tongue from the classroom has received much support, it being felt that such a measure would preclude interference of the first language with what was being learned. It was also felt that fluency and command of the new language would gain in this way. E. B. de Sauzé's "Cleveland Plan" is typical of early twentieth-century experimentation: "Very early in our experiment we found that classes in which the foreign language was used exclusively as a medium of instruction were showing appreciably better results than others in which English was used for part of the time."[318:18] This idea remained one of the bases of orthodox classroom behavior during the rest of the century.

Two hundred years of formal methodology between the Renaissance and our time have made us forget that it was not until about the middle of the eighteenth century that the possibility of using the mother tongue extensively even occurred to language teachers. Most grammatical scholarship existed in Latin until Port-Royal insisted on using French as a medium of instruction. Learning grammar rules in Latin had been considered a desirable way of exercising the language. A few tried to apply the technique to modern languages, one such being de Lévizac: ". . . it is from a grammar written in French that one must study the principles of that language."[306:vii]

The Middle Ages took it for granted that the school language was Latin, and teachers of the early Renaissance saw every advantage in perpetuating the system: "Only by rapid practice in oral composition can fluency and readiness be gained. And this will be further secured if the class is accustomed to speak in Latin."*[223:164] Though the practice later came under attack, there were many who, like Brinsley, thought that speaking "must be begunne from the very first entrance into construction."[155a:215] The long discussion of this question in the *Ludus litterarius* insists on the necessity of making Latin a normal vehicle of speech behavior to ensure that other uses of the language are fluent and correct.

Opposition to the system had been growing since the fifteenth century. Ascham was one who opposed speaking Latin in class, fearing that it would weaken stylistic sense. Opinions were certainly not unanimous, and from the comment of Comenius in the mid-seventeenth century, we can assume that it was usual to conduct the Latin class in Latin: "The first sin of modern methodology is that children are forced to learn an unknown language, Latin, in the abstract without a previously formed knowledge of things."[252:72] The quarrel continued during the eighteenth century, Rollin taking up a moderate position:

> It seems to me that, in this matter, there are two extreme positions that are equally noxious. One is to exclude all other languages besides Latin from the classroom; the other, to abandon entirely efforts to make them speak the language.
>
> 1740 (Rollin) 965: I: 198

Spoken Latin died in the classroom for social reasons, as prowess in this area became irrelevant outside. With the advent of logical and rule-governed approaches to language teaching, the oral approach to modern languages lost ground too. It was not until the efforts of the Direct Method that pupils were made to speak in the classroom, unless one takes account of isolated experimenters like Pestalozzi and Basedow. Though one tends to think of modern languages in this connection, classical languages had some share in this development. Walter Ripman, Rouse, and certain Jesuit teachers tried to popularize spoken Latin but, owing to the lack of a Latin-speaking community and the overriding importance of Ciceronian style, experiments of this kind remained few and were ignored. Since stylistic problems in living languages were not felt to the same extent, this same division of opinion did not exist there, at least until the end of the nineteenth century.

The reforms in language teaching that took place at the time threw into relief the difference between the situation of classical and modern languages. For various reasons, some merely camouflage for the teachers' inability to speak modern languages, the move towards using them as instructional media was bitterly opposed. The main justification brought forward by the reformers was that language was made to be spoken:[614:75] others spoke of creating a foreign environment in which pupils would see their new language in its proper perspective. Both justifications remained current through the 1960's. Yet the vexed question remained: was it necessary to exclude the mother tongue from the classroom, or was it even desirable? In the answers to this question, there was no consensus.

13.1.2 Other Subjects in Foreign Languages

Twentieth-century teachers tried to make a virtue out of what was a necessity during the Middle Ages: teaching subjects in a foreign language or out of foreign-language textbooks. This scheme operated in Roman Catholic seminaries until well into this century, Latin texts being used for philosophy, theology, and canon law. This is also one of the conditions of life for the graduate student in a foreign university.

Gouin saw teaching other subjects by cycle methods as an extension of his technique: "Why should not the lesson on physics or history be employed as the theme of a lesson in German or French?"[468:342] The passage in which this sentence occurs is not clear whether the main object was to teach languages or these other specialized subjects. In the hundred years preceding Gouin, there were isolated attempts to set up foreign-language medium schools in Europe: the *Französisches Gymnasium* of Berlin was one of the important schools of the nineteenth century. Similar experiments were carried out during the eighteenth century by Basedow, who founded the *Philanthropinum,* and Pestalozzi, to whom modern kindergartens owe many of their methods.

In bilingual countries, this means of teaching the second language is more to hand. The types of school possible range from unilingual schools in which all the instruction is given in the second language to the various types of bilingual school.

In 1959 the Soviet Union instituted foreign-language schools along the lines of the *Französisches Gymnasium.* By 1963 there were thirty-two of them, most of them in European Russia. Besides devoting almost double the amount of time to the foreign language as the schools in the ordinary system, they taught the whole curriculum in the language of the school. Pupils and teachers were carefully selected and the pupil-teacher ratio was ten or twelve to one. Russian was used where necessary in the first three years, but from the fourth on, it was excluded. Each school was left free to develop its own methodology; hence methods ranged, even in Moscow, from that based on an approach including both reading and speech, to those which depend on the exclusion of the written word. Within the limits imposed by the necessity to teach the Soviet view of things, the cultural atmosphere of the schools was modeled on the foreign culture, the teachers in many places speaking the foreign language at all times within the school.[*106:122-123]

The above schools should be distinguished from the bilingual schools which catered to Russia's many ethnic minorities in which both Russian and the local language were languages of instruction.[*106:73-79] Such schools are common wherever two languages are spoken in the community. They fall into three groups. The most comprehensive give all their teaching in both languages; others divide the curriculum up between the languages; the third type gives only what is of particular interest to each culture in its own language. An example of the possibilities is found in the Collège militaire royal de S.-Jean, a bilingual military college near Montreal. There, although most of the teaching is given in the mother tongue of the student, the college itself is run in English and French, alternating by fortnights. By an ingenious system of incentives and rewards, the necessity for skill in both languages is impressed on the young officers who attend.[248:31] Unfortunately, it is only during the last hundred or so years that practices such as these have been documented, but bilingual schools have existed for many years in Belgium, Alsace-Lorraine, and Eastern Europe.

In officially unilingual countries with large populations who speak another language, the school has played an important role as an instrument of linguistic suppression. For example, in the Roman Empire and some parts of the United States, languages were forcibly suppressed by schools where the very existence of any means of expression other than that recognized by law was ignored. It must be emphasized that the loss of the minority language was considered as desirable and was actively sought by the authorities, and in many cases, by the minority group, who saw their own language as a block to their advancement.[*65:45] Likewise, a conquering power which regards foreign territory as its own will try to impose its own language through the schools. In 1870 and 1918, for instance, Alsace-Lorraine was ceded to Prussia and France respectively, and the language of the schools changed accordingly. The aim is not the creation of bilinguals, but a forcible shift in language loyalty.

13.2 LEARNING LANGUAGES OUTSIDE SCHOOL

As language exists for purposes other than use in school, language learning can take place in the home, or in society at large.

13.2.1 The Home

Through force of circumstances, the home is often the first place in which a child meets two or more languages. This is especially true when the parents belong to two different language groups, a situation inevitable where two cultures are in contact. Here the bilingual character of the society is an extension of the home, and the child grows up in close contact with both his parents' languages. In addition, even though the parents might share the same mother tongue, the predominance of a foreign language in cultured society has often dictated its use in the home. This was the case with Greek in ancient Rome and with Latin during the Middle Ages. During the Renaissance, Latin slowly became restricted to the world of churchmen and scholars, and French, which had been gaining importance since the late Middle Ages, became one of the languages of European society. The other was Italian, which, as it occupied the same territory as Latin once had, was made the central language of art and culture. English and French held this position in many underdeveloped countries during the mid-twentieth century. As the colonial powers gradually left their colonies to their own devices, the former colonial languages became languages of commerce and government. One peculiar example of this is pidgin English, which, though spoken by few as a mother tongue, is the medium of trade and administration in Melanesia.

The governess or private tutor has become part of the folklore of Western society. Yet the first of the type were slaves: in the great slave markets of Delos, an educated Greek could fetch as much as ten work slaves. By reading between the lines in the Plautine comedies, one can infer that such tutors were already common in the second century B.C., there being no question that they were the rule among the Roman aristocracy during the golden and silver ages. From that day to this, foreign-born tutors pop in and out of the literature, especially in noble families for whom the knowledge of a foreign language was considered necessary. Thus, as part of his scheme of reforging the links between East and West, Charlemagne engaged a Greek tutor for his sister, who was to marry the Emperor of Byzantium. And during the nineteenth century, foreign tutors were especially common in the rich European middle class.

The French linguist M. Grammont said that for effective language learning, every person in close contact with a child should speak only one language, thus localizing its use and avoiding a confusing choice the child would have to make between languages when talking to those in his immediate circle. This idea, *la formule Grammont,* was followed by Werner Leopold in the education of his daughter, Hildegarde. The idea first appeared, it seems, during the Renaissance, as an implication of the use of the Latin-speaking tutor (Montaigne, *Essais* I:xxv). The idea was stated again during the seventeenth century: in England, Alberic Gentili taught his son French, English, and Latin by having members of his family talk to the boy exclusively in the language of their choice.[776:I:441] It seems that this was the first time the practice was erected into a principle, though Roman children had undoubtedly learned Greek from unilingual slaves in this manner.

13.2.2 Language Learning in Society

The aspect of language that most strikes the ordinary person is its relevance as a social tool. Hence, many have believed that the most efficacious way of learning it is by using it in real situations. It is pointed out that one important reason for the profound knowledge of Latin that existed once was due to its use as a language of scholarship and communication in the church and in secular society. We have already seen that French was the language of polite society from the sixteenth century until the nineteenth; likewise, for a short period during the Middle Ages, Provençal was the language of artistic society in southern Romance Europe.

Besides these social developments there were others peculiar to the scholastic world. Latin was a required language in school until the mid-seventeenth century: most school statutes contained a clause like the following: "Games will be allowed for relaxation, and for the purpose of extended practice of Latin."[*84:81] This arrangement spread to modern languages during the eighteenth century and has become a feature of immersion courses during which the pupils live in the school. Speaking Latin at meals survived in the European universities as late as the seventeenth century, and some universities were still accepting Latin theses at the beginning of this century. Owing to the important position of Latin in the Roman Catholic Church, the Roman universities (i.e., those of the Vatican) still require theses in Latin.

Informal arrangements between pupils to use foreign languages have always been encouraged. In his instructions to the young prince of Bohemia, Piccolomini (later Pope Pius II) wrote: "You should be surrounded by truthful boys.... Some of these should speak Hungarian, some Czech, some your own language, and all Latin in turn. Thus, without effort and in playing you will learn all these languages."[878:134] These arrangements still exist, but since the nineteenth century they have been supplemented by the club, which has become a normal part of undergraduate life and is not unknown in secondary schools. In the schools they date from the 1890's.[421:46] In his memoirs Sir Frederick Hamilton, a British diplomat of the turn of the century, describes the workings of a businessmen's club that flourished in Leipzig in the 1870's: "For an hour and a half the members of the club had to talk English or French as the case may be under a penalty of a fine of one thaler for every lapse into their native German."[*79:171] Such rigor is rare among modern clubs, but many cultural organisations that developed during the twentieth century, for instance, the *Alliance française* and the *Goethe Society*, usually require their members to speak the language of the society they are interested in. During the Renaissance and the two centuries immediately following, there were several suggestions of a city in which only Latin would be spoken.[776:I:425] But they came to nothing.

Through fear of contaminating the fine Latin style they were aiming at, many Renaissance teachers rose up against forcing pupils to speak Latin outside class. Opposition to the idea came as early as Ascham and was debated by Brinsley, who saw no harm in it. But criticism of the practice mounted during the seventeenth century, the arguments for it carrying less and less weight: "Objection. Those who chat in Latin, corrupt the language. Reply. Practical use dominates in the arts, and there does not exist a discipline in which one does not make mistakes at the learning stage" (Perizonius).[858:774] Yet in spite of this attitude, the eighteenth century was the heyday of extempore oral composition of Latin and Greek verse.

Travel has always been the most widely recommended method of adding a polish to linguistic knowledge. The custom spans two thousand years from the great schools of Athens, which received Roman boys on the threshold of a public career, to the modern graduate student, who very often studies in a foreign-language university. This reached its peak during the Middle Ages, when the universities of Oxford, Cambridge, and Paris were truly international societies, with all the teaching in Latin. The ancient classical university course was associated with a tour of the Greek East. In time this was separated from university study and the grand tour became the crown of a young man's education, until the higher cost of travel and the savage wars of this century made it almost impossible to continue the practice.

There were some reservations: Sweet remarked that, before one goes to live in a foreign country, one should know enough of the language to benefit by it.[1054:76] Many people, conscious that it is possible to remain isolated in a foreign society, suggested various ways of integrating. Going to divine service in another language was a favorite Renaissance way of exercising comprehension skills at least. In any case, churchgoing was a favorite amusement owing to the histrionics indulged in by preachers. Religious authorities were, of course, inclined to regard this as an abuse. Theatergoing was also regarded as a most important means of practicing the second language, some adding to this pleasure others not so desirable: "There are two ways of learning French commonly recommended: take a mistress and go to the comedie."[*213:19] This remark was passed to an acquaintance by John Adams, one of the first American ministers in France.

The idea that friendship was a possible tool in learning a second language gave rise to the twentieth-century idea of "twinning." This rose out of efforts by countries that had not been seriously affected by the Second World War to help the other part of the world rebuild itself. Cities of comparable size and character initiated programs of cultural and educational exchange consisting of correspondence and, more important, of exchange of pupils, teachers, and ordinary citizens. This allowed people to enter more fully into the community life of their "twinned" city, as barriers encountered by strangers who enter a city were broken down by the mere fact of twinning, and unlike ordinary tourists, visitors found that the interest they had in their twinned city was eagerly reciprocated. This was especially valuable for Americans, whose world-wide aid plans had this counterpart in the educational systems of both the helper and the helped. Other important schemes related to this were the less ambitious "au pair" systems, whereby students were welcomed as unskilled workers and housed in families that had volunteered. Thus language learning and international understanding went hand-in-hand, realizing one goal that had been put forward as early as Comenius.

13.2.3 Letter Writing

During the nineteenth century, as a result of the great improvement in international postal services, language learners began writing to pen pals in foreign countries. Cultural organizations, such as the *Alliance française,* seized on this method of promoting cultural exchange, matching foreigners with nationals of their own interests. Despite the wars which occurred regularly during the twentieth century, the practice became very popular. Often such exchanges worked to the common benefit of both correspondents, each writing in the language of the other. Even classical languages shared in this development. An exchange service for Latin-writing pen pals was instituted during the 1950's by the Society for Latin as a Living Language.[264:26] As far as modern languages are concerned, the idea does not go back further than the last years of the nineteenth century. Bainvel, a Jesuit educator, ascribes the idea to an article which appeared in the *Review of Reviews* during the 1890's.[74:342]

Nothing is said about correspondence in modern languages before this time, but epistolatory style was a fairly important part of all Latin composition. During the Middle Ages and Renaissance, it was taught by techniques of imitation already discussed (see §6.2.3). Whether any of the letters written were actually sent is another matter. During the twelfth to the fourteenth centuries, the art of letter writing was a separate discipline, the *ars dictaminis.* This creation of the law faculties of Italy rose out of the necessity of drafting documents clear and precise enough for legal purposes. It was, of course, a lucrative business, being made even more so by several unscrupulous lawyers who made sure that legal documents were as incomprehensible to the layman as possible. It became immensely popular, contributing greatly to the decline of scholarship that immediately preceded the Renaissance.

Having traced the ideas in practice, we will now examine their origins.

PART VI

WHERE HAVE THE IDEAS COME FROM?

INTRODUCTION

While linguistics, in its traditional dress as grammar, has had a long connection with language teaching, it is only in the last century that psychologists have attempted to rationalize what teachers have known from experience.

The first analyses of language were made by philosophers especially for the purpose of teaching. Their interest was not merely in grammatical analysis, but in stylistic training as well, so that logic, grammar, and rhetoric were all thought of as facets of the same reality of language use. Not until Roman times were the three formally separated, but it was still unthinkable that one should be taught without the other. By the Renaissance they were definitely discrete, only to be brought back together again by the exponents of general grammar during the early nineteenth century, the word linguistique *first being used by Charles Nodier in 1834.*[801] *At first linguistics was concerned with the history of languages. This has left its mark on the contemporary approach. With Saussure, however, the importance of description of synchronic states became the main object of the science, a development foreshadowed by Sweet and Viëtor. This in turn fell in with the new orientation to language teaching in the twentieth century.*

Psychology began as a science which dealt with the soul as the principle of life, becoming restricted to the treatment of human behavior only during the eighteenth and nineteenth centuries. It was not finally separated from philosophy until the late nineteenth century. The treatment of learning as a separate form of behavior is foreshadowed in the work of Kant and Herbart, but was not made into a subject of specialization until the twentieth century.

As the early grammarians had worked in the whole field of

philosophy, they saw no incongruity in laying down approaches to teaching as well as to language. Just as the science of philosophy was ultimately one, so too was the art of teaching languages. One of the last indications of this classical and medieval attitude is the book of Vivès on education, De anima et vita. *This recalls the medieval attitude that all knowledge was a property of the soul. The early humanists, like their medieval counterparts, formed their ideas from this background, but the Renaissance impatience with medieval scholarship occasioned abandonment of the philosophical background of both grammar and pedagogy. The science of education began to develop independently of grammar. But as much classical scholarship was still produced by churchmen, for whom philosophy was a required subject of study, there continued to be some cross influence between the two.*

But as this new generation of grammarians was not trained in the full corpus of the old scholastic philosophy, the sciences of education and grammar diverged. By the nineteenth century they were completely separate. The tendency was accelerated by the diminished importance accorded classical languages in education. Learning problems were not seen in a linguistic light, but under the more general aspect of the learning of skills.

Control over separate disciplines has gradually passed from the teaching body to the analytic scientists, who legislate on what is to be taught and the methods to be used. Concepts of language have changed from those directed towards the teaching of analysis and rhetoric to behavioral ideas. Besides causing the creation of interdisciplinary sciences, such as psycholinguistics, this has resulted in the formation of schools of linguists that try to take the modern concepts into account, while preserving the old analytical bias. In language teaching, those linguists who have gone into the field have learned from the psychologists, and have loudly proclaimed as their own ideas drawn from psychology. In addition, twentieth-century linguists, not being psychologists themselves, have a tendency to adhere to psychological ideas that the psychologists themselves have doubts about. Both sciences have shown an inclination to trespass on the territory of the other, and the question of the provenance of ideas is far from clear.

14

PSYCHOLOGY AND LANGUAGE TEACHING

To learn a language is, as we have said, to translate one's individuality into that language.

1880 (Gouin) in 468: 284

Few theories of language learning are peculiar to the twentieth century, but modern psychological research has given them a point and clarity they had lacked, while clothing them in language that disguises their relationship to older ideas. Under the influence of the Natural and Direct Methods, emphasis slowly shifted from the knowledge of grammar rules to the habit and skill aspect of language. Such a shift had already occurred during the Renaissance, to be set aside by the proponents of general grammar. But during the twentieth century, psychologists developed a view of language that was complementary to that of the linguists and pedagogues. For them, language was an aspect of behavior, and learning a type of conditioning.

14.1 CONCEPTUAL PROBLEMS

Two problems have interested those who design language courses: the nature of language, and what constitutes language learning. The skill aspect of language predominated during the classical, Renaissance, and modern periods; while in the intervening centuries, the knowledge aspect was taken as the most important. This, in turn, has affected the importance of the various means of teaching that suggest themselves.

14.1.1 The Nature of Language

In considering language, psychologists have concentrated on two of its facets, treating it either as an aspect of human behavior or as a factor in social activity.

Considerations of language as behavior differ according to the school of the psychologist. In general, the behaviorists headed by Skinner, adopted a mechanistic approach, while the neobehaviorists allowed more freedom of action to the individual.

For the behaviorists language was a series of stimulus-response mechanisms. The Skinnerian analysis of verbal behavior supposed two types of 'repertoire', formal and thematic. This division was used as a basis for programed instruction:

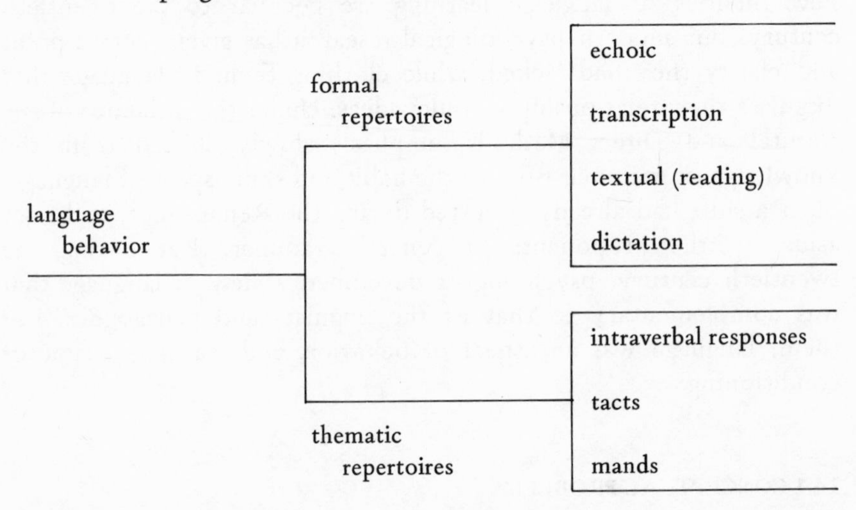

Formal repertoires depend on exact reproduction of a verbal stimulus, while thematic ones entail a linguistic reaction to the stimulus concerned. Formal repertoires are self-explanatory. These imitative activities progress to thematic repertoires in which the stimulus is not reproduced. Intraverbal responses are based on transformations of grammatical patterns, e.g. 'I saw him/ I did not see him'; or on translation. Tacts are linguistic reactions to non-verbal stimuli, so that, depending on the class, the picture of a house will produce sentences like: 'That is a house.'/'C'est une maison.'/'He whare tera.' In all cases some sort of reinforcement follows. A mand is a verbal response to a verbal stimulus with some sort of result. Formulas of politeness are good examples. Opening a door for a person and the resultant verbal behavior would go something like the following: the door is opened, the reply is 'Thank you' and the acknowledgement is 'You're welcome.' In France the sequence would be: door opened, 'Merci', 'Il n'y a pas de quoi.' In French Canada the last phrase would be replaced by 'Bienvenu.' In each case the last reply is a 'mand'. It is clear that all of these classifications of behaviour were traditional teaching techniques, even if labels had not been coined for them.[644:281-290]

The neobehaviorists, while agreeing that language is a form of behavior, see speech as an activity which directs and transforms other behavioral functions. Speech is a mediated response to stimuli, the mediation being effected by emotional factors and by cognition. Language directs motor behavior and restructures cognitive processes. It is therefore a much less automatic process than that postulated by Skinner's school.

Though the twentieth century was the first to treat language from a purely psychological point of view, the modern concept of language as a skill or habit has been current for some time: it was such a concept that inspired the Natural and Direct Methods. Firmery put it well: "We are to transform dead knowledge into living practice, to substitute 'can' for 'know how to.' "[406:332] A similar idea was at the base of all the attempts to eliminate grammar from language courses before this time. Locke seems to have been the first to regard education, and through it, language teaching, as a conditioning process: "The great thing to be minded about education is what habits you settle."[*49:231]

The school of psychologists who collaborated in building up the theory of the Direct Method followed Herbart and Humboldt. From Humboldt they took the idea of *innere Sprachform,* which was the psychological set peculiar to a speech community, and which shaped the expressive uses of language. This conception had close affinities with Gestalt psychology, because the idea of a complex and organised body of knowledge and skills was uppermost in their concept of language.[614:25] Kappert noted that the *innere Sprachform* varied slightly from individual to individual,[614:28] and Flagstad remarked that differences in language depended on differing views of the world:

> The differences between languages are due to two facts: first, concepts are transmitted through peoples or other external, visible means which differ for each language. Second, each concept of the whole that forms an impression comes from a truly conventional form, which supplies a foundation for communication.
>
> 1915 (Flagstad) 410: 162

The resemblance of this idea to the linguistic view of Saussure will be apparent (see §15.1). The link with both behavioral conceptions of language is also clear; formation of appropriate linguistic behavior was recognised by Jespersen as the central aim of the Direct Method: "Our ideal must be rather the nearest possible approach to the native command of the language, so that the words and sentences may awaken in us the same ideas as in the native."[587:54]

At the beginning of the nineteenth century, Humboldt had specifically rejected any mechanistic concept of language that reduced it to a mere response to stimuli. In this, he anticipated both the neobehaviorist school of psychology, for whom mediation was a mental operation essential to language, and the psychomechanic school of Guillaume, who postulated that owing to the analysis of experience that dominated the mental processes behind language, linguistic knowledge, in even the most ignorant of men, resembled the corpus of knowledge in a speculative science.[496:276] Humboldt owed to Schlegel the idea that language was a creative activity which expressed the personality of the user.[215:26] For Schlegel, the distinguishing characteristics of language were its freedom from external stimuli and its role of self-expression. He compared the normal uses of language to artistic creation, a concept taken up by the theorists of the romantic movement in both England and Germany.[215:16]

In this form the concept goes back to Descartes. His school argued that free response to stimuli, or actions for which there were no outside stimuli, were proper to the human race; speech was the most obvious form of this type of behavior. He himself attacked the theory current among some of his contemporaries that it was merely the lack of speech organs that precluded animal speech.[215:4] This position was confirmed by anatomical research that identified in animals organs resembling the "speech organs" of human beings, and assigned normal physiological functions to human speech organs. Though none of the scholars in question made the connection, their ideas on language as a series of concepts underlying speech has some affinity with the theory of universals, which from Aristotle on is a constant theme in philosophy. The universal was a general concept based on specific experience. Cultural factors governed the formation of these concepts. By St. Augustine's time the idea of *lingua mentis,* which was no one language, but a generalization of experience which gave form to attempts at linguistic expression, was a commonplace in philosophical thought.

Equally relevant to the history of language teaching is the idea of language as communication or as a social tool. There has been some reaction against it, for example, Abercrombie, professor of phonetics at Edinburgh, wrote: "The definition of language as 'a means of communicating thoughts' is nowadays held to be, as a partial truth, more misleading than illuminating; a more fruitful definition is that language is a means of social control."[4:2] In the minds of language teachers and language-teaching theorists the social implications of language had never been forgotten, but they had been overlaid by the necessities of teaching language as an individual form of behavior. The difficulties that such an approach entailed were not fully realized until the Second World War, when one of the goals of the ASTP was to reduce the clash between the American cultural values of the soldiers and the cultural values of those among whom they were to be fighting. The basic relationship of language and culture was most forcefully summed up in a MLA publication which appeared in 1961: "Every such national language [i.e., Asian/African] is imbedded in a *cultural matrix* which differs in striking ways from the cultural matrix of European languages, and the language is ultimately related to this matrix."[762:3]

While this principle was slowly working in language teaching in the field of social psychology, there developed an approach to the psychological behavior of language users in use situations. The basic question was: "How does language act as a tool of social interaction?" One of the basic concepts of this approach to language was that of "domain," defined as "a constellation of social situations, each of which is composed of combinations of specific times, settings and role relationships."[268:200] This is a sociological and psychological restatement of the linguist's idea of availability. The techniques described in Cooper's article are not unlike those evolved by St-Cloud to define *le vocabulaire disponible.* The role relationship is a culturally defined set of expectations in a person-to-person relationship. This has a rough parallel in the linguistic concept of "register" (see §7.2.1).

In themselves, these concepts did not have any direct influence on language teaching. But the continuing emphasis on social factors, which was one of the Direct Method's major contributions, broadened language lessons in the twentieth century to include social as well as literary uses of the language. A brief perusal of the dialogues of the Renaissance and following centuries will show that the practical implications of the social psychologist's theories were already too commonplace to be mentioned, though social interaction theories were certainly not current. One of the most interesting facets of social consciousness in language teaching was in classical languages. Even though classical literature had had the character of forbidden sweets during much of the Middle Ages, practitioners realized that it was impossible to handle Latin with any finesse without a knowledge of its written and unwritten culture. Hence the importance given to aspects of Roman life, and in Biblical criticism, to Hebrew life, in the comments of the medieval scholiasts.

The conclusions of twentieth-century psychologists largely confirmed what had already been known about learning behavior, but they were also instrumental in putting an end to a large number of abuses that had crept into the classroom. These ideas fitted in very neatly with the direction of structural linguistics, so neatly, in fact, that linguists tended to be unaware that there was any division between the two sciences, and sold the psychologists' conclusions as their own.

14.1.2 Learning a Foreign Language

From their concept of the nature of language, psychologists have enunciated four principles taken up by the linguists who developed audio-lingual methods:

1. that learning a foreign language implies the formation of new habits and skills;
2. that the only really natural method of tackling foreign langugaes is to teach oral skills before written;
3. that the student should work out for himself the grammar of a new structure before seeing the official analysis; and
4. that one should take account of cultural facts in learning a language.[959:10]

The twentieth-century structuralist scorned rule learning, pointing out that this was absorbing analysis, not language. As the stimulus-response theory of Skinner was the ruling theory of behavior at the time structuralism ventured into language teaching, endless repetition was at the core of the method developed by Bloomfield and his school.[123:12] It was not until the late 1950's that this procedure was questioned by psychologists who investigated the element of fatigue associated with frequent repetition. In their view fatigue prevents learning beyond a certain point. The work of Lambert and Jacobivits at McGill University would suggest that satiation by intensive repetition brings about a rejection mechanism that actually inhibits learning and retention.

As early as 1956 teachers were questioning "the paralyzing belief that in our courses, drill is enough."[859:113] Educational psychologists began to put forward the idea that it was only by trial and error that a student would develop sufficient flexibility to deal with the demands of the foreign language.[959:78] The dilemma was this: by drill students learned how to handle what they were given in class, but the method did not allow for transition to free behavior. By 1967 J. B. Carroll had arrived at the position held by Erasmus, three hundred years before, that both deductive and inductive methods are to be used in teaching concepts, one reinforcing the other.[193:578] Likewise programed learning specialists tended to repudiate the "sunburn method" of Bloomfield on the grounds that it ignores "the remarkable plasticity of human behavior."[644:251]

In Russia there was more emphasis on the reasoned learning of language concepts. They tended to question the whole idea of language habits:

> The distinguishing characteristic of the Soviet method of teaching foreign languages is considered to be the principle of consciousness, which required that pupils should be so taught as to have a thorough understanding of the teaching material assimilated by them. It has been proved that the conscious assimilation of any school subject is more effective than the mechanical assimilation that takes place when students learn material by rote through frequent repetitions made without understanding.
>
> 1959 (Belyayev) 97: 95

To the element of unconscious behavior they added knowledge of the elements involved.

Far from being the property of the Russians, the "Soviet method of teaching" had been a commonplace of the classical, medieval, and Renaissance periods. While respecting analysis for what it could offer, Quintillian had fired the first blast against it: ". . . it is one thing to speak Latin, another to speak grammatically."[923:I.vi.27] No attempt was made to impugn the important role of memory, but both its nature and the use to which it was put were questions demanding clarification. St. Augustine put forward a theory based on the Greek idea of universals that resembles quite closely the neobehaviorist ideas of mediation. He claimed that what a person hears is processed according to a definite set of mental concepts before it is understood and acted on.[60:1216] On this idea he based an approach roughly resembling the Direct Method, but tempered by the needs of rhetorical training. Six hundred years later, Hugo of St.

Victor decried parrot repetition, recommending active participation by the pupil in learning.[565:57] The theoretical basis from which he worked was still felt to be valid by Vivès in the sixteenth century: "The course of learning goes from senses to imagination, and then from there to the mind."[1123:87] Erasmus translated this general principle into practical terms: "The best concept of memory is the following: full understanding, and ordered knowledge of what is understood, and then repetition of what you want to remember."[377:512A] This concept, though based on medieval practice deriving from the classification of the soul's powers into memory, understanding, and will, was strengthened by classical authority. Alcuin, like Erasmus, had already drawn heavily on Cicero: "I cannot improve on what Cicero says: Memory is the storehouse of everything and unless it guards the thoughts, words, and things we have arrived at and we understand them all, as orators we are useless."[25:941B]

Comenius stood in the same line of development. For him, efficient learning and retention depended on good representation. He agreed with the authorities of the high Renaissance that understanding preceded memory, and that efficient ordering materially helped understanding.[256:142] The most important aspect of representation was that this was a task in which the pupil participated through his sense impressions.[256:130] Examples were another essential part of representation, as they supplied the pupil with the means to make his own as he became more expert. Everything that Comenius had to say had already been said by experts as diverse as Quintillian and Erasmus, but his peculiar contribution is summing up all the trends of the preceding seventeen hundred years in a clear, coherent method based on a sound theory of learning.

Despite Comenius's own movement to formalism, the germs of what he taught remained. There is an echo of both Comenius and Quintillian in this statement from Robert Lowe, one of the lesser known enthusiasts for the Natural Method:

> Learning the grammar is a joke compared with learning the language. The Grammar is one thing, and the language another. I agree with the German wit, Heine, who said, 'How fortunate the Romans were that they had not

to learn the Latin language, because if they had done so they would never have had time to conquer the world.'

1867 (Lowe) *49: 430

Habit formation was rather brutally brought to the attention of many nineteenth-century teachers and pupils by the necessity to learn languages that did not conform to the pattern of those hitherto learned. The extension of trade and missionary activity in America, Asia, the Pacific, and Africa demanded that the appropriate languages should be learned quickly and efficiently without recourse to either grammar or written analysis. The normal way out of this dilemma is summed up in the preface to Howse's grammar of Cree:

Notwithstanding the peculiarities in the structure of this and other American tongues, Habit will, with attention on the reader's part, so familiarize them to the mind that they may, after the lapse of many years, become as spontaneously the vehicle of thoughts as the mother tongue.

1844 (Howse) 561: xiv

Herbart's theories of education and learning were the basis of the teaching practice of the Direct Method. As language was a matter of organised perception, teaching it involved observation lessons (*Anschauungsunterricht*), which gave the pupil direct experience of the language and its reality. The five steps of the Herbartian lesson can be seen in every treatment of the Direct Method: they were preparation (revision of old material), presentation (imparting new facts), association (of the new with the old), systematization (recapitulation of the new work in its context), and application (practice).[*49:350] Skill in the language was to come from organization of the apperception masses presented to the pupil; a liking for the language (sympathy) was dependent on the interest in the matter itself and on the attitude of the teacher to both pupil and language.

The second principle of twentieth-century methodology is the primacy of oral skills, first laid down by Vivès: ". . . there is no organ through which we learn more readily than the ear."[1120:13] We have already noted that in Renaissance practice, modern and classical languages were generally treated differently, an oral approach being used for the first and a mixed oral-written approach for the second. It was Pestalozzi who formulated the principle of complete reliance on oral-aural training in the first stages of a new language. The idea was applied in earnest by Gottlieb Heness and publicized by Lambert Sauveur. The principle was invoked with ever-increasing rigor by the Direct Methodists and more extreme theorists of the twentieth century.

Though it was generally agreed that as far as children were concerned, this was the more valid approach, there were rumblings of discontent from those who believed that audio-lingualism confused the order of analysis with the order of teaching. A strong body of opinion, headed by Michael West, counseled the use of reading as a beginning, this being the easiest approach for one who could already read his own language. The matter, then, was far from settled.

The third point, relying on analogy to make the foreign learner conscious of good usage, rests on the principle that one retains easily what one has to work out for oneself. It is, nevertheless, disputable whether this understanding results in the formulation of a rule: the aim is rather the development of a sure instinct of what is right and wrong:

> The processes which govern quick hearing and understanding of language, lead us to the reflection that in the teaching of foreign language we must take into account all the factors which help us to master the reception/integration and emission/reproduction of the language.
>
> 1964 (Guberina) 490: 11

Research into programed learning indicated that progression from rules to language inhibited the development of fluency by setting up a cast of thought that is unnatural to the native speaker.[644:286]

Both of these ideas were already current at the beginning of the twentieth century. Sweet, followed by Palmer, had fixed on association as the key factor in language learning.[1054:102] From Herbart, the Direct Method had taken the ideas of apperception masses. As far as language was concerned these were not sets of rules, but examples of language in use, it being the pupil's task to arrange these in a unified whole, and then to analyze them. This fitted in with two concepts from Humboldt: *innere Sprachform,* to which we have already referred, and the notion that language learning was *Selbstschöpfung der Individuen* (fashioning of a person by himself).[215:64] It will be remembered that Gouin adopted this conception of language learning, and reference to the headnote of Chapter 16 will show that it lived on into the twentieth century.

The philosophical tone of grammar during the seventeenth and eighteenth centuries demanded application of analogy in another form. Whereas in the approach just described the pupil was called on to extrapolate from structure to structure, in this approach he was made to extrapolate from the rules of one science to the rules of another. Condillac regarded grammar as the first part of the art of thinking: "In order to discover the principles of language, we must observe how we think; we must look for these principles in the very analysis of thought."[261:4] Rollin required that his pupils should be quite familiar with the consequences and implications of something learned by heart, otherwise, in his view, pupils were wasting their time.[965:I:205]

The Herbartian idea of analysis, without its Platonist overtones concerning the independent life of ideas, had alrady appeared in Comenius:

> XCVII. We become acquainted with the parts of anything by means of analysis.
> XCVIII. We come to know them more completely if we also employ synthesis.
> XCIX. We come to know them most completely if, in addition, we employ syncrisis.
> C. When we seek exact knowledge of things, we must combine the analytic, synthetic and syncritic methods.
>
> 1648 (Comenius) 256: 137

He was merely summing up the Renaissance point of view, aiming at both the instinctive mastery of the native speaker and the analytical knowledge of the scholar.

Hoole, as usual with Renaissance pedagogues, put the whole matter succinctly: "Till the memory and understanding go hand in hand, a child learns nothing to any purpose."[551:II:12] Though living languages were taught mainly by intuitive methods, classical languages were based firmly on a progression to rules, which were normally derived from copious examples. Pupils were expected to go in both directions, from examples to rules, as in the disputations, and from rules to correct usage. In its turn this was a Renaissance survival of the medieval use of analogy derived from the practice of the ancient grammarians.

Cultural awareness was critical to the methods developed during the twentieth century. Cultural material figured largely in the ASTP, and under the name of "area programs" became an important part of the course in the United States. Owing to the work of cultural anthropologists like Sapir and Malinowski, the symbiotic relationship was investigated and found to be of capital importance for language teaching. Modern theorists were inclined to put the matter in behavioral terms (see §14.1.1).

The Direct Methodists had seen the problem in terms of reactions: the learner should react to material in the same way as a native speaker would.[410:164] The problem of cultural awareness was sharpened by contact between Europeans and the peoples they were colonizing. Indeed, in preventing wars between colonizers and colonized, understanding of culture became a key issue. Sir George Grey, who is largely responsible for the pacification of New Zealand under the British crown, tried to head off the Maori wars (1840-1865) by collecting Maori legends and having them taught to his liaison staff: ". . . I could neither successfully govern, nor hope to conciliate, a numerous and turbulent people, with whose language, manners, customs, religion and modes of thought I was quite unacquainted."[*4:231] Necessity forced him to the realization that in order to understand all the ramifications of what a Maori said to him, especially on a formal occasion, he had to know to the full his intellectual and social background. The neglect of this principle during the previous two hundred years' teaching had followed from the impression that languages were merely a body of knowledge.

Difficulties with interpretation of Scripture had underlined the necessity of knowing Hebrew and Hellenistic culture. Melancthon, for instance, writes: "Paul says: 'Put on the bowels of mercy.' What can a Latinist understand from such an outlandish turn of phrase? This was a common metaphor among the Jews, who used the word 'bowels' to mean any deep emotion."[741:872] Something of the same attitude lay behind the highly unpopular and suspect attempt by Erasmus to apply normal philological techniques to Biblical criticism. Vivès generalized the principle, claiming that "no language is worth learning if nothing is sought beyond the linguistic aspect."[*105:20] Something of this idea had been behind the scholia that had become increasingly common from the fourth century. They were never meant as anything but scholarly information to provide the cultural background necessary for the proper understanding and elegant handling of Latin.

14.2 ACQUISITION PROBLEMS

As a result of the present-day interest in learning problems sparked largely by the philosophers and psychologists of the nineteenth century, an attempt was made to place language teaching techniques on as sophisticated a base as the content. Fields that have been of great interest to modern researchers are the ideal age for acquiring a foreign language, relationships between intelligence and learning ability, relation of method to student characteristics, and the question of motivation.

14.2.1 Age of Learning

Since classical times Western teachers have speculated about the ideal age for language learning. Two main schools of thought can be traced: the traditional one sees immense advantages in introducing a child to a foreign language as young as possible; it is only in the last four hundred years that this has been disputed and the pattern of late language learning arose in European and American schools. In addition, there is a small middle group which according to circumstances inclines one way or the other. The most coherent statement on early language learning came from Quintillian. It seems that in spite of the prevailing Roman practice of starting Greek early, there was some disagreement over its advisability. Quintillian tried to settle the question, reminding his readers that "by nature we retain best what is learned in our tenderest years."[923:I.i.5]

The medieval practice was related to the manner in which the Church recruited its clergy. Philosophical and theoretical considerations of age were not entertained: beginning Latin was governed by the age at which boys entered the monastic schools; they learned Latin and began their education at the same time. Thus the beginning age for Latin was between seven and ten; one entered the university at about fifteen, or earlier. The early humanists found little to quarrel with in this, though they imperceptibly lowered the age of language introduction to about five. In the hands of the fifteenth-century humanists it was a matter of principle, Vergerius remarking that "this age is more receptive to learning than the others."[1104:461] Erasmus is explicit that:

> As far as languages are concerned, this age is so supple, that within a few months a German child learns French unknowingly while doing other things. Such learning is never more effective than when carried out in the earliest years.
>
> 1529 (Erasmus) 377: 501

He puts it down to the ease with which children imitate.[375:714] In some statements of policy from this time there is a little confusion: most avoid it by using the word *puer,* meaning a young boy, but those who use the word *iuvenis* leave themselves open to ambiguous interpretation, as in certain technical contexts this could mean a person of military age.

Comenius was quite clear, noting that the *prima aetas,* (i.e., the first seven years of life) was especially adept at studies involving memory. He was followed by Pestalozzi and Basedow. Basedow was inclined to deny the sense of teaching languages to anyone over sixteen,[81:109] but the tendency of the time did favor a late introduction. There were two reasons for this: the first was the introduction into the schools of the mother tongue as a subject of study: the second, derived from the first, demanded that a pupil should be familiar with the grammar of his own language before tackling another. It seems that by the late eighteenth century the normal age of introduction was twelve, setting the pattern for the next two hundred years. It was left to the Natural and Direct Methods to focus attention on the advantages of early language learning.

After 1900 the argument continued in a desultory fashion. In an effort to settle the question on medical grounds, the head of the Institute of Neurology of McGill University, Wilder Penfield, tried to place the idea on a scientific basis. His experiments with the human brain pointed to the flexibility of the child. Observation of aphasic patients showed that children recover speech more quickly than adults. Further observation of the patterns of loss and recovery of speech showed that speech, including the use of two languages, was centered in the same part of the brain, thus providing a neurological theory for interference. The logical outcome was a very strict application of the *formule Grammont* (see §13.2.1). Unlike many educational theorists, Penfield had sufficient faith in his own theories to experiment on his own children. He sent them to nursery schools in which only a foreign language was spoken. In this way they learned English, French, and German with a negligible amount of interference.

Penfield's article produced a scandalized reaction from Michael West, who pointed out the greater capabilities of the adult mind. He also questioned the validity of Penfield's assumptions, claiming that the miraculous learning power of children was largely conditioned, in his experience, by ideal environmental conditions, and that even then the speed of learning was quite slow.[1150] Opposition to the Penfield hypothesis was also implicit in the work of the Belgian educationist, Franz Closset:

> Foreign language study rests on analysis, synthesis, and comparison, three procedures which demand a maturity which we just begin to glimpse in children of twelve and thirteen. It is only from this age that the child shows the intellectual capacities which the serious study of a foreign language requires.
>
> 1963 (Closset) 237: 73

This is, in sum, the position of the Swiss psychologist, Piaget, who sees early bilingualism as harmful to a child. As the learning of language accompanies concept formation, he holds that the introduction of two methods of conceptualization is harmful and confusing. Experiments in bilingual children carried out during the 1920's and 1930's confirmed this hypothesis, as far as the development of intelligence was concerned. Doubt has been cast on the validity of these experiments, especially by Lambert, whose own experiments, controlled for sociological factors, give an opposite result and led him to question the experimental validity of the earlier studies.

14.2.2 Intelligence and Language-Learning Ability

Among the many traditional ideas that came under attack during the twentieth century was the equation of intelligence and language-learning ability. Henry Sweet was convinced that there was no necessary link between intellectual capacity and ability to learn a language. As proof he quoted the appalling command many of his scholarly colleagues had of foreign languages.[1054:79] Though this early heretical opinion passed without notice, twentieth century scholars seized on the supposition of a necessary link and found that indeed there was no cutoff point in the IQ scale below which a pupil was incapable of learning a language.[242:451] These experiments of the twenties were repeated by those interested in preparing courses for special purposes, and the earlier conclusions were confirmed. Some even went further, claiming that linguistic ability was a function of immaturity.[567:6] This lent support to the findings of Penfield and confirmed opinions on early language learning held since classical times.

14.2.3 Student Characteristics and Second-Language Teaching

Though language teaching is a personal affair, methodology has often been founded on the peculiarities of the subject, those of the pupil being left to chance. However, it has long been known that methods of handling a student vary according to his age, previous experience, and psychological make-up.

Following the Erasmian dictum that imitation was the appropriate way for children to learn, Hoole recommended activity methods:

> . . . it is very hard to teach a childe in doing of a thing to heed, much less to judge what he doth till he feel some use of reason, in the meantime, he will profit more by continual practice and being kept still (as he loves to be) doing, than by knowing why and being called upon to consider the causes wherefore he doth this or that.
>
> 1660 (Hoole) 551: II: 10

This attitude was also that of Comenius. Port-Royal had an almost contradictory viewpoint. In their view, as children were not really capable of constructive reasoning, they demanded that they proceed from rules parrot-fashion, in contradistinction to adults, who could proceed by analogy.[47:xii]

The question of relating method to age and maturity received little further attention until George Ticknor, professor of modern languages at Harvard, delivered his *Lecture on the Best Methods of Teaching the Living Languages* in 1832. As a general principle, he laid down that spoken and active methods were preferable, that one should start in early childhood, and that grammar was not to be introduced until the age of thirteen at the earliest. (In many twentieth-century circles this was still regarded as a progressive doctrine.) Failing this state of things, Ticknor recommended an oral translation method, with a little grammar for those who start in their teens. In spite of the current fashion, he did not consider a philosophical approach to grammar allowable, but recommended that any necessary explanations should be short and plentifully exemplified. For those unfortunates who start later he considered that a modified Grammar-Translation Method was suitable. He does not recommend an oral approach for them, as their imitative faculties will have atrophied with age.

The Natural Methodists did not consider that age affected the kind of learning a pupil was capable of; it was taken for granted that all people learned in the same way, no matter what their age or educational standard was. This unspoken assumption was one that the Direct Methodists attacked vehemently. In the words of Henry Sweet, "the fundamental objection, then, to the Natural Method is that it puts the adult into the position of an infant, which he is no longer capable of utilising, and at the same time, does not allow him to make use of his own special advantages."[1054:75] Many exponents of the Direct Method were not afraid to explain a point of grammar when they considered it helpful or necessary.[685:97] There was always the possibility that the pupil in need of an explanation would fabricate one for himself, usually with doubtful results owing to his lack of information.

In an attempt to put this pragmatic observation on a scientific foundation, psychologists divided pupils into four age groups, each with different learning characteristics. From birth to about eight was termed the age of assimilation; eight to thirteen, the age of analysis; thirteen to sixteen, the age of logical thought; sixteen to nineteen, the age of objective thought.[614:61-64] In his discussion of these divisions, Kappert saw no reason why "natural" methods of teaching should not be reinforced by analytical methods in all age groups except the first. Flagstad had already denied that a child could benefit from the Natual Method after the age of seven.[910:192]

According to the testimony of Richards, as late as 1943 "there remains one widespread misconception, with roots deep in human stupidity . . . : the half-conscious identification of the language learner with the young child."[952:88] As confirmation it is easy to cite courses that demanded mindless imitation and research into language learning that was not controlled by age or education factors. But psychologists tended to handle this problem with kid gloves, for lack of firm research on the way adults learn a new language.

Harold Palmer had already resumed many of the above ideas and had called attention to other aspects of the problem. While denying it was a proven fact that language-learning ability necessarily varied according to nationality, he admitted that this factor was important, as environment would force certain stereotypes of themselves on the students. In determining how to handle a student, teachers should also take temperament into account.[836:50] Likewise, a student who already knows the foreign language is not to be handled as a tyro: he has concepts set by previous experience of his role as a learner, and because of his background, he will react differently to the material presented to him.

To explain failures of good pupils with the Direct Method, Hovelaque postulated that there were two types of pupil: those who learn primarily through their eyes (visuals), and those who learn through their ears (audials). This distinction was largely ignored, being swallowed up by the doctrinaire trends of later methodology. It is tempting to surmise that control over language teaching, as well as passing between the logician and the linguist, has also been dominated by audials and visuals in turn.

14.2.4 Motivation

Effective teaching rests on inducing the pupils to work harder than the teacher. There are two directions in which a teacher may work to achieve this: the negative and the positive.

Testimony to the strength and accuracy of the teacher's right arm can be found from Plautus to Rudyard Kipling. The normal attitude was a moral one: "He who spares the rod has no concern for the welfare of the child," as Arnulf remarked.[52:101] Protests against the indiscriminate use of the cane are found in Quintillian and reach a chorus during the Renaissance. In spite of the general knowledge that motivation of this sort often turned the pupil against his subject, the teacher in the field was not lightly parted from this aid to establishing order in the classroom.

The Jesuits tried to avoid ill effects by entrusting all punishment to a layman on the administrative staff of the school. At the end of the nineteenth century, Bainvel put forward the idea that though it was important to use the foreign language as a vehicle of instruction, punishments should be given in the mother tongue to avoid unpleasant associations with the language taught.[935:80] By the middle of the twentieth century, punishment was slowly disappearing from the schools, being replaced by various expedients: with better trained teachers, the necessity for it likewise diminished.

As a key concept in teaching theory, motivation is a twentieth-century term. In the precise domain of language learning it was examined during the 1950's by Lambert, who distinguished two types: instrumental and integrative. The first type, the weaker when judged on long-term results, rests on factors outside the language: course prerequisites, employment opportunities, etc.; the second, on an interest in the language itself and in the community which speaks it. As the second type of motivation affects the learner's behavior, rather than his intellect, all things being equal, it makes for more effective initial learning and for longer retention. Throughout the history of language teaching little is said about the first: the "usefulness" of languages was taken, it seems, for granted. But the second type has had a long history. Just what makes up effective motivation is hard to pinpoint. It is convenient to rest our account of it on attitudes to the language itself and relationships with the teacher.

St. Augustine was well aware of what was later to be called integrative motivation: "It is clear enough that free curiosity has a more positive effect on learning than necessity and fear."[62:I:14] Quintillian, less interested in the general principle, laid down a caution: "The teacher must take special pains to make sure that the pupil does not come to dislike subjects he will in time come to appreciate. For if once he hates them, this will remain with him into adulthood."[923:I.i.20] In his letter to Laeta St. Jerome repeats this counsel almost verbatim, and he, in his turn, is plagiarized by Abelard.[3:325] The idea was taken up by the humanists: Sadoleto emphasized the importance of home attitudes in transmitting to the child a cast of mind that would allow him to enjoy learning at school;[988:103] Vida added that the teacher was important in maintaining motivation by intelligent handling of both child and subject. Cardinal Wolsey, himself an ex-teacher, advised teachers to give their classroom exercises point in such a way that it was meaningful to the child;[797:15] the way in which this was done is quite obvious from the racy flavor of the sixteenth-century *vulgaria.*

All those points recurred in the thinking of Comenius. In addition, he was one of the first to consider the idea of language-learning readiness, though he did not consider how this was to be measured, merely relying on the pupil's expressed wish to learn. Both intellectual and emotional factors came under his consideration; he is insistent that it is the responsibility of the teacher both to create and preserve the pupil's eagerness to learn. In this all the resources of his personality and skill are to be exerted. Except for a few isolated experiments like the *Anthropinum* these ideas were forgotten during the next two centuries. Lemare gives a very good indication of the mood of the times: "We have substituted for the infallible guide of need our own ideas and pet theories in the study and teaching of languages, and our tedious way has been sown with thorns."[655:xiv]

More concern with the pupil's motivation needs was shown by the exponents of the Natural and Direct Methods, as otherwise the teacher could not survive in the classroom, because the methodology was not designed to keep the children quiet. Viëtor attacked the old methodology on the grounds that children were not interested in rules. And much of the literature on the Direct Method that was written in the first years of the twentieth century was concerned with the ways of awakening the child's interest and keeping it.

The Herbartian school transmitted to the Direct Method the principle that motivation or "willing interest" should rise out of the subject itself,[410:365] thus repeating the idea St. Augustine had put forward sixteen hundred years before. For the psychologists who worked in language teaching, the key factor was the importance of having the pupil work things out for himself and the sense of achievement and discovery which followed.[410:353] Twentieth-century theorists developed the matter further. To truly motivate the student the method should generate its own interest.[141:93] This came from various sources: the pupil had to be made to feel that the language he was learning was an instrument flexible enough to satisfy his needs;[141:93] and, as well, the student was to find intellectual satisfaction both in the challenge offered him and in the means he was given to meet it.[190:4] The word "motivation" became common property in the work of psychologists. The movement away from direct compulsion in the classroom underlined the necessity for willing co-operation from the pupil, as noncompliance with the teacher's directions became harder to camouflage, and the influence of one obstinate pupil had more effect on the rest of the class.

Work done by the American linguist, Nida, with missionary candidates who inexplicably failed to reach a good linguistic standard, uncovered the role of subconscious attitudes in language learning. With many such cases, two important factors recurred: many who were perfectionists in their own language were inhibited in language learning by the fear of making mistakes, which would, apparently, bring rejection real or imagined, by the community in which they were working. The intensely nationalistic and chauvinistic character of American society also had its effect:

> What apparently happened in Mr. D . . . .'s case was that a resentment against the foreignness of his (immigrant) parents (of which the foreign language served as a trigger symbol) served to produce an emotional resistance against the learning of any foreign language.
>
> 1957 (Nida) 799: 9

Adulation of a great teacher is common enough to draw attention to this means of creating motivation. But while scholars praised the effect their masters had had on them, few reflected on the damage a bad teacher could cause. One who did think of it was Comenius, who was inclined to blame the shortcomings of the pupil on bungling by the teacher.[256:360] Erasmus saw that respect and liking for a good teacher is often transmuted into high performance in school.[377:503E] Just how a teacher was to gain this respect was never really gone into: it seemed to be accepted that a man either had the peculiar brand of warm humanity, scholarship, and teaching skill that drew his pupil's praise or he did not. Beyond generalities on teachers' enthusiasm for both subject and pupils little could be said.[242:207] One application of this principle occurred in an experiment at Loyola University, Chicago. Languages were taught to small groups by techniques akin to those used in psychological counseling. The fundamental drive to learn was supplied by the development of a warm and almost dependent relationship between the pupils and their teacher.[280]

Before the perceptive articles of Gerald Fleming on humor in the classroom, few counted on the teacher's sense of humor as a factor in pupil motivation. Scholarly humor has a sardonic quality that is aptly pilloried in Rudyard Kipling's Mr. King of *Stalky & Co.,* and this has destroyed more pupils than the teaching profession has ever deserved to have. However, much of the teaching effectiveness of a John Brinsley or an Erasmus rested on deft observation of their pupils and a perceptive pointing of fun at them. This quality was shared by the eleventh-century abbess, Hroswitha, in her playlets, and by Michael West. One of the climaxes of this sort of gentle humor is the incongruous translation of A. A. Milne's *Winnie the Pooh* into Latin by Alexander Lenard. The rolling language, fit for the heroes of Livy, contrasts oddly with the fairy-tale content, so that the book has had some success as a Latin text. But many teachers have taught successfully with a more savage humor, directed at targets outside the classroom which pupils enjoy attacking too. Thus the Erasmian colloquies became social satires, and were promptly placed on the *Index librorum prohibitorum* by a sensitive ecclesiastical bureaucracy; and many of Brinsley's colloquies were directed at unpopular parts of school life, like the *asini* (see §12.2.1). The more solemn post-Comenius classroom did not encourage such attitudes, and satire never really was reinstated as a teaching tool. But the role of humor in showing that the teacher too is a human being has never really been forgotten.

We have seen how psychology has gradually crystallized from the *psychologia* of the ancient and medieval philosophers, and some effects of its principles on language teaching. We shall now turn to the other source of ideas, linguistics.

15

LINGUISTICS AND LANGUAGE TEACHING

It is clear that grammar is governed by three factors: nature, authority, and custom.

A.D. 825 (Erchambertus Frisingensis) in 711: 3

Since the Stoics, linguistics and second language teaching have been so closely associated that grammarians and linguists have habitually arrogated to themselves the role of teacher, psychologist, educational theorist and arbiter of manners. Unaware of the limitations of their science, linguists have controlled many of the crucial developments in language teaching. The first schemes for teaching Greek as a foreign language were developed by grammarians of classical Greece; Renaissance linguists killed medieval linguistic traditions in Latin teaching by ridicule of the accepted standards; grammarian-philosophers brought about the formal reorientation of language teaching after the Renaissance; and linguists concerned primarily with analysis of unrecorded dialects developed the structural methods of teaching common in the first half of the twentieth century.

This confusion has led some linguists to assume roles for which they are neither suited nor trained. By right, the linguistic contribution is: an analysis and a coherent theory of language, which can facilitate a teacher's understanding of his subject, and, therefore, his imparting of it.[507:26]

15.1 THEORIES OF LANGUAGE

The nature of language itself has been an absorbing preoccupation with linguists and grammarians, and the opinions that have received a hearing during various periods have shaped the classroom approach. Debates on this matter have polarized around four questions: whether language was due to nature or convention; whether it was to be equated with the observable realities of speech; whether the essential core of language was its role in human communication; and whether it was essentially an assembly of structures or an assembly of units.

15.1.1 Nature or Convention

For the classical grammarians, the first question was the only one worth debating. Judging from the surviving literature, the naturalists had the upper hand. Lucretius (*fl.* 60 B.C.) expressed the dominant opinion when he wrote in the *De rerum natura:* "Nature constrained us to produce various sounds with our tongues, and necessity shaped the names of things" (v. 1028-9). Grammarians of the end of the Empire took matters further, seeing grammatical categories like gender and tense as necessarily linked to a quality in the thing represented; likewise, mood was said to be an expression or a tendency or attitude of mind, as the sentence was being formed.[915:VIII.xii;63]

During the thirteenth century, philosophers tried to hold a middle ground, claiming that language itself was a natural quality, but that it was molded by convention. This view was rejected by the philosophers immediately following, who returned to the narrowly naturalistic view of language. Thus it was taken that language could conform to only one pattern, that familiar to them in Latin and Greek to which vernacular languages were made to conform. Our previous discussion of etymology has already underlined the attitude that the original meaning of a word was taken as the only authentic one and that later developments were taken as aberrations. Renaissance thought, prompted by scholarly attention to languages other than Latin, inclined to a conventionalist viewpoint, a tendency taken to extremes by Rousseau two hundred years later. However, in the meantime, the naturalist idea returned, giving rise to the theories of general grammar. Rousseau's ideas took time to filter into the modern-language classroom. As late as 1797 Meidinger could claim that grammatical gender was a reflection of sex differences.[733:9] The typical eighteenth-century scholar was still inclined to regard language as a natural faculty governed by rules rooted in natural modes of thought.

The linguistic research of the nineteenth century gave grounds for challenging this opinion. Saussure's work culminated this tendency. He took language as conventional, coining the term *l'arbitraire du signe* to express the conventional nature of the link between sign and reality.[317:100] This view accorded very well with the new attention to cultural facts in language emerging through the new Direct Method. It also allowed linguists to investigate new ways of analyzing language and put the traditional Latinate view of grammar in perspective. The historical orientation to nineteenth-century linguistics had cast considerable doubt on the theory that words deviate from an original meaning that is the only correct one. Etymological approaches to vocabulary teaching almost disappeared for a while under the realization that words and things had no necessary link and that one could evolve independently of the other. For similar reasons the logical approach of general grammar, which had lasted well into the nineteenth century, disappeared with the realization that logic tends to vary with language and cultural climate.

15.1.2 "Mentalism" and "Antimentalism"

This controversy, a purely modern one, deals with two subjects: whether language is merely the observable realities of sound and writing, or whether the mental operations behind phonation are fit material for linguistics. The quarrel is thus twofold: over the nature of language and over the boundaries of the science of linguistics.

Mentalist linguistics takes its rise from Saussure's famous dichotomy of *langue* and *parole.* The first is the possession of the whole linguistic community; the second is the use each person makes of it. This concept became the property of the Geneva school, which postulated that there was no support for linguistic facts, observable and observed, unless a basic system common to the whole community existed. Gustave Guillaume refined the dichotomy, introducing the idea of "system of systems" that had already been elaborated by the Prague school and extended the bounds of *langue* to include every act of mental representation that resulted in speech. He also abandoned the term *parole* for *discours,* arguing that this was a more exact term.

This idea had little direct effect on language teaching, but it did harmonize easily with the Direct Method's preoccupation with culture in language teaching. When the Direct Method began drawing on Gestalt psychology, this idea of *langue,* which, as we have seen, existed in Humboldt as the *innere Sprachform,* was part of the theoretical stock of the method. But Saussure's enunciation of his theories really came too late to have any real effect, and the idea of language systems was transmitted to teachers in psychological terms.

During the 1950's and 1960's the dichotomy returned in a more formal dress in the work of Chomsky. In his analysis, language was made up of "deep structures" and "surface structures." Deep structures were a basic series of shapes from which all surface structures could be derived by using certain rules. His theories made language into a series of mathematically induced relationships between words and structures. Again the effect of his theories on language teaching was not direct. But with the rising importance of the computer in linguistic analysis the Chomsky approach smoothed out problems in gradation and the selection of basic structures to be taught.

The antimentalists preferred to leave the no-man's land of conceptualization of language to the psychologists, claiming that language was merely what could be observed. They regarded languages either as arrangements of discrete units, or else as a series of units that are slightly changed to make them fit together. The units and the rules governing their use were together known as the "code." It was this code that was embodied in the drills so popular among language teachers of the twentieth century.

The attention given to the phenomenon of bilingualism had its effect on language teaching. The traditional opinion was that mixed languages were unthinkable, as W. D. Whitney, the noted American Sanskritist, put it. And the question of whether mixed codes were possible was still being debated sixty years later. It was, indeed, one of the subjects which caused the hottest debate at the Moncton Seminar held in June, 1967. That there may be a connection between the data yielded by the study of bilingualism and teaching a second language was obvious to linguists like Braunshausen, but firmly applicable theories of what happened to languages in close contact were not developed until the work of Einar Haugen on Norwegian in America and the more general work of Uriel Weinreich were published.

The direct effect of this work and of the refinement of the new concept of bilingual interference was minimal, but it helped to give point to the interest in contrastive linguistics that language teachers had manifested since the 1930's.

15.1.3 Language and Communication

It has always been normal to consider language as merely a means of communication. Vivès, for instance, remarks that language is an instrument of human society,[1122:298] a position later taken up by Rousseau. A common twentieth-century view is:

> From the social function of language which is its essential condition, as well as from the structural form of the language itself, it is obvious that a language is, first of all, a means of communication among people and that the spoken language with all its necessary elements—sound, intonation, pause, rhythm, intensity and time—is the structural basis of language.
>
> 1964 (Guberina) 490: 6

As teaching is a process of communication, and one can communicate only what is visible, it is not surprising that it is this view which has contributed most to language teaching. The twentieth-century oral approach, like those of the Renaissance and classical periods, aimed at training in communication; and cultural training and other side issues were subordinated to that end. Another important effect was the decreasing importance of classical languages, whose communicative utility was slight.

But though communication is undoubtedly a most important function of language, the research of several modern linguists called this ruling opinion into question. The work of Christine Mohrman on sacral and poetical languages emphasizes the importance of language as expression rather than communication. In the schools of Saussure and Guillaume, the communicative functions of language were considered an outgrowth of a means of self-expression shared by a linguistic community. Such a view of language postulates mental processes which produce language but which do not lead to communication. The antimentalists see the process from the other end: monologued uses of languages are a type of communication with self, an aberrant practice merely worthy of a facetious comment.

15.1.4 Structure and Meaning

The twentieth century prides itself on the discovery of the idea of structure: "A language is primarily a system of vocal symbols and of devices for indicating grammatical structure: it is only secondarily a collection of words."*44:72 What the structural theories meant to language teaching was more specifically detailed by Fries:

> This 'structuralism' of American linguistics has resulted in a changed view of the nature of human language—a changed view of what constitutes the basic functioning units of a language. Consequently it has led to a new understanding of the precise problems involved in learning and teaching a foreign language.
>
> 1957 (Fries) 431: 265

The idea of structure gave theoretical support to the drill methods popular during and after the Second World War. Indeed these drill methods, as we have seen in Chapter 4, were derived from theories by the Bloomfield school of linguistics.

It was Saussure who had forced the concept of structure on the world of linguistics. From this came the idea of language systems, a concept found in Saussure but developed by Prague and Guillaume. But the idea of structure had been thought of long before this. During the eighteenth century, for instance, Pluche felt it necessary to warn scholars that language was concerned not only with words, but also with "structural entities" (see Lemare).[655:115]

Rival modern schools were not inclined to go so far as the followers of Bloomfield in their reverence for structure. They tried to strike a compromise between what seemed to be two extremes: the modern emphasis on structure and the traditional emphasis on meaning. The old view, which was expressed in the theories of *modus significandi* of the late Middle Ages, in general grammar, and in the traditional attitude that language learning was merely the acquisition of a new series of meaningful units, had survived for several thousand years without any real opposition. Thus Cordier could write that the principal task of a person learning Latin was "to try to understand not only words but especially their meanings."[273:i] And a close examination of ancient grammars shows that the principle concern was over the correct way of using words. Structure was derived from word usage, not treated as a separate entity worthy of attention.

15.2 ANALYSES OF LANGUAGE

Four levels of analysis are often distinguished. The phonological level deals with sounds; the grammatical with system and structure; the lexical with words; and the semantic with shades of meaning. In this section we group these levels into analyses of sounds, sentences, and words. Though the history of all four levels of analysis is equally long, it is grammatical analysis that has been most prominent. Lexical and semantic analyses were not distinguished from prescriptions on spelling and usage, and unless one excepts the Hindu linguists of the sixth century B.C., phonological analysis was the least developed of the four until the late nineteenth century.

15.2.1 Analysis of Sounds

There are two interconnected sciences of analysis which deal with speech sounds: phonetics and phonology. Phonetics studies sounds as physical entities, while phonology takes them as units in the transmission of meaning. In practice, one science does not make sense without the other, and it is only in this century that they have been separated. For phonology even to exist, some sort of phonetic consciousness is necessary; while phonetics, unless guided by phonological considerations, becomes a physical science rather than a branch of linguistics.

15.2.1.1 Phonetics. One is inclined to forget that both sciences have existed in the West for about 3,000 years and in the East, notably India, for about 4,000. The Greeks treated phonetics as a part of grammar, a custom the Romans followed slavishly. Between them, they left to the Middle Ages a fourfold classification of the sound (*vox*) that shows how inextricably mixed phonetics and phonology were:

> There are four different kinds of vocal sound: articulate, inarticulate, literate, and illiterate. Articulate sounds are those linked together to convey a meaning, as, "My song is of arms and the man–." Inarticulate sounds convey no meaning, as a creaking or roaring sound. Literate sounds can be written, illiterate can not.
>
> A.D. 775 (Alcuin) 23: 854D

This passage also shows the degree to which a speech sound had become identified with the letter which represented it–indeed the word *sonus* had long been replaced by *littera* in the language of the grammarians.

Vowels and consonants were distinguished by phonological criteria—their ability to appear as the center of the syllable in Latin and Greek: "Vowels can be produced by themselves and form a syllable; consonants can not be pronounced alone, nor do they form syllables."[23:855B] What are now termed consonants were divided according to voicing. The four liquid consonants, l/m/n/r, were put into a class of their own. This classification was, however, reinforced by some articulatory criteria: it was known that vowels were produced by uninterrupted passage of air through the vocal organs, and that in the production of consonants, some constriction or blockage of the vocal passages was necessary. The consonants, however, were classified on the basis of what could be observed by watching the speaker. For certain sounds, notably the labial and dental consonants, this was as accurate as any modern analysis. Matters rested here until the Renaissance. As yet, no phonetic alphabet was envisaged, as the Roman alphabet in use still represented fairly well the sounds of European languages.

Renaissance scholars were forced to refine their analytical techniques when they dealt with modern languages, especially with the vowels. The classical and medieval analyses of the consonants were sufficiently vague to cover the possibilities offered by the cultural languages of the time, but the vowels had altered so much that the classical sounds were not even numerous enough to cover the field. Part of the difficulty rose from identifying the units to be described with the letters which symbolized them. Louis Meigret, it seems, was the first to distinguish between open and closed varieties of vowels, as between [e] and [ɛ]. He also saw that length had little to do with vowel quality. This aspect of phonetics was later to be developed during the seventeenth century.

The ancient division of the consonants into *mutae* and *liquidae* was further refined by Port-Royal's fourfold classification:

Muettes	Liquides	Sifflantes	Aspiration
BPFV	LR	S	H
CQGI	MN	XZ	
DT			

The vowels, following Meigret and de Bèze, were divided into open and closed. But Port-Royal confined its attention to the classical languages. By the end of the century, the *consonnes muettes* of Port-Royal had been divided into voiced and unvoiced by de Dangeau. The table from Cooper's *Grammatica linguae anglicanae* (Figure 26) shows a transitional stage between this classification and that of the IPA. It is especially notable that the position of the tongue tip is described and some idea of areas of articulation is obvious. The idea of variation in aperture is likewise in evidence. However it was difficult to shake oneself free from the influence of spelling: GH [dʒ] and CH [tʃ] are not guttural sounds in spite of the fact that /k/ and /g/ can be.

Phonetic experimentation was a common recreation of the learned during the eighteenth century. Stoddart describes a primitive speech synthesizer which consisted of a vibrating cord whose frequencies were altered to recognizable vowel sounds by a resonator which changed volume and shape. From his description it seems that this was a balloon of some sort attached directly to the string. But this remained a scientific toy.

Owing to the Renaissance development of the natural sciences, specialists in anatomy became interested in the physiological aspects of speech. By the mid-eighteenth century, the shape, biological functions, and speech functions of the organs of the mouth, nose, and throat were well known, at least to medical men. The functions of the brain were still conceived in metaphysical terms, so that the neurological aspects of speech were still not apparent. Neither was there any connection made between hearing and speech.

Though the phonetic research of the nineteenth century was given direction by the discovery of the work of Panini and the other Sanskrit grammarians, the most significant work was done by A. M. Bell, whose *Visible Speech* appeared in 1874. Bell was especially interested in the problems of teaching the deaf; and by very careful observation, he refined the traditional analysis of speech sounds into a rigorous classification in which the position and movements of every part of the mouth are minutely detailed. With the founding of the International Phonetic Association (IPA) by Paul Passy in 1886,

Locetur ad pag. 37. C. Collocantur literae secundum earum naturam. 1. Cum respectu organorum, quibus formantur. 2. Sonorum: Semivocalium, Aspiratarum, Semimutarum, Mutarum. 3. Variorum graduum appertionis vel clausurae instrumentorum et soni.

	sive Vocales			*sive Consonantes quae formantur* à labiis. *superioribus inferioribus: vel ambobus.*			à linguae *extremitate motâ vel fixâ.*						à linguae *medio*	in Gutture *à linguae radice* inferiori palato fixâ		
	Linguales.	Labiales.	Gutturales	extremitate amborum labiorum	labia inferi: dentibus superi:	labis occlusis.	dentibus inferioribus.	magis crassa per dentes occlusos.	superioribus dentibus.	Gingivis, per nares efflata.	anteriori palato	tremulâ ad medium Palatum	ad medium palatum.	per os efflata.	per nares efflata.	
apertae	a	o	*a*	W	V	M	Z	Zh	Dh	N	L	R	Y	Gh	Ng	*Semivocales.*
intermediae	*a*			Hw	F	Hm	S	Sh	Th	Hn	Hl	Hr	Hy	Ch	Hng	*Aspiratae.*
intermediae	e					B			D					G		*Semimutae.*
clausae	ee	oo	u			P			T					C		*Mutae.*

u radix est vocalium

Tres mutae sunt consonarum radices à quibus variè formantur caeterae in variis sedibus, secundum diversos formandi modos.

Figure 26. Phonetic Table from Cooper, *Grammatica linguae anglicanae.*[601:27]

Bell's ideas were given extended recognition and were widely promulgated because of the educational utility of phonetics, as the new science was called. For perhaps the first time, *littera* and *sonus* were differentiated.

The association has been identified with the more glamorous task of preparing a phonetic alphabet, thus obscuring the more fundamental work of its members. The early members of the association, notably Daniel Jones and Paul Passy, took an interest in instrumental aids to analysis. From his early work with X-ray photography, Jones established the standard vowel trapezium and confirmed Bell's refinement of the traditional method of classifying consonants. Rousselot, though not a member of the association, carried out similar work, using the kymograph, which gave a rough picture of the vibrations emanating from various parts of the vocal apparatus, distinguishing very clearly the voiced from the unvoiced, and the aspirated from the unaspirated.

Palatography was developed to show precisely where the areas of contact between tongue and palate were in the production of speech sounds. The tongue was painted and the trace it left on the roof of the mouth was examined. At first, a thin artificial palate was moulded to the roof of the mouth and removed for examination. During the early 1960's a method of doing the experiment by photography without the use of foreign bodies in the mouth was developed.

After the Second World War electronic spectographs were used in an attempt to analyze exactly the wave forms of speech sounds. This type of analysis was taken up by communications engineers to help in the design of telephones, radios, and transmission lines. It became relevant to teaching with the development of the language laboratory, in which phonetics, as well as grammar and vocabulary, was to be taught. Research carried out at Laval University, Quebec, cast some doubt on the accuracy of the trapezium in use. By X-ray photography, it was shown that the most stable conformation of the vocal organs took place in the pharynx, the standard articulations in the mouth varying according to the other sounds associated with the phoneme in question.

The effect of this research can be gauged from the third chapter of this book. Until the beginning of the Direct Method, pronunciation had been taught according to instinct. But in 1884 Trautmann introduced the findings of the new science of phonetics into the classroom, thus touching off a controversy that was never settled, even within the ranks of the Direct Methodists. But it was agreed that even if the teacher did not teach phonetics along with pronunciation, he should be guided by its findings.

15.2.1.2 Phonology. The science of phonology is equally ancient: the Sanskrit linguists of the millenia before Christ were phonologists, as were the early grammarians who gave us our modern alphabets. The passage quoted from Alcuin earlier in this chapter (page 334) shows that one can equate the medieval term "*littera*" with the modern "phoneme."[23:854D] But one sees the phonological preoccupations of the ancients most clearly in the treatment of features like tone and length. The famous Greek accents that have plagued beginners for centuries were devised during the second century B.C.

by Aristophanes of Byzantium to guide foreigners through the tone system of Greek. Likewise, those who have to read or write classical Latin or Greek verse will be aware of the phonological importance of length and accent. The modern confusion over the relationship of these two features is due to their gradual merging in the classical languages, and the consequent misunderstanding of classical grammarians by later scholars.

The phoneticians of the late nineteenth century used phonological criteria to separate significant sounds one from another and to group variants of phonemes. Such an approach was necessary to determine what to teach and how to teach it. Though a Polish linguist contemporary with the early Direct Methodists, Badouin de Courtenay, formulated the concept of the phoneme as a distinctive speech sound, it was left to the school of Prague, under Prince Nicholas Troubetzkoy, to develop the idea.

Phoneticians had hitherto concentrated on the reproductive aspect of the phoneme, seeing it as a cluster of slightly differing articulations. Troubetzkoy approached the problem from the receptive angle: in its most extreme form, his theory regarded the phoneme as a mental ideal to which the speaker tried to approximate when he spoke, and to which he related speech sounds he heard from other people. On this, Troubetzkoy based a whole theory of sound interference which rested not merely on the effects of untrained motor muscles, but also on faults in perception of new and strange sounds. He and his school were likewise interested in problems relating to the catenation of sounds, the realization slowly dawning that nonphonetic features like length and sequence of sounds could make the difference between good reception, faulty interpretation, and mystification.

The effect on language teaching was profound, especially as Paul Passy had already undertaken a comparative analysis of the phonetic resources of the standard languages. Such a task would have been impossible on phonetic grounds alone. In America the phonological doctrine took very deep roots, phonetic and phonemic analyses being regarded as necessary preliminaries to making language courses. The IPA absorbed the phonological approach by making explicit in later editions of the *Principles* what was already implicit.

15.2.1.3 Phonetic Symbolization. The first attempts at phonetic writing were the alphabets, but as the spoken and written languages evolved at different rates, it was thought, when modern languages entered the schools, that auxiliary alphabets or spelling reform would ease the path of the learners. The question was complicated by two factors. The first was the phonetic evolution of language that had outstripped that of spelling. The second was reverence for etymology. In an effort to link the vernacular word with its etymon, etymological letters were freely inserted. Printers had a large hand in this last development, but their influence was confusing. Though their consciences demanded the insertion of these letters (like "b" in "debt") they felt free to omit these letters at will, such flexibility being demanded by the chancy techniques of justifying printed lines. During the Renaissance the proponents of phonetic spelling fell into two groups. The radicals, like Meigret, aimed at replacing the spelling in use with a fully phonetic system; some even went far toward creating a new alphabet. The other group produced systems that could be used as auxiliaries to normal alphabets. Jacques Dubois, for instance, used superscripts over normal letters to indicate the correct pronunciation (see §3.2.2.2). It is from these experiments that the French accents developed. In England Sir Thomas Smith and John Hart produced alphabets rivaling in acuteness that of the IPA, formulated three hundred years later. Of these reformers Hart was the only one who succeeded in shaking himself completely free from etymology and in making provision for combinatory variation.[588:25]

The above alphabets were based mostly on the Roman, and thus were conventional in representation. Two hundred years later A. M. Bell tried to evolve a system in which the symbol shapes suggested articulatory movements. The open shapes were meant to suggest the open mouth, and the obstructions proper to consonants are represented by bars or by distorting the open shape.[*149:10] Nasals were represented by the tilde. The general symbol for a vowel (I) suggests the shape of the vocal cords in contact, while the various modifications of the shape were to show place and type of articulation. "Narrow" and "wide" refer to lip position. While Sweet's revision kept to Bell's symbols, Jones and Passy modified them considerably, while respecting the conventions. They also replaced the terms "wide" and "narrow" by "écarté" and "arrondi."*[149:11]

The most successful, in language-teaching terms, of the modern alphabets was that evolved by the International Phonetic Association. The IPA preferred to use an alphabet based on Roman, as its symbols were evocative enough for a European. As far as possible diacritics were kept for special purposes, e.g., indicating variants special to dialects. Modifications to the alphabet are not undertaken lightly. Before a new symbol is accepted it is discussed in the pages of the *Maître phonêtique,* and a decision of the council of the association is necessary.[576:19]

Various types of transcription are possible. A "broad transcription" corresponds to the modern phonetic transcription, and is recommended for teaching. By the use of diacritics and less flexible symbols, various "narrow" transcriptions are possible for scientific purposes, or even for teaching. Though other alphabets exist, this has received most general acceptance.

15.2.2 Analysis of the Sentence

It is only in this century that linguistics has finally succeeded in separating the normative from the descriptive. The few linguists before our time who treated linguistics as a speculative science were ignored, as the aim of analysis was, in the first place, to prepare teaching materials. The root procedure was analysis of language in use. This developed two almost inseparable branches, grammar proper and rhetoric (in modern terms, stylistics). The principles and techniques developed by this method were often used to analyze other languages. Thus Latin was analyzed according to a Greek framework of grammar, and later other languages were made to conform to this Latin frame. The early interest of philosophers in language caused a third type of analysis to rise, logical analysis.

15.2.2.1 Literature, Rhetoric, and Structural Analysis. Ancient Greece transmitted to Rome a tradition of grammatical scholarship that was based on rhetoric. The philosophers who first thought to analyze language were impelled not by the problems of teaching Greek as a second language, but by the need to develop and pass on the art of rhetoric, which held a key place in Greek society. Thus a normative approach to grammar was inherent in the discipline. It was the Stoic rhetoricians who first taught grammar in Rome. In 160 B.C. while on an embassy from Attalus II of Pergamum, Crates of Mallos broke his leg in a Roman drain and whiled away his convalescence by teaching. The climate had already been prepared: as Rome began to absorb the Greek colonies of the south of Italy and marched into Sicily to contain the menace of Carthage, its soldiers returned with a taste for Greek art and amusements. Among the Greek slaves they brought back was Livius Andronicus, who first adapted Greek genres to Latin and translated Homer into Latin. In abandoning the native Saturnian and Faliscan meters for the classical hexameter, he had to create a climate of taste that would accept his innovations. This he did by founding schools of grammar and rhetoric in Rome.[*16:128]

The Greek approach ruled classical grammar. Rhetoric being an application of both literary taste and logic, grammar, its handmaiden, followed suit. Logic was a necessary tool in codification, but classical grammar was a discipline based on literary analysis. The range of authors was sharply restricted, and every ruling was based on an apposite quotation from a writer whose claim to greatness was uncontested by the pundits.

Levels of style were sharply distinguished according to genre and subject matter. The language of poetry was a thing apart, drawing on colloquialisms and archaisms for its peculiar effect. In both poetry and prose something very like the modern distinction between registers was in force. Three broad levels of style were distinguished: the low for narration of everyday affairs, the intermediate for more important matters, and the sublime for speaking of the great.[218:XXIX.101] During the first century B.C. the literary basis for rhetoric was tied to this congruence between style and subject and to a certain measure of archaism by the Alexandrian school, which had its imitators in Rome during the golden age. The maintenance of sound linguistic customs was essential to public and private morality, an attitude which still survives: "There is a vicious circle which goes from substandard language to slavery," wrote the French-Canadian author, J.-P. Desbiens (better known as *le frère Untel*), referring to *joual,* one of the varieties of French spoken in Canada, and the unfavorable position of those who speak it.

Under the impetus of Alexandrianism, Latin became an incisive and harmonious instrument of controversy and law, and a graceful poetic language. Archaism ran riot in the brilliant experiments of Tacitus, who fused the languages of poetry and prose to achieve a sublime style suitable for history, but a balance was restored during the fourth century. Renaissance opinion to the contrary, literary scholarship was a key factor in rhetoric for the medieval scholar, but the concept of style was shaken by the rise of Christianity and by the new requirements of an apostolate among a cultivated public.

It is notorious that the early Christian forms of Latin were not to the classical taste. As well as being shot through with interference from Hebrew and Hellenistic Greek, by comparison with the aristocratic standard consecrated by the golden and silver ages they were uncouth, as befits a language spoken mainly among the lower class. Yet for the effective spread of the religion, Christian oratory had to be developed to woo the cultivated class. That is the reason why St. Augustine spent much of his definitive tract *De doctrina christiana* discussing the idea of style. The paradox was that according to classical precedent only the sublime style could be used to discuss the divine,[59.4.18] while the consecrated language of the Scriptures was definitely in the low style. He changed the relationships of the three styles so that the low style became the vehicle of narration and the high a vehicle of persuasion. This effectively overturned the classical ideal: style became a tool geared to specific audiences rather than to subject matter.[*6:33-39] As the medieval canon of authors was constantly expanding to take in the Fathers and the medieval theologians, the balance between style and purpose changed too. In not seeing the purpose of medieval rhetoric, classicists of later ages calmly assumed that it did not exist.

To the classical teacher or grammarian, analysis was only the beginning of grammar. It was not merely a speculative or a descriptive science, but a normative which set out the correct way of using language. As rhetoric was an expected sequel to grammar, a start had to be made in the arts of composition. The Greek or Roman schoolboy was introduced to stylistic criticism even before his own style was formed, in the hope that this forced growth would make good style instinctive. Thus Quintillian could write of grammar: "Now this subject . . . is divided into two parts: accurate knowledge of the conventions of speech, and interpretation of the poets."[923:I:iv:2] It seems that knowledge of structure was taken for granted: Cassiodorus amplified Quintillian: "Grammar is the science of interpreting poets and historians, and the codification of the conventions of writing and speech. It is both the origin and the first step in studying the liberal arts."[195:595B] It can easily be seen that there was a large area of overlap between the two disciplines, and fierce jurisdictional quarrels broke out between the various parts of the classical educational system.

The grammatical scholarship of the Roman Empire is refreshingly free from rules for rules' sake. It is no accident that in writings of the time, from the inspired dilettantism of Aulus Gellius to the plodding scholarship of Priscian, we find many snippets of authors now lost. Stylistics and grammar were not separated. The immense range of the discipline given in Isidore's *Etymologiae* goes from the eight parts of speech to the conventions of literary genres. Faults in grammar as such seem to have been of little interest to these authors, it being the basic faults of rhetoric that took up most of these books.[577:I:v.4]

Donatus and Priscian dominated the medieval period. As far as standards went, a certain amount of conflict arose as Christians extended the allowable canon to include the Vulgate and the Fathers (see §7.2.1). There were, of course, objections from the purists. But these were in the minority. One force working against literary scholarship was the medieval attitude to the pagan origins of classical scholarship. For instance, though Alcuin set his grammar and rhetoric in a classical mold, he advised against reading classical literature, regarding it as a danger to faith and morals. Smaragdus, abbot of St. Mihiel, resolved all stylistic conflicts very easily: "I do not follow Donatus, for I hold that the Scriptures have the higher authority."*[162:181] In spite of people like the reverend abbot, medieval remembrance of the dimly remembered glories of classical Latin drove scholars to the classics, Vergil, Juvenal, and Cicero especially, and rhetorical imitation is one of the results of this close acquaintance.

But many preferred to take their grammar secondhand to avoid moral contamination, and for this reason much of the medieval grammar was based on medieval *collectaneae* and on the *libri manuales.* Matters came to a head in the thirteenth century. By this time the break between linguistic and literary studies was complete. What was happening was described by Henri d'Andeli in a pseudo *chanson de geste, La Bataille des sept ars,* in which he parodied the popular epic form and poked fun at the open warfare between the universities of Paris and Orléans over the place of literature: Paris had rejected it while Orléans remained the center of literary study in France. The long-term result was the definitive divorce of grammar and rhetoric.

It was about this time that living languages received the accolade of formal study. As originally with Latin, the impetus was literary. The development of literary competitions by the jongleurs and troubadours demanded a fairly objective standard of grammatical and literary judgement and consequently manuals of French and Provencal were developed for this purpose, and the movement died when Provençal lost its importance as a literary language. (see §§16.1; 17.1)

The classical learning of the Renaissance was based on literature. The discovery of Quintillian weakened reliance on grammar and to a large extent destroyed the logical approach. But literary study was a necessary consequence of an introduction to grammar. Scaliger, for instance, looked to the creation of a science of stylistics to bridge the gap: "There is only one purpose for the existence of a grammarian: to teach correct speech. His discipline falls into two parts: one concerns the parts of speech themselves: the other, the niceties of composition. . . . It is not an art, but a science."[999:3]

Erasmus observed this distinction, borrowing it from Quintillian.

The important distinction here is between *verba* (words) and *res* (things or ideas). For the Renaissance, the importance of Erasmus's book lies in its copious reference to great classical writers like Cicero and Quintillian. In a sense the *De copia* is a continuation of medieval tradition in its reliance on the *Ad Herrenium* as a source. But the most important and significant feature of the book is its wholeness of vision. Grammar is subordinated to style which in turn is subordinated to literature, a definite reversal of St. Augustine's merging of the three classical styles and their use. It is here that stylistics was brought to the attention of the Renaissance world.

Stylistics itself was first developed as a branch of philology. In its traditional form it was an analysis of the composition techniques of great authors and formed a resource for *praelectio* and its descendants. During the twentieth century comparative stylistics was developed as a means of comparing the expressive resources of two literary languages (see §2.3). The ancestry of this approach goes back to the *copiae* of the Renaissance and like the Renaissance approach found its pedagogical expression in translation. But the modern approaches bypassed the classical languages, mainly because the importance of writing them had gone.

15.2.2.2 Linguistic Criteria. As an independent speculative science grammar has little real existence until late in the medieval period. And linguistics as a science was not separated from grammar until the nineteenth century; but the techniques of grammatical and linguistic observation were well established by the Greeks before the Romans entered the field.

The first grammarian who tried to free himself from both philosophy and rhetoric was Dionysius Thrax, who codified the work of the Stoics. He left his mark so solidly on linguistic analysis that the categories he laid down are still in use. Language manuals as diverse as the Port-Royal grammars, Kennedy's *Latin Primer* (1890), and Grévisse's *Le bon usage* (1950) are founded on the plan Thrax used himself. The important legacy of Thrax was the formalization of the classical idea of analogy into rules, the formalization of the eight parts of speech, and the normative orientation of the science based on relationships between structures and their parts.

This was picked up by Varro, who consecrated the idea that an analysis drawn up for one language could be adapted to fit another. Varro's own analysis provided the archetype for practically all grammatical work for the next two thousand years. His techniques were continued by Quintillian and the Late Latin grammarians, including Donatus and Priscian, who dominated grammatical scholarship until the rise of the *grammatica speculativa* during the eleventh century of the Christian era. The literary preoccupations of these grammarians were clear. Cassiodorus (*fl.* A.D. 550) opens his *De grammatica* with the following definition: "Grammar is the grace of elegant speech which comes from acquaintance with famous poets and orators. Its function is to lay the ground for faultless composition in prose and verse."[195:1152]

It was this aspect of grammar that gave it its importance during the Carolingian Renaissance. Not only was it felt that the standards of rhetoric needed raising, but the actual command of basic linguistic structures was defective. To this end Charlemagne in his famous *Encyclica de literis colendis* ordered a complete overhaul of Latin scholarship in his empire. The role grammar was to play in this was well symbolized by the sixth-century author Martianus Capella, whose description was repeated by Theodulphus, a friend and pupil of Alcuin's and, two hundred years later, by John of Salisbury:

> . . . Martianus in the *Marriage of Mercury and Philology* depicted Grammar carrying a scalpel, a cane, and a jar of ointment. Let her cut away the vices of the mouth with her scalpel, and she will trim down the tongues of children who are to go on to philosophy, receiving food and guidance from her. At the same time she will be teaching them not to blurt out grammar mistakes and unfitting turns of phrase. . . .
>
> 1182 (John of Salisbury) 593: 852

The aim was a return to the norms of Ciceronian Latin, but not even the written language conformed in all respects to this rather unrealistic goal. It could not because the texts commented on included the Bible and the Fathers, classical texts being considered dangerous from a religious point of view. Indeed, the Vulgate was commented on from a grammatical standpoint and much of the doctrinal interpretation of the time rested on a grammarian's analysis of the text. We find this flourishing by Bede's time, a hundred years earlier than Charlemagne, and the technique was still in vogue in the twelfth century. Walafrid Strabo's *Glossa ordinaria* is a thorough grammatical exegesis of the Vulgate from the beginning of Genesis until the end of the Apocalypse. But the Carolingian Renaissance was the last flourish of grammar as grammar during the Middle Ages.

During the next three hundred years, the balance swung toward a logical approach to grammar, a tendency reversed at the Renaissance. Subsequent return to a linguistic standard was due to two factors: the coming of age of the vernaculars, and a violent reaction against medieval linguistic scholarship. The growing stature of the vernaculars demanded realistic and acceptable techniques of analysis, so that the frame developed for classical languages was applied.

Vernacular grammars first appeared in the fourteenth century. In French, the Englishman John Barton published the *Donet franceis* at the beginning of the century. In Provençal, the *Donatz proensals* (Faidit) and the *Razos de trobar* (de Bezalu) were the two earliest grammars of the type. They followed Donatus section by section, forcing the Latin analysis on the languages:

> There are six cases: nominative, genitive, dative, accusative, vocative, and ablative. The nominative is shown by *lo:* as in *lo reis est vengutz;* the genitive by *de,* as in *aquetz destrier es del rei;* the dative by *a* as in *mena la destrier al rei;* the accusative by *lo,* as in *eu vei lo rei armat* . . .
>
> 1400? (Uc Faidit) 399: 4

From this beginning, applying Latinate frames to modern languages spread, until by the end of the seventeenth century descriptive-normative grammars of this type were common for all the languages of Europe.

In Latin Donatus and Priscian gave place to the *Doctrinale* of Alexander de Villa Dei and the *Graecismus* of Eberhardus de Béthune, and if one is to believe Henri d'Andeli, not without dissension. However, like all new trends, the new grammar conquered all opposition and rapidly acquired the respect usually accorded theology. This did not escape the notice of the humanists. Numerous satires were written on grammar and its exponents including a murderously funny parody on the Athanasian Creed which appears in the *Epistolae virorum obscurorum.*[877:II:36] This extols the virtues of the *Doctrinale,* which by now was out of date, but was still used by traditionally-minded teachers. Like most medieval parodies, it takes its peculiar force from its original, which, as part of the Divine Office, was known by heart by practically every priest and monk in Europe. The attack was all the more stinging as the creed had been written as a summary of Church belief during one of the early heresies. And Humanism certainly had the air of heresy as it gleefully overturned the bases of medieval scholarship, returning to the pagan sources that scholars regarded as regrettably indispensable but dangerous.

During the Renaissance some attempt was made by people like Ramus to counter this tendency; he tried to get away from the ordinary formalistic subdivisions of the Latin system to an arrangement based on his own observations. More important for the learners of living languages, pundits were laying down standards of usage based on observation of speech and writing. Ramus took part in this, but the most famous names in the field are Malherbe and Vaugelas, who exercised a reign of terror over the literary world. Similar movements in the rest of Europe resulted in the forming of academies to establish standards in all departments of language use. The only two still active are the *Acadêmie française,* founded by Cardinal Richelieu in 1635, and the *Academia Española,* which establishes standards for Spanish.

Though the medieval Latinate grammars were by now forgotten, given the tenets of general grammar, it was inevitable that the traditional Latin frame should be used to analyze modern languages. Though this became orthodox and actually invaded the teaching of the first language, there were some who departed from the principle for their own purposes. At first these rebels were dealing with non-Indo-European languages. Missionaries penetrating into the East found that languages like Chinese did not yield to the traditional Latin analysis.[*67:735] In 1741 an M. Harriet published a French grammar for the Basques in which he analyzed French according to categories he had worked out for Basque. The system is not unlike the twentieth-century structural approach.

Examination of nineteenth-century grammars for languages as diverse as New Zealand Maori and those of the American Indians show that there was an increasing lack of respect for traditional schemes of analysis. True, there were those who forced the whole classical apparatus on these languages, but many tried to adapt the traditional categories to new realities. In Maori, Williams recognized the peculiarities of the Maori verb by rejecting the notion of tense (while keeping the word itself) for that of aspect, which fitted the reality. On the American continent, Howse accepted the categories traditional from Aristotle's time, but on structural grounds assimilated the adjective with the verb,[561:24] on morphological grounds claimed that Cree had only two genders, animate and inanimate,[561:18] and created a whole new terminology of verb tenses. In European languages, however, though there was dissent from people of the stature of William Hazlitt and Girault-Duvivier, there was an ordered progression in the schools from a Latinate analysis of the mother tongue to the classical languages, or to modern languages analyzed in the traditional form.

The tendency towards analyzing all languages according to one traditional frame was due to the logical orientation grammar regained during the seventeenth century. The primary effects of this will be described in the next section. Revolt against this situation began early in the nineteenth century: the naturalists had no use for logical criteria, and at the end of the century Gouin rejected out of hand the logical requirement of symmetry in analysis that had been thrust on language by scholars of the previous two centuries. Parallel with this was more thorough philological analysis: one of its aims was to clean out of the grammars of classical languages the analogical forms that had been created to fill gaps in paradigms that the Greeks and Romans who had spoken these languages had never felt the need to fill. The final blow came from Saussure: "Necessary divorce: grammar is the enemy of logic and logic of grammar."[*108:103]

Preoccupation with non-Indo-European languages and a reorientation toward the spoken language confirmed the unsuitability of traditional methods of attack. Rejecting the word "grammar" with its tainted overtones, linguists adopted the word "structure," and following the approach adopted by the physical sciences, analyzed the language as one would a physical compound. The movement rejected meaning as a criterion for the analysis of structure, a direct reversal of the classical approach to the problem. It is for this reason that drill methods, which do not really require full understanding of what is being said, appealed so much to structural linguists.

The structural approach to language analysis rested on phonology and grammar, taking its cue from the techniques used by Boas and his team to analyze Amerindian languages. In their zeal for reform, the structuralists abandoned the traditional type of analysis altogether and applied structural analysis to all the languages they were dealing with.

15.2.2.3 The Logical Approach. Grammar has never managed to escape from its philosophical origins. In spite of its early acceptance as a linguistic discipline, it has continued to draw quite freely on philosophy for its methods and aims. The most recent manifestation of this tendency is transformational grammar, which its authors trace to the rationalist linguistics of the eighteenth century. But in its methods and aims, like the general grammar of the eighteenth century, it resembles the philosophical grammar of the Middle Ages.

The core preoccupation of transformational theory is the question of competence, i.e., how a normal speaker can generate an indefinite number of sentences from a finite stock of material and be understood. It is postulated that he does this by applying "rules" to the material.[216:51] and it is the goal of generative or transformational grammar to discover these rules. Unlike the structuralist theories many transformationalists seek to supplant, transformational theory distinguishes between the rules of language and the rules by which it is analyzed, thus laying its proponents open to the comment that they theorize about grammar and not about language. One facet of this preoccupation with rules of analysis is the rejection of personal intuition as a guide in finding the norms which govern linguistic behavior.

In contrast to structural linguistics, which concentrated on the peculiarities of given languages, transformational grammar looks to the discovery of rules which are applicable to all languages. Like other mentalist or near-mentalist theories, transformational grammar is concerned with uncovering the underlying system of language, but unlike them, it conceives the system in mathematical terms. Indeed, transformationalism found such a congenial tool in the computer that it was wrongly identified with mathematical linguistics. The theory of structural formation by generation instead of by simple juxtaposition lent itself very easily to mathematical expression and opened the way to drawing on philosophical concepts like symbolic logic, and to an approach to linguistic analysis through postulates that are treated as working hypotheses until they are disproved.

The previous flourish of logical grammar lasted for approximately two hundred years, from the early seventeenth century to the last editions of the Bescherelle French grammar in the 1860's, the high point being the mid-eighteenth century. Acceptance of grammar as a department of logic had been justified by Condillac on the grounds that as language depends on thought and thought on logic, so grammar depends on logic.[261:35]

It follows, then, that the principles which govern the grammar of all languages are the same. This basic tenet of general grammar was modified by postulating that the peculiarities of each language were different modifications of the general principles.[1041:21] From this developed the dichotomy of the art and science of grammar: all treatments of general grammar were part of the science; facts dealing with the individual languages were the art.[1041:22] As general grammar never concerned itself with languages outside the Indo-European complex, no obstinate contradictions became apparent. Any difficulties were explained away by appeals to etymology.

Most of the development work in general grammar was done by the scholars of Port-Royal. They took over the phrase from Alsted, who invented the concept in 1606.[33:278] In his later years Comenius had taken up the idea, seeing Latin teaching as basic in the formation of the intellect. The polyglot textbooks of the Comenius method confirmed the tendency, and Comenius changed his approach to a doctrinaire formalism in his old age.

Arnauld and Lancelot, the authors of the Port-Royal grammars, dealt with most of the important languages of Europe, but uncovered nothing that would disturb their idea that the languages they studied were basically similar. Their analysis was an attempt to explore basic thought processes and to regulate them, their approach being deeply influenced by the philosophy of Descartes. But the scheme of logic current at the time had very strong affinities with that current in the classical world. It is little wonder, therefore, that what differences they perceived were minimal.

The slow development of this logical approach paralleled a similar trend during the late Middle Ages. The medieval reorientation of grammar as a philosophical discipline rose from a remark made by Peter of Helias, that Priscian and Donatus had neglected to give "reasons" for their rulings. Evrard de Béthune, in the preface to *Graecismus,* expanded the criticism:

> As Priscian did not teach grammar by calling on every possible type of knowledge, his rules are of less value to us. He describes many constructions, without assigning any reason other than usage by ancient grammarians. For this reason he does not teach, for only those who give reasons for their rulings may be said to teach.
>
> 1200? (Evrard de Béthune) 396: 5

This important statement of policy is the basis of the *grammatica speculativa.*

The exponents of *grammatica speculativa* were known as *modistae,* from their custom of relating everything to the *modi significandi.* These were of two types, active and passive. It is only the first which concerns us here. The *modus significandi activus* was a property of the word, and, as such, had no connection with lexical meaning: it was essentially concerned with the way the word was linked into the sentence.[1076:5] This was divided into the *modus significandi essentialis* and *modus significandi accidentalis.* The first part of speech had a necessary relationship to its referent: thus content words belonged to this class. The second were grammatical words, that were dependent for their function and meaning on other words in the sentence. From this division a whole scheme of grammar was erected. It was taken as universal, even though no attempt was made to apply it outside Latin: According to Roger Bacon, "the substance of grammar is one and the same in all languages, even if there are accidental variations."*[108:15] The early grammarians of the school had admitted the possibility of several varying basic grammars, but this self-contradictory position had disappeared with further development of the doctrine.*[108:15]

It is not to our purpose to trace the early development of grammar as a branch of logic, as this was concerned with Greek as a first language, having but little direct effect on foreign language teaching.

15.2.3 Analysis of the Word

The question of the exact nature of the word has caused linguists endless trouble. The earliest attempts at definition centered round its function of meaning and representation:

> A word is the smallest part of connected discourse, that is, of composition. It is a discrete unit, in that it designates a whole and transmits a complete sense. I make this distinction to prevent attempts to divide units like *vires,* as *vi* and *res,* or some such division. This is not designed to facilitate comprehension of a whole.
>
> A.D. 550? (Priscian) 915: II.iii.14

This definition was echoed 1,300 years later by Saussure, who pointed out the difficulty of delimiting the word from the stream of speech.[317:145] Any approach to the problem is complicated by the fact that words are not the only units of speech that have meaning. Hence, Saussure was reluctant to use the word *mot,* and substituted *unité.*

Harold Palmer met the difficulty by abandoning the concept *word* in favor of three types of significant units: the "monolog," the "polylog," and the "miolog." The first is a functionally independent unit, the second is a linguistic sign made up of two or more monologs (e.g., in deaf-mute); the third is a morpheme that exists only in composition (re- in "redo").[836:15] It is important to note that our concept of the word has long been clouded by the written language. Though separation of word from word arrived late in the history of writing, the very act implied one was conscious of a separation, as is quite clear from the way in which the ancients tackled the problems of analysis.

The ancient science which dealt with the word itself was termed *orthographia,* and it continued until the early Renaissance. While it was not concerned with the very nature of the word, the science, despite its title, which would seem narrow to a modern, dealt with more than spelling: "the Book of Caper, which deals with spelling, meanings, and distinctions between words."[15:113] It covered four fields: spelling, meaning, usage, and etymology. In practice the four were lumped together in the same treatise without any attempt to separate them.

Though there are traces of the science during the classical age of Rome, it was not until the silver age that *orthographia* reached its definitive form. The most famous author was Palaemon (the reputed teacher of Juvenal), the fragments of whose *Orthographia* are preserved in some of the manuscripts of Suetonius. Palaemon drew together all the threads of the science of the word, as the Romans knew it.

By the time of Palaemon, the regulation of spelling had become of critical importance. The spoken language had begun to evolve away from the written, and scholars were divided over whether to alter spelling to fit pronunciation, or vice versa. The archaist tendencies of the second century resisted any attempt to legitimize contemporary pronunciation by changing spelling, and the written word was used as a brake to the evolution of the spoken. Owing to the frequency of spelling mistakes this particular aspect gained in importance, gradually pre-empting the term, orthography.

Consideration of meaning involved two different approaches: definition and delimitation of paronyms and synonyms. This had been a Roman preoccupation since before classical times, but became an integral part of the grammarian's activity as classical purism gained ground in Rome. The importance of fine distinctions for legal purposes also had some influence; synonymy was a valued tool for making sure that a law was comprehensive, covering all possibilities. For instance, in the *Senatus consultum de Bacchanalibus* (185 B.C.), which was enacted to stop Orphic worship in Italy, there are four words meaning *to plot,* each one of them throwing some part of the process into relief. Even Cato the Censor (*fl.* 200 B.C.), who was inclined to regard linguistic quibbles as beneath his dignity, remarked that *properare* and *festinare* (both meaning to hurry) were two different concepts. The consideration of usage revolved around questions of flexion and governance. Here the principle of analogy was of utmost importance. Palaemon has: "*Honos/honor:* if the nominative was *honos,* as in *nepos, dos, sacerdos* the genitive case would be *honotis,* as in *dotis, sacerdotis.* We say, therefore, *honor,* as in *arbor, honoris* as in *arboris.*"[834:307] Thus the ancient form was legislated out of the language.

Yet, despite contradictory behavior like the above, most grammarians were convinced that etymology was the final court of appeal. Palaemon remarks that "all the harmful effects of custom have been reversed by appealing to the ancients."[834:310] This statement set the keynote for all the pre-Renaissance treatment of the word as an entity, but was applied only when it suited the grammarian in question. As exemplified in Latin it led to some odd results: Varro gave two etymons for every word, one from Greek and one from Latin; many phonetic tendencies, especially assimilation, were reversed: *inlustrare* was written for *illustrare, inpotens* for *impotens,* for instance; similar word configurations caused forced and absurd derivations: *terra ex quo teritur,* for example.

The medieval taste for allegory had its roots in Roman practice: *lepus* (rabbit) was derived from *levipes* (light of foot) by Aulus Gellius (A.D. 100) who was also responsible for tracing *spica* to *spes* as the ear of corn gives hope (*spes*) of the harvest.[63:XII:14] Varro makes the point that if it were not for the etymological mechanisms in the language, remembering it would be a crushing task.[1101: § VI.36] Though he regarded flexion and derivation as two different things, later grammarians failed to follow his example. By now the Greek treatments of etymology had become the norm to which all similar aspects of Latin scholarship were made to conform.[744:756]

The medieval *orthographiae* followed the lines laid down during the classical era, but had a tendency to specialize in spelling problems. The seventh-century *Appendix probi* shows a number of different influences at work. The first was an effort to adhere to imaginary Greek originals: thus spellings like *vyr* and *vyrgo* are prescribed in favor of the authentic *vir* and *virgo.*[*55:29] Other prescriptions show the effect of the evolution of Vulgar Latin. They include attempts to preserve atonic short vowels (*speculum* non *speclum*), to counter the ancient tendency to drop final *m* (*pridem* non *pride*), and to prevent spirantization of plosive consonants (*Baculus* non *vaclus*). In fact all the evolutionary tendencies of early Romance receive attention.[*55:28-34] It is not absolutely certain that this list was meant for second-language teaching; it was probably directed towards young Latin speakers whose speech was beginning to show these peculiarities. But later *orthographiae* followed the same lines. Agroecius (A.D. 700?) attacks the same faults, for example the Vulgar Latin confusion between [e] and [I]: "One binds (*ligat*) with a chain but deeds (*legat*) in a will."[15:124]

In the delineation of meaning, definition, even without the preliminary step of distinguishing between synonyms, became important. Alcuin (A.D. 775) wrote about the word *probo: "Probo* has two meanings: we *probamus* (approve of) what we choose. And it also means to test: 'Proba me Deus.' "[24:914A]

Until the work of the *modistae,* there was little extended consideration of the word and its relationship with the thing it represented. The *modistae* distinguished three levels of analysis: *modus essendi, modus intelligendi,* and *modus significandi.* Lexical consideration of the word was determined by the *modus significandi passivus,* which was a property of the thing signified. This rested on the *modus intelligendi passivus,* which was a property of the thing as it was perceived. Both rested on the *modus essendi,* the conditions of existence of the thing. The most important feature of their approach is the emphasis on the intervention of the cognitive faculties in the creation of the signifier: in many ways, the *modistae* look forward to Saussure and Guillaume.

The Renaissance approach to the Latin word was governed by stylistic considerations. The Renaissance Latin *copiae* follow directly along the lines of the medieval *orthographiae,* reverting the classical preoccupation with fine distinctions:

> Between *frondes* and *folia* (leaves): only trees have *frondes;* both trees and flowering shrubs have *folia.* Between *excubiae* and *vigiliae:* (guard duty) *Excubiae* pertains to both day and night; *vigiliae* to night duty only.
>
> 1491 (Valla) 1095: 53

Spelling is an incidental matter, the Carolingian standards being accepted, and etymology loses, at least temporarily, its overriding importance in word study. Because it was felt that modern language could gain finesse only under the tutelage of Latin, extensive borrowing and remodeling, guided by etymology, took place.

Etymology proved to be a double-edged weapon. Though it became more scientific during the seventeenth and eighteenth centuries, it still regulated spelling and meaning, prevailing over popular usage as far as educated speech and writing were concerned. It was not until the twentieth century that the science of *orthographia* finally split into four parts: orthography, etymology, semantics, and lexicology.

Language teachers of the nineteenth century looked into the problem of the word from several angles. Dufief, in dividing vocabulary into "sense-words" and "link-words," looked both forwards and backwards.[345:xi] On the one hand he recalled the Aristotelian classification of *ὄνοματα*, *ῥῆματα* (nouns and verbs) and *σύνδεσμοι* (all the other parts of speech) and on the other he anticipated the distinction between form and content words that is at the base of the structural approach to teaching grammar. Seventy years later, Gouin, relying on what Saussure was later to call *valeur,* classified the stock of vocabulary that he taught into objective and subjective language.

Discovery of the relationship of the languages of the Indo-European complex caused a revival and reorientation of etymology. Basing themselves on the newly discovered rules of phonetic change, linguists, most of them Germans, traced the ancestry of modern Indo-European languages, even building a hypothetical common Indo-European. The most complex corpus of knowledge existed in Romance languages, because the ancestor of the group was still known. This group of linguists, the neogrammarians, dominated linguistics until well into the first half of this century. At their prompting, attempts were made to apply their findings to language teaching: however, the vogue of this approach was short.

It was Saussure who pointed out that, while historical studies in linguistics were of great interest, studies of languages in their modern form were equally rewarding. In putting forward the concept of "states of language," he provided a framework which would allow a language to be analyzed at every stage of its development. In lexicology and semantics this gave rise to several developments. One of the most fruitful was the theory of the semantic field. Some hint of it occurs in Humboldt, but it was first elaborated by Jost Trier.[*152:123] The lexical resources of language were regarded as falling into a mosaic in which each piece set bounds to the meaning of its neighbors. This is quite like Saussure's figure of pieces disposed on a chessboard.[317:126] As in the linguistic field, the movement of one piece would upset the whole pattern of relationships. This was a good way of approaching the difficulties of finding equivalences between languages. Saussure's idea of *valeur* also provides a linguistic approach to the problem of cultural orientation of words and ideas, a preoccupation of the Americans and French who entered the field of language teaching.

The traditional approaches to which we have referred tended to take the word separate from structures. This separation was first shaken by Ogden and Richards, who selected words for teaching on both their range of meaning and their adaptability to structures (see §7.4). A similar analysis technique was applied in the "levels analysis" devised by the Firth school.[175] While admitting that their theories are still in their infancy, linguists of this school attempted to define words by the twin ideas of *collocation* and *set.* Collocation is co-occurrence, i.e., the environment in which a word can appear.[506:152] Words which can appear in similar collocations are in the same set. This is a theoretical basis for the selection procedures of availability and coverage discussed in Chapter 7. It also is a throwback to Saussure's idea of defining a word by the relationships into which it can enter.

The transformationalists took the approach much further, postulating the idea of semantic structure. Proceeding from the key idea of competence, they phrased the problem of semantics as follows: why is it that certain grammatically correct sentences are seen by competent speakers of the language as nonsense?[615:485] Their explanation does contain certain elements of the Firthian theory of collocation, but on the level of formal analysis they base the characterization of a word on the mental operation of proceeding through increasing degrees of specificity. This adapts well to processing by computer. But at the same time, it is an approach with similar bases to the medieval analysis of the *modi significandi.* The tree graph by which they express the semantic structure of word meaning takes into account both structural implications (*modus significandi activus,* in medieval terms) and the actual shades of meaning *(modus significandi passivus).*

Only during the twentieth century has linguistic analysis separated itself from a teaching aim. In the past, all branches of linguistics and grammar were oriented to normative usage. Today, linguistics is concerned with describing what is, rather than laying down what should exist.

In these two chapters we examined the sciences which gave rise to the ideas of language teaching. We will now look at their fate.

PART VII

WHAT HAS HAPPENED TO THE IDEAS?

INTRODUCTION

The total corpus of ideas accessible to language teachers has not changed basically in 2,000 years. What have been in constant change are the ways of building methods from them, and the part of the corpus that is accepted varies from generation to generation, as does the form in which the ideas present themselves. Here we consider the reasons for the birth, development, and death of the ideas discussed in the previous parts of the book.

The basic factor in progress from discovery, to full implementation, and then to abandonment is the peculiar tendency of any idea to be choked by formalism. This is a trend which the art of education shares with the fine arts. When an idea first appears and appeals to the most creative in the field, it is developed little by little. At all stages of the development of ideas and methods, the less original follow the successful innovators like sheep, accepting as received doctrine what is really a transitional stage. Inevitably the idea reaches the limit of its growth. At this stage, it is applied slavishly by the unoriginal, who are always in the majority, catches the attention of the interested dabbler, and repels the creative who turn elsewhere. Thus an idea develops to sterility and dies by neglect, to be rediscovered later; and then it goes through the same cycle of tentative development, doctrinaire enforcement, and rejection.

Very few inherently bad ideas have ever been put forward in language teaching. The reason for their evolution is to be found in the society in which teaching takes place and in the men who practice the art.

Formative relationships between education and society as a whole are reciprocal, and language teaching has shared fully in them. Basically the fate of language teaching ideas depends on the sensorium, i.e., the way in which cultures react to their environment. Thus ideas have to be tied to the role language plays. As the sensorium is unconscious and so self-evident that no one analyzes it, it is more powerful than any factor external to ideas. An orally based culture will operate differently from a written or electronic culture. This produces a series of value clusters which vary widely, but in predictable patterns. Language teaching depends on a changing balance of aims, techniques, and attitudes derived from the modalities of social intercourse and on what is considered essential to the intellectual life of each society.

Thus, language teaching has been shaped by both the professional and the amateur. As educational administrators usually come from society at large rather than from among professional educators, the amateur viewpoint has had tremendous influence. Indeed, it is remarkable that so many people whose practical experience was severely limited have put forward theories of education and teaching that have had a formative influence on the field. Rousseau is a case in point. Educational ideas which fit in with contemporary thought and prejudices find ready acceptance, while others, which may be just as sound, but which run counter to the orthodox thought of the time, die for lack of support. One of the most important variables has been the relative importance of church and state in society as a whole: this has affected both the choice of languages taught and the method of teaching.

Though the teaching body itself has not had much influence on the provenance of philosophies of education, it has had much on the practice of individual subjects. Ideas are usually judged, not on their theoretical worth, but on their feasibility under prevailing circumstances and on their relation to the aims recognized by the profession, which need not coincide in all respects with those recognized by the administrators or the public. A teacher's receptivity to new ideas is also conditioned by the fact that he himself is a member of the society in which he lives, and shares its views. Likewise his training is also an important factor in forming his attitudes, as are his pride in his profession and his own sense of experimentation. Thus the discovery, development, and survival of an idea depend on two factors: the public and the teacher.

16

THE PUBLIC AND LANGUAGE TEACHING

The learning of a second language must be regarded as a necessary part of total personality formation in the modern world since it should enable a person to live and move more freely in more than one culture and free him from the limitations imposed by belonging to and being educated within a single cultural group and a single linguistic community.

1963 (Stern) in 1036: 15

Education is one of the few professional fields that is controlled at most levels by amateurs and interested outsiders. This is natural, considering the social importance of education and the fact that teaching is a fundamental human activity that everybody, at some stage of his life, is forced to do. Thus public opinion acts as an efficient control, preventing the promulgation of ideas that are contrary to the accepted values of society. The matters of interest to the public and the educational administrator fall under three heads: the choice of language to be taught, the moral and religious consequences of teaching and learning, and the intellectual and social values that regulate both subject matter and methodology.

16.1 THE CHOICE OF LANGUAGE TAUGHT

In the West, language teaching has been dominated by Latin and Greek, their position being effectively challenged only during the twentieth century.

Since the intellectual life of Rome was entirely formed by Greek ideas, Greek was the prerequisite for the educated and cultured. But outside a restricted area in Italy, Latin was a foreign language; and as any advancement was dependent on a good knowledge of Latin, it too was a necessity for any ambitious provincial. The local languages had no status whatsoever and did not enter into consideration. Even the Greek dialects succumbed to the pressure of Attic and the *κοινή* (Hellenistic Greek), which remained the second language of the Empire until it was divided.

It seems that the decline of Greek antedates the complete separation of the two empires. An enemy of St. Jerome, Rufinus, claims that before St. Jerome became interested in theology, he did not know Greek and adds the comment *mecum pariter* (like me) (see *PL* 21:590D). There is also evidence to show that St. Augustine's Greek was not very good.[*47:140] The picture of the later Empire that emerges is of brilliant Greek scholarship confined to a circle of archaists that became smaller as time went on.[*47:142] By the sixth century even the popes were ignorant of the language. Gregory the Great confessed that: "We are neither acquainted with Greek, nor have we ever written in Greek."[481:Ep.xi:55] It seems that the decline of Greek was largely due to political reasons, though the difficulties of learning Greek and Latin together probably contributed to its demise as well, for both were foreign languages in parts of the Empire. As the Romance vernaculars diverged more and more from Latin, Greek became the preserve of diplomats and scholars, leading a precarious existence among the Romance-speaking elite and in certain monasteries in Germany and Ireland.

Formal instruction in the Romance vernaculars began some time in the thirteenth century, without, however, coming into conflict with Latin. Much of the impetus for this movement came from the troubadours, who, in the manner of the Greek dramatists, recognized different dialects as appropriate for different genres.[926:71] By the late thirteenth century French was already spreading throughout Europe as a language of culture: Brunetto Latini and Martino da Canale both remark on its beauty and on its wide acceptance in European society.[*36:23] This was especially noticeable in the princely and royal courts, laying the foundation for the later predominance of French as the language of diplomacy. In Sicily and the south of Italy, as well as in the East, Greek was still the first language of most of the society. The arrival of cultured refugees from Constantinople during the fifteenth century once again forced on Romance Europe the Roman conviction that the basis of their secular and religious culture was Greek.

While Latin dominated scholarship during the Renaissance, Greek dominated religion, and Italian, polite society. In a movement parallel to the Carolingian Renaissance, Erasmus went to the roots of Christian belief and attempted to put the sacred books on a solid scholarly foundation, this time by compiling a critical Greek text. In this he was inspired by the example of St. Jerome, for whom he had a deep admiration. The *textus receptus,* on which the Authorised Version of the Bible (1611) is based, is largely due to him. The reformers received his initiative with delight, thus rendering it suspect to theologians in the universities. But French never really lost the place it had held in medieval Europe. In England, for instance, it was the language of Henry VIII's court.[*111:78] But in spite of this, the position of Latin as the language of controversy and scholarship was not assailed.

By deliberately abandoning the vigorous, if unclassical, Latin of the Middle Ages for the self-conscious polish of the Roman golden age, Renaissance scholars contributed to the decline of classical studies. This change of emphasis in itself would have had little effect on the survival of the discipline, had interest not been growing in the vernaculars. Convinced Latinists regarded the vernacular as a tool for classroom teaching, but many others regarded skill in the mother tongue as one of the marks of the educated gentleman. Even during the fourteenth century the *ars dictaminis* of the University of Bologna had been concerned with Italian as well as Latin. Dante, despite his excellent Latin scholarship, looked forward to the maturing of the vernaculars; Cardinal Antoniano remarked that it was reprehensible to find a gentleman who scarcely knew his mother tongue.[*225:67]

The same qualities of grace and exactness required in Latin were being expected in modern languages. The first stages of self-consciousness in the vernaculars caused furious attacks on the influence of other living languages, especially Italian. As yet, Latin was spared, as it had a seemingly unbreakable monopoly over scholarship, and until the eighteenth century it often acted as a vehicle through which other languages were taught. But during the seventeenth century its rights were questioned. The comment of Lelaboureur was typical: "It is a dead language, and one whose sleep we do not wish to disturb: ours [i.e., French] is living and we can even say that it has assumed the rights of succession."[654:16] Even so, the list of modern languages taught was quite restricted. Italian, French, Spanish, Portuguese, German, and English were the most common. Catalan and the Provençal dialects, which had been of prime importance during the late Middle Ages, had lost their relevance to literature and were no longer taught.

Attacks on the classical languages became more common during the nineteenth century, but modern languages remained on the fringe of the curriculum. It was not until the Direct Method movement brought them to the attention of the public at the end of the century that the decline of classical languages was accelerated. By the end of the nineteen-sixties, classical Greek rarely appeared in the curriculum; and Latin was no longer the center of a good education.

The European zeal for colonization that reached its peak during the nineteenth century brought the languages of America, Africa, Asia, and Oceania to the attention of Europe. As missionaries often penetrated where colonizers were unwilling to go, the first analyses of these languages for the purposes of teaching were made by missionaries, and often the first book translated was the Bible. This was still going on in the 1960's, but as many of the territories colonized during the nineteenth century are now independent, their vernaculars have become national languages.

This poses a problem of choice for those in these territories whose language is not the national language,[660:14-44] as well as for foreigners who wish to enter into diplomatic or trade relationships. Thus the corpus of teachable languages suddenly expanded from the traditional list to cover languages which had gained political importance.

Another important factor in the choice of a language to learn was the ideological struggle going on between the Communist and Western blocs after the Second World War. For the purposes of propaganda, the languages of the newly independent countries had to be known by both sides, and an undignified competition ensued as to which bloc could command the most languages.

The question of the order in which a number of foreign languages should be taught raised some debate. In general, it has been preferred to teach easier languages first. Thus Esperantists have suggested that Esperanto, being a language designed without irregularities, could be taught to show pupils the mechanics of language learning.[404:92] In traditional practice, however, Latin was taught first as the foundation of all scholarship, and other languages were taught through it. It has been suggested that cognate languages should be taught first: thus an English speaker would start with German and the French speaker with Italian or Spanish. However, this idea drew little support.

16.2 RELIGIOUS, MORAL, AND SOCIAL AIMS

Society looks to education to provide more than mere knowledge: it must provide an ethical and moral component which has always been of utmost importance to the pupil's later absorption into adult society. In the case of classical languages, their value as tools of established religion was most important. In addition, the effort involved in learning any language has been accorded a role in character formation. Lastly, knowledge of foreign languages has traditionally been expected to bring about a tolerance for foreign cultures.

16.2.1 Religious Aims

As the religious tradition of Europe depends on documents written in Latin, Greek, and Hebrew, these three languages have always held an important place:

> There are three sacred languages: Hebrew, Greek and Latin, which have great value for the whole world. For these languages were written over the Lord's cross by Pilate to detail the reason for his death. For this reason, and because of the veiled language of Sacred Scripture, knowledge of these three languages is necessary.
>
> A.D. 600 (Isidore) 577: IX.i.3

The requirements of Biblical exegesis provided much of the motivation for classical study, and in the Latin rite sections of the Roman Catholic Church, which used an entirely Latin liturgy until 1965, a good command of Latin was necessary for the clergy at least. In the Protestant world, Greek and Hebrew were needed for Biblical scholarship and Latin was necessary for the study of basic documents from the Reformation period.

Owing to the mythological content of classical literature and the ethical aims of the classical poets, literary studies fell under the suspicion of the Christian church. About the middle of the third century arose what Bolgar called "the Christian dilemma."[*17:12] The comprehension of grammar and literature in one discipline, coupled with the emergence of a Christian literature in both Latin and Greek, brought about a crisis of conscience that was never resolved on the continent of Europe. In the face of a literature dealing with divinities whose morals in many cases did not measure up to Christian standards, Christians began to ask themselves whether a pure Latinity or a sound Greek style were worth the risk to their faith and morals. Yet refusal to have anything to do with ancient literature would have isolated them from their intellectual heritage, making the work of apostolate almost impossible. The question was further complicated by the rise of Christian dialects with their roots in popular Latin and Greek, heavily affected by the κοινη of the Greek Bible. Finally, as many Christians were teachers, religious sanctions against classical studies would have destroyed their living.

In spite of this, rigorists like Tertullian (whose Latin is nothing to boast of) advocated complete abandonment of the classics.[*17:50] Moderates advised careful selection of what was useful. St. Basil (*fl.*

A.D. 350) recommends: "And just as in plucking the blooms from a rose bed we avoid the thorns, so also in garnering from such writings whatever is useful, let us guard against what is harmful."[82:393] This was the attitude of St. Augustine, who was one of the formative writers of the Christian tradition.[*17:54] Though he used a classical style in his most formal writings addressed to a pagan audience, he was careful to use a popular style in his sermons.[*161:181] Failure to perceive this distinction led to stylistic confusion during the Middle Ages.

But in Ireland, where the classical languages were the vehicle of the Christian religion, the dilemma did not arise. There, paganism was associated with the druidic writings in Gaelic, and the Irish saw Christianity in all classical literature. The common Messianic interpretation of Vergil's Fourth Eclogue, which refers to the birth of a child who will bring peace to the Roman world, is an example of this sort of identification.

For the later Middle Ages, classical scholarship had value outside the narrowly exegetical sphere. After the Carolingian Renaissance scholars tended to regard correct Latinity as an honor to God: According to Aelfric: "It seems better to me to pay due honor to God the Father with the syllables lengthened in the correct way than to shorten them in the English fashion. God is not to be subjected to Grammar."[11:2] This was an echo of the attitudes of the Carolingian Renaissance, which was set afoot for the sole purpose of revising the sacred books and the liturgical books of the Gallican liturgy. One is inclined to suspect that pleasing the royal ears when their owner was in chapel ranked with honoring God. A more serious reason, which remained current until the time of St. Thomas Aquinas, was the opinion that a sacramental formula mangled by the priest was invalid.[70:107] The only religious value accorded living languages arose out of the Crusades: a knowledge of Eastern languages was necessary for those who wished to convert the heathen.

Yet the early Christian division of opinion was perpetuated through the Middle Ages to the early Renaissance. In spite of attempts to preserve classical literary standards, the literature was regarded with suspicion. In his letter to his brothers at York, Alcuin counsels them to read poets in the Christian tradition, like

Fortunatus and Ambrose, and to avoid "pollution by the flowery eloquence" of Vergil.[25:§10] As the Cluniac movement spread in Northern Europe, monasteries consistently neglected the classics: Peter Damian (*fl.* 1000) was overjoyed to find that they had no schools for little boys, which often cause the rigor of the holy life to slacken."[866:621] One can picture the dilemma of cultivated courts like those of Charlemagne and the Norman kings of southern Italy, which took much of their inspiration from the classics while remaining militantly Christian.

In spite of their enthusiasm for the classics, Renaissance educators shared the disquiet of medieval scholars. Antoniano, for example, thought it "better to see Christians with good morals and little eloquence, rather than see them unworthy of the name of Christ despite the brilliance of their eloquence."[*226:63] This attitude slowly disappeared as the classical languages became tools of controversy, and as stylistic considerations dominated. One can gauge the importance of style from the numerous versions of the Bible that were produced in classical Greek and Latin by Renaissance scholars, and by the revision of the Roman breviary undertaken at the order of Pope Urban VIII. All the medieval hymns were polished until they conformed to the educated taste of the time.

The humanist devotion to Greek was considered dangerous by many scholars; and experience with the reformers led to bitter slogans such as: "Beware of Greek, otherwise you will apostatize" (see introduction to 53). Secular studies in Greek, given the religious turmoil of the time, tended to be overshadowed by religious motivations for the language. The care Erasmus took to establish a Greek text and the enthusiasm with which this was greeted by Luther and the evangelicals seemed to confirm the worst fears of the faculties of theology. The Erasmian foundation of the *Collegium trilingue* at Louvain was greeted with intense hostility, which was not made any better by the quarrel that broke out between Erasmus and Edward Lee, who, it seems, had the support of Louvain University, over a set of notes the latter had written on the Erasmian New Testament. Studies of Greek were eagerly embraced by the reformers, and for its own protection the Roman Catholic Church at the Council of Trent enjoined Greek studies on candidates for the priesthood.

16.2.2 Moral Aims

In considering the moral worth attributed to language studies, one has to deal with an ambivalence in attitude. In spite of what has already been said about Christian suspicions of classical literature, many writers in both classical and medieval periods were impressed with its moral relevance. Abelard advised a pupil to "love the discipline of letters, and you will not love the sins of the flesh."[3:310] This is taken textually from St. Jerome's letter to Laeta (A.D. 350?), written in answer to a request for advice on educating a young girl.

Christian though this idea is, it had its roots in the practice of ancient Greece and Rome. In his *Dialogus de oratoribus* (A.D. 80?) Tacitus attacks the contemporary schools of rhetoric that taught only the arts of elocution, pointing out that the ancients considered a moral training, gained through sound schooling in a good home, to be essential to a future orator.[1057:31] The truth was even more complicated than this. It had always been considered that scholarship and probity went together; and the essence of the oratorical discipline was the training of good moral attitudes and the art of persuading hearers to adopt them. The unscrupulous demagogue was, to the Romans and Greeks, a contradiction in terms of which they were very afraid.

As oratorical training was in the hands of the Greeks the attitude was ambivalent. Greek orators were expelled from Rome twice. This attitude was partly due to the questionable content of much Greek literature, partly to the reputation Greeks had acquired in Rome for licence and debauchery. It disappeared only during the seventeenth century, as Greek had become identified with Biblical scholarship and fascination with the old pagan values had become a thing of the past.

The moral relevance of rhetoric was a medieval commonplace, as is shown by the derivations commonly ascribed to the word *ars:*

> We use the word, *ars,* because by its rules we are bound (*arctare*) and hold to a certain course of action (*constringere*). Others claim that the word comes from the Greek, ἀρετή, that is from the virtues of teaching, which brings knowledge of good to learned men.
>
> A.D. 550 (Cassiodorus) 195: 1151

Medieval scholars followed this line of thought exactly, seeing an art as dealing only with what was good. An unknown scholar glossed the word in the *Morale Scholarium* of John of Garland thus: "All arts, insofar as they are arts, deal with the good and the classification of good. Any abuse is evil."[591:190]

Notwithstanding this attitude, later scholars, to account for the moral value of language study, seized on literature as the valuable element. The great classical poets were regarded as the embodiment of every conceivable moral goodness. In addition, the discipline required to plow through the aridity of the first stages of language study was looked on, not as the result of bad teaching, but as desirable in the formation of character. Moral relevance of classical languages to the art of government was an important tenet of the Carolingian court:

> There is nothing more effective in directing one's life according to the best moral standards, nothing more necessary to the exercise of kingly power, than the riches of wisdom, a high regard for learning, and deep erudition.
>
> A.D. 800 (Alcuin) Ep. 43: *PL* 101:209

The long life of this idea ended only during the early twentieth century, a classical education being considered necessary for the most gifted, especially for those going into public service. One will recall that in the various treatises published during the Renaissance on the education of the prince, a classical education played a most important role. This simply follows a tradition that goes back to the Gracchi, who, it seems, were the first Romans educated in Greek to hold public office.

Common belief from the classical age until after the Renaissance was that a country that was morally sound spoke a well-ordered, forceful language. The Alexandrian school of poets and critics tried to bring back the greatness of Greece by reforming the language and restoring it to the classical standard of the fourth century B.C. They had their imitators in Augustan Rome who tried to freeze the language to that stage of development in the hope that the republican virtues would not die out under the emperors. This philosophy was one of the root causes for the Renaissance return to classical Latin: "For mark all ages: look upon the whole course of both the Greek and Latin tongue, and ye shall surely find that when apt and good words began to be neglected . . . then also began ill deeds to spring. . . ." (Ascham)[53:134]

We have already referred to the uninhibited content of many Renaissance colloquia (see §4.3.1). Erasmus came under attack for this reason, and later editions of his *Colloquia* carry his *De utilitate colloquiorum*[374a:654-672] as an appendix, a tract in which he points out that each of the major conversations in his book has a definite social, ethical, or religious purpose. Thus he satirizes abuses, especially those in religion that impinge on social conditions, like forcing unsuitable subjects into the religious life, looseness of morals, and superstitious religious practices. In many ways, his *Colloquia,* as he himself claims,[374a:655] are a Christian tract in the style of the classical dialogues on morals and religion.

The modern languages did not share this development, being taught at first for practical reasons, having no tradition, and lacking a religious aura. But to be accepted in the schools as having the same educational, moral, and intellectual values as Latin, they had to be taught with the same methods and according to the same analysis.

16.2.3 Social and Political Aims

It is rare that a society does not consider language as one of its distinguishing marks, and does not feel some kinship with another group that speaks its language. Thus the Greeks designated foreigners by the unflattering name of *βαρβαροι* (stammerers) and transmitted the pejorative undertones of the word to the Latin *barbari,* and to its derivatives in the modern European languages. However, any community that adopted the Greek language as an ordinary vehicle of social life was welcomed into the Greek nation: hence, when Greek became the official language of the court of Philip V, the father of Alexander the Great, Macedonia was given the right to compete in the Olympic games, which was the prerogative of the Greek community of states.[*213:91]

In the late Roman Empire, with grants of full citizenship to all freeborn persons and the increasing number of freed slaves, the inculcation of a true Roman pride in the imperial heritage seemed a pressing necessity: hence the growing official interest in education. Sporadic attempts were made to Latinize the East, centers of Latin learning being founded at Berytus (Beirut) and Byzantium.[*132:349] Roman officials tried to carry on imperial business in Latin, even requiring the use of interpreters on official occasions. For some time after the division of the Empire, Latin remained the official language of the Byzantine court. In the West, the most serious problem was the Romanization of the peoples of the frontier. Settlement by Germanic tribes was encouraged, provided they adopted Roman institutions and the Latin language. So oratory, which had fallen into a decline following its banishment to the classroom under the totalitarian emperors of the first centuries of the Empire, acquired a new lease of life as a vehicle of cultured persuasion.[*39:309] This movement was fed mainly from the excellent schools of the south of Gaul, and was transmitted to Ireland through the efforts of missionaries like St. Patrick.

After the destruction of the Empire of the West, Latin remained the international language of culture, so overshadowing the Romance vernaculars that for six centuries they had no intellectual standing and little political significance. The rise of linguistic nationalism can be dated from the Renaissance. Linguistic jingoism was a natural outcome of the new pride men felt in their own language, and mythical beliefs like *"la clarté française"* are a direct outcome of the period. One tends to forget that the same claim was made for all the great European languages, but as French cultural influence dominated Europe, the claims of Frenchmen for the logical efficacy of their own language drowned out those of all other nationalities. Thus the idea of language as a unifying or divisive influence appeared as well, and suppression of minority languages became one of the goals of nation builders and colonizers. The main instrument of this was, at the time, the school, though during the twentieth century mass media and general population mobility have played an even more important part.

Thus, after the French Revolution, the new rulers of France tried to stamp out all the dialects and patois spoken outside the Ile-de-France; after the English conquest of Canada, attempts were made to assimilate the French by a deliberate policy of denying them schools in their own language, a policy reversed at the beginning of the nineteenth century. In colonies of other European nations, the same thing was done, but usually a little more tactfully. Portugal, for instance, offered full citizenship to any of the inhabitants of its colonial empire who could speak Portuguese. It is a general pattern that higher education and advancement depend on an efficient command of the official language.

Multilingual countries, like South Africa and Russia, tried to ensure some national unity by teaching the most important languages throughout the school system. Still others, mainly former colonies, opted, often temporarily, for the colonizer's language, as no native language was sufficiently widespread for general adoption, and the political and emotional consequences of preferring one native language to the others seemed more ominous than choosing an outside language. India and Malaysia are cases in point.[660:53-76] Another formula that was used, especially in Europe, was adopting the dialect of one area as the official language. Usually the social and cultural development of this area made any other choice impossible. Thus the dialect of the Ile-de-France became accepted as French and Tuscan became Italian. In all cases, the instrument of transmission was the school system.

16.2.4 Cultural Aims

Knowledge of foreign cultures has always loomed large in the thoughts of language teachers. It is now commonly accepted that the culture of other language groups must be known for the purpose of effective communication with them, for the vaguer aim of "sympathy and knowledge," and for full understanding of one's own culture.

The cultural orientation of language teaching has always been one of its unstated aims. Otherwise it is impossible to explain the hold Greek literature, history, and attitudes had over Roman thought. It is likewise noteworthy that the scholia so frequent in medieval editions of the classics dealt as often with cultural facts as with grammar. We have already mentioned the importance of the Renaissance colloquy in teaching basic etiquette (see § 4.3.1). In addition, scholars of the Renaissance recognised the utility of languages as a medium of international understanding:

> And thus the science of letters is an excellent and precious thing, and like an inspiration of God given to men through his infinite goodness, to serve as a help and to give us a clear understanding of human nature. This acquisition and magnificent gift must serve us as an antidote and balancing influence more of divine value than of human. . . .
>
> 1574 (Budé) 169: 16

The religious aspect of the Renaissance position is notable, but it gave way to the humanitarianism of the eighteenth and nineteenth centuries. At the end of the nineteenth century Gouin devoted a whole chapter of his book to the importance of culture, a theme developed by the Direct Methodists.[410:273] Though the cultural orientation of the Direct-Method language courses is often regarded as something grafted onto the teaching of language, those in the main stream realized it went deeper, taking in all aspects of teaching. Strohmeyer, one of the later Direct Methodists, laid it down that introducing the pupil to the foreign culture was one of the overriding aims of language teaching.[1047:79] The psychological orientation of language toward behavior accepted by the structuralists brought this idea to the forefront after the Second World War, though even in the short time between the Direct Method and the beginning of the war cultural training had been neglected.

In Soviet Russia, the teaching of cultural material in the foreign language was first deliberately rejected, then subordinated to political indoctrination. Following the ideas of Ščerba, it was considered that one of the main intellectual purposes of foreign languages was to teach the value of one's own culture by comparing it with others.[*106:9] But as the authorities carefully fostered the idea that the way of life of the Soviet state was immeasurably superior to that of other nations, in practice foreign cultures were neglected, or elements of foreign life were chosen to throw into relief the advantages of living under the Communist system. Thus the general pattern of foreign life was distorted and, in English especially, the curriculum included literature depicting the miseries of the Industrial Revolution, or oriented towards the development of socialist and communist thought in the West.[*106:29] Extracurricular activities, clubs, correspondence, and songs were given the same bias.[*106:94-103] Ideological education was inextricably mixed with cultural.

In the West, though cultural teaching had varying fortunes in modern languages, under the name of "antiquities" it was an essential part of the classics course. It returned to the modern-language course during the Second World War. The most sophisticated modern approach to the problem was worked out in the United States. "Language and area programs" were elaborated at many universities as interdisciplinary courses in which the history and geography departments collaborated with the requisite language departments. These were the outcome of certain aspects of the wartime ASTP programs, in which some attempt was made to prevent American soldiers from offending the sensibilities of those whose language they were learning.[*2.4]

The fact was ignored that similar programs had been in use in the classics since the early Middle Ages. The traditional classics course includes a thorough treatment of both the history and geography of the Roman Empire and an account of daily life in classical times, in other words, a full area program subordinated to the literary and linguistic content. Owing to the allusive quality of most classical literature, such an approach was unavoidable.

16.3 ATTITUDES TOWARD AIMS AND IDEAS

It is the general pattern of education that few people question aims and methods generally accepted, but they raise a tremendous outcry when any change is suggested.

The greatest safeguard for any curriculum is public snobbery, a fact obvious during all ages, but not closely analyzed until the nineteenth century:

> The Culture which is supposed to plume itself on a smattering of Greek and Latin is a culture which is begotten by nothing so intellectual as curiosity; it is valued either out of sheer vanity or ignorance, or else as an engine of social and class distinction . . .
>
> 1867 (Matthew Arnold) 49: 442

The growing interest in modern languages as a school discipline became especially vocal as education ceased to be a monopoly of the rich and came to be regarded as an essential to advancement in society, not merely as something conferring graces on those whose livelihood was already assured. The acid comment of Petronius has a modern ring: "Children in school become immensely stupid because they hear or see nothing that is in common use" (Satyricon 1). This opinion has, at various times, had important effects on what is taught. The long exclusion of modern languages from the schools and the modern decline of classical languages are alike partly due to this factor.

We have noted elsewhere that one of the values ascribed to language study is mental discipline. In spite of its importance it has usually been appealed to as an emergency device when the other aims of language teaching are becoming confused: "Language teaching suffers because its aims are ill-defined. We have never decided if we should teach languages for use or merely as a discipline. Wavering between these objectives, we are hampered in both."[1070:5] The real confusion rested on two points: just what "mental training" was, and how important. The founders of the FLES programme saw knowledge of the foreign language as a "necessary element in total personality formation,"[1036:15] by which children's appreciation of the world around them was heightened. This point had been seen dimly by certain pioneers of the Direct Method: "What I desire to emphasize is that the culture of the taste and refining influence of literary knowledge must be sought equally with the discipline of a rigid grammatical knowledge."[536:34] In this there are echoes of the Renaissance and the classical schools of rhetoric.

Richards was quite disturbed by the twentieth-century emphasis on acquiring the mechanisms of language: "only in so far as the second language develops a mind's powers, does it become truly worth having."[953:132] It is true that this attitude had become twisted during the two hundred years preceding him and had produced abominations, but it was the most important factor in classical and Renaissance methodology. In the classical era, the study of grammar was considered fundamental to all disciplines. Classical educators transmitted to the Middle Ages and the Renaissance the idea that all knowledge entered into one vast discipline of which grammar was the foundation: "Every section of the liberal arts is contained in an interlinked body of knowledge," was Cicero's claim in the *De oratore.*[220:III:vi.21] But the grammar concerned was Latin grammar.

As a discipline, modern languages grew up outside this scheme. Though several attempts had been made during the late Middle Ages and early Renaissance to tie them to a formal grammar, they were not accepted as part of school education until the early seventeenth century, and even then, they remained on the fringe. Fleury characterizes classical languages as *études utiles* and modern as *études curieuses.*[415:10] But it is interesting to note that the mother tongue was an *étude nécessaire.* Acceptance of the mother tongue as a necessary part of education stems from the Renaissance, but everything else was subordinated to it by Port-Royal. There were parallel movements in other countries, and with the acceptance of the various languages of Europe in the schools of their own countries, they entered the schools of other countries as well. It is not unexpected that languages like Provençal, Basque, and dialects that were not accorded recognition on their own territory were not taught elsewhere.

Twentieth-century authorities approached the teaching of languages in an iconoclastic spirit, confident that what they were doing was immeasurably better than what had gone on in any other period of history:

> No period in the history of living languages has shown as noticeable progress as the last few years. Everywhere, under the impetus of the necessities of modern life, the teaching of foreign languages has undergone profound reforms, whose happy results can now be seen.
>
> 1903 (Schweitzer and Simmonot) 1007: 1

In one sense they were right: the pace of evolution was quite rapid, but this is typical of the usual attitude of language teachers of any age. They glance at the past, only to reject it. The pattern established by the Direct Method continued during the twentieth century. Depending on the need felt by the community at large and the powers of persuasion of those supporting particular techniques, the pace of adoption of new ideas has varied in different countries. In Europe, for instance, the Direct Method was adopted at the beginning of the century, as it was obvious that a good knowledge of foreign languages was advantageous. In England and America it was never officially accepted, though widely followed, and it took a war to bring Direct Methodology to the attention of the public. Much also depended on the financial state of the community that was to foot the bill. Thus, mechanical teaching has been accepted more readily in the United States than elsewhere. In addition the purchase, maintenance, and replacement of the machines can only be done in a nation that has access to a well-developed electronics industry.

In deliberately laying aside the oral aim for grammatical exactness and translating ability, the eighteenth and nineteenth centuries merely followed the intellectual tendencies of the time. The Cartesian approach to knowledge place analysis above all else. Hence the practice of language was not rated highly. This was a direct reversal of the Renaissance attitude toward modern languages. Grammatical knowledge was not highly valued, while a fluent command of the classical languages ranked with competent handling of grammar. The language-teaching world aimed at a balance between the four language skills and a philosophical knowledge of grammar and literature, after the pattern laid down by Quintillian. During the Middle Ages, it was the knowledge of grammar that was emphasized at the expense of speaking knowledge, though written composition was also very important.

In every case the determining factor has been the needs felt by the community that was being served. Until this century it was a relatively small aristocratic community that controlled policy. With the advent of universal education, those who learned languages were usually the more intelligent, those who aimed at professional careers. In these cases a philosophical approach was desirable. But as attempts were also made to teach languages to an unselected group, a functional approach was indicated, as it was easier for the pupils to understand and more interesting as well.

Having seen the effect society at large has had on the corpus of ideas in language teaching, let us see how it has fared in the hands of the teacher.

17

IDEAS AND THE TEACHER

Those who can, do; those who can't, teach.
G. B. Shaw

In language teaching the life and death of an idea rests mainly on the teacher who is to apply it. The fate of an idea in the classroom depends on the concepts and instincts a teacher has received from his training and the amount he is required to do. Another factor that can have some bearing on the development of ideas is the status of the profession in the community, for this governs the teachers' freedom of action in both their private lives and their work.

17.1 THE EFFECT OF TRAINING

The issue of teacher training has already been discussed (see §12.1.2), and it will be recalled that specialized training for language teachers is not very old. Even so, language teaching had been going on since Roman times, at first under the control of the imperial civil service, then under the Church. As a rhetorical and philosophical training was all that teachers before the Renaissance had, except for a minority that were more interested in teaching itself than in their subject, methods were transmitted with little change from generation to generation. This did, however, leave a freedom of experiment to the individual that the more centralized modern systems do not. Hence, at that time, evolution of language teaching was controlled from within the classroom.

The predominance of clerics in language teaching had several important effects. It was assumed that by virtue of his training, a priest was a teacher. Thus the seventh-century Council of Constantinople enacted that: "Priests must run schools in the towns and villages. And if any of their flock wish to entrust their sons to them to learn letters, they are not to be refused, but taken in and taught with the utmost kindness."[*131:XI:1004] This directive was repeated by Charlemagne two centuries later.[208] The relative importance of the Fathers of the Church and a suspicion of classics were among the obvious results of such a policy. Less obvious, but equally significant, was the status of modern languages. Aelfric, it seems, had met some opposition to his use of English during the ninth century.[11:2] While it would be totally false to put the lack of scholarly importance entirely at the door of the clerical establishment, the fact that there was little use for modern languages in the philosophical and rhetorical curriculum during the Middle Ages was not without importance. They did, however, exist on sufferance as tools of teaching: they were part of the construe which was well established in the schools of Western Europe by the thirteenth century.

The first modern languages to be taught were, as we have seen, the Romance vernaculars of southern France and Spain. The decline of Provençal and Catalan, and the subsequent passing of cultural power to the north of France, is partially due to the climate created by the Albigensian heresy of the thirteenth century. While there was no direct connection in the minds of churchmen between Provençal dialects and the activities of the Provençal courts, they had long looked askance at the morals of those who flourished there. So while these courts were suppressed for political expediency by the king of France, the Church was relieved to see them go.[*55:394-395] And without political and cultural importance, these languages were of little relevance to education.

Modern languages were, from the first, a layman's preserve. In ancient Rome, where Greek was the only contemporary language systematically taught, its teachers were academics with no special training beside their scholarship. It is no wonder that their approach was little different from the philosophy and rhetoric classroom. During the Middle Ages, modern languages were taught by the troubadours, who were not clerics, and during the Renaissance, largely by cultured refugees who had been professional men in their own country. It was only after the Renaissance that modern languages became the property of the schoolmaster.

Thus, while the classical languages were taught mainly for literary, scholarly, and religious needs, it was the social purpose of modern languages that was important. The only exception to this was the use of French by Calvin and his disciples, who wished to influence the common people who knew no Latin. It is noticeable that the first clerics who systematically dealt with modern languages were the scholars of Port-Royal (1650). But even then, modern languages remained on the fringe of the curriculum until the state assumed control of education and teacher training.

The advent of teacher training did little to help the specialty of language teaching, general training being the aim. As the teacher who could teach anything, provided a book lay open in front of him, gradually took over in the classroom, the Grammar-Translation Method was consolidated, and skill in handling the language itself was no longer required of the teacher. Indeed, specialist training for young language teachers was comparatively rare before the Second World War, but in the 1950's and 1960's became much commoner, though by no means universal.

One phenomenon of the 1950's was the advent of teacher training for the use of a particular method. Only teachers trained specifically in the method were allowed to use it. While some attempt was made by all those who owned such methods to give a rounded pedagogical training, in practice many teachers who held these specialized diplomas were extremely uncomfortable with any other method. An example of this was the training for *Voix et Images de France*. In addition, as some of these methods were regarded by their exponents as the last word in pedagogical finesse, it was difficult to dislodge them when something better came along: the teachers resisted because of the danger to their position and their convictions, and the administrators refusd to abandon the investment they had made.

It is an interesting phenomenon of the twentieth century that many of the ideas in teaching came from abstract research, instead of arising spontaneously from classroom situations. This aroused the suspicion of practicing teachers owing to a pragmatism which is the result of a tradition of self-sufficiency. It was generally agreed that the classroom itself was a valuable training ground for a tyro, but some teachers extended this to believing that training colleges were refuges for utopians: an anonymous teacher capped the Shaw quotation at the head of this chapter by remarking that "those who can't teach, teach teachers." As training colleges and their equivalents are the main disseminators of ideas, this often led to scepticism on the part of older teachers to both the ideas they produce and the teachers they train.

17.2 WORK LOAD

A teacher's willingness and ability to apply new ideas and go outside his routine is also partly governed by what he is required to do. Until this century, we have had little information about the time a teacher was required to devote to his pupils. In Rome we can conjecture that he spent the morning in the classroom, and we can see the amount of classroom time expanding over the whole of the history of teaching.

However, nobody knows how much time the teacher puts into preparation, marking, and other duties essential to efficient teaching. During this century the teaching profession has shared the unrest of the working class, claiming that classroom teaching takes up less than half the time of the conscientious teacher, and that those other duties are not accounted for in determining salary, responsibility, and duties. Thus ideas are apt to be measured not by their theoretical results, but by their effect on the teacher's reserves of energy, stamina, and knowledge. In part, this was the objection to the Direct Method: Dodson claimed that "Only the brilliant teacher seems to be assured of success under Direct Method teaching. The average and less-than-average teacher becomes quickly frustrated, worn-out and disheartened when using the Direct Method."[332:10]

The matter of class size is just as important. It is no accident that oral and direct methods were used with such success until the end of the seventeenth century. For the most part, classes were small, and large classes were dealt with by calling on outside help. By the time classes had become too large to handle by informal methods, the Grammar-Translation Method was universal. This enabled the pupil to be kept busy and learn without requiring too much *expertise* from the teacher—in either teaching or language. Thus, introduction of "modern methods" in all but experimental or commercial situations was badly hampered by the size of the average class.

17.3 THE TEACHER IN SOCIETY

What the profession expects of its members is conditioned largely by what society expects of the profession. There are three elements here: the degree to which society wishes to control its teachers, social attitudes toward the teacher, and what he has to give.

In Rome the first reactions of officialdom were guarded and then hostile: Greek rhetoric was seen as an influence that went counter to the traditional values of Rome. Consequently, on two occasions, in 161 B.C. and 92 B.C., schools of rhetoric were forcibly closed and their teachers expelled. The Greeks, being a more sophisticated people, easily acquired a reputation for moral depravity and dishonesty which, if one is to believe the satirists, was amply lived up to by slaves in Rome. Yet, despite the misgivings of the legislative assemblies, educated Greeks were valued by many families. Educated Greeks to whom the education of young Romans could be entrusted fetched very high prices in the slave market, and when freed they were often taken into the circle of their former owners. And with increasing dealings with the Greek East, the demand for Greek education grew in Rome. It is little wonder, then, that each of these decrees became a dead letter within five years.

In classical Rome education was a private affair in the hands of tutors and freed slaves. But the period between the early Empire and the fall of the Western Empire is marked by increasing interest in education on the part of the state. As its political importance became more obvious to the rulers of Rome, the state gradually regularized administration of education. Near the end of the first century of the Christian era, Vespasian endowed a chair of Greek and Roman rhetoric in Rome, and then founded imperial chairs in other major cities of Italy. Antoninus Pius extended the system all over Europe, and by the time of Diocletian teachers had a salary scale based on a promotion system.[*16:80] Constantine granted teachers and doctors immunity from taxes and military service, a recognition few other societies have accorded.

With the crumbling of the Empire, the Christian church took over the custody of learning. To the medieval mind this was not unjustified: "Go and teach all nations" had been Christ's mandate, and along with the Gospel, missionaries spread classical learning. The teaching body was made up of clerics, and the best of them, Bede, Alcuin, John of Salisbury, for instance, rank extremely high in the general history of education. The sudden influx of Byzantine scholars during the fifteenth century upset the clerical monopoly of teaching in the West. Though these people received a warm welcome, they were part of a status problem teaching has faced for most of the existence of the profession.

The profession, and to a large extent, the language-teaching part of it, has traditionally been the refuge for educated people who have failed elsewhere. Thus teachers in classical Rome were people who had lost their freedom in the first instance. Romans did not take over in the classroom until fairly late, but in so doing ushered in a period in which public respect was quite high. The Middle Ages solved the problem by confining teaching to clerics; yet the clergy was not so hand-picked as one would have liked, and holy orders make one a priest, not a teacher. The attitude of levity towards the clergy that was one of the factors in the Reformation was reinforced by distrust of their scholarship and teaching prowess, though this situation seemed to correct itself during the late Renaissance with more stringent controls on clerical morals and scholarship by both Catholics and Protestants.

Classics teachers were largely protected by the respect accorded their discipline, and there was a minimum of governmental interference, though England did impose the Lily grammar on the schools, with the blessing of the profession. In modern languages, however, the refugee status of many modern-language teachers did not help matters, and the social and economic status of the profession was low. The religious tensions engendered by the Reformation ensured that control of education devolved on the churches. In many places they issued licenses and certificates to teachers until the mid-nineteenth century. In certain places this continued right up to the early years of the twentieth century. Few states entered the educational field until the nineteenth century; but they gained control of training, certification, and, often, placement.

It is implied by Thomas Hughes's account of life at Rugby that many teachers during the nineteenth century had come into teaching as disappointed men, who had aimed at law and the church. And Lichtenberger states outright that French and German teachers were in teaching because they could find nothing better to do. Language teaching was not regarded as anything special:

> . . . the feeling is, anybody can teach French and German, or what is just as dangerous, anybody can teach English. By introducing scientific methods we shall show before very long that everybody can not so teach, that the teacher must be as specially and as scientifically trained for his work in our department as well as in any other.
>
> 1885 (Brandt) 146: 60

Pupil performance was affected, especially as languages became marginal in the curriculums of many countries. In addition, of all the learned professions, teachers have had the least possibilities of social advancement, or of controlling their own destinies as a group. This has had its effect on the quality of recruits, especially in societies that were otherwise well developed.

This picture cannot, of course, be taken as universal, as various societies at all times have placed the teacher on a level with the other professionals. It is noticeable that in those societies where the teacher was respected, language teaching was freer, and spontaneous experimentation widely practiced, the art of teaching evolving more readily. Low status for any profession inhibits the desire to find the best ways of performing its functions, as it is directed from outside by either prescription or the weight of amateur opinion. This, of course, has a double result in teaching: while it usually leads to conservatism, it can also mean that the directing authorities can impose the results of linguistic and psychological experiment either through directives or through training.

Thus the teacher is at once a positive and a negative influence on the history of ideas in language teaching; for an idea is accepted not only on its intrinsic worth, but also because of its appeal to those who are to apply it. And it evolves according to the manner in which the individual teacher thinks it will fit into his scheme of teaching.

With this discussion of the teacher's role, we have come to the end of our account of ideas in isolation. Let us now see what pattern emerges.

CONCLUSION

ERA	PARENT SCIENCES	ART								CRITICAL SCIENCES
		AIMS						METHODS		
		Lit.		Scholarly		Social		Informal	Formal	
		CL	ML	CL	ML	CL	ML			
Classical	Logic Grammar Rhetoric Philosophy Theology	Gr X	Gr X	Gr X	Gr X	Gr X	Gr X	Introduction at home & in Society	Literary & Rhetorical schooling	
Middle Ages		X		X		Y			Teaching by book–social uses of Latin secondary–contemporary languages taught for literary purposes.	Parent sciences with normative bias–observations erected into rules to govern activities drawn from them.
12th–15th centuries			X							
Renaissance	Education Grammar Rhetoric	X	X	X		Y	X	Methods in ML mainly oral–example followed by some Classics teachers	Methods in CL follow medieval pattern–ML enter translation teaching for literary purposes	
17th, 18th & 19th centuries	Grammar Philosophy Education Rhetoric	Y		X	X				Logical orientation of grammar–social purposes of language subordinate–grammar-translation evolves	
19th & early 20th	Linguistics Psychology Education Anatomy			X	Y		X	Natural & Direct methods, etc. predominate–experimentation in Direct and 'structural' methods for Latin	Classical languages continue 19th-century practice–many modern-language teachers do likewise.	Experimental Psychology. Language Didactics, Methods Analysis.

X Main aim
Y Most important subsidiary aim

CL Classical Languages
ML Modern Languages

Gr Greek
Lit. Literature

Figure 27. Schema of Evolution of Second Language Teaching.

CONCLUSION

To account for the changes of direction described in this book we must distinguish between an art, its basic sciences, and its critical sciences. Any art can ultimately trace its procedures to the principles of a science or group of sciences that are not necessarily known or practiced by the artist. Out of the reaction between these basic sciences and practice grows a science of criticism by which both performance and new ideas are judged. This science is usually pragmatic, basing its norms on what proves successful, rather than on what should prove successful according to theory. An element of tension thus arises between theoretician and artist: in the eyes of the artist his colleague is a utopian, while the theoretician often sees himself as a misunderstood prophet and the artist as either a dangerous radical or an unredeemed conservative.

Like an art, which is sensitive to social pressure and the innate decay of ideas referred to on page 363, its critical science is always evolving. Its evolution is, however, one step behind the *avant-garde* sections of the art, so that new approaches are greeted with mixed enthusiasm and outrage. Then, if they prove successful, they are added to the corpus of ideas. It is likewise not unusual for ideas no longer useful in their context to be "disproved" by new discoveries and to drop out of use.

The critical science, or its equivalent, the normative sections of the basic sciences, holds a key place in the evolution of ideas. For the training of the artist is usually based on these sciences of criticism. It is the critics, rather than the artists themselves, who take in hand the training of young talent, artists often becoming impatient with the different problems of teaching their techniques. Thus, though the sciences of criticism are derivative, it is through them that the art is transmitted to beginners. New ideas found by the creative artist have to survive the scrutiny of the critic: this is part of a process whereby unworkable ideas are filtered out before they have a chance to gain acceptance. It is also one factor in the death of ideas which appear before their time or which have outlived their usefulness.

While one can ascribe a linear development to sciences, the development of an art is cyclical. Old approaches return, but as their social and intellectual context are changed, they seem entirely new. Very often the creative artist seeks inspiration from the past, but transforms the idea in taking it over, as did Bartok, for instance, with the contrapuntal techniques of Bach. Language teaching has shared neither the honesty nor the self-knowledge of the fine arts. Whereas artists are willing to seek inspiration from the past, teachers, being cursed with the assumption that their discoveries are necessarily an improvement on what went on before, are reluctant to learn from history. Thus it is that they unwittingly rediscover old techniques by widely differing methods of research.

In an art, success is merely conformity with an aim that is so taken for granted that the artist is often only dimly aware of it. Each period determines its aim according to social and intellectual factors that have little to do with scientific validity. Ends and means vary from age to age. Education is in constant movement to suit the needs of its milieu, and the various parts of education tend to lag in their reaction to social demands, so that there is always scope for reformers; and one has the impression of constant improvement when what is really happening is a constant updating.

In language teaching three broad aims can be distinguished: the social, the artistic (or literary), and the philosophical. The first aim demands that language should be regarded as a form of social behavior and a type of communication. The artistic aim treats language as a vehicle for creativity, demanding both appreciation of creative activity and creative activity itself. This aim is often split into its active and passive aspects. The philosophical aim demands training in analytical techniques and often confuses linguistics with language teaching. At each period in history one of these has become predominant, generating its own approach to method.

It is the regular changing of these aims that produced the cyclic progression which is such a noticeable feature of language-teaching development. The classical, Renaissance, and modern periods have enough points of similarity to allow us to contrast them with the Middle Ages and the age of reason. The basic aim of the first group was communication (with the other aims subordinated), while the other periods aimed at analysis above all else.

In classical Rome, Greek filled the functions of both classical and modern languages, being taught for a range of purposes from social chitchat to transmission of literary and philosophical thought. The apex of education was the *orator* whose faultless command of language showed a fitting moral standing and strong social and political consciousness. This could only be obtained through study of the great minds of the literary world and imitation of them. Greek held equal place with Latin until the Greek communities of the West were almost completely absorbed, and the East became a separate political reality. During this period all aims were in balance, one flowing into the other from the social needs of the bilingual home and society, to the intellectual trials in the schools, to the scholarly and administrative requirements of the bilingual Roman in the Greek communities of the Empire.

The Renaissance distinguished between the functions of ancient and modern languages. The Humanists thought to reform Europe by remaking the *orator* on the classical model. However, the philosophical aim had no existence apart from its usefulness in assuring acceptable usage in contemporary Latin literature. The social aim was taken for granted—it was unthinkable that an educated man could not speak Latin. Though they were by now literary vehicles of some stature, modern foreign languages were taken by the Renaissance gentleman as primarily social implements. In scholarship they had little more than curiosity value and were not considered to have the lasting power necessary for literature. Hence early attempts, like that of John Palsgrave, to analyze them along formal lines were not commercially successful, while the opposite approach which inculcated speech skills monopolized the market.

Though definitely launched in 1882 by Viëtor's famous pamphlet, the modern period had been in preparation since the beginning of the nineteenth century. Modern languages, but not classical, had once more asserted themselves as social tools. Creation of literature was gratefully abandoned, and in the most doctrinaire schools of the twentieth century, the value of even reading was widely questioned. Since languages were taught as behavioral entities, schemes of analysis were not regarded as valuable, except as reinforcement of behavior. Owing to their lack of social relevance, classical languages retained the philosophical aim and the passive aspect of literary study and appreciation. Among a few dedicated classicists, literary production in Latin and Greek lingered on as a pastime.

In contrast, the parallelism between the eighteenth and nineteenth centuries and the Middle Ages is equally close. It would be unfair to claim that the communication aspects of languages were lost sight of, but the balance had shifted towards written and analytical skills.

During the Middle Ages, Latin was taught as a highly sophisticated vehicle of argument and artistic creation. The oral dimension, although not entirely abandoned, was merely an important side issue which grew out of classroom teaching. The key disciplines of theology and philosophy, which depended on exact usage and on sharp analytical thinking, demanded close attention to intricacies of grammar, while the need for forceful expression kept alive the discipline of rhetoric. This tendency towards written composition reached its height in the development of the *ars dictaminis* during the fourteenth century. But as this was mainly a creation of the law schools, it did not affect too deeply the literary and philosophical aims of the older and more traditional schools.

It is no accident that the first vernacular languages to be formally taught were those of the troubadours, for it was only in these languages that literary conventions as sophisticated as those of Latin had arisen. Hence Romance dialects were not taught orally, but as vehicles of poetic genres. In itself grammatical analysis was not important, but, as in Latin, it was a useful introduction to rhetorical form.[399:647:926]

The Cartesian spirit of the seventeenth and eighteenth centuries matched the zeal of the *grammatica speculativa* for grammatical analysis. The Renaissance was succeeded by an age which valued performance less than coherent theorizing about reality: the shift in emphasis is well illustrated by Comenius, who changed from a teacher favoring active teaching to one who expected his pupils to derive practice from theory. Language teaching fell under the control of the logicians, for whom language was governed by logic and, at times, was part of it. As the headquarters of the movement was in France, claims for *la clarté française* outweighed similar pretensions of other languages of culture. Where this age differs from the medieval period is in the position of literary creation. In modern languages it was unheard of; in classical it was still a valid aim, but owing to the declining importance of Latin as a scientific language, it became less important and even had to struggle for its life on the continent before going under in the early nineteenth century. In England the struggle was more protracted, courses in free composition being found even now. But apart from an exceptional few who were interested in the intellectual challenge free composition entailed, the only aim envisaged for classical languages was "mental discipline."

At no period was the ruling aim universally accepted, or any one aim, until the eighteenth century, completely excluded. The cyclic evolution we have observed is largely based on alternation between the social and philosophical aims of language teaching with the literary aim acting as a balance. The need for forceful and elegant expression implied by this third aim kept the other two from going to excess. Thus, on its disappearance in the eighteenth century, first modern languages, then classical languages became arid and utopian manipulations of units and rules. The swing to the social objective of the late nineteenth century brought about similar doctrinaire espousals of the oral language and violent denials of the important stabilizing role of writing in both real life and the classroom.

The difference in the length of the two cyclic phases is striking. From the final abandonment of classical methodology (in this we include the social teaching of language as well as the formal) to the

Renaissance is more than a thousand years; from Comenius, who marks the end of the Renaissance, until the development of the Direct Method is about 300 years. This is doubtless due both to social forces and to the means of transmission available. As a language of scholarship and administration, Latin remained important until well into the seventeenth century. Its usefulness as an auxiliary language had been considerably lessened by the well-intentioned and successful efforts of the Renaissance to set aside medieval developments and restore it to its classical shape. This antiquarianism was reinforced by the religious importance of Greek, Latin, and Hebrew. During the Renaissance traces of the medieval internationalism in Europe ensured that foreign languages were taught as vehicles of communication. Both French and Italian, for historical reasons, were intensely important as cultured languages for the educated. As linguistic nationalism spread across Europe, languages lost their international importance to a large extent, with dire effects on the balance of aims. With improved communications during the nineteenth century and greater contact among the peoples of Europe, needs in language mastery changed once again.

Technology kept pace with these social changes. For various reasons books were not common before the Renaissance. The invention of the printing press made this aid widespread enough to ensure diffusion of ideas and knowledge to a wide circle, lay and clerical. Unconventional ideas were given the permanence of print, and the book had a wider sale than the manuscript it superseded. The early humanists realized the importance of this new medium and took control of it themselves. Other media, including the phonograph, television, and films, had a similar effect during the twentieth century. These were first exploited commercially, and after the public were familiar with their uses in entertainment and business, they were adapted to the classroom.

What have these cyclic changes meant in terms of approach? The classical period shows an ordered progression from active teaching in the home to very sophisticated grammatical and rhetorical training in the schools of Rome and Athens. During childhood Greek was picked up through contact with bilingual tutors, slaves, and social peers. The school, not having to bother with elementary skills, used extremely formal techniques based on a rigid analytical scheme starting from letters and phonemes and finishing with a complete oration. The aim was not merely communication, but graceful and forceful communication. To achieve this the teaching corpus was based on a selection of the best authors and both the analytical and the artistic powers of the pupil were developed by methods based on guided imitation and textual criticism. As the Roman learned both Latin and Greek in childhood, there was no real need to distinguish between first and second language. This came only when Rome ceased to be bilingual and the Greek communities of the Empire, which had disdained Latin during the golden and silver ages, began to learn Latin to avoid becoming a subject race with no say in their destiny.

By the third century, the social support for Greek had almost gone and bilingualism was at a discount. A brief trial of translation methods was made in Alexandria and the Greek-speaking parts of Gaul, and the transition to medieval methods had begun. In the West, once the East had been cut off, Latin was stabilized as the only second language. But as it was thought of merely as a cultivated register of Romance, a whole stage dropped out of the learning process: except for a cursory introduction in the choir schools, pupils began their Latin with grammar and passed to rhetoric, which retained its classical rigor while expanding the basis for selection of material.

In non-Romance Europe, where Romance-speaking missionaries brought classical learning with Christianity, there was, it seems, no thought given to suiting the approach to local conditions. In any case Latin was now the only language in Western Europe in which scholarship was possible; and the rigorous methods of Romance Europe held good in the monasteries which were being founded among the barbarians. Though the Middle Ages by no means ignored classical precedent, they tended to be eclectic in their choice of models and overlaid classical methodology with approaches drawn from their own treatment of religion, philosophy, and literature. As Phrysius, Erasmus's secretary, was to realize, the boundary between philosophy and theology was far from clear; and much can be said for the view that during the second part of the Middle Ages, methods in scholarship were dictated by theology. In language teaching this was reflected in reliance on infallible authority, in this case the *Doctrinale* and *Graecismus.* Yet Latin teaching was extremely vital, as can be seen from the sheer volume of excellent secular and religious literature produced for both enjoyment and worship. The only antirhetorical development of the Middle Ages was the *ars dictaminis,* which, dealing with drafting legal documents, explicitly rejected literary models as irrelevant. Despite the attention this new development caused, it did not really disturb classroom method, which kept its rhetorical cast, this time on a broader base of models and needs. If we include poetry under rhetoric, an attitude not supported by Aristotle, but the *de facto* position in both classical and medieval schools, it is not hard to see why the first formal approaches to the languages of the troubadours were written not oral, or why Donatus, the great fourth-century grammarian, was the expository model chosen for modern-language grammars of the time.

Two types of method rose from the double aim current during the Renaissance: in classical languages ancient rhetorical methods continued, but humanist emphasis on stylistics brought into question the medieval acceptance of spoken Latin in class, causing a series of debates in methodology which were never resolved. The new-found respectability of the vernaculars, together with the need to forge from them languages as subtle as Latin, occasioned an elaborate typology of translation and a careful assessment of its utility in class. In contemporary languages, however, as they were considered social rather than scholarly assets, the first fully documented appearance of many techniques often considered proper to the twentieth century produced an oral methodology which in no way relied on linguistic analysis. This was not without effect in the classical classroom, where clairvoyant teachers saw that unless Latin and Greek were accorded other than scholarly importance, they would slowly die.

The age of reason, as far as language teaching was concerned, was ushered in by general grammar. The Cartesian attitude, which sought to relate appearances to deterministic laws, emphasized once again the science of grammar, reducing quite considerably the role of rhetoric, in which law had been tempered by artistic taste. In this language scholarship followed the temper of the times. It seems that introduction to language through pronunciation and socially oriented drills was abandoned. As all languages were related to the same first cause, logic, grammatical studies in the mother tongue became the introduction to foreign-language learning, the categories of one being easily applied to the other. Translation, which had served as an introduction to the arts of literature during the Renaissance, became a general work horse. Both speech and finesse of style were neglected; even composition came under attack as a utopian exercise. What mattered was establishing correspondences between home and target language. At first, the remaining traces of the old rhetorical approach kept Latin and Greek free from this method, now known as "Grammar-Translation." But as the social aim was now dead and the literary the property of a few enthusiasts, the philosophical approach invaded classical languages at the beginning of the nineteenth century and reached its greatest development there.

While the age of reason went to one extreme, the modern period went to another. Reaction against written methods in a situation imposing an oral aim produced a rigid stand in favor of approaches through the spoken language. Like the previous two hundred years, the modern age lacked the stabilizing influence of the literary approach, so that there was little brake on the adoption of the view that one could learn a language only through speech and that all else was artificial. Thus teaching was tied to the oral language by selection methods developed by linguists and conditioning methods built first on intuition, then on learning psychology, and then on conditioning theory. As the emphasis was on communication, minimal standards of competence were aimed at, rather than finesse. Where the emphasis had been once on the matter of the course and method taken for granted, in line with the tendency in general education method was carefully worked out to get tangible results quickly and matter was restricted to suit. Thus language teaching became akin to training musicians or sportsmen, with a series of procedures based on drills that did not require theoretical understanding but faultless performance of a well-graded series of relatively simple operations.

Given the prime role of educational objectives in language teaching, we must view with skepticism the notion of a cause-and-effect relationship between human sciences and language teaching. Yet the question remains: how do intellectual pressures react with scientific ideas to produce method?

The idea of an applied science is peculiarly modern. Before the nineteenth century it seems to have been accepted that grammar and rhetoric were arts. The only science of language that existed was codification of existing practice for the purpose of teaching. In this way both grammar and rhetoric were developed and transmitted. However, it is clear that ancient and medieval language teachers drew on philosophy for their basic concepts and methods. Language learning was a preparation for philosophy, and there was a circular relationship between logic and grammar that kept the link close. Logic in the beginning had been based on analysis of Latin and Greek in use, but after a few centuries was used as a tool to analyze that from which it had sprung. There was equally a rudimentary science of education: to take but a few examples, Cicero, St. Augustine, Alcuin, and John of Salisbury were extremely conscious of the needs of both pupil and teacher, but all of their recommendations were *ad hoc* statements based on their experience in the classroom.

It was not until the Renaissance that conformity of practice and theory began to suggest that some aspects of practice might profitably follow theory; but one is never sure whether appeals to theory are brilliant hindsight or not. It is clear that the structural techniques of Erasmus and de Sainliens owe nothing to contemporary language theory, though the grammatical scheme of Petrus Ramus was worked out for class use. Likewise the phonetic investigations of the sixteenth century certainly come from research, and we have reason to conjecture that certain teachers used Renaissance phonetics in the classroom. In learning theory Vivès called on the medieval concept of the powers of the soul to create a philosophy of teaching that went beyond languages. But as he was a teacher himself, how much of this was rationalization of his own practice we do not know. It was left to Comenius to codify teaching theory, but again this certainly was based on his own experience.

Comenius, by his change from spontaneous teaching of the Renaissance type to an approach governed by grammatical principle, was in tune with seventeenth-century developments. By now the prime discipline was Cartesian logic, which sought to relate everything to one logical model. In language this meant that all languages shared a basic grammar which could be deduced from the mother tongue. It is to this development that we owe the Grammar-Translation Method. During the next century Rousseau confirmed that theorists whose prowess in the classroom was nil could have an effect on educational theory and practice. While his influence was not widely felt until the Natural Method of the nineteenth century, he opened the gates to educational philosophers like Kant, Herbart, and Dewey.

While educators had handled only the able and interested in the exclusive schools of pre-nineteenth-century Europe, the pressure on teaching skills exerted by the opening of schools and language classes to increasing numbers of pupils who did not share their parents' motivation, brought about a deeply felt need for workable theories. Consequently, the character of books on language teaching began to diversify. Along with the standard type of treatise drawn from classroom experience, came the type of book which related teaching theory to human development. The Natural Method was the first result of this approach. Having observed salient facets of natural language learning, Natural Methodists from Pestalozzi to Gouin bent Rousseau's ideas on the primacy of nature to language teaching. These ideas combined with those of Herbart on learning and Humboldt on language to provide the theoretical basis of the Direct Method. Contemporary with this was the structural method of Prendergast, which too was inspired by the *idée fixe* of Rousseau while looking forward to the 1940's.

This was not immediately obvious at the time since the major scientific contribution, in the eyes of the Direct Method, was phonetics. Almost for the first time a linguistic theory affected teaching practice instead of being developed to answer a teaching need. That there was now a distinction between linguistics and language teaching was clear to at least some people (cf. Glauning's remark that a teacher must know phonetics but need not teach it as such in class).[462:11] This simple distinction operated in the best applications of the Structural Method and other modern methods derived from it.

As the stimulus-response view of language came to be accepted, Herbartian psychology was largely replaced by behaviorism. It is to this and similar theories that the structurally based methods of the 1940's owe their pedagogy. The comparative success of the Direct Method had made respectable teaching practice based on scientific experiment and theory rather than on experience.

The modern development of the critical sciences in language teaching was partially due to the replacement of rule making in linguistics by observation, and to the specialization of the roles of scientist and teacher. The first linguistic scientists were primarily teachers; hence as the descriptive side of linguistics developed, so did the normative. This is strikingly illustrated by the Carolingian reform, which set in train a school of philology whose sole aim was the revision of sacred and scholarly texts, and the reform of classroom teaching. The first analyses of modern languages were equally normative until linguists became interested in "exotic" languages for scientific and religious reasons. In these, rule making was rejected and, by extension, was outlawed even in treatments of languages which had been taught for centuries. Similar descriptive orientations appeared in other sciences concerned with language teaching. The need was felt for a science of teaching that would fill this gap.

It was assumed that prior to the Direct Method language teaching had been a hand-to-mouth affair. It thus seemed reasonable for Sweet to write that his aim was

> . . . first to determine the general principles on which a rational method of learning foreign language should be based, and then to consider the various modifications these general principles undergo in their application to different circumstances and different classes of learners.
>
> 1898 (Sweet) 1054: vi

Twenty years later Palmer went even further, declaring that: "It is time that language study should be placed on a scientific foundation, and to that effect it would be well to institute a general inquiry into the whole question."[836:21] Such an inquiry was in effect made by the Modern Language Association of America, which between 1927 and 1931 published the American and Canadian Foreign Languages Study in seventeen volumes covering all aspects of the matter.

While Sweet and Palmer had been interested in teaching, attempts at placing language teaching on a scientific foundation, of which the MLA study is typical, rested on testing the results of certain methods and comparing them from a psychological viewpoint. But just after the Second World War attention shifted to the methods themselves, and the orientation recommended by Sweet and Palmer was followed. Methods analysis was developed by a group of linguists and teachers in England,[700:150] and elsewhere applied linguistics developed its own norms. Both approaches depend almost equally on psychology and descriptive linguistics, deducing principles of teaching whereby findings of grammarians and linguists can be applied in the classroom.

That the expert in language teaching acts with the purity of motive and design expected from a scientist is demonstrably untrue. Discoveries are filtered by social and educational needs, and what suits the circumstances is what is considered proved. Thus, during the last twenty years it has been taken for granted that the written language, as an artificial construct, would be played down. But this was certainly not a universal opinion: Slama-Cazacu is quite clear that ". . . it is not justified to identify language solely with spoken expression."[1020:22] Yet, in the stampede towards the spoken language this and other similar opinions by equally reputable linguists and psychologists were ignored.

Such filtering of scientific data is accompanied by the remorseless torpedoing of men in the field who are out of step. Erasmus and his conventional colleagues did not allow G. H. Cominius to have any but a minor effect, though the moderns who have discovered him recognize a sympathetic theorist and practitioner. James Webbe and Pestalozzi suffered the same fate. Palsgrave is remembered for a brilliant attempt at formal analysis of French, though he was a teacher rather than a grammarian. Every age, in fact, has its rebels whose teaching techniques, though scientifically justifiable, failed to gain acceptance because they did not fit the atmosphere of the time. Teaching, being an art, looks to its market and takes from the parent sciences what will sell.

Those who swim against the current can be divided into three groups. The majority are those whom the evolution of philosophy and aim have left behind. The second are those who through wits or good luck sense a change and contribute to its acceptance. The third group comprises the innovator who takes his stand on scientific proof and is unaware of the social forces which isolate him. It is possible to distinguish the second group from the third only in retrospect. So what are we to make of Chomsky's statement in a BBC interview in 1968 that "the evidence is very convincing that the [habit-structure] view of language is erroneous, and that it is a very bad way—certainly an unprincipled way—to teach language"?[217:690] How are we to judge the importance of Susan Ervin-Tripp's insistence on the creative aspect of child learning?[385:29] Are we to expect that this presages another stage in the evolutionary cycle of language-teaching theory, or will these two experts and others like them suffer the fate of Cominius and Webbe?

It is clear that ideas do not exist on their worth alone. If this were so there would have been no evolution after the formation of a definitive corpus, and development would have stopped with Quintillian or Erasmus. Two factors have worked against this state of affairs: the changing perception of needs in the teaching profession; and the tendency of ideas to become sterile and men doctrinaire, causing independent minds to rebel and strike out on their own. These have been the motivations that have occasioned teachers to develop as many resources as possible to meet the changing problems of the transmission of knowledge. As in the fine arts, needs, approaches, and resources change, and one generation's heresy becomes the orthodoxy of the next.

BIBLIOGRAPHY

1. *Abbreviations*

AHR	*American Historical Review.*
AL	*Archivum Linguisticum.*
BAGB	*Bulletin de l'association Guillaume Budé.*
BHR	*Bibliothèque d'humanisme et de renaissance.*
BZ	*Byzantinische Zeitschrift.*
CJ	*Classical Journal.*
CP	*Classical Philology.*
CR	*Classical Review.*
Diderot	Diderot, D., et al. *Encyclopédie ou dictionnaire raisonné des sciences, des arts et des métiers.* 17 vols. Paris and Neufchâtel, 1751-1765.
E	*Education.*
EC	*Les études classiques.*
ELA	*Etudes de linguistique appliquée.*
ELT	*English Language Teaching.*
Faral	Faral, E. *Les arts poétiques du XIIe et du XIIIe siècle.* Paris, 1958.
FdM	*Le français dans le monde.*
Firth	Bazell, C. E., et al. *In memory of J. R. Firth.* London, 1966.
Fodor and Katz	Fodor, J. A., and J. J. Katz. *The Structure of Language, Readings in the Philosophy of Language.* Englewood Cliffs, N. J., 1964.
FR	*The French Review.*
G	*Gnomon.*
Guessard	Guessard, F. *Grammaires provençales.* Paris, 1858.
H	*Hispania.*
IRAL	*International Review of Applied Linguistics.*
Jacobovits and Miron	Jacobovits, L.A., and M. S. Miron. *Readings in the Psychology of Language.* Englewood Cliffs, N. J., 1967.

JASP	*Journal of Abnormal and Social Psychology.*
Keil	Keil, H. *Grammatici latini.* 8 vols. Hildesheim, 1961.
Kelly	Kelly, L. G., ed. *The Measurement and Description of Bilingualism, An International Seminar.* Toronto, 1969.
KFLQ	*Kentucky Foreign Language Quarterly.*
L	*Latinitas.*
La	*Latomus.*
Li	*Library.*
LL	*Language Learning.*
LM	*Les langues modernes.*
MF	*Le maître phonétique.*
MGH	*Monumenta germaniae historiae.* 50 vols. Hanover, 1826-1913.
MGP	*Monumenta germaniae paedagogicae.* 18 vols. Berlin, 1887-1904.
MH	*Medievalia et humanistica.*
MLJ	*Modern Language Journal.*
MLN	*Modern Language Notes.*
MLR	*Modern Language Review.*
MS	*Medieval Studies.*
PBA	*Proceedings of the British Academy.*
PL	Migne, J-P., ed. *Patrologia latina.* 222 vols. Paris, 1841-86.
PMLA	*Publications of the Modern Language Association.*
PQ	*Philological Quarterly.*
Pulgram	Pulgram, E., ed. *Applied Linguistics in Language Teaching,* Washington, 1954.
R	*Romania.*
RACL	*Revue de l'association canadienne de linguistique.*
RF	*Romanische Forschungen.*
Rice	Rice, W. H., ed. *Planning the Modern Language Lesson.* Syracuse, N. Y., 1946.
RLV	*Revue des langues vivantes.*
RR	*Revue de la renaissance.*
RSS	*Revue du seizième siècle.*
RU	*Revue universitaire.*
S	*Speculum.*
T	*Traditio.*
Wright	Wright, T., ed. *A Volume of Vocabularies.* London, 1857.

PRIMARY SOURCES

1. Abbo of Fleury. *Quaestiones grammaticales, PL,* CXXXIX, 522-534.
2. Abbott, O. L., "A Defense of Grammar," *MLJ,* XL (1956), 357-358.
3. Abelard, P. *Epistula nona, PL,* CLXXVIII, 325-336.
4. Abercrombie, D. *Problems and Principles: Studies in the Teaching of English as a Second Language.* London, 1956.
5. *Abrégé des particules.* Paris, 1736.
6. Adams, J. *Euphonologia linguae anglicanae.* London, 1794.
7. Adams, J. *The Herbartian Psychology Applied to Education.* Boston, 1879.
8. ——— , ed. *The New Teaching.* London, 1919.
9. Adler, G. J. *Ollendorf's New Method of Learning to Read, Write and Speak German.* New York, 1845.
10. ——— . *Ollendorf's Method of Learning German.* New York, 1854.
11. Aelfric. *Ars grammatica et glossarium,* ed. J. Zupitza. Berlin, 1880.
12. ———. *Colloquium,* ed. B. Thorpe. *Analectica Anglosaxonica,* London, 1858, 18-36.
12a.———. *ibid., Wright,* 5-96.
13. Agard, F. B., and H. B. Dunkel. *An Investigation of Second Language Teaching.* Boston, 1948.
14. Aggeler, W. F., "The Army Language School, An Appraisal," *MLJ,* XXXIV (1950), 189-195.
15. Agroecius. *Ars de orthographia, Keil,* VII, 113-125.
16. Ahern, J. *Leçons d'anglais par la méthode naturelle.* Quebec, 1895.
17. Ahn, F. *A New Practical and Easy Method of Learning German.* 2 vols. Philadelphia, 1859.
18. ———. *German Grammar.* New York, 1867.
19. A. I. *Italian Dialogues.* Cambridge, 1774.
20. Alanus de Insulis (Alain de Lille). *Anticlaudianus, PL,* CCX, 482-578.
21. Albertus, L. *Certissima ratio discendae, augendae, ornandae, propagandae, conservandaeque linguae alemanorum sive germanorum,* (1573) ed. C. Muller-Fraureuth. Strasbourg, 1895.

22. Alciat, A. *De verborum significatione,* Lyons, 1530.
23. Alcuin. *De arte grammatica, PL,* CCI, 850-901.
24. ———. *De orthographia, PL,* CCI, 902-919.
25. ———. *De rhetorica et virtutibus, PL,* CCI, 920-975.
26. ———. *Disputatio Pippini cum Albino, PL,* CCI, 975 ff.
27. Aldhelm. *Liber de septenario et de metris, aenigmatis, ac pedum regulis, PL,* LXXXIX, 95-99.
28. ———. *Epistola Aethilwaldo, PL,* LXXXIX, 100.
29. Alexander of Neckham. *De utensilibus, Wright,* 96-120.
30. Alexander de Villa Dei. *Doctrinale, MGP,* XII (whole volume).
31. Allen, E. D. "Effects of the Language Laboratory on the Development of Skill in a Foreign Language," *MLJ,* XLIV (1960), 355-358.
32. Allen, J. H., and J. B. Greenough. *A Latin Grammar.* Boston, 1879.
33. Alsted, J. H. *Encyclopedia universalis,* Herbornae Nassouiorum, 1630.
34. *Amplificationes latines graduées.* Paris, 1831.
35. Andersson, T. *The Teaching of Foreign Languages in the Elementary School.* Boston, 1953.
36. Andrews, E. A. *First Lessons in Latin.* Boston, 1843.
37. ———, and S. Stoddart. *A Grammar of the Latin Language.* Boston and New York, 1872.
38. Angiolillo, P. "French for the Feeble-minded," *MLJ,* XXVI (1942), 267-271.
39. Anselm of Canterbury. *De grammatica,* ed. D. P. Henry. New York, 1964.
40. Anthon, C. *An Introduction to Latin Prose Composition.* New York, 1875.
41. Antoniano, S. *Dell' educazione christiana dei figliuoli.* Rome, 1584.
42. Anwykyll, J. *Compendium totius grammaticae,* Oxford, 1483, U. M. Film.
43. Aristotle. *The Basic Works of Aristotle,* ed. R. McKeown. New York 1941.
44. Aronstein, P. *Methodik des neusprachlichen Unterrichts.* 2 vols. Leipzig, 1926.
45. Arnauld, A., and C. Lancelot. *Nouvelle méthode pour apprendre la langue latine,* 3rd ed. Paris, 1656.
45a.———,and ———. *ibid.,* ed. A. Duclos. Paris, 1819.
46. ———, and ———. *La grammaire de Port-Royal,* Paris, 1810.
47. ———, and ——— . *Nouvelle méthode pour apprendre la langue grecque.* (1655) Paris, 1758.
47a.———, and ———. *ibid.* (after ed. of 1754). Paris, 1819.
48. ———, and ——— . *Abrégé de la nouvelle méthode pour apprendre la langue grecque,* 2nd ed. Paris, 1656.

49. ———, and ———. *Le jardin des racines grecques* (1657), ed. J.-A. Regnier. Paris, 1861.
50. Arnold, T. K. *A Practical Introduction to Greek Prose Composition.* London, 1849.
51. ———. *First and Second Latin Books,* ed. J. H. Spencer. New York, 1864.
52. Arnulf of Louvain. *Deliciae cleri,* ed. J. Huemer *RF,* XI (1899), 211-246.
53. Ascham, R. *The Scholemaster* (1570), London and New York, 1909.
54. Assn. of Assistant Mistresses in Secondary Schools. *Memorandum on Modern Language Teaching.* London, 1952.
55. Atkins, H. G., and H. L. Hutton. *The Teaching of Modern Foreign Languages in School and University.* London, 1920.
56. Aue, C. E. *German Grammar,* Edinburgh, 1901.
57. Auger, A. *Discours choisis de Cicéron à l'usage des classes.* 3 vols. Paris, 1786.
58. St. Augustine. *De doctrina christiana, PL,* XXXIV, 16-120.
59. ———. *De grammatica, PL,* XXXII, 1385-1408.
60. ———. *De magistro, PL,* XXXII, 1193-1220.
61. ———. *De musica, Oeuvres de S Augustin.* VII. Tournai, 1947.
62. ———. *Confessiones.* W. H. D. Rouse. 2 vols. ed. Loeb Classical Library, 1950.
63. Aulus, Gellius. *Noctes atticae,* ed. J. C. Rolfe. 3 vols. Loeb Classical Library, 1960.
64. Ausonius, *Opera omnia,* ed. H. G. E. White. 2 vols. Loeb Classical Library, 1951.
65. B____. G. *L'interprète américain.* New York, 1849.
66. Bacci, A. "Adversus grammatistas ac minutioris eruditionis amatores," *L,* IV (1956), 91-98.
67. Bachi, P. *Conversazione italiana,* Cambridge, 1835.
68. Bacon, F. *The Advancement of Learning* (1606), ed. G. W. Kitchin. London and New York, n.d.
69. Bacon, R. *Greek Grammar* (1272), ed. E. Nolan and S. A. Hirsch. Cambridge, 1902.
70. ———. *Opus maius III (The Study of Tongues),* tr. R. B. Burke. New York, 1962.
71. Badois, C. *Grammaire anglaise après le system d'Ollendorf* (1852), New York, 1861.
72. Bahlsen, L. *The Teaching of Modern Languages,* tr. M. Blakemore-Evans. Boston, 1905.

73. Baillius, W. *De quantitate syllabarum graecarum.* Lyon, 1612.
74. Bainvel, R. P. *Causeries pédagogiques.* Paris, 1898.
75. Ball, C. Y. *Teaching Modern Languages to Adults.* London, 1917.
76. Barbour, H. M. *L'anglais dans un coup d'oeil.* New York, 1912.
77. Baret, A. *La première année d'anglais.* Paris, 1902.
78. Barlement, N. *Colloquia et dictionariolum septem linguarum belgicae, teutonicae, anglicae, gallicae, latinae, hispanicae, et italicae* (1592). Antwerp, 1616 (Reprinted Nederlandsche Boekhandel, Antwerp, 1925).
79. Barré, F. T. *English Accentuation, Speller and Reader.* New York, 1909.
80. Basedow, J. B. *Das Elementewerke.* Leipzig, 1785.
81. ———. *Ausgewählte Schriften,* ed. H. Göring. Langensalza, 1880.
82. St. Basil. "Letter to Young Men on Reading Pagan Literature," *Complete Works,* ed. R. J. Deferrari and M. R. P. McGuire. Loeb Classical Library, 1961, 378-435.
83. Bathe and White. *Janua linguarum quadrilinguis or a Messe of Tongues* (1611). London, 1617.
84. Batiffol, H. *Grammaire latine.* Paris, 1886.
85. Bayley, C. *An Entrance into the Sacred Language.* London, 1782.
86. Bazouin, A. "Le latin plus facile, par une meilleure ponctuation," *RU,* XXXVII (1928), 223-230.
87. St. Bede. *Cunabula grammaticae artis Donati a Beda restituta, PL, XC,* 613-623 (dubious attribution).
88. ———. *De arte metrica, Keil,* VII, 227-260.
89. ———. *De schematibus et tropis, PL,* XC, 175-180.
90. ———. *Epistola ad Egbertum, PL,* XLIV, 657-668.
91. ———. *Opera historica,* ed. J. E. King. Loeb Classical Library, 1954.
92. Beinhauer, W. *Spanische Umgangssprache.* Bonn, 1958.
93. Bell, A. M. *Visible Speech,* London, 1867.
94. ———. *Hand-book of World English.* New York and London, 1888.
95. ———. *Speechtones,* Washington, 1894.
96. Bellarmine, R. *Institutiones hebraicae* (1580). Antwerp, 1606.
97. Belyayev, B. V. *The Psychology of Teaching Foreign Languages* (1959), tr. R. F. Hingley. New York, 1964.
98. Bembo, P. *De Imitatione* (1513), in *Insignia quotquot exstant opuscula.* Basle, n.d.
99. Bénédict, G. *L'enseignement vivant des langues vivantes par la méthode directe progressive.* Lausanne, 1930.
100. Bennet, J. *Collectio sententiarum, exemplorum, testimoniorum necnon et similitudinum in usum scolasticae iuventutis.* London, n.d. (1790?).

101. Benzies, D. *Learning Our Language.* London, 1940.
102. Berger, F. *Méthode d'anglais.* Paris, London, and New York, 1903.
103. Berlitz, M. D. *Method for Teaching Foreign Languages, English, Books 1 & 2.* New York, 1922.
104. ———. *Français, 1e et 2e livres.* New York, 1905.
105. ———. *Erstes Buch.* London, 1929.
106. Bernard of Clairvaux. *De conversione ad cleros sermo, PL,* CLXXXII, 834-856.
107. Bernard, E. G. "Using Slides and Films Effectively," *MLJ,* XXIII (1939), 557-561.
108. Berry, T. *La vraie méthode pour apprendre l'anglois.* Rouen, 1788.
109. Bertenshaw, T. H. *Complete Grammar.* London, 1902.
110. Berthon, H. E. *Grammaire française.* London, 1902.
111. Bescherelle, L.-N. *Grammaire nationale.* Paris, 1835.
111a.———. *ibid.* 12e ed. Paris, 1864.
112. Beuzelin. *Nouvelle méthode pour étudier l'hébreu.* Paris, 1826.
113. Beynel, V. *Guide pratique pour la version latine.* Paris, 1930.
114. Bézard, J. *Comment apprendre le latin à nos fils.* Paris, 1914.
115. Biagioli, G. *Grammaire italienne élémentaire et raisonnée.* Paris, 1808.
116. Biarnois, A. *A Practical and Theoretical Method of Learning the French Language.* New York, 1868.
117. Bierman, H. "Original Dramatisation in Modern Languages," *MLJ,* I (1916), 242-246.
118. Bitzer, D. L., E. R. Lyman, and J. A. Easley. *The Uses of PLATO, a Computer-controlled Teaching System,* Urbana, Ill., 1965.
119. Blackwall, A. *An Introduction to the Classics.* London, 1719.
120. Blair, T. *Some Short and Easy Rules, Teaching the True Pronunciation of the French Language.* Boston, 1720.
121. Blebel, T. *Grammaticae hebreae sanctae linguae institutiones.* Witebergae, 1578.
122. Blondin. *Précis de la langue française.* Paris, 1790.
123. Bloomfield, L. *Outline Guide for the Practical Study of Foreign Languages.* New York, 1942.
124. ———. *Spoken Dutch.* New York, 1944.
125. Blouin, M. E. *An Eclectic Method of Teaching French.* Greensburg, Pa., 1942.
126. Bloume, E. *Une première année de latin.* Paris, 1872.
127. Bodin, E. *Bericht von der Natur und Vernunfft Didactica.* Hamburg, 1621.
128. ———. *Ars Mnemonica per imagines.* Giessen, 1626.

129. Bodin, J. *Oratio de instituenda in republica iuventute ad senatum populumque tolosanum*. Toulouse, 1559.
130. Boethius. *De musica, PL,* LXIII, 1167-1196.
131. ———. *De rhetoricae cognatione, PL,* LXIV, 1218-1222.
132. Boinvilliers, J. E., and J. F. Boinvilliers. *Grammaire latine théorique et pratique*. 7th ed. Paris, 1808.
133. Bolmar, A. *A Book of the French Verbs*. New York, 1831.
134. Bohlen, A. *Methodik des neusprachlichen Unterrichts*. 3rd ed. Heidelberg, 1958.
135. ———. *Bild und Ton im neusprachlichen Unterricht*. Dortmund, 1962.
136. Boldyreff, T. W. "Phonograph versus Phonetics," *FR,* ii (1929), 205-213.
137. St. Boniface. *Ars grammatica,* ed. A. Mai. *Auctores classici,* Rome, 1828-1838, VII.
138. Bottke, K. G. "French Conversational Laboratory," *FR,* XVIII (1944), 54-56.
139. Bouchendhomme, E. *De l'enseignement du français*. Paris, 1912.
140. Boulouffe, J. "La progression des exercices," *RLV,* XXIX (1963), 245-256.
141. Bouton, C. "Motivation et enseignement des langues," *ELA,* I (1962), 85-94.
142. Bovée, A. G. "A French Course of Study," *MLJ,* III (1919), 193-213, 251-276, 300-324, 368-376. 368-376.
143. ———. "Some Fallacies of Formalism," *MLJ,* VIII (1923), 131-144.
144. Boyer, A. *A New Methodical French Grammar*. London, 1696.
145. Boyer, P., and N. Speranski. *Manuel pour l'étude de la langue russe*. Paris, 1935.
146. Brandt, H. C. G. "How Far Should Our Teaching and Textbooks Have a Scientific Basis?" *PMLA,* I (1885), 57-63.
147. Braunfels, W., and F. White. *Schillers William Tell with Interlinear Translation*. London, 1859.
148. Braunshausen, N. *Le bilinguisme et les méthodes d'enseignment des langues étrangères*. Liege, 1933.
149. Bréal, M. *De l'enseignement des langues anciennes*. Paris, 1891.
150. Brebner, M. *The Method of Teaching Modern Languages in Germany*. London, 1898.
151. Brenkmann, C. *Hossfeld's New Practical Method for Learning the German Language,* ed. M. Happe. London, 1900.
152. Brereton, C. *Modern Language Teaching in Day and Evening Schools with Special Reference to London*. London, 1930.

153. Breul, K. *The Teaching of Modern Foreign Languages and the Training of Teachers* (1898). 4th ed. Cambridge, 1913.
154. Bridel, A. *Chambaud's Exercises.* London, 1810.
155. Brinsley, J. *Ludus literarius or the Grammar Schools.* London, 1612.
155a.———. *ibid.* (2nd ed) (1627), ed. E. T. Campagnac. Liverpool, 1917.
156. ———. *Pueriles confabulatiunculae.* London, 1617 (UM Film).
157. ———. *A Consolation for Our Grammar Schools.* London, 1622 (UM Film).
158. ———. *The Posing of the Parts.* London, 1633.
159. ———. *Virgil's Eclogues with his Book de Apibus.* London, 1633.
160. Briod, E. *L'étude et l'enseignement d'une langue vivante.* Lausanne, 1922.
161. Bronstein, M. *Méthodes d'enseignement des langues étrangères aux adultes.* Paris, 1937.
162. Brooks, N. *Language and Language Learning.* New York, 1960.
163. Brooks, N. C. *Ross's Latin Grammar,* Philadelphia, 1844.
164. Bruno, P. "De lingua latina rite excolenda peropportuna monita," *L,* VI (1958), 115-120.
165. Buchanan, M. A. *A Graded Spanish Wordbook.* Toronto, 1927.
166. Budé, G. *Commentarii linguae graecae,* Paris, 1529.
167. ———. *De Studio litterarum* (1532), reprinted Stuttgart-Bad, 1964.
168. ———. *De transitu hellenismi ad christianismum.* Paris, 1535.
169. ———. *De l'institution du prince.* Paris, 1547.
170. Bullions, P. *The Principles of Latin Grammar.* New York, 1865.
171. Bunn, N. H. H. *Practical German Exercises.* London, 1933.
172. Bureau pour l'enseignement de la langue et de la civilisation françaises a l'étranger. *Colloque international sur les problèmes des langues secondes,* Quebec & Paris, 1966.
173. Burgdorf, I., et al. *Méthode audio-visuelle de l'allemand.* Paris and Brussels, 1962.
174. Burnouf, J. L. *Méthode pour étudier la langue latine.* Paris, 1841.
175. ———. *Premiers principes de la grammaire latine,* 3 ed. Paris, 1842.
176. Bursill-Hall, G. L., "Levels Analysis: J. R. Firth's Theories of Linguistic Analysis," *RACL,* V (1960), 124-135; 164-191.
177. Bushnell, D. D., and D. W. Allen. *The Computer in American Education.* New York, 1967.
178. Buswell, G. T. *A Laboratory Study of the Reading of Modern Foreign Languages.* New York, 1927.
179. Butin, R. *Progressive Lessons in Hebrew.* Washington, 1915.
180. Butler, F. *The Spanish Teacher.* New York, 1845.

181. Buxtorfius, J. *Hebreae epitome grammaticae.* Basle, 1605.
182. Bythner, V. *Lingua eruditorum.* London, 1664.
183. ———. *Clavis linguae sanctae.* Cambridge, 1648.
184. Caius, J. *De pronunciatione grecae et latinae linguae.* London, 1574.
185. Camden, W. *Institutio graecae grammatices compendaria in usum scholae westmonasteriensis.* London, 1595.
185a.———. *ibid.*, ed. I. W. London, 1793.
186. Canadian Legion. *Latin.* 3 vols. Ottawa, 1941.
187. ———. *Conversation anglaise.* 4 vols. Ottawa, 1941.
188. Capella, Martianus. *De nuptiis Philologiae et Mercurii,* ed. U. F. Kopp. Frankfurt, 1836.
189. Carniero, L. A. *O ensino das linguas vivas.* São Paulo, 1935.
190. Carr, W. L. *The Teaching of Elementary Latin.* London, 1929.
191. Carroll, J. B. "Wanted, a Research Basis for Educational Policy on Foreign Language Teaching," *Harvard Educational Review,* XXX (1960), 128-140.
192. ———. "A Primer of Programmed Instruction in Foreign Language Teaching," *IRAL,* I (1963), 115-141.
193. ———. "Words, Meanings and Concepts," in *Jacobovits and Miron,* 567-586.
194. Cartledge, H. A. "Verse Speaking in the English Class," *ELT,* XIII (1958), 67-72.
195. Cassiodorus. *De artibus ac disciplinis liberalium literarum, PL,* LXX, 1149-1218.
196. Cassirer, H. R. *Television Teaching Today.* Paris, 1960.
197. Catford, J. G. "Intelligibility," *ELT,* V (1950), 7-15.
198. Caussin, N. *De eloquentia sacra et humana.* 7 ed. Lyons, 1551.
199. Caxton, W. *Vocabularie Frenche and Englishe.* London, 1480.
200. Ceporinus, J. *Compendium grammaticae graecae.* London, 1585.
201. Chagnon, P. E., and G. C. Kettelcamp. "The Mirrophone as a Teaching Device," *MLJ,* XXIX (1945), 517-520.
202. Chall, J. *Learning to Read.* New York, 1967.
203. Chambaud, L. *Grammar of the French Tongue.* 3 ed. London, 1764.
204. ———. *French and English Dialogues.* 5 ed. London, 1779.
205. Chamberlain, J. L., "Some Aids in Teaching a Spoken Foreign Language," *MLJ,* XXXVIII (1954), 331-346.
206. Chambers, R. L., and K. D. Robinson. *Septimus, a First Latin Reader.* Edinburgh and London, 1936.
207. Chapman, L. R. H. *Teaching English to Beginners.* London, 1958.

208. Charlemagne. "Encyclica de literis colendis," *MGH* Leges I, 52-53.
209. Charpentier. *De l'excellence de la langue françois.* Paris, 1683.
210. Cheydleur, F. D. *French Idiom List.* New York, 1929.
211. Chifflets, L. *Grammaire françoise.* Paris, 1660.
212. Chompré, P. *Introduction à la language latine par voie de la traduction.* Paris, 1743.
213. ———. *Moyen d'apprendre les langues et principalement le latin.* Paris, 1757.
214. Chomsky, N. *Syntactic Structures.* The Hague, 1957.
215. ———. *Cartesian Linguistics.* New York, 1966.
216. ———. "Current Issues in Linguistic Theory," in *Fodor and Katz,* 50-118.
217. ———, Stuart Hampshire, and Alisdair MacIntyre. "Philosophy and Linguistics," *The Listener,* LXXIX (1968), 685-691.

Cicero, Marcus Tullius. Rhetorica, ed. A. S. Wilkins. 2 vols. Oxford, 1903.

218. ———. *Orator, Rhetorica* II.
219. ———. *Partitiones oratoriae, Rhetorica* II.
220. ———. *De oratore, Rhetorica* I.
221. Cioffari, V. "The Teaching of Foreign Languages in the Elementary School–a Realistic Analysis of the Present Movement," *MLJ,* XXXVIII (1954), 142-157.
222. Clajus, J. *Deutsche Gramatik* (1587). Strasbourg, 1894.
223. Clare, W. *A Compleat System of Grammar, English and Latin.* London, 1699.
224. Clarke, C. C. "The Phonograph in Modern Language Teaching," *MLJ,* III (1919), 116-122.
225. Clarke, G. H., and C. J. Murray. *School Grammar of Modern French.* London, 1900.
226. Clarke, J. *Essay upon the Education of Youth in Grammar Schools.* London, 1720.
227. ———. *Lucii Annaei Flori epitome rerum romanarum cum versione anglica.* London, 1744.
228. ———. *Corderii colloquiorum centuria selecta.* 26 ed. London, 1786.
229. ———. *An Introduction to the Making of Latin.* London, 1798.
230. Cleland, J. *Ἡρω-παιδεία or the Instruction of a Young Gentleman,* (1607) ed. M. Molyneux. New York, 1948.
231. Clemens, Scotus. *Ars grammatica,* ed. J. Tolkiehn. *Philologus,* Supplementband 20, Heft 3, 1928.
232. Clenardus (Kleynaerts), N. *Peregrinationum, ac de rebus machometicis epistolae elegantissimae.* Louvain, 1551.

233. ———. *Epistolarum libri duo,* Hanover, 1606.
234. ———. *Institutiones absolutissimae in graecam linguam.* Lyon, 1610.
235. Closset, F. *Les langues vivantes dans l'enseignement,* Liège, n.d.
236. ———. *Didactique des langues vivantes.* 2 ed. Paris and Brussels, 1953.
237. ———. "Le probleme du bilinguisme et l'enseignement des langues vivantes," *RLV,* XXIX (1963), 70-75.
238. Cobbet, W. *Le maître d'anglais,* ed. Davies. Paris, 1819.
239. Cochran, A. *Modern Methods of Teaching English as a Second language.* 2 ed. Washington, 1958.
240. Codret, A. *Les rudimens, ou les premiers principes de la langue latine.* Paris, 1694.
241. Cohen, M., et al. *Le français élémentaire, NON.* Paris, 1955.
242. Cole, R. D. *Modern Foreign Languages and Their Teaching.* New York, 1931.
243. ———, and J. B. Tharp. *Modern Foreign Languages and Their Teaching.* New York, 1937.
244. Coleman, A. *Experiments and Studies in Modern Language Teaching.* Chicago, 1934.
245. Colet, J. *Libellus de octo orationis partium* (1513). Paris, 1530.
246. ———. *Preces, hymni, et catechismus graece et latine in usum scholae S Pauli fundatore Joanne Coleto* (1515). London, 1896.
247. Collège de Montréal. *Grammaire grecque.* Montreal, 1837.
248. Collège militaire royale de S. Jean. *Annuaire.* Ottawa, 1966.
249. Colombo, C. *Manuel du latin commercial.* Paris, 1904.
Comenius, J.A. Opera didactica omnia (1657).6 vols.Reprinted by Academia Scientiarum bohemo-slovenica, Prague, 1957.
250. ———. *Ianua linguarum reserata* (1631). Amsterdam (1665?).
251. ———. *Vestibulum,* Opera VI, 301-317.
252. ———. *Novissima linguarum methodus* (1648), Opera I, 1-292.
253. ———. *La grande didactique* (1657), tr. J.-B. Pichetta. Paris, 1952.
254. ———. *Eruditionis scholasticae atrium.* Noribergae, 1659.
255. ———. *Schola-Ludus, seu encyclopedia viva, hoc est, ianuae linguarum praxis comica.* London, 1664.
256. ———. *The Analytic Didactic of Comenius,* ed. V. Jelinek. Chicago, 1953.
257. ———. *Orbis sensualium pictus* (1648). (ed. of 1658) Prague, 1942.
257a.———. *Orbis sensualium pictus latina, germanica, hungarica, bohemica.* Leutschoviae, 1658 (Reprinted Czech Government, 1958).
258. ———. *Orbis pictus, Švet v Obrazích, Die Welt in Bildern, Le monde en tableaux, renovatus et emendatus.* Prague, 1883.

259. ———. *Orbis pictus,* ed. C. W. Bardeen. published privately, Syracuse, N. Y., 1887.
260. ———. *Pampaedia,* ed. D. Tschizewsky, H. Geissler, and K. Schaller. *Pädagogische Forschungen* V. Heidelberg, 1960.
261. Condillac. *La grammaire.* Paris, 1802.
262. *Congrès international des professeurs de langues vivantes.* Paris, 1931.
263. *Premier congrès international pour le latin vivant.* Avignon, 1956.
264. *Deuxième congrès international pour le latin vivant.* Lyon, 1959.
265. Conybeare, W. D. *Letters and Exercises of the Elizabethan Schoolmaster, John Conybeare.* London, 1905.
266. Cooley, A. W. *Language Teaching in the Grades.* Boston, 1913.
267. Cooper, J. *Domus mosaicae clavis.* London, 1673.
268. Cooper, R. "How Can We Measure the Roles Which a Bilingual's Languages Play in His Everyday Behaviour?" *Kelly,* 191-206.
269. Copineau. *Origine et formation des langues.* Paris, 1774.
270. Coppa, I. "De italica ratione latinae linguae docendae," *L,* IV (1956), 199-210.
271. Corder, S. P, *English Language Teaching and Television.* London, 1960.
272. ———. "A Theory of Visual Aids in Language Teaching," *ELT,* XVII (1963), 82-87.
273. Cordier, M. *Principia latine loquendi scribendique, sive selecta quaedam ex Ciceronis epistolis, ad pueros in lingua latina exercendos, adjecta interpretatione gallica et (ubi opus visum est) latina declaratione* (1556), tr. T. W. London, 1575.
274. Cornelius, E. T. *Language Teaching, a Guide for Foreign Language Teachers.* New York, 1953.
275. Cotgrave, R. *Dictionarie of the French and English Tongues* (1611), ed. W. S. Woods. Columbia, S. C., 1950.
276. Crawford, C. C., and E. M. Leitzell. *Learning a New Language.* Los Angeles, 1930.
277. Crombie, A. *Gymnasium Abridged.* London, 1846.
278. Cruice, M. *Le Narrateur anglais.* Paris, 1845.
279. Cummings, T. F. *How to Learn a Language.* New York, 1916.
280. Curran, C. A. "Counseling Skills Adapted to the Learning of Foreign Languages," *Bulletin of the Menninger Clinic,* XXV (1961), 78-93.
281. D'Andeli, H. *La bataille des sept ars* (13th Century), ed. L. J. Paetow. Memoirs of the University of California, IV.i. Berkeley, Calif., 1914.
282. Dante, A. *De vulgari eloquentia,* ed. J. G. Trissini. Florence, 1840.

283. Darbelnet, J. "Pour une révalorisation des exercices de traduction dans l'étude des langues," *Culture,* XXIV (1963), 348-355.
284. Daubichon, J. *An English Exercisebook for the French Language.* Dublin, 1769.
285. de Arteaga, J. *Correspondance commerciale espagnole.* Heidelberg, 1907.
286. de Beauzée. "Méthode," *Diderot,* X, 446-462.
287. ———. *Abrégé de la grammaire générale.* Paris, 1790.
288. de Bèze, T. *De francicae linguae recta pronunciatione tractatus* (1584), ed. A. Tobler. Berlin, 1868.
289. de Bigault-d'Harcourt, R. *De la manière d'enseigner les humanités.* Paris, 1819.
290. de Bouge, X. *L'italien sans maître.* Paris, n.d. (1880?).
291. ———. *Le portugais sans maître en quatre mois.* Paris, n.d.
292. ———. *L'espagnol sans maître.* Paris, n.d.
293. de Brisay, C. T. *Latin Mastered in Six Weeks.* Toronto, 1897.
294. ———. *Analytical Latin Method.* 4 vols. Toronto, 1897.
295. de Bustamente, A. L. *Grammaire espagnol de Sobrino.* Paris, n.d.
296. de But, Adrianus. *The Rhetorica nova (1464) attributed to Jacobus Izelgrinus,* ed. Sister Mary Frances Laughlin. Washington, 1947.
297. *Les déclinaisons.* Paris, 1612.
298. de Clugny. *Dialogues français-latins.* Paris, 1819.
299. de Corro, A. *The Spanish Grammar: with certain rules teaching both the Spanish and the French tongues,* tr. Thorius. London, 1590.
300. de Dacia, Iacobus Nicholaus. *Liber de distinccione metrorum,* ed. A Kabell. Upsala, 1967.
301. de Dangeau, L. C. *Opuscules sur la grammaire* (1660), ed. M. Ekman. Upsala, 1927.
302. de Fivas V. *New Grammar of French Grammars.* New York, 1871.
303. ———. *An Introduction to the French Language.* New York, 1847.
304. de la Villeglé, L. *Grammaire anglaise.* Paris, 1894.
305. de Launay. *Nouvelle méthode pour apprendre la langue latine.* 4 vols. Paris, 1756.
306. de Lévizac. *L'art de parler et d'écrire correctement la langue française.* Paris, 1818.
307. ———. *A Theoretical and Practical Grammar of the French Tongue.* 8th ed. rev. S. Pasquier. London, 1819.
308. *Les délices de la langue latine.* Paris, 1769.
309. Denes, P. B., and E. N. Pinson. *The Speech Chain.* Baltimore, 1963.
310. *De praecipuis graecae,* Paris, 1627.

311. de Sainliens, C. *The French Schoolemaster.* London, 1573.
312. ———. *The French Littleton* (1576). London, 1583.
313. ———. *The Treasurie of the French Tong.* London, 1580.
314. ———. *A Dictionarie French and Englishe.* London, 1593.
315. ———. *The Italian Schoolemaster.* London, 1597.
316. de Saint-Sulpice. *Grammaire latine.* Montreal, 1847.
317. de Saussure, F. *Cours de linguistique générale,* ed. C. Bally and A. Sechehaye. Paris, 1915
318. de Sauzé, E. B. *The Cleveland Plan for the Teaching of Modern Languages* (1929). Philadelphia, 1946.
319. ———. "Teaching French in the Elementary Schools of Cleveland," *FR,* XXVI (1953), 371-376.
320. ———. *Nouveau cours pratique pour commençants.* Philadelphia, 1946.
321. Despautres, J. *Universa grammatica* (end C 16). Rouen, 1684 and Limoges, 1710.
322. Destutt de Tracy. *Élémens d'idéologie.* 4 vols. Paris, 1803.
323. De Witt, N. J. "Spoken Latin," *CJ,* XXXVII (1941), 106-112.
324. Diderot, D. "Langage," in *Diderot,* IX, 242-243.
325. *Dialogues français et allemands à l'usage des deux nations.* 12th ed. Strasbourg, 1822.
326. Diller, E. "The Linguistic Sequence in Learning Foreign Languages," *MLJ,* XLVI (1962), 259-260.
327. Dimnet, E. *Grammaire anglaise simplifiée.* Paris, 1922.
328. *Disticha Catonis* (3rd Century), ed. M. Boas. Amsterdam, 1952.
329. *Les disticques de Caton,* tr. Adam de Suel (13th Century), in J. Ulrich. "Traductions d'Adam de Suel et de Jean de Paris ou du Chastelet," *RF,* XIV (1903), 41-149.
329a. *Ibid.* in P. Meyer. "Notice de manuscrit Arsenal 5201," *R,* XVI (1887), 65-66.
330. *Les distiques de Caton.* Parallel Latin-French version, see Codret (240), 108-135.
331. Dixson, R. J. *Practical Guide to the Teaching of English as a Foreign Language.* New York, 1960.
332. Dodson, C. J. *The Bilingual Method.* Aberystwyth, 1962.
333. Dolet, E. *La manière de bien traduire à une langue dans une autre.* Paris, 1540.
334. ———. *Commentariorum linguae latinae tomi duo.* 2 vols. Lyon, 1536-1538.
335. ———. *Formulae latinarum locutionum illustriorum,* Lyon, 1539.

336. Donatus. *Ars grammatica. Keil,* IV, 367-402.
337. ———. *Ars minor. Keil,* IV, 355-366.
338. Dostert, L. "The Georgetown Language Program," *PMLA,* LXVIII (1953), March issue, 3-15.
339. Doyle, H. G., et al. *A Handbook on the Teaching of Spanish and Portuguese.* Boston, 1945.
340. Drach, D. P. L. B. *Pius philohebraeus.* Paris, 1853.
341. Dryden, J. "Preface to Ovid's Epistles," in ed. W. P. Ker, *Essays.* Oxford, 1900. I, 230-237.
342. du Bellay, J. *Deffence et illustration de la langue francoyse* (1550), ed. E. Person. Paris, 1887.
343. Dubois, J. *In linguam gallicam isagoge.* Paris, 1531.
344. Dubois, P. *De recuperatione terrae sanctae,* ed. C. V. Langlois. Paris, 1891.
345. Dufief, N. G. *Nature Displayed in Her Mode of Teaching Languages to Man* (1804). 5th ed. Philadelphia, 1823.
346. Dugrès, G. *Breve et accuratum grammaticae gallicum compendium.* Cambridge, 1636.
347. Dumarsais, C. *Exposition d'une méthode raisonnée pour apprendre la langue latine.* Paris, 1722.
348. ———. *Principes de grammaire.* Paris, 1793.
349. Dunchad. *Glossarium martianum,* ed. C. E. Lutz. Lancaster, Pa., 1944.
350. Dunkel, H. B., and R. A. Pillet. *French in the Elementary School.* Chicago, 1962.
351. Duplan. *Les racines de la langue latine.* Paris, 1789.
352. du Ploiche, P. *A Treatise in English and Frenche.* London, 1578.
353. Durand, D. *Nouvelle méthode d'apprendre la langue latine.* Paris, 1710.
354. Durand, D. *Claude Mauger's French and English Grammar.* 26th ed. London, 1751.
355. Dutrey. *Nouvelle méthode de la langue latine.* Paris, 1843.
356. Duwes (Duguez), G. *An Introductorie for to Learn French.* London, 1534.
357. Ebeling, C., and G. Vitali. *Manuel de conversation, français, anglais, allemand, italien.* Paris, n.d.
358. Edwards, T. W. C. *Eton Latin Grammar.* London, 1856.
359. Egbertus Leodiensis. *Fecundia ratis,* ed. F. A. E. Voigt. Halle, 1889.
360. Ehrke, K. *Methodik des neusprachlichen Arbeitsunterrichts.* Berlin, 1928.
361. Eliot, J. *Ortho-epia gallica.* London, 1593 (UM Film).
362. Elliott, A. V. P., and P. Gurrey. *Language Teaching in African Schools.* London, 1940.
363. Ellis, W. *A Collection of English Sentences.* London, 1842.

364. Elyot, T. *The Boke named the Governour* (1531), ed. H. H. S. Croft. London, 1883.

Erasmus, D. Opera omnia. 10 vols. Leyden, 1703-1706 (Gregg Reprint, London, 1960).

———. *Erasmi opuscula*, ed. W. K. Ferguson. The Hague, 1933.

365. ———. *Moriae encomium* (1509). Opera IV (whole volume).

366. ———. *De recta latini graecique sermonis pronuntiatione* (1510). Opera I, 913-1068.

367. ———. *De ratione studii* (1512). Opera I, 521-528.

368. ———. *De copia verborum et rerum* (1512). Opera I, 3-116.

369. ———. *Institutio principis christiani* (1516). Opera IV, 561-611.

370. ———. *Collectanea adagiorum veterum* (1517). Opera II.

371. ———. *Theodori Gazae grammatices* (1518). Opera I, 117-489.

372. ———. *Chonradi Nastadiensis germani dialogus bilinguium et trilinguium* (1519). Opuscula 206-224.

373. ———. *Apologia quae Jacobo Latomo inscribitur* (1519). Opera IX, 79-100.

374. ———. *Colloquiorum liber* (1524). Opera I, 629-913.

374a.———. *ibid.* Amsterdam, 1662.

375. ———. *Christiani matrimonium institutio*. Opera V, 615-723.

376. ———. *Ciceronianus* (1528). Opera I, 528-629.

377. ———. *De pueris statim ac liberaliter instituendis* (1529). Opera I, 489-521.

378. ———. *Epitome in elegantiis Laurenti Vallae* (1534). Opera I, 1069-1100.

379. Erbacher, Joseph P., ed. *Carmen,* Prentice-Hall Programmed Reading French Series, Englewood Cliffs, N. J., 1965.

380. Eriksson, M., I. Forest, and R. Mulhauser. *Foreign languages in the Elementary School.* Englewood Cliffs, N. J., 1964.

381. Ermanricus. *Fragmenta grammatica, PL,* CXVI, 26-30.

382. Ernesti, J. C. T., *Lexicon technologiae graecorum rhetoricae* (1795) Hildesheim, 1962.

383. Erpenius, R. *Rudimenta linguae arabicae* (1620). 2nd ed. Leiden, 1628.

384. ———. *Grammatica arabica,* Leiden, 1656.

385. Ervin-Tripp, S. "Comment on Jones, R. M., 'How and when do Persons become bilingual?' " *Kelly,* 26-35.

386. *An Essay on a System of Classical Instruction Combining the Methods of Locke, Milton, Ascham and Colet.* London, 1829.

387. Essen, E. *Methodik des Deutschunterrichts.* 3rd ed. Heidelberg, 1962.

388. Estienne, C. *De recta latini sermonis pronunciatione et scriptura libellus.* Paris, 1540.

389. Estienne, H. *Ciceronianum lexicon graeco-latium.* Paris, 1557.
390. ———. *In Marci Tulli Ciceronis quam plurimos locos castigationes Henrici Stephani: partim ex eius ingenio, partim ex vetustissimo quodam et emendatissimo exemplari.* Paris, 1557.
391. ———. *De latinitate falso suspecta.* Paris, 1576.
392. ———. *De Plauti latinitate dissertatio et ad lectionum eius progymnasma.* Paris, 1576.
393. ———. *La précellence de la langue françoise* (1579), ed. F. Huguet. Paris, 1896.
394. Eton School. *Graece grammatices.* London, 1812.
395. ———. *Graecae grammaticae rudimenta.* Oxford, 1868.
396. Evrard de Bethune. *Eberhardi Bethuniensis graecismus,* ed. J. Wrobel. Breslau, 1887.
397. *Exercitatio grammatica in primam concionum domini Joannis Chrysostomi de sacris precibus.* Rouen, 1681.
398. Fabritius, H. *Das Büchlein gleichstimmender Wörter* (1532). ed. J. Meier. Strasbourg, 1895.
399. Faidit, Uc. *Donatz proensals, Guessard,* 28-66.
400. Fasquelle, L. *A New Method of Learning the French Language.* New York, 1860.
401. Fénélon. *Education des filles* (1688). *Oeuvres,* Paris, 1854, IV, 240-346.
402. Ferri de St-Constant, J-L. *Rudimens de la traduction.* Angers, 1801.
403. Filelfo, F. *Oratio in suo legendi principio habita.* Florence, 1429.
404. Findlay, J. J. *Modern Language Learning. A concise Sketch of Principles and of a Programme for the Introductory Stage.* London, 1929.
405. Finocchiaro, M. *Teaching English as a Second Language in Elementary and Secondary Schools.* New York, 1958.
406. Firmery, J. "La première période d'enseignement des langues vivantes," *RU,* XI (1902), 329-350.
407. *First Reader in English and Blackfoot.* Montreal, 1886.
408. Fishman, J. "Bilingualism, Intelligence and Language Learning," *MLJ,* XLIX (1965), 227-237.
409. Flad, M. *Le latin de l'église,* Paris, 1938.
410. Flagstad, C. B. *Psychologie der Sprachpädagogik.* Leipzig, 1913.
411. Fleming, C. *Grammaire anglaise.* Paris, 1853.
412. Fleming, G. "Language Teaching with Cartoons," reprint from *Film User,* June, 1964.
413. ———. "Attitudes to Modern Language Teaching Aids," *Audio-Visual Language Journal,* III (1966), 1-7.

414. ———. "The Didactic Organisation of Pictorial Reality in the New Language Teaching Media," *Praxis* (1967), 160-174.
415. Fleury, C. *Traite du choix et de la méthode des études* (1675). Paris, 1686.
416. Florio, J. *Florio his Firste Fruits* (1578). Facsimile reprint by Arundell del Re, Taikohu Imperial University, Formosa, 1936.
417. ———. *Florio his Second Frutes* (1591). ed. R. C. Simonini. Gainesville, Fla., 1953.
418. Forbes, J. *The Principles of Gaelic Grammar.* Edinburgh, 1848.
419. Fotitch, T. *Teaching Foreign Languages in the Modern World.* Washington, 1961.
420. Fowler, M., et al. "Linguistics and the Classical Languages," *CJ,* LII (1957), 259-278.
421. Francois, A. "La conversation et la lecture dans l'étude," *RU,* III (1902), 45-48.
422. Franke, F. *Die praktische Spracherlernung auf Grund der Psychologie und der Physiologie der Sprache* (1884). 3rd ed. Leipzig, 1896.
423. Franklin, M. "Latin up-to-date," *CJ,* XXXVI (1941), 564-567.
424. Fraser, F. L. *Lehrverfahren and Lehraufgaben.* Marburg, 1926.
425. French, F. G., *First Year English. What and How to Teach.* London, 1943.
426. ———. *The Teaching of English Abroad.* 3 vols. London, 1948-50.
427. ———. *Teaching English as an International Language.* London, 1963.
428. Frères des écoles chrétiennes. *Cours de langue anglaise.* Montreal, 1878.
429. Frères de l'instruction chrétienne. *La classe en anglais.* Montreal, 1914.
430. Frères du Sacré Coeur. *Cours élémentaire de langue anglaise.* Montreal, 1917.
431. Fries, C. C. *Teaching and Learning English as a Foreign Language.* Ann Arbor, Mich., 1945.
432. ———. "As We See It," *LL,* I (1948), 12-17.
433. ———, and A. C. Fries. *Foundations for English Teaching.* Tokyo, 1961.
434. Frisby, A. W. *Teaching English; Notes and Comments on Teaching English Overseas.* London, 1957.
435. Froissart, J. *L'Espinette amoureuse,* ed. A. Fourrier. Paris, 1963.
436. Fungerus, J. *Etymologicum latinum.* Frankfurt, 1605.
437. Furstenhoff, J. *De l'adoption du francais.* Paris, 1908.
438. Gaede, W. R. "Some Guiding Principles for Outside Reading," *MLJ,* XXIII (1939), 251-255.
439. Gaffiot, F. *Méthode de la langue latine.* Paris, 1910.
440. Gands, P. *Clef de la méthode Ollendorf.* Frankfurt, 1853.
441. Gantrelle, L. *Nouvelle grammaire de la langue latine d'apres les principes de la grammaire historique.* 10th ed. Paris, 1880.

442. Gardner, R. G., and W. Lambert. "Motivational Variables in Second Language Acquisition," *Canadian Journal of Psychology,* XIII (1959), 266-272.
443. Garnerius, J. *Institutio gallicae linguae, ad usum iuventus germanicae.* Marburg, 1558.
444. Gatenby, E. V. "The Training of Language Teachers," *ELT,* VI (1951), 199-207.
445. ———. *English as a Foreign Language. Advice to non-English Teachers.* London, 1944.
446. Gaudin, J. *La grammaire de Despautre abregée.* Fontenay, 1703.
447. Gaultier, L. *Phrases et periodes graduées.* Paris, 1809.
448. ———. *Méthode pour entendre grammaticalement la langue latine.* Paris, 1839.
449. Gauntlett, J. *Teaching English as a Foreign Language.* London and New York, 1957.
450. Gautbert (Gozbert). *Grammaticorum* διαδοχη in L. Delisle, "Notices et extraits," 35.I.311, n.d.
451. Gen Ca (Jacques Bellot). *Le maistre d'escole anglois* (1580). ed. T. Spira. Halle, 1912.
452. Gendron, J.-D. "La méthode radiographique appliquée à la comparaison des articulations vocaliques en français canadien et en français parisien," *Proceedings of the Fourth International Congress of Phonetic Sciences, Helsinki, 1961,* The Hague, 1962.
453. Genzardi, N. E. *Le français et l'italien.* Turin, 1891.
454. Geoffroi de Vinsauf. *Poetria nova, Faral,* 197-262.
455. ———. *Documentum de modo et arte dictandi et versificandi, Faral,* 265-320.
456. ———. *Summa de coloribus rhetoricis, Faral,* 321-327.
457. Gessler, J., ed. *Fragments d'anciens traités pour l'enseignement du français en angleterre.* Paris, 1933.
458. ———. *Le livre des mestiers de Bruges et ses dérivés.* Bruges, 1931.
459. Gianella, A. F. "The Use of Flashcards for Drill in French," *MLJ,* I (1916), 96-99.
460. Gill, A. *Logonomia anglica* (1621), ed. O. L. Jiriczek, *Quellen und Forschungen* XC, Strasbourg, 1903.
461. Glaum, P. *Disputatio castellani de methodo docendi artem quamvis intra octiduum.* Giessen, 1661.
462. Glauning, F. *Didaktik und Methodik des englischen Unterrichts.* Munich, 1903.

463. Goodwin, W. A. B. *Direct Method of Learning English.* London, 1960.
464. Gottsched, J. C. *Le maître de la langue allemande* (1754). 16th ed. by A. Koenig. Paris and Strasbourg, 1814.
465. Goudar, L. *Grammatica francese e italiana.* Nizza, 1787.
466. Gougenheim, G., et al. *L'élaboration du français élémentaire.* Paris, 1956.
467. Gouin, F. *L'art d'énseigner et d'étudier les langues* (1880). 6th ed. Paris, 1925.
468. ———. *The Art of Teaching and Studying Languages,* tr. H. Swan and V. Bétis. London, 1894.
469. Gourio, E. *The Direct Method of Teaching French.* Boston, 1921.
470. *Grammaire angloise pour facilement apprendre la langue angloise.* Paris, 1625.
471. *La grammaire de Despautère abrégée et corrigée.* Bordeaux, 1700.
472. *Grammaire françoise et latine.* Paris, 1832.
473. *Grammaire françoise pour servir d'introduction à la grammaire latine.* Montreal, 1811.
474. *Grammaire latine.* Montreal, 1811.
475. Granger, T. *Syntagma grammaticum.* London, 1616.
476. Gras, P. *Methode aisée pour apprendre la langue grecque.* Paris, 1699.
477. Gray, M. D. *The Teaching of Latin,* New York, 1929.
478. Board of Education (Great Britain). *Suggestions for the Teaching of Classics.* London, 1939.
479. Greene, F. *Companion to Ollendorf.* New York, 1853.
480. Greenleaf, J. *Grammar Simplified; or Ocular Analysis of the English Language.* 5th ed. Montreal, 1823.
481. St. Gregory the Great, *Epistolarum libri IV, PL,* LXXVII, 431-1326.
482. Greimas, A. J. "Observations sur la methode audio-visuelle de l'enseignement des langues," *ELA,* I (1962), 137-155.
483. Gretserus. *Rudimenta linguae graecae.* Lyon, 1656.
484. Groisy, M. A. *Manuel du jeune latiniste.* Paris, 1840.
485. Guarino, B. *De ordine docendi et studendi* (1459). see Woodward (*223), 159-178.
486. ———. *Breviloquus vocabularius cum arte diphthongandi, accentuandi et punctuandi.* Cologne, 1487.
487. ———. *Erotemata.* Ferrara, 1509.
488. Guarna, A. *Grammaticae opus novum.* Cremona, 1511.
489. Guberina, P. "La méthode audiovisuelle structuro-globale," *RLV,* XXIX (1963), 431-441.
490. ———. "The Audiovisual Global and Structural Method," Courses given at Ohio State University, 1964 (typescript).

491. Guénot, J. "Télévision et l'enseignement d'une langue vivante," *LM,* LVI (1962), 208-219.
492. Guérard, A. L. "The Teaching of French Civilisation," *MLJ,* VII (1923), 257-267.
493. Gueroult, P. C. B. *Nouvelle méthode pour apprendre le latin.* Paris, 1805.
494. Guibert de Nogent. *De vita sua, PL,* CLVI, 838-1018.
495. Guichard, L. *Exercices sur les mots italiens.* Paris, 1898.
495a.———. *Petite grammaire italienne.* Paris, 1902.
496. Guillaume, G. *Langage et science du langage.* Paris and Quebec, 1964.
497. Gullette, C. C., Keating, L. C., and Viens, C. P. *Teaching a Modern Language.* New York, 1942.
498. Gurrey, P. *The Teaching of Written English.* London, 1954.
499. ———. *Teaching English as a Foreign Language.* London, 1955.
500. Haden, E. F. "Descriptive Linguistics in the Teaching of a Foreign Language," *MLJ,* XXXVIII (1954), 170-176.
501. Hagboldt, P. "An Experiment in Reading Known Material in Beginners' Classes," *MLJ,* X (1925), 345-352.
502. ———. *Language Learning.* Chicago, 1935.
503. Hale, W. G. *The Art of Reading Latin and How to Teach It.* Boston, 1887.
504. Haller, A. *De partibus corporis humani.* vols. VII and VIII. Berne and Lausanne, 1778.
505. Halliday, M. A. K. "Linguistique générale et linguistique appliquée," *ELA,* I (1962), 5-42.
506. ———. "Lexis as a Linguistic Level," *Firth,* 148-161.
507. Halliday, M. A. K., McIntosh, A., and Strevens, P. *The Linguistic Sciences and Language Teaching.* London, 1964.
508. Hamilton, J. *Essay on the Usual Mode of Teaching Languages.* New York, 1816.
509. ———. *History, Principles and Practice and Results of the Hamilton System for the Last Twelve Years,* Manchester, 1829.
510. ———. *Gaii Iulii Caesaris commentariorum libri quinque priores, with an analytical and interlineal translation.* London, 1829.
511. ———. *Selections from Ovid,* ed. G. W. Heilig. Philadelphia, 1861.
512. Hammond, R. M. "A Campaign for the Rehabilitation of Grammar," *MLJ,* XXXVIII (1954), 420-421.
513. Handschin, C. H. *Methods for Teaching Modern Languages.* New York, 1924.
514. Hankwitz, C. E. "A Series—a Light Approach to a Serious Matter," *H,* XXVIII (1945), 593-543.

515. Harper, W. R., and W. E. Waters. *An Inductive Greek Method.* New York, 1888.
516. Harriet, M. *Grammatica escuarez eta francesez.* Bayonne, 1741.
517. Harris, J. *Hermes–a Philosophical Enquiry concerning Universal Grammar.* London, 1751.
518. Hartig, P., and H. Strohmeyer. *Moderner neusprachlicher Unterricht.* Braunschweig, 1929.
519. Hartlib, S. *A True and Ready Way to Learne the Latin Tongue.* London, 1654.
520. Harvard, J. *German for Pleasure.* London, 1962.
521. Hauch, E. F. *German Idiom List.* New York, 1929.
522. Haugen, E. "Linguistics and the Wartime Programme of Language Teaching," *MLJ,* XXXIX (1955), 243-245.
523. Haughton, H. P. *The Middle System of Teaching Classics.* London, 1844.
524. Haygood, J. D. "The Amount and Composition of a Minimum Essential French Reading Vocabulary," *MLJ,* XVIII (1933), 177-189.
525. Hayne, T. *Linguarum cognatio seu de linguis in genere et de variarum linguarum cognatione dissertatio* (1634), ed. T. Crenius. *Analectica philologico-critico-historica.* Amsterdam, 1699.
526. Hébert, M. H. *L'anglais sans maître.* Toronto, 1909.
527. Hempl, G. *German Orthography and Phonology.* Boston, 1897.
528. Heness, G. *Der Leitfaden für den Unterricht in der deutschen Sprache.* Boston, 1875.
529. ———. *Der Sprachlehrer unter seinen Schulern.* New York, 1878.
530. Henmon, G., et al. *Prognosis Tests in the Modern Foreign Languages.* New York, 1929.
531. Henn, P. *Ahn's First German Reader.* New York, 1875.
532. Henry, M. A. *La version latine.* Paris, 1890.
533. Herrade de Landsberg. *Hortus deliciarum,* ed. A. Straub and G. Keller. Strasbourg, 1879.
534. Hess, J. A. "The Use of Pictures in the German Classroom," *MLJ,* I (1916), 308-314.
535. Hetch, M. *De l'étude des langues vivantes.* Orléans, 1867.
536. Hewett, W. T. "Aims and Methods of Collegiate Instruction in Modern Languages," *PMLA,* I (1885), 25-36.
537. Hicks, W. C. R., and M. A. Haycocks. *Modern Language Teaching on the Decline.* London, 1937.
538. Hildemarus. *De recta legendi ratione, PL,* CVI, 395.
539. H. M. S. O. *Modern Languages in Secondary Schools.* Edinburgh, 1950.

540. *Hisperica famina* (9th century), *PL,* XC, 1185-1196.
541. Hoadly, S. *The Natural Method of Teaching.* London, 1683.
542. Hockett, C. F., and Fang Chaoying. *Spoken Chinese.* New York, 1944.
543. Hocking, E. *Language Laboratory and Language Learning.* Department of Audio-visual Instruction, United States National Education Association, 1964.
544. Hodgson, F. M. *Learning Modern Languages.* London, 1955.
545. Hoenigswald, H. *Spoken Hindustani.* 2 vols. New York, 1945.
546. Hollyman, K. J. "A Quantitative Method of Predicting Areas of Phonemic Interference," *Te Reo,* VII (1964), 36-43.
547. Holmes, D. T. *The Teaching of Modern Languages in Schools and Colleges.* Paisley, 1903.
548. Holt, J. *Lac Puerorum,* London, 1500? (photocopy).
549. Honorius Augustodunensis. *De animo exsilio et patria, seu de artibus, PL,* CLXXII, 1242-1246.
550. Hood, M. H. "Foreign Language Methodology in Europe and America," *MLJ,* XLII (1958), 279-283.
551. Hoole, C. *A New Discovery of the Old Art of Teaching School,* ed. E. T. Campagnac. Liverpool, 1913.
552. Horace. *Ars poetica,* ed. E. C. Wickham. Oxford, 1901.
553. Horman, W. *Vulgaria.* London, 1519.
554. Horn, E., and C. F. Ward. *Minimum French Vocabulary Testbook.* Iowa City, Iowa, 1923.
555. Hornby, A. S. *A Guide to Patterns and Usage in English.* London, 1954.
556. ———. *The Teaching of Structural Words and Sentence Patterns.* 2 vols. London, 1959-1961.
557. Horwill, H. W. *The Right Method of Studying the Greek and Latin Classics.* Oxford, 1887.
558. Hovelaque, E. *Deux conférences sur l'enseignement des langues vivantes.* Paris, n.d.
559. ———. "La progression dans l'enseignement des langues vivantes," *RU,* XIV (1905), 200-208; 287-302.
560. ———. "L'enseignement des langues vivantes dans le deuxième cycle," *RU,* XIX, 1 (1910), 293-310; XIX, 2 (1910), 1-16; 93-114.
561. Howse, J. *A Grammar of Cree.* London, 1844.
562. Hroswitha. *Comoediae sex Hrotsuithae, PL,* CXXXVII, 975-1062.
563. Huebener, T. *The Reading Aim in Foreign Language Teaching.* Monograph 6, Board of Education, New York, n.d.
564. Huebner, W. *Didactik der neueren Sprachen,* Frankfurt, 1933.

565. Hugo de Sancto Victore. *Didascalion de studio legendi,* ed. C. H. Buttimer. Washington, 1939.
565a.———. *ibid. PL,* CLXXVI, 741-1000.
566. Huse, H. R. *The Psychology of Modern Foreign Language Study.* Chapel Hill, N. C., 1931.
567. ———. *Reading and Speaking Foreign Languages.* Chapel Hill, N. C., 1931.
568. Huss, J. *Orthographia bohemica* (1400?), ed. A. A. Sembera. Vienna, 1857.
569. Hutchinson, J. L. *Modern Foreign Languages in the High School–the Language Laboratory.* Washington, 1961.
570. Incorporated Association of Assistant Masters. *The Teaching of Modern Languages.* London, 1952.
571. ———. *The Teaching of Classics.* London, 1954.
572. Ibarra, F., and C. V. Coelho. *Brazilian Portuguese Self-Taught.* New York, 1943.
573. International Correspondence Schools. *A Textbook on German.* Scranton, Pa., 1902.
574. ———. *Méthode d'anglais,* Scranton, Pa., 1903.
575. *Introduction à la langue latine.* Paris, 1761.
576. International Phonetic Association. *Principles.* London, 1949.
577. Isidore of Seville. *Etymologiarum libri viginti, PL,* LXXXII, 73-728.
578. ———. *Differentarum libri duo, PL,* LXXXIII, 9-98.
579. Ivo Carnotensis. *Epistolae, PL,* CLXII, 11-286.
580. Jacobovits, L. and W. E. Lambert. "Verbal Satiation and Changes in Intensity of Meaning," *Journal of Educational Psychology,* LX (1960), 376-383.
581. Jacobus Comes Purliliarum. *De generosa liberorum educatione* (1492), Pädagogischer Schriften 6, 1880.
582. Jacotot, J. *Enseignement universel des langues étrangères.* Paris, 1830.
583. Jamieson, E. I. "A Standardised Vocabulary for Elementary Spanish," *MLJ* (1924), 325-334.
584. Jean Lemaire de Belges. *La Concorde des deux langues,* ed. J. Frappier. Paris, 1947.
585. Jehan le Teinturier d'Arras. *Le mariage des sept ars* (suivi d'une version anonyme), ed. A. Langfors. Paris, 1923.
586. St. Jerome. *Epistola ad Laetam, PL,* XXI, 107.
587. Jespersen, O. *How to Teach a Foreign Language,* tr. S. Y. Bertelson. London, 1904.
588. ———, ed. *John Hart's Pronunciation of English 1569 and 1570.* Anglistische Forschungen 22. Heidelberg, 1907.

589. Joannes Scotus. *Commentarium in Martianum Capellam,* ed. C. E. Lutz. Cambridge, 1932.
590. John of Garland. *Ars Grammatica, PL,* CL, 1578-1600.
591. ———. *Morale scolarium,* ed. L. J. Paetow. Memoirs of the University of California, IV.ii, Berkeley, Calif., 1927.
592. ———. *Dictionarius, Wright,* 120-138.
593. John of Salisbury. *Metalogicon, PL,* CXC, 823-945.
594. ——— *De septem septenis, PL,* CXC, 945-1000.
595. ———. *Epistolae,* ed. W. J. Millon and H. E. Butler. London, 1955.
596. Johnsen, J. E. *Basic English.* New York, 1944.
597. Johnson, C. L. "Vocabulary Difficulty and Textbook Selection," *MLJ,* XI (1927), 290-297.
598. Johnson, S. *Grammaire anglaise.* Paris, 1847.
599. Joly, A., and P. Virey. *L'anglais par l'explication des textes.* Paris, 1963.
600. Jones, D. *An Outline of English Phonetics* (1909). 8th ed. Cambridge, 1956.
601. Jones, J. D., ed. *Cooper's Grammatica linguae anglicanae.* Halle, 1912.
602. Jones, R. M. *System in Child Language.* Unpublished Ph.D. thesis, University of Wales. Aberystwyth, 1965.
603. ———. "Situational Vocabulary," *IRAL,* IV (1966), 165-173.
604. ———. "How and When do people become bilingual?" *Kelly,* 12-25.
605. Jorgensen, A., and M. Ringberg. "La méthode directe," *MF,* VIII (1904), 37-41.
606. Josse. *Nouvelle grammaire raisonnée* (1799). 2 vols. Paris, 1818.
607. ———. *A Grammar of the Spanish Language with Practical Exercises.* 2 vols. Boston, 1822.
608. Joynes, E. S. "Reading in Modern Language Study," *PMLA,* V (1890), 33-46.
609. ———, and Meissner, C., *A German Grammar.* Boston, 1902.
610. Julian of Toledo. *Ars grammatica,* ed. W. M. Lindsay. St. Andrews University Publications 15, 1922.
611. Jump, J. *Grammaire de la langue anglaise.* Paris, 1829.
612. Juvenal. *Satires,* ed. A. E. Housman. 3rd ed. Cambridge, 1931.
613. Juvencus, J. (Jouvancy). *Ratio discendi et docendi.* Lyon and Paris, 1764.
614. Kappert, H. *Psychologische Voraussetzungen des neusprachlichen Unterrichts.* Halle, 1915.
615. Katz, J. J., and Fodor, J. A. "The Structure of a Semantic Theory," *Fodor & Katz,* 479-518.
616. Kaulfers, W. V. *Modern Languages for Modern Schools.* New York, 1942.

617. ———, and H. D. Roberts. *A Cultural Basis for the Language Arts.* Stanford, Calif., 1937.
618. Keating, R. E. *A Study of the Effectiveness of Language Laboratories.* New York, 1963.
619. Kendrick, A. C. *Greek Ollendorf.* New York, 1852.
620. Keniston, H. *Spanish Idiom List,* New York, 1929.
621. Kennedy, B. H. *A Revised Latin Primer,* ed. J. F. Mountford. London, 1930.
622. *Key to Ollendorf's Greek Grammar.* New York, 1854.
623. Khouri, A. *Nouveau syllabaire français à l'usage de la jeunesse arabe.* Beyrouth, 1889.
624. Kimmins, C. W., and B. Rennie. *The Triumph of the Dalton Plan.* London, n.d.
625. Kingdon, R. *The Groundwork of English Intonation.* London, 1958.
626. ———, and M. Kingdon. "The Use of Dictation," *ELT,* VI (1951), 11-15.
627. Kirkman, F. B. *The Teaching of Foreign Languages.* London, 1909.
628. Kittson, E. *Theory and Practice of Language Teaching.* Oxford, 1918.
629. Kleyntiens, J. *Grammaire flamande.* Tournai, 1882.
630. Klinghardt, H. *Ein Jahr Erfahrungen mit der neuen Methode.* Marburg, 1888.
631. ———. *Drei weitere Jahre Erfahrungen,* Marburg, 1892.
632. Konrad of Hirschau. *Dialogus super auctores sive didascalion* (14th century), ed. E. Schepps. Wurzburg, 1889.
633. Krause, C. A. *The Direct Method in Modern Languages.* New York, 1916.
634. Kristeller, P., ed. *Exercitium super Pater Noster* (1418). Berlin, 1908.
635. Kron, R. *Die Methode Gouin oder das Seriensystem in Theorie und Praxis.* Marburg, 1895.
636. Krysto, G. "Bringing the World to Our Foreign-Language Soldiers," *National Geographic Magazine,* XXXIV (1918), 81-90.
637. Labbe, P. *Tirocinium linguae graecae.* Paris, 1683.
638. ———. *Regulae accentuum et spirituum graecorum.* Paris, 1694.
639. Lado, R. *Linguistics across Cultures.* Ann Arbor, Mich., 1957.
640. ———. *Language Teaching.* New York, 1964.
641. Lambert, W. E. "Developmental Aspects of Second Language Acquisition," *Journal of Social Psychology,* XLIII (1956), 83-110.
642. ———, R. C. Gardner, H. C. Barik, and K. Tunstall. "Attitudinal and Cognitive Aspects of the Intensive Study of Second Languages," *JASP,* LXVI (1963), 358-368.

643. Lambertus. *De recta legendi ratione, epistola ad Albericum regem. PL,* CVI, 398-399.
644. Lane, H. L. "Programmed Learning of a Second Language," *IRAL,* III (1964), 249-300.
645. Lanfredini. *Nouvelle méthode pour apprendre l'italien.* Paris, 1683.
646. Larew, A. "The Optimum Age for Beginning a Second Language," *MLJ,* XLV (1961), 203-206.
647. *Las Leys d'amors* (C 14), ed. J. Anglade. Toulouse, 1920.
648. Laudenbach, H., P. Passy, and A. Delobel. *De la méthode directe dans l'enseignement des langues vivantes.* Paris, 1899.
649. Leavitt, L. W. *The Teaching of English to Foreign Students.* London, 1940.
650. Lee, W. R. "Linguistics and the 'Practical' Teacher," *ELT,* XIII (1958), 159-170.
651. ———. "Grading," *ELT,* XVII (1963), 107-112; XVIII (1964), 82-88.
652. Legrand, E. *Manuel de conversation grec-français.* Paris, 1900.
653. Leibnitz. *Nouveaux essais sur l'entendement humain.* Amsterdam and Leipzig, 1765.
654. Lelaboureur. *Avantages de la langue française sur la langue latine.* Paris, 1669.
655. Lemare, P. A. *Cours de la langue latine.* 3rd ed. Paris, 1819.
656. Lentulo, S. *Italian Grammar,* tr. H. Grantham. London, 1574 (UM film).
657. Léon, P. "De l'allemand au français: problèmes phonétiques et phonèmiques," *FdM,* IV (1961), 45-48.
658. ———. *Laboratoire de langues et correction phonétique,* Paris, 1962.
659. ———, and M. Léon. *Introduction a la phonétique corrective.* Paris, 1964.
660. LePage, R. B. *The National Language Question, Linguistic Problems of Newly Independent States.* London, 1964.
661. LeRoy, P. *Reforme de l'enseignement.* Quebec, 1875.
662. Le Tourneux, J.-H. *Introduction à l'anglais ultra-rapide.* Quebec, 1942.
663. Lévy, A. *Methode pratique de la langue allemande.* Paris, 1880.
664. Levy, B. "Foreign Language Teaching Aims and Methods in the Light of ASTP," *MLJ,* XXIX (1945), 403-410.
665. Lévy, J. *Thorough Method vs. Natural Method: a Letter to Dr. L. Sauveur.* Boston, 1878.
666. Lewis, E. G. *Foreign and Second Language Teaching in the USSR,* British Council, 1962.
667. Lewis, M. M. *Language in School,* London, 1942.
668. Leygues, G. "Projet d'instructions relatives a l'étude des langues vivantes dans les lycées et collèges," *MF,* XII (1902), 37-39.

669. Lhomond. *Élémens de la grammaire latine.* Paris, 1805.
670. Lichtenberger, F. *How to Teach and Learn Modern Languages.* London, 1880.
671. Lilly, W. *Brevissima institutio seu ratio grammatices cognoscendae.* London, 1513.
672. ———. *Absolutissimus de octo orationis partium constructione libellus.* Basle, 1517.
673. ———. *A Short Introduction of Grammar generallie to be used and set forth.* London, 1574.
674. ———. *English Grammar by R. R.* London, 1651.
675. Linacre, T. *De emendata structura latini sermonis libri sex.* Paris, 1527.
676. ———. *Rudimenta grammatices ex anglico sermone in latinum versa,* tr. G. Buchanan. Lyon, 1559.
677. Lindsay, W. M. "Etyma latina Philoxeni," *CR* (1917), 128-138.
678. ———, et al., ed. *Glossaria latina.* 5 vols. Paris, 1926-31.
679. Lindquist, L. "A Unit in General Language," *Rice,* 11-26.
680. Lion, C. T. *Die praktische Erlernung und Verwertung der neueren Sprachen.* Leipzig, 1909.
681. Lipsius, J. *De recta pronunciatione linguae latinae* (1549), Opera omnia I. Versailles, 1675.
682. Listov, J. *Engelsk Elementarbog.* Copenhagen, 1875.
683. Locke, J. *New Method of a Commonplace Book.* London, 1686.
684. ———. *Some Thoughts Concerning Education.* London, 1693.
685. Lockhart, B., and A. Jones. "The Danger of the Reform Method," *MF,* XIV (1908), 96-98.
686. Lockhart, L. W. *Word Economy.* London, 1931.
687. Löpelmann, M. *Erzeihung und Unterricht an der höheren Schule.* Frankfurt, 1938.
688. Lott, B. "Graded and Restricted Vocabularies and Their Use in the Oral Teaching of English as a Foreign Language," *ELT,* XIV (1959), 3-12; 65-69.
689. Lubinus, E. *Clavis ac fundamenta graecae linguae.* Amsterdam, 1657.
690. Lucensi, S. P. *Observationes in linguam hebraicum.* Paris, 1546.
691. Lugné-Philipon, J.-R. *The New English Grammar.* Paris, 1908.
692. Luna, Jean de, *Dialogues Spanish and English with the Grammar of César Oudin.* London, 1622 (UM film).
693. Luneau de Boisgermain, P. *Cours de langue italienne.* 3 vols. Paris, 1783.
694. ———. *Cours de langue angloise.* 2 vols. Paris, 1784-1787.
695. ———. *Cours de langue latine.* 4 vols. Paris, 1789.

696. MacEnery, G. *L'anglais mis à la portée de tout le monde.* Paris, 1878.
697. Mackey, W. F. "Shipboard Language Teaching," *ELT,* XI (1957), 86-94.
698. ———. "Language Teaching and Applied Linguistics," *Vuosikirja* IV, 23-34.
699. ———. *Language Teaching Analysis.* London, 1965.
700. ———. "Method Analysis; a Survey of Its Development, Principles and Techniques," *Georgetown University Monographs* XVIII (1965), 149-162.
701. Macrobius. *Oeuvres complètes.* Paris, 1854.
702. Macropedius, G. *Methodus de conscribendis epistolis.* Cologne, 1570.
703. Madvig, I. N. *A Latin Grammar,* tr. G. Woods. Oxford, 1849.
704. ———. *Lateinische Sprachlehre für Schulen,* tr. L. H. F. Oppermann. Braunschweig, 1867.
705. Mair, J., ed. *Gaii Julii Caesaris de bello gallico.* Edinburgh, 1770.
706. ———. *An Introduction to Latin Syntax.* Edinburgh, 1842.
707. Malebranche, N. *Recherche de la vérité* (1674). 7th ed. Paris, 1721.
708. Mallinson, V. *Teaching a Modern Language.* London, 1953.
709. Malsachanus. *Ars grammatica,* ed. M. Roger. Paris, 1905.
710. Manesca, J. *A Philological Recorder Adapted for the Oral System of Teaching Living Languages.* New York, 1843.
711. Manitius, M., ed. *Erchamberts von Freising Donatkommentar, Philologus,* LXVIII (1913), 369-409.
712. Manutius, A. *Orthographiae ratio.* Venice, 1561.
713. ———. *Purae, elegantes et copiosae latinae linguae phrases.* Cologne, 1571.
714. ———, ed. *Gaii Julii Caesaris commentarii.* Venice, 1588.
715. Mapheus Vegius Laudensis (1406-1458). *De educatione liberorum.* 2 vols. libri 1-3, ed. Sr. Maria Walburg Fanning; libri 4-6, ed. Sr. Anne Stanislaus Sullivan. Washington, 1933-1936.
716. Marbodus. *Liber de ornamentis verborum, PL,* CLXXI, 1677-1684.
717. Marcel, C. *Language as a Means of Mental Culture and International Communication: or the Manual of the Teacher and Learner of Languages.* 2 vols. London, 1853.
718. ———. *The Study of Languages Brought Back to Its True Principles.* New York, 1869.
719. Marchand, L. *L'enseignement des langues vivantes par la méthode scientifique.* Cahors, 1927.
720. Martin, D. *Les colloques français et allemands* (1627), ed. J. Hatt. Paris, 1929.
721. Marty-Laveaux, C. *Etudes de langue française.* Paris, 1901.
722. Mason, G. *Grammaire anglaise* (1622), ed. R. Brotanek. Halle, 1905.

723. Massoul, H. *Pour comprendre l'italien.* Paris, 1934.
724. Massoul, H. *Pour comprendre l'allemand.* Paris, 1935.
725. Mathieu, G. "A Brief Guide to Sound Labmanship," *MLJ,* XLIV (1960), 123-126.
726. Mathy, M. *Vocabulaire de base du latin.* 2 ed. Paris, 1957.
727. Matthew, R. J. *Language and Area Studies in the Armed Services.* Washington, 1947.
728. Matthieu de Vendôme. *Ars versificatoria, Faral,* 109-193.
729. Maugard. *Cours de langue française et de langue latine comparée.* 5 vols. Paris, 1809.
730. Maupas, C. *Grammaire françoyse* (1607). Latin version, Lyon, 1623.
731. Mays, R. *A Guide for Teachers of Foreign Languages.* Dallas, Tex., 1930.
732. Meiden, W. E. "A Technique of Radio French Instruction," *MLJ,* XXII (1937), 115-126.
733. Meidinger, J. V. *Praktische französische Grammatik.* Liege, 1783.
734. ———. *Nouvelle grammaire allemande pratique.* Liege, 1797.
735. Meier, J., ed. *Porney's Syllabaire française.* New York, 1841.
736. Meigret, L. *Le tretté de la grammere francoeze* (1550), ed. W. Foerster. Heilbronn, 1888.
737. Meilleur, J. B. *Nouvelle grammaire anglaise.* Montreal, 1854.
Melancthon, P. Opera omnia quae supersunt. 28 vols. Halle, 1834-1852 (Johnson Reprint, New York and London, 1963).
738. ———. *Declamationes* (1517), Opera, XI, 600-769.
739. ———. *Grammatica graeca* (1521), Opera, XX, 100-146.
740. ———. *Grammatica latina* (1526), Opera, XX, 246-335.
741. ———. *De studio linguae hebreae* (1549), Opera, XI, 770-890.
742. Menon, T. K. N., and M. S. Patel. *The Teaching of English as a Foreign Language.* Baroda, 1957.
743. Méras, A. *A Language Teacher's Guide.* New York, 1954.
744. Mercator. *Sermones Nestorii, PL,* XLVIII, 699-1218.
745. Mercier, N. *Le manuel des grammariens.* Paris, 1673.
746. *Méthode phonique de la langue anglaise.* Montreal, 1922.
747. *Méthode rationnelle pour apprendre la langue latine.* Paris, 1830.
748. *Methods of Teaching Modern Languages, a Collection of Essays by a Group of Specialists.* Boston, 1893.
749. Meyer, E. "Le thème latin et la méthode directe," *RU,* XVII, 2 (1908), 117-126.
750. Michéa, R. "Rapports de la fréquence avec la forme, le sens et la fonction des mots," *LM,* XLV, (1951), 191-196.

751. ———. "Limitation et sélection de vocabulaire dans l'enseignement actif des langues vivantes," *RLV,* XXII (1956), 467-474.
752. Midant, P. "Latin et la méthode directe," *RU,* XXX, 2 (1921), 194-197.
753. ———. "Le latin vivant," *RU,* XXXI, 1 (1922), 271-275.
754. Miège et Boyer. *Grammaire angloise-françoise.* Paris, 1745.
755. Miller, D. C. "Beginning to Teach English," London, 1963.
756. Milns, W. *The Well-bred Scholar.* London, 1794.
Milton, J. Complete Works. 21 vols. New York, 1931-1938.
757. ———. *Ad patrem* (1645), Works I, 268-277.
758. ———. *Of Education* (1644), Works IV, 275-291.
759. Ministry of Education. *Language, Some Suggestions for Teachers of English and Others.* London, 1954.
760. ———. *Language Teaching in the Primary Schools.* London, 1945.
761. Minsheu, J. *Ductor in linguas the Guide into Tongues, in novem linguis.* London, 1625.
762. Modern Language Association. *Second Language Learning as a Factor in National Development in Asia, Africa and Latin America.* Washington, 1961.
763. *Modern Studies, Being the Report of the Committee on the Position of Modern Languages in the Educational System of Great Britain.* London, 1918.
764. Moffat, C. W. P. *Science German.* London, 1907.
765. ———. *Science French.* London, 1912.
766. Monroe, R. E. "Radio Instruction in Languages," *MLJ,* XVI (1931), 212-217.
767. Montaigne, M. de. *Essais* (1580-1588), ed. P. Villey and V. L. Saulnier. Paris, 1965.
768. Moore, H. E. *Modernism in Language Teaching.* Cambridge, 1924.
769. Moquotus, S., ed. *Nicolai Clenardi grammatica graeca.* Paris, 1656.
770. Moraud, M. I. "Teaching Machines and the Programming of Foreign Languages," *KFLQ,* XI (1964), 24-32.
771. Mordente, J. E. *A New Easy and Complete Grammar of the Spanish Language.* London, 1810.
772. Moreux, T. *Pour comprendre le latin.* Paris, 1931.
773. Morgan, B. Q. *German Frequency Word Book.* New York, 1928.
774. ———. "The Coleman Report and the 'Reading Method'," *MLJ,* XIV (1930), 618-623.
775. ———. "A Minimum Standard Vocabulary for German," *MLJ,* XVIII (1933), 145-152.

776. Morhof, D. G. *Polyhistor literarius, philosophicus et practicus cum accessionibus virorum classicorum Joannis Frichii et Joannis Molleri Flensburgensis.* 2 vols. Lübeck, 1747.
777. Morris, I. *The Teaching of English as a Second Language.* London, 1945.
778. “Vocabulary Control,” *ELT,* I (1946); *ELT,* II (1947).
779. ———. “Grammar and Language, the Prescriptive and Descriptive Schools,” *ELT,* VI (1951), 55-60.
780. ———. *The Art of Teaching English as a Living Language.* London, 1959.
781. Morton, F. R., “The Teaching Machine and the Teaching of Languages: A Report on Tomorrow,” *PMLA,* LXXV (1960), 1-6.
782. Mosellanus. *Paedologia* (1518), ed. H. Michel. Berlin, 1906.
783. ———. *Oratio de variarum linguarum cognitione paranda.* Berlin, 1519.
784. Moulton, W. G. “Applied Linguistics in the Classroom,” *PMLA,* LXXVI (1961), 1-6.
785. Müller, G. *Methodik des neusprachlichen Unterrichts.* Leipzig, 1914.
786. Müller, M. *Kursbuch für den neusprachlichen Lesestoff.* Leipzig, 1929.
787. Mueller, H. “Wall-pictures, an Old Teaching Device Reshaped,” *Pulgram,* 19-27.
788. Mueller, T. “An Audiovisual Approach to Modern Language Teaching,” *MLJ,* XXXIX (1955), 237-239.
789. Münch, R. *Die dritte Reform des neusprachlichen Unterrichts.* Frankfurt, 1936.
790. Münch, W. *Didaktik und Methodik des französischen Unterrichts.* Munich, 1910.
791. ———. *Vom Arbeitsunterricht in der neueren Sprachen.* Leipzig, 1927.
792. Munck, A., and G. Guibillon. *Germania.* Paris, 1930.
793. McBriarty, W. J. *The French-Canadian's Guide in English Grammar.* Quebec, 1935.
794. McHenry, L. J. A. *A New and Improved Spanish Grammar.* London, 1823.
795. Nairn, J. A., and G. A. Nairn. *Greek through Reading.* London, 1952.
796. Nantel, A. *Nouveau cours de la langue anglaise selon la méthode Ollendorf.* Montreal, 1868.
797. Nelson, W., ed. *A Fifteenth-Century Schoolbook.* London, 1956.
798. Neuse, W. *Vom Bild zum Wort.* 2nd ed. New York, 1958.
799. Nida, E. A. *Learning a Foreign Language.* 2nd ed. New York, 1950.
800. ———. “Some Psychological Problems in Second Language Teaching,” *LL,* VIII (1967), 7-15.
801. Nodier, C. *Notions de linguistique.* Paris, 1834.
802. Noël, F., ed. *Gradus ad Parnassum.* Paris, 1755.

803. Noël and Chapsal. *Grammaire française.* Paris, 1838.
804. ———. *Langue française et grammaire, cours supérieur.* New York, 1860.
805. North, M. A., and A. E. Hillard. *Greek Prose Composition for Schools.* London, 1889.
806. *Nouveaux dialogues, français-italiens.* Paris, 1819.
807. *Nouvelle méthode pour apprendre la langue allemande.* Strasbourg, 1701.
808. Nunn, H. P. V. *The Elements of New Testament Greek.* Cambridge, 1916.
809. Oertel, H. *Lectures on the Study of language.* New York, 1901.
810. O'Grady, H. *The Teaching of Modern Foreign Languages by the Organised Method.* London, 1915.
811. Ollendorf, H. G. *Methode, eine Sprache in sechs Monaten lesen, schreiben und sprechen zu lernen.* Frankfurt, 1783.
812. ———. *New Method of Learning to Read, Write and Speak the French Language.* New York, 1846.
812a.———. *ibid.,* ed. V. Value. New York, 1850.
813. ———. *New Method of Learning to Read, Write and Speak the Spanish Language.* New York, 1848.
814. ———. *Clef de la nouvelle méthode appliquée à l'italien.* Paris, 1872.
815. ———. *La nouvelle méthode appliquée à l'allemand.* 21st ed. Paris, 1873.
816. ———. *Nouvelle méthode pour apprendre l'italien.* 9th ed. Paris, 1874.
817. Ölinger, A. *Grammatica seu institutio vera germanicae linguae* (1573), ed. W. Scheele. Halle, 1897.
818. Omphalius. *De elocutionis imitatione ac apparatu.* Paris, 1555.
819. Ontario Curriculum Institute. *Technology in Learning, an Interim Report of the Study Committee on Instructional Aids and Techniques.* Toronto, 1965.
820. Ornstein, J. "Structurally Oriented Texts and Teaching Materials since World War II," *MLJ,* XL (1956), 213-222.
821. Orthological Institute. *Learning the English Language.* 3 vols. Boston, 1942.
822. Oliver, T. E. *The Modern Language Teachers' Handbook.* Boston, 1935.
823. Otten, G. *Die Verwertung der Ergebnisse der Sprachwissenschaft im französischen und englischen Unterrichte.* Leipzig, 1914.
824. Otto, E. *French Conversation Grammar.* Boston, 1864.
825. ———. *Elementary German Grammar.* Heidelberg, 1900.
826. ———. *German Conversation Grammar.* New York, 1908.
827. ———. *Methodik und Didaktik des neusprachlichen Unterrichts.* Leipzig, 1925.
828. ———. *Kulturkunde und neusprachlicher Unterricht.* Marburg, 1929.

829. Oudin, C. *Grammaire espagnole.* Bordeaux, 1660.
830. ———. *Grammaire italienne.* Paris, 1670.
831. Pace, R. *De fructu qui ex doctrina percipitur* (1517), ed. F. Manley and R. F. Sylvester. New York, 1967.
832. Pachtler, G. M., ed. *Ratio studiorum et institutiones scolasticae societatis Jesu per Germaniam olim vigentes, MGP,* II, V, IX, XVI (whole volumes).
833. Painter, F. V. N. "A Modern Classical Course," *PMLA,* I (1885), 112-117.
834. Palaemon. *Fragmenta orthographiae.* see Suetonius (1051), 300-320.
835. Palmer, G. W. *Cours d'anglais.* Montreal, 1918.
836. Palmer, H. E. *The Scientific Study and Teaching of Languages.* London, 1917.
837. ———. *The Principles of Language Study* (1920). London, 1964.
838. ———. *The Teaching of Oral English.* London, 1940.
839. ———, and H. V. Redman. *This Language-learning Business.* London, 1932.
840. Palsgrave, J. *L'esclaircissement de la langue francoyse* (1530), ed. F. Genin. Paris, 1832.
841. Pannonius, J. *Panegyricus in Guarinum Veronensem* (1500), ed. L. Juhasz. Budapest, 1934.
842. Papias Grammaticus. *Ars grammatica, PL,* CXLI, 1437-1450.
843. Pargment, M. S. "On Learning a Foreign Language," *MLJ,* XXIX (1945), 198-209.
844. Parker, W. R. "The Case for Latin," *CJ,* XL (1964), 1-10.
845. Pascal. *Pensées* (1669), ed. E. Havet. Paris, 1883.
846. Passy, J., and A. Rambeau. *Chrestomathie française.* London, 1926.
847. Passy, P. *Sons du français.* Paris, 1887.
848. ———. *De la méthode directe dans l'enseignement des langues vivantes.* Cambridge, 1899.
849. ———. *Petite phonétique comparée.* Leipzig and Berlin, 1922.
850. ———. *La phonétique et ses applications.* Cambridge, 1929.
851. Patenaude, W. J. *L'anglais rendu facile.* 2 vols. Montreal, 1934.
852. Patterson, A. S. "Some Psychological Aspects of Reading a Foreign Language," *MLJ,* XVII (1933), 575-578.
853. Paulinus Pellaeus. *Eucharisticon.* see Ausonius (64) II, 304-351.
854. Payne, J. *A Compendious Exposition of the Principles and Practice of Professor Jacotot's Celebrated System of Education.* London, 1830.
855. Peal, E., and W. E. Lambert. "The Relation of Bilingualism to Intelligence," *Psychological Monographs.* whole number DXXXVI, 1962.

856. Penfield, W. G. "A Consideration of the Neurophysiological Mechanisms of Speech and some Educational Consequences," *Proceedings of the American Academy of Arts and Sciences,* LXXXII (1953), 199-214.
857. ———, and L. Roberts. *Speech and Brain Mechanisms.* Princeton, N. J., 1959.
858. Perizonius. *Minerva.* Lyon, 1789.
859. Perkins, M. L. "General Language Study and the Teaching of Languages," *MLJ,* XL (1956), 113-119.
860. Perotti, N. *Cornucopiae linguae latinae.* Venice, 1494.
861. Perreault, J. F. *Nouvelle méthode pour apprendre la langue anglaise.* Quebec, 1823.
862. Perret, J. *Latin et culture.* Bruges, 1947.
863. Perrin, J. *Grammar of the French Tongue.* Philadelphia, 1779.
864. ———. *The Elements of French Conversation.* 6th ed. London, 1810.
865. Pervy, A. *L'audiovision et l'enseignement des langues vivantes.* Unpublished thesis, Université Laval, Quebec, 1949.
866. St. Peter Damian. *Opuscula, PL,* CXLV (whole volume).
867. Petit, N. *Epithetorum parvum opus.* Paris, 1649.
868. Petitmangin, H. *Les mots latins classés par familles.* Paris, 1935.
869. *Petit trésor de la belle latinité.* Paris, 1755.
870. Petrarch, F. *Prose Works.* Milan, 1955.
871. Petrus Victorius. *Commentarii in tres libros Aristotelis de arte dicendi.* Florence, 1548.
872. Petty, W. *The Advice of W. P. to Mr. Samuel Hartlib for the Advancement of some Particular parts of Learning.* London, 1648.
873. Peyton. *Elémens de la langue angloise.* London, 1765.
874. Pfrimmer, P. "Après un demi-siècle de la méthode directe," *LM,* XLVII (1953), 201-209.
875. Philip of Harveng. *De institutione clericorum, PL,* CCIII, 665-204.
876. Philo Iudaeus. *On Mating with the Preliminary Studies,* ed. R. Marcus. Loeb Classical Library, 1953.
877. Phrysius, J. (attributed). *Epistolae virorum obscurorum* (1514), ed. A. Bömer. Heidelberg, 1924.
878. Piccolomini, A. S. *De liberorum educatione,* ed. J. S. Nelson. Washington, 1940.
879. Pick, E. *Dr Pick on Languages—French, a New Method of Studying Foreign Languages.* London and Edinburgh, 1863.
880. Pierce, R. *A New French Spelling Book.* London, 1780.
881. Pierre de Blois. *Epistola 66, PL,* CCVII, 195-210.

882. Pillot. *Gallicae linguae institutio.* Paris, 1581.
883. *Pinax,* in *Tabula qua vitae humanae prudenter instituendae ratio continetur.* Basle, 1561.
884. Pinloche, A. *Vocabulaire par l'image de la langue française.* Paris, 1923.
885. *Pinnock's Catechisms, Rhetoric, English Grammar.* 3 vols. London, 1822.
886. Piroch, G. "The Importance of Bilingual Description to Foreign Language Learning," *LL,* VI (1955), 51-61.
887. Pitschel, E. *Eindrücke und Beobachtungen während eines Studienaufenthaltes in Frankreich.* Frankfurt, 1909.
888. Pizarro, J. A. *Original Dialogues in Spanish.* Baltimore, 1851.
889. *A Plaine Pathway to the French Tongue.* London, 1575.
890. Plecher, H. *Handbuch für die Methodik des deutschen Sprachunterrichts.* Leipzig, 1927.
891. Ploetz, G. *Sprachlehre auf Grund der Schulgrammatik von K. Ploetz.* Berlin, 1911.
892. Ploetz, K. *Elementarbuch der französischen Sprache.* New York, 1865.
893. ———. *Vocabulaire systématique et guide de conversation française.* Berlin, 1879.
894. ———. *Schulgrammatik der französischen Sprache.* Berlin, 1894.
895. Pluche. *La mécanique des langues et l'art de les enseigner.* Lyon, 1811.
896. Politzer, R. "Linguistics and the Elementary Language Course," *MLJ,* XXXV (1951), 314-318.
897. ———. "The Controlled Auto-didactic Approach," *H,* XXXVII (1954), 214-216.
898. ———. "Phonetics, Phonemics and Pronunciation Theory," *Pulgram,* 19-27.
899. ———. "On the Relation of Linguistics to Language Teaching," *MLJ,* XLII (1958), 65-68.
900. ———. *Teaching French.* Boston, 1960.
901. ———, and C. N. Staubach. *Teaching Spanish—a Linguistic Orientation.* Boston, 1961.
902. Polivanov, E. L. "La perception des sons d'une langue étrangère," *Travaux du cercle linguistique de Prague,* IV, 79.
903. Pomey, F. *Les particules reformés.* Rouen, 1699.
904. Pond, Sr. Mary Lelia. "The Multiple Approach Method of Teaching French vs. the Grammar Method," *FR,* XIII (1940), 475-482.
905. Pope, H. *Why Not Learn Greek?* New York, 1941.
906. Pope, M. K. "The Tractatus Orthographiae of T. H., Parisii Studentis," *MLR,* V (1910), 185-193.
907. Porney. *Syllabaire française.* New York, 1829.

908. Posselius, J. *Familiarium colloquiorum libellus graece et latine auctus.* London, 1660.
909. Postgate, J. P. "The Reformed Pronunciation of Latin," *CR,* I (1887), 40-42.
910. Powers, F. F., and M. Hetzler. *Successful Methods of Teaching English to Bilingual Children.* Washington, 1937.
911. Prendergast, T. *Handbook to the Mastery Series.* New York, 1870.
912. *The Primitives of the Greek Tongue.* Boston, 1812.
913. Prince, J. R. "Philology at Work," *MLJ,* XXXVIII (1954), 75-79.
914. *Les Principes de la langue latine à l'usage des collèges de Bretagne.* St. Malo, 1780.
915. Priscian. *Ars grammatica, Keil,* II and III (whole volumes).
916. Pseudo-Boethius. *De disciplina scholarium, PL,* LXIV, 1223-1238.
917. Pseudo-Dositheus. *Hermeneumata Pseudodositheana,* ed. G. E. Loewe and G. Goetz. *Corpus glossarium latinorum.* Leipzig, 1889-1923. III, 637-638.
918. Pujol, L., and D. C. van Norman. *The Complete French Classbook.* New York, 1870.
919. Pulgram, E. "Preparation for Language Teaching," *Pulgram,* 75-85.
920. Purin, C. M. "The Direct Teaching of Modern Foreign Languages in American High Schools," *MLJ,* I (1916), 43-51.
921. ———. *The Training of Teachers of Modern Foreign Languages.* New York, 1929.
922. Quaife, P. "Programming a Remedial Pronunciation Course," *Te Reo,* VIII (1965), 41-52.
923. Quintillian. *Institutionis oratoriae libri duodecim,* ed. E. Bonnel. Leipzig, 1861.
924. Rabelais, F. *Gargantua* (1532), ed. P. Grimal. Paris, 1957.
925. Radonvilliers, C. D. *De la manière d'apprendre les langues.* Paris, 1768.
926. Raimon Vidal de Besalu. *Las razos de trobar, Guessard,* 67-100 (see also *137 for extracts).
927. Rambeau, A. "Phonetics and the Reform Method," *MLN,* VIII (1893), 321-331; 385-398.
928. Ramus (de la Ramée), P. *Pro philosophica parisiensis academiae disciplina oratio.* Paris, 1550.
929. ———. *Scholae grammaticae.* Paris, 1569.
930. ———. *Petri Rami grammatica.* Paris, 1572.
931. ———. *La grammaire de Pierre de la Ramée.* Paris, 1572.
932. ———. *Grammatica graeca.* Hanover, 1605.

933. Randonnet, A. *Trésor de la langue française, revu et augmenté par J. Nicot* (1621). Photographic reproduction by Fondation Singer Polignac, 1960.
934. Rapper, H. *Psychologische Grundlagen des neusprachlichen Unterrichts,* Leipzig, 1914.
935. *Rapport de la Commission royale d'enquête sur l'éducation dans la province de Québec.* 5 vols. Quebec, 1964.
936. Ratichus (Ratke), W. *In methodum linguarum generalia.* Halle, 1615.
937. ———. *Methodus institutionis nova quadruplex.* Leipzig, 1617.
938. Regberg, R. *English as a Second Language.* Tel Aviv, 1958.
939. Regnier-Desmarais, F.-S. *Traité de grammaire française,* Paris, 1706.
940. Remigius Autissiodorensis (Rémi d'Auxerre). *Remigii Autissiodorensis commentum in Martianum Capellam,* ed. C. E. Lutz. Leiden, 1962.
941. ———. *Commentarium in artem Donati minorem,* ed. W. Fox. Leipzig, 1892.
942. ———. *Remigii inedita.* ed. M. De Marco. *Aevum,* XXVI (1952), 495-517.
943. Renard, R. *L'enseignement des langues vivantes par la méthode audio-visuelle et structure-globale.* Brussels, Paris, and Montreal, 1965.
944. Renauld, E. "Le latin et les langues vivantes," *RU,* XXX, 1 (1923), 26-33.
945. Reuchlin, J. *De rudimentis hebraicis.* Pforzheim, 1506.
946. Revell, R. J. "Sign and Sound in the Study of Written Texts," *RACL,* XIII (1967), 24-33.
947. Rhabanus Maurus. *De clericorum institutione, PL,* CVII, 293-420.
948. ———. *Excerptio de arte grammatica Prisciani, PL,* CXI, 64-75.
949. ———. *Glossaria, PL,* CXII, 1575-1583.
950. Rheinfelder, H. *Vergleichende Sprachbetrachtung im neusprachlichen Unterricht.* Munich, 1926.
951. Rice, W. H. "General Considerations on Unit Lesson Plans in Modern Language Teaching," *Rice,* 1-10.
952. Richards, I. A. *Basic in Teaching, East and West.* London, 1935.
953. ———. *Basic English and Its Uses.* New York, 1943.
954. ———. "Responsibilities in the Teaching of English," in I. A. Richards, *Speculative Instruments.* London, 1955. 91-106.
955. Riégel, L. "Les croquis et leur utilisation dans la classe de langue," *LM,* LV (1961), 247-261.
956. Reimann, O., and H. J. E. Goelzer. *Grammaire latine complète.* Paris, 1924.
957. Riggs, J. D. S., and H. F. Scott. *In latinum.* Chicago, 1892.
958. Ripman, W. *A Handbook of the Latin Language.* London and New York, 1930.

959. Rivers, W. M. *The Psychologist and the Foreign Language Teacher.* Chicago, 1964.
960. ———. "Comment on Jones, R. M., 'When and How do Persons Become Bilingual?' " *Kelly* 35-41.
961. Robbins, F. E. "A Ten-day Program of Preparation for Language Learning," *LL,* X (1960), 157-160.
962. Roche, A. J. *L'étude des langues vivantes.* Paris, 1955.
963. Rocklyn, E. H., and W. E. Montague. *A Brief Review of Extreme Massing of Practice and Stress on Foreign Language Acquisition.* Alexandria, Va., 1965.
964. Roehrig, F. L. O. *The Shortest Road to German.* Ithaca, N. Y., 1873.
965. Rollin, G. *De la manière d'enseigner et d'étudier les belles lettres.* 2 vols. Paris, 1725.
966. Roman-Cornut, R. *Grande grammaire grecque et latine.* Paris, 1844.
967. Rondeau, G., and J.-P. Vinay. *Le français international.* Montreal, 1966.
968. Roques, P. "La culture européenne et l'enseignement des langues vivantes," *RU,* XLVII (1938), 111-119.
969. ———. "Allemand et latin," *RU,* XXXIX, 1 (1930), 13-19.
970. Roscius, L. V. *De docendi studendique modo.* Basle, 1541.
971. Rosenthal, R. S. *The German Language.* New York, 1901.
972. Röttgers, B. *Methodik des englischen und französischen Unterrichts.* Berlin, 1913.
973. Rouse, W. H. D. *Demonstrations in Greek Iambic Verse.* Cambridge, 1899.
974. ———. "Latin Composition," *CR,* XXI (1907), 129-131.
975. ———. "Translation," *CR,* XXII (1908), 105-110.
976. ———. *Latin Stories.* London, n.d.
977. ———, and R. B. Appleton. *Latin on the Direct Method.* London, 1925.
978. Rousseau, J. J. *La nouvelle Héloise* (1758), ed. D. Mornet. Paris, 1925.
979. ———. *Emile ou de l'éducation* (1780). Paris, 1961.
980. Rousselot, J. P. *Précis de prononciation française.* Paris and Leipzig, 1902.
981. ———. *Principes de phonétique expérimentale.* Paris, 1908.
982. Royal Commission on Education in Ontario. *Report.* Toronto, 1950.
983. Ruddiman, T. *The Rudiments of the Latin Tongue.* 17th ed. Edinburgh, 1769.
984. Russell, H. J. "Phonetic Suggestions for Teachers," *MLJ,* XVII (1933), 349-354.
985. Ruteboeuf. *Poèmes concernant l'université de Paris,* ed. H. H. Lucas. Paris, 1952.
986. Sack, F. L. *Vom Englischunterricht.* Berne, 1941.

987. Sadler, P. *Grammaire pratique de la langue anglaise.* Paris, 1879.
988. Sadoleto. *De liberis recte instituendis, Opera Omnia.* Verona, 1738. III, 66-126.
989. Sallust. *Opera omnia quae extant, edidit Crispinus in usum Delphini.* London, 1776.
990. Saporta, S. *Psycholinguistics, a Book of Readings.* New York, 1961.
991. Sauer, C. M. *Nouvelle grammaire italienne,* rev. A. Tozza. Paris, 1909.
992. Sauveur, L. *Entretiens sur la grammaire.* New York, 1875.
993. ———. *Causeries avec mes élèves.* Boston, 1875.
994. ———. *Introduction to the Teaching of Living Languages without Grammar or Dictionary.* Boston, 1875.
995. ———. *Talks with Caesar, de bello Gallico.* New York, 1879.
996. ———. *Introduction to the Teaching of Ancient Languages.* New York, 1882.
997. Savory, D. L. *Deutsches Reformlesebuch.* Oxford, 1908.
998. Sawyer, J., and S. Silver. "Dictation in Language Learning," *LL* 11 (1961), 33-42.
999. Scaliger, J. C. *De causis linguae latinae.* Lyon, 1540.
1000. Scherping, E. *Englischer Unterricht auf der Oberstufe.* Marburg, 1926.
1001. Schickard, W. *Horologium ebraeum* (1623). London, 1702.
1002. Schmidt, J. *Methodik des französischen Unterrichts.* Leipzig, 1928.
1003. Schmidt, O. *Methodik des englischen Unterrichts.* Bonn, 1929.
1004. Schneider, C. H. *The Edinburgh High School French Conversation Grammar.* Edinburgh, 1874.
1005. Schopenhauer, A. "De usu et praestantia linguae latinae," *L,* VI (1958), 44-47.
1006. Schweitzer, C. "Methodologie des langues vivantes," *RU,* CXXII (1903), 1-10; 105-115.
1007. ——— and E. Simmonot. *Methodologie des langues vivantes.* Paris, 1903.
1008. Scioppius, G. *De paedia humanarum ac divinarum literarum.* Padua, 1636.
1009. ———. *Consultationes de scholarum et studiorum ratione.* Padua, 1636.
1010. Sears, B. *The Ciceronian or the Prussian Method of Teaching the Elements of the Latin Language.* Boston, 1845.
1011. Sébillet, T. *Art poétique* (1548), ed. E. Gaiffe. Paris, 1932.
1012. Segal, L. *Russian Grammar and Self-Educator.* London, 1943.
1013. Seidenstücker, J. H. *Elementarbuch zur Erlernung der französischen Sprache.* Berlin, 1811.
1014. Sergius. *Explanationes in artem Donati, Keil,* IV, 475-584.
1015. Sidonius Appollinaris. *Epistolae et carmina, PL,* LVIII, 435-752.

1016. Siertsema, B. "Language Learning and Language Analysis," *Lingua,* X (1961), 128-147.
1017. Sigwalt, C. *De l'enseignement des langues vivantes.* Paris, 1903.
1018. Siret, M. *Elémens de la langue anglaise.* 25 ed., ed. M. MacCarthey. Paris, 1828.
1019. Slack, A., et al. *Parlons français,* 8 vols. Boston, 1961.
1020. Slama-Cazacu, T. *Langage et contexte.* The Hague, 1961.
1021. Smaragdus. *De Smaragdi Arte* (Code Bernensis), *Keil,* VIII, 239-300.
1022. Smetius, H. *Prosodia promptissima.* Rouen, 1626.
1023. Smith, D. A. "The 'Madras Snowball'–an Attempt to Retrain 27000 Teachers of English to Beginners," *ELT,* XVII (1963), 3-9.
1024. Smith, H. A. "Outside Reading," *MLJ,* XVIII (1933), 1-20.
1025. Smith, J. *Grammar of the Greek Language.* Boston, 1809.
1026. Smith, Sir Thomas, *De recta et emendata linguae anglicae scriptione dialogus* (1568), ed. O. Deibel. Halle, 1913
1027. Spencer, H. *Education.* New York, 1861.
1028. Spiers, A. *Grammaire raisonnée de la langue anglaise.* Paris, 1845.
1029. Spyridis, G. *Living Greek Language.* Athens, n.d.
1030. Stack, E. M. *The Language Laboratory.* Fair Lawn, N. J., 1960.
1031. Stanbridge, J. *Vulgaria* (1519), ed. B. White. Early English Text Society 187. London, 1932.
1032. ———. *The Long Accidence.* London, n.d. (UM film).
1033. ———. *Accidence.* London, n.d. (UM film).
1034. ———. *Libellus grammaticus latinus, Longe parvula* (1509), ed. H. Varnhagen. Erlangen, 1906.
1035. Stepney, W. *The Spanish Schoolmaster,* London, 1591.
1036. Stern, H. H., ed. *Foreign Languages in the Primary School,* Hamburg, 1963.
1037. ———. ed. *International Congress on Modern Foreign Language Teaching,* vol. IV Reports. Berlin, 1965.
1038. Stevens, C. M. *Swedish-English Conversation Teacher.* Chicago, 1905.
1039. Stevick, E. W. *Helping People to Learn English.* New York, 1957.
1040. Stockwood, J. *Progymnasma scholasticum.* London, 1597.
1041. ———. *Disputatiuncularum grammaticalium libellus.* London, 1598.
1042. Stoddart, J. *Universal Grammar.* 2nd ed. London, 1849.
1043. Stott, D. H. *Language Teaching in the New Education.* London, 1946.
1044. Streubler, A. *Neuere Sprachen.* Breslau, 1925.
1045. Strevens, P. *Spoken Language.* London, 1956.
1046. ———. *Papers on Language and Language Teaching.* London, 1965.

1047. Strohmeyer, H. *Methodik des neusprachlichen Unterrichts.* Braunschweig, 1928.
1048. Sturm, J. *De literarum ludis recte aperiendis Argentorati.* Strasbourg, 1538.
1049. ———. *Epistolae classicae.* Strasbourg, 1565.
1050. ———. *Onomasticon puerile argentinense.* Strasbourg, 1571.
1051. Suetonius. *De grammaticis,* ed. C. Roth. *C. Suetonii Tranquilli quae supersunt omnia.* Leipzig, 1907. vol. II.
1052. Sulpitius, J. *Grammatices comendium perutile* (1505). Venice, 1536.
1053. Sweet, H. *History of Language.* London, 1900.
1054. ———. *The Practical Study of Languages* (1898). London, 1964.
1055. Sweet, W. E. "The Linguistic Approach to the Learning of Latin," *LL,* IV (1952), 42-54.
1056. Tabouret-Keller, A. "Comment on MacNamara, J., 'How Can One Measure the Extent of a Person's Bilingual Proficiency?' " *Kelly,* 102-106.
1057. Tacitus. *Dialogus de oratoribus,* ed. W. Peterson. Loeb Classical Library, 1958.
1058. Taillon, L. *"Présentation dialoguée versus enseignement structurel."* Paper given at the annual meeting of the Canadian Linguistics Association, 1964 (unpublished MS).
1059. Talbot, G. H. *French Translation Self-taught.* Boston, 1855.
1060. ———. *Philosophy of French Pronunciation,* 2nd ed. New York, 1856.
1061. Tamborra, J. "The What, Why and When of Phonetics in Learning French Pronunciation," *MLJ,* XIX (1935), 511-518.
1062. Tan Gwan Leong and R. Gauthier. *"Tan-Gau, a Natural Method for Learning a Second Language,"* mimeographed Leaflet, n.d.
1063. *Teaching Modern Languages; the Report of a Seminar in the Interests of Education by the Canadian Teachers' Federation.* Ottawa, 1963.
1064. Terence. *Phormio,* ed. A. Sloman. Oxford, 1899.
1065. Tharp, J. B. "The Basic French Vocabulary and its Use," *MLJ,* XVIII (1935), 123-131.
1066. ———. "Unit Lesson in Extensive Reading," *Rice,* 83-112.
1067. Theodulphus of Orleans. *Opera omnia, PL,* CCV.
1068. *Thesaurus purioris et elegantioris latinitatis.* Rouen, 1647.
1069. Thiergen, O. *Methodik des neusprachlichen Unterrichts.* Leipzig, 1914.
1070. Thimann, I. C. *Teaching Languages.* London, 1955.
1071. Thimm, F. *Spanish at a Glance.* New York, 1884.
1072. ———. *Italian Self-taught.* New York, 1877.

1073. ———. *German Self-taught.* New York, 1877.
1074. Thomas, C. (Chairman). *Report of the Committee of Twelve of the Modern Language Association of America.* Boston, 1901.
1075. Thomas de Erfurto (pseudo-Duns Scotus). *Grammatica speculativa.* Paris, 1891.
1076. Thomas, F. *Les langues étrangères et la vie.* Paris, n.d.
1077. Thomas, W. *Principal Rules of the Italian Grammar* (1550). London, 1567.
1078. Thompson, A. R. *Russian and English Dialogues.* London, 1882.
1079. Ticknor, G. "Lecture on the Best Methods of Teaching the Living Languages" (1832), *MLJ,* XXII (1937), 19-31.
1080. Tikhomirov, O. K. "Review of Skinner, B. F., *Verbal Behavior,*" *Word,* XIV (1959). 362-367.
1081. Timmermans, W. F. C. *La réforme de l'enseignement des langues vivantes, le débat des méthodes.* Groningen, 1937.
1082. Tisken, T. *Der englishe Unterricht.* Heidelberg, 1931.
1083. Todiere, L. P. *Nouvelle grammaire anglaise.* Tours, 1834.
1084. Tomatis, A. *L'oreille et la langue.* Paris, 1961.
1085. Tondini, H. "De ciceronianae imitationis ortu et progressione ad exordio renatarum litterarum ad P. Bembem," *L* VII (1959), 166-181.
1086. Transtagano, A. V. *A New Portuguese Grammar.* London, 1768.
1087. Tricot. *Les rudimens de la langue latine,* Paris, 1785.
1088. *Troisième congrès international des professeurs des langues vivantes.* Paris, 1937.
1089. Trubetzkoy, N. S. *Principes de phonologie* (1939), tr. J. Cantineau. Paris, 1949.
1090. Tursellini, H. *De particulis.* Paris, 1662.
1091. Twaddell, W. F. "Meaning, Habits and Rules," *LL,* II (1949), 2-11.
1092. Udall, J. *The Key of the Holy Tongue.* Leyden, 1593.
1093. UNESCO. *L'enseignement des langues vivantes et compréhension internationale.* Paris, 1953.
1094. Vachek, J. *The Linguistic School of Prague.* Bloomington, Ill. and London, 1966.
1095. Valla, L. *Elegantiae linguae latinae.* Venice, 1491.
1096. Valpetre, J. *Petit cours de la latinité.* Paris, 1828.
1097. van Eenenaam, E. "The Teaching of Languages in the Elementary Schools," *MLJ,* XXXVIII (1954), 309-313.
1098. Vanière, C. *Cours de latinité.* Paris, 1749.

1099. van Teslaar, A. P. "Learning New Sound Systems: Problems and Prospects," *IRAL,* III (1965). 80-93.
1100. Varenne, G. "Le rôle de la grammaire dans l'enseignement des langues vivantes," *RU,* XIV, 1 (1905), 12-25.
1101. Varro. *De lingua latina,* ed. R. G. Kent. Loeb Classical Library, 1958.
1102. Vaudelin, G. *Nouvelle manière d'écrire comme on parle en France.* Paris, 1713.
1103. Veneroni. *Maître italien.* Lyon, 1745.
1104. Vergerius, P. P. *De liberalibus studiis* (1392), Basle, 1541.
1105. *Veteres panegyrici (Gaii Plinii Secundi).* Caen, 1653.
1106. Vergilius Maro Grammaticus. *Ars grammatica, Keil,* VIII, 189-201.
1107. Victor, Claudius. *Ars grammatica, PL,* LXI, 970-1000.
1108. Vida, G. J. *Ars poetica* (1535), in ed. A. S. Cook, *The Art of Poetry.* New York, 1926.
1109. Vidon-Varney, J. "Comment enseigner l'intonation," *MLJ,* XVIII (1934), 516-520.
1110. Viëtor, W. *Der Sprachunterricht muss umkehren! Ein Beitrag zur Überbürdungsfrage* (1882). Heilbronn, 1886.
1111. Vieyra, A. *A Grammar of the Portuguese Language.* 14th ed. London, 1878.
1112. Vinay, J.-P., and J. Darbelnet. *Stylistique comparée du français et de l'anglais.* Paris, 1963.
1113. Vincent de Beauvais *De eruditione filiorum nobilium,* ed. A. Steiner, A. Cambridge, Mass., 1938.
1114. ———. *Speculum doctrinale.* 2 vols. Venice, 1494.
1115. Vingutt, F. J. *Ollendorf's New Method of Learning to Write, Read and Speak Spanish.* New York, 1862.
1116. Vitruvius. *De architectura,* ed. F. Granger. Loeb Classical Library, 1955.
Vivès, J. L. Opera omnia. Valencia, 1782 (Gregg reprint, London, 1964).
1117. ———. *Campo di fior,* tr. C. de Sainliens. London, 1583.
1118. ———. *Linguae latinae exercitatio* (1538), Opera, I, 283-432.
1119. ———. *Epistolae I et II de ratione studii puerilis* (1523), Opera I, 257-280.
1120. ———. *Introductio ad sapientiam* (1524), Opera I, 1-48.
1121. ———. *De causis corruptorum artium* (1531), Opera VI, 77-105.
1122. ———. *De disciplinis tradendis* (1531), Opera VI, 243-409.
1123. ———. *De anima et vita* (1538), Photographic reproduction of Basle edition. Turin, 1959.
1124. Voegelin, C. F., and S. Adams, S. "A Phonetic Study of Young Children's Speech," *Journal of Experimental Education,* III (1934), 107-116.

1125. von Jagemann, H. C. G. "On the Use of English in Teaching Foreign Languages," *PMLA,* I (1885), 218-226.

1126. Vossius, G. J. *Latina grammatica.* 2 vols. Amsterdam, 1662.

1129. Waititi, H. R. *Te Rangatahi.* 2 vols. Wellington, 1962-1964.

1130. Walafrid Strabo. *Glossa ordinaria, PL,* CXIII, 67-1316; CXIV, 9-752.

1131. Walter, M. *Zur Methodik des neuspraechlichen Unterrichts mit Ausländern* (1912). Wolfenbüttel, 1936.

1132. Wanostrocht, N. *A Grammar of the French Language with Practical Exercises.* London, 1798.

1133. Ward, C. F. *Minimum French Vocabulary Testbook.* New York, 1926.

1134. Warshaw, J. "Automatic Reactions in Practical Foreign Language Work," *MLJ,* IX (1924), 151-158.

1135. Waxman, S. M. "Foreign Languages and the U. S. Army," *E,* LXV (1945), 553-557.

1136. Webbe, J. *An Appeale to Truthe.* London, 1622.

1137. ———. *Petition to the High Court of Parliament.* London, 1623.

1138. ———. *Usus et authoritas.* London, 1626.

1139. ———. *Pueriles confabulatiunculae, or Children's Talke: Claused and Drawn into Lessons.* London, 1627.

1140. Weinstein, R. H. "Phonetics, Phonemics and Pronunciation," *Pulgram,* 28-38.

1141. ———. "The Preparation of Phonology Tapes in Language Teaching," *LL,* V (1953), 135-138.

1142. Wells, P. F. *Notes for Trainees.* Auckland, N. Z., 1959 (mimeographed).

1143. Werner-Spanhoofd, A. *Lehrbuch der deutschen Sprache.* Boston, 1905.

1144. West, M. P. "Simplified and Abridged," *ELT,* V (1950), 48-52.

1145. ———. "Catenising," *ELT,* VI (1951), 147-151.

1146. ———. "Is a Textbook Really Necessary?" *ELT,* VIII (1953), 64-67.

1147. ———. *The Teaching of English: a Guide to the New Method Series.* Toronto, 1953.

1148. ———. "Vocabulary Selection and the Minimum Adequate Vocabulary," *ELT,* VIII (1954), 121-126.

1149. ———. *Learning to Read a Foreign Language.* London, 1955.

1150. ———. "At What Age should Language Study Begin?" *ELT,* XIV (1959), 21-26.

1151. ———. "Learning English as Behaviour," *ELT,* XV (1960), 3-10.

1152. ———. *Teaching English in Difficult Circumstances.* London, 1960.

1153. ———. *Language in Education.* London, 1929.

1154. ———, and J. G. Endicott. *The New Method English Dictionary, Explaining the Meaning of 24,000 Items within a Vocabulary of 1490 Words*. Paris, 1941.

1155. Wetenhall, E. *Graece grammaticae institutio* (17th century), ed. P. Lynch. Dublin, 1809.

1156. Whipple, C. A. *English Is a Foreign Language*. Washington, 1952.

1157. White, D. S. *The Teaching of Latin*. Chicago, 1941.

1158. Whittinton, J. *Vulgaria* (1519), ed. B. White. Early English Text Society (CLXXXVII), 1932.

1159. Widgery, W. H. *The Teaching of Languages in School*. London, 1888.

1160. Williams, H. W. *First Steps in Maori* (1845). Auckland, 1952.

1161. Willot, A. "L'étude des langues vivantes," *EC* XXV (1940), 207-226.

1162. Wilson, P. G. *A Student's Guide to Modern Languages*. London, 1939.

1163. Wiseman, C. *A Complete English Grammar*. London, n.d. (1780?).

1164. Withers, A. M. "On Learning Modern Languages," *MLJ*, XXXIV (1950), 475-477.

1165. Wolff, H. "Fact and Distortion in Language Teaching," *LL* XI (1961), 1-11.

1166. Worman, J. H. *First German Book after the Natural or Pestalozzian Method*. New York, 1880.

1167. ———. *First and Second French Books after the Natural or Pestalozzian Method*. New York, 1881.

1168. ———, and A. Rougemont. *Grammaire française*. New York, 1883.

1169. Yamagiwa, J. K. *The Japanese Language Programs at the University of Michigan during World War II*. Ann Arbor, Mich., 1946.

1170. Young, C. W., and C. A. Choquette. "An Experimental Study of the Relative Effectiveness of Four Systems of Equipment for Self-monitoring in Teaching French Pronunciation," *IRAL*, III (1965), 14-50.

1171. Zidler, C. *L'enseignement du français par le latin*. Paris and Quebec, 1912.

SECONDARY SOURCES

*1. Abelson, P. *The Seven Liberal Arts.* New York, 1906.

*2. Agard, F. B., et al. *A Survey of Language Classes in the ASTP.* New York, 1944. (Commission on Trends in Education.)

*3. Allen, W. S. *Phonetics in Ancient India.* London, 1953.

*4. Alpers, A. *Maori Myths and Tribal Legends.* Auckland, 1964.

*5. Angiolillo, P. F. *Armed Forces Foreign Language Teaching.* New York, 1947.

*6. Auerbach, E. *Literary Language and Its Public in Late Latin Antiquity and in the Middle Ages* (1958), tr. R. Manheim, New York, 1965.

*7. Bagster-Collins, E. W., et al. *Studies in Modern Language Teaching.* New York, 1930.

*8. Baldwin, T. W. *Shakespere's Smalle Latin and Lesse Greeke.* Urbana, Ill., 1944.

*9. Barwick, K. "Clemens Scotus," *G,* VI (1930), 385-395.

*10. Bennet, H. S. "A Checklist of Robert Whittinton's Grammars," *Li* VII, V (1952), 1-14.

*11. Benson, M. "The New Soviet Foreign Language Program," *MLJ,* XL (1956), 173-174.

*12. Bischoff, B. "Elementarunterricht und *probationes pennae* in der ersten Hälfte des Mittel-Alters," ed. L. W. Jones, *Studies in Honor of E. K. Rand.* New York, 1938, 9-20.

*13. ——— "Das grieschische Element in der abendlandische Bildung des Mittelalters," *BZ,* XLIV (1951), 27-55.

*14. Bloomfield, L. "Why a Linguistic Society?" *Language,* I (1925), 1-5.

*15. Boas, F. *Handbook of American Indian Languages.* Washington, 1911.

*16. Boissier, G. *Etude sur la vie et les oeuvres de Varron.* Paris, 1861.

*17. Bolgar, R. R. *The Classical Heritage and Its Beneficiaries.* London, 1958.

*18. Bonaventure, Bro. F. S. C. "The Teaching of Latin in Later Medieval England," *MS,* XXIII (1961), 1-20.

*19. Bongers, H. *The History and Principles of Vocabulary Control.* Woerden, 1947.

*20. Boyd, W. *The History of Western Education.* London, 1947.

*21. Breal, M. "La tradition du latin en France," *Revue des deux mondes,* CV (1891), 551-570.

*22. Breymann, H., and C. Steinmüller. *Die neusprachliche Reformliteratur von 1876-1909.* 4 vols. Leipzig, 1895-1909.

*23. Brunot, F. *Histoire de la langue française dès les origines à 1900.* 8 vols. Paris, 1913.

*24. Buchanan, M. A., and E. D. MacPhee. *Modern Language Instruction in Canada.* 2 vols. Toronto, 1938.

*25. Bureau international de l'éducation. *L'enseignement des langues vivantes.* Geneva, 1937.

*26. ———. *L'enseignement des langues anciennes.* Geneva, 1938.

*27. Bursian, C. "Die Grammatik des Winfried-Bonifacius," *Sitzungberichte* III, Munich, 1873.

*28. Bursill-Hall, G. L. "Medieval Grammatical Theories," *RACL,* IX (1963), 40-54.

*29. Butts, R. F. *A Cultural History of Education.* New York, 1947.

*30. Cadet, F. *L'Education à Port-Royal.* Paris, 1887.

*31. Callaey, F. "La vie belge au temps jadis d'après les manuels de conversation," Conférence faite à l'Institut historique belge de Rome, le 31 mars, 1925.

*32. *Cambridge Ancient History.* 12 vols. London, 1923-39.

*33. *Cambridge Medieval History.* 8 vols. London, 1924-1936.

*34. *The New Cambridge Modern History.* 13 vols. London, 1957.

*35. Carré, T. *L'enseignement secondaire à Troyes.* Paris, 1888.

*36. Chaytor, H. J. *From Script to Print.* Cambridge, 1950.

*37. Clarke, M. L. *Greek Studies in England.* London, 1945.

*38. ———. *Classical Education in Britain.* London, 1959.

*39. Cochrane, C. N. *Christianity and Classical Culture.* London, 1944.

*40. Cole, P. R. *Later Roman Education in Ausonius, Capella and the Theodosian Code.* New York, 1909.

*41. Coleman, A. *The Teaching of Modern Languages in the United States.* New York, 1931.

*42. ——— and R. H. Fife. *An Analytical Bibliography of Modern Language Teaching.* 3 vols. New York, 1933-1949.

*43. Compayré, A. Articles "oratoire," "Port-Royal," in F. Buisson, *Nouveau dictionnaire de pédagogie et d'instruction.* Paris, 1911.

*44. Conseil scientifique pour l'Afrique. *Colloque sur le multilinguisme.* Brazzaville, 1962.
*45. Cosenza, M. E. *Biographical and Bibliographical Dictionary of the Italian Humanists.* Boston, 1962.
*46. Courcelle, P. *Les lettres grecques en occident de Macrobe et Cassiodore.* Paris, 1943.
*47. Croll, F. "Juste Lipse et le mouvement anti-cicéronien," *RSS,* II (1914), 200-242.
*48. Curtius, E. R. "Das mittelalterliche Bildungswesen und die Grammatik," *RF,* LX (1947), 1-26.
*49. Curtis, S. J., and M. E. A. Boultwood. *A Short History of Educational Ideas.* London, 1953.
*50. Darlington, O. G. "Gerbert the Teacher," *AHR,* LII (1946), 456-476.
*51. Dartigues, G. *Le traité des études de l'abbé Claude Fleury.* Paris, 1921.
*52. Dassonville, M. "De la Ramée et la dialectique" (unpublished thesis, U. Laval, Quebec, 1952).
*53. Desbiens, J.-P. *Sous le soleil de la pitié.* Montreal, 1965.
*54. Eichelkraut, P. *Beiträge zur Kentnis der Didaktik des Wolfgangs Ratichius.* Jena, 1895.
*55. Elcock, W. D. *The Romance Languages.* London, 1951.
*56. Elder, J. P. "Did Remigius of Auxerre Comment on Bede's *de Schematibus et tropis?" MS,* IX (1947), 141-150.
*57. Escher, E. "Essay on the Sources and History of the Direct Method of Teaching Modern Languages," unpublished M.A. thesis (Chicago, 1919).
*58. ———. "The Direct Method of Studying Foreign Languages: A Contribution to the History of Its Sources and Development" (unpublished Ph.D. thesis, Chicago, 1928).
*59. Ewert, A. *The French Language.* London, 1933.
*60. Farrell, A. P. *The Jesuit Code of Liberal Education.* Milwaukee, 1938.
*61. Febvre, L., and H. J. Martin. *L'apparition du livre.* Paris, 1958.
*62. Ferguson, C., and W. A. Stewart. *Linguistic Reading Lists.* Washington, 1963.
*63. Fife, R. H. *A Summary of Reports on the Modern Foreign Languages.* New York, 1931.
*64. Findlay, J. J. *Arnold of Rugby.* London, 1897.
*65. Fishman, J. A., et al. *Language Loyalty in the United States.* The Hague, 1966.
*66. Fletcher, H. F. *The Intellectual Development of John Milton.* Urbana, Ill., 1956.

*67. Fraenkel, J. "The Decline of Latin as a Model for Linguistic Analysis," *Proceedings of the Ninth Congress of Linguistics*, ed. H. G. Lunt. The Hague, 1964, 730-737.
*68. François, A. *La grammaire du purisme.* Paris, 1905.
*69. Frisch, J. C. "Grammatical Suppositions to the Treatise, *De Trinitate,* in the *Summa Theologica*" (unpublished paper, Faculty of Philosophy, U. Laval, Quebec, 1968).
*70. Gabriel, A. L. *The Educational Ideas of Vincent de Beauvais.* New York, 1962.
*71. Gallup, J. "De Saussure: de l'existence d'un double signe et d'un double signifié" (unpublished MS, Faculty of Philosophy, U. Laval, Quebec, 1968).
*72. Ganss, G. E. "Changing Objectives and Procedures in Teaching Latin, 1556-1956," *CJ*, LII (1957), 15-22.
*73. ———. *St. Ignatius' Idea of a Jesuit University*. Milwaukee, 1956.
*74. Graves, F. P. *A History of Education during the Middle Ages.* New York, 1910.
*75. ———. *Petrus Ramus and the Educational Reform of the Sixteenth Century*. New York, 1912.
*76. Groulx, L. *L'enseignement français au Canada.* Montreal, 1933.
*77. Gwynn, A. *Roman Education from Cicero to Quintillian.* London, 1926.
*78. Haarhoff, T. J. *Schools of Gaul.* London, 1920.
*79. Hamilton, F. S. *The Days before Yesterday*. London, 1920.
*80. Hans, N. *Comparative Education.* London, 1949.
*81. Harmer, L. C. *The French Language Today*. London, 1954.
*82. Harnois, G. *Les théories du langage en France de 1660 à 1821*. Paris, 1929.
*83. Harris, C. W. *An Encyclopedia of Educational Research.* New York, 1960.
*84. Haskins, C. H. *Studies in Medieval Culture.* London, 1921.
*85. ———. *Studies in the History of Medieval Science*. Cambridge, Mass., 1924.
*86. ———. *The Renaissance of the Twelfth Century*. London, 1927.
*87. ———. *The Differentiae dictionum latinarum of William of Corbeil.* Bruges, 1930.
*88. Hay, D. *The Italian Renaissance in Its Historical Background.* London, 1961.
*89. Highet, G. *The Classical Tradition.* London, 1949.
*90. Hill, W. K. *William Henry Widgery, Schoolmaster.* London, 1894.
*91. Horkan, V. J. *The Educational Theories of Maffeo Vegio.* Washington, 1953.
*92. Hughes, T. *Tom Brown's School Days.* London, 1879.
*93. Hulubei, A. "Virgile en France au XVIe siecle," *RSS,* XVIII (1931), 74-76.

*94. *Encyclopédie pratique de l'éducation en France,* Institut pédagogique national. Paris, 1960.

*95. Ising, E. *Wolfgang Ratkes Schriften zur deutschen Grammatik, 1612-1630*. Berlin, 1959.

*96. Jacobsen, E. *Translation a Traditional Craft*. Copenhagen, 1958.

*97. Jakobson, R. "Henry Sweet's Paths towards Phonemics," *Firth,* 242-255.

*98. Johnston, M. C. *Modern Foreign Languages in the High School.* Washington, 1958.

*99. Jourda, P. "Un humaniste italien en France, Theocrenus, 1480-1536," *RSS,* XVI (1929), 40-46.

*100. Jullian, C. *Ausone et Bordeaux,* Bordeaux, 1893.

*101. Jullien, E. *Les professeurs de littérature dans l'ancienne Rome,* Paris, 1885.

*102. Kelly, L. G. "Un problème linguistique à propos du chant grégorien," *Bulletin des jeunes romanistes,* X (1964), 9-13.

*103. ———. "L'enseignement du style latin pendant la renaissance," *Revue de l'université d'Ottawa* XXXVII (1967), 573-577.

*104. ———. "Aim and Approach in Language Teaching," *LM,* LXII (1968), 370-381.

*105. Kress, D. M. "Juan Luis Vivès, a Study in Renaissance Theories in Methodology in Foreign Language Instruction," *MLJ,* XXV (1940), 20-30.

*106. Kreusler, A. *The Teaching of Modern Foreign Languages in the Soviet Union.* Leiden, 1963.

*107. Kroeh, H. "Methods of Teaching Foreign Languages," *PMLA,* II (1887), 169-185.

*108. Kukenheim, L. *Esquisse historique de la linguistique française et de ses rapports avec la linguistique générale.* Leiden, 1962.

*109. ——— *Contributions à l'histoire de la grammaire grecque, latine, et hébraique à l'époque de la Renaissance.* Leiden, 1951.

*110. Laistner, M. L. W. *Thought and Letters in Western Europe.* London, 1931.

*111. Lambley, K. *The Teaching and Cultivation of the French Language in England during Tudor and Stuart Times.* Manchester, 1920.

*112. Langlais, J. *"L'éducation en France avant le XVIe siècle,"* *RR,* VI (1905), 91-103.

*113. Leach, A. F. *The Schools of Medieval England.* London, 1915.

*114. Leclercq, J. *L'amour des lettres et le désir de Dieu.* Paris, 1957.

*115. Lewis, G. L. ed. *Bilingualism in Education, Report on an International Seminar, Aberystwyth, Wales, 20 August–2 September, 1960.* London, 1965.

*116. Lindsay, W. M. *The Corpus, Epinal, Erfurt and Leyden Glossaries.* London, 1921.

*117. Livet, C. L. *La grammaire française et les grammairiens du XVIe siècle.* Paris, 1859.

*118. Lugol, P. "Une éducation classique au XVIIe siecle," *RU,* II (1893), 16-21.

*119. Lupton, J. H. *A Life of John Colet.* London, 1887.

*120. Lutz, C. E. "Remigius' Ideas on the Classification of the Seven Liberal Arts," *T,* XII (1956), 65-86.

*121. McClain, W. "25 Years of the Cleveland Plan," *E,* LXV (1945), 541-547.

*122. McKeon, R. "Rhetoric in the Middle Ages," *S,* XVII (1942), 1-32.

*123. McKnight, G. H. *Modern English in the Making.* 2 vols. New York, 1928.

*124. McMahon, C. P. *Education in Fifteenth-Century England.* Baltimore, 1947.

*125. McMurray, M., et al. *Modern Foreign Languages in France and Germany.* New York, 1930.

*126. Maître L. A. *Les écoles épiscopales et monastiques en occident, (768-1180).* Paris, 1886.

*127. Malye, J. "L'enseignement parallèle du latin et du français aux Etats-Unis," *BAGB,* XVII (1927), 28-39.

*128. Malherbe, E. G. *The Bilingual School, a Survey of Bilingualism amongst Pupils and Teachers in South African Schools.* Capetown, 1946.

*129. Mandonnet, P. "La crise scholaire au début du XIIIe siècle et la fondation de l'ordre des frères prêcheurs," *Revue d'historie ecclésiastique,* XV (1914), 34-49.

*130. Manitius, M. *Geschichte der lateinischen Literatur des Mittelalters.* 3 vols. Munich, 1911-1931.

*131. Mansi, G. D. *Sacrorum consiliorum nova collectio.* 53 vols. Paris, 1901-1913.

*132. Marrou, H. I. *Histoire de l'éducation dans l'antiquité,* 2nd ed. Paris, 1950.

*133. Massebiau, L. *Les colloques scolaires de XVIe siècle et leurs auteurs, 1480-1570.* Paris, 1878.

*134. Matthews, W. K. "The Soviet Contribution to Linguistic Thought," *AL,* II (1950), 1-23.

*135. Matthias, A. *Geschichte des deutschen Unterrichts.* Munich, 1907.

*136. Meyer, K. *Learning in Ireland in the Fifth Century and the Transmission of Letters*. Dublin, 1912.
*137. Meyer, P. "Traités catalans de grammaire et de poétique," *R,* VI (1887), 431-458; *R,* VIII (1889), 181-210.
*138. Michaud, G. L. "Luis Vivès and Rabelais' Pedagogy," *PMLA,* XXXVIII (1923), 419-424.
*139. Millet, A. *Les grammariens et la phonétique*. Paris, 1933.
*140. Mohrmann, C. *Liturgical Latin: Its Origins and Character*. London, 1959.
*141. Monceaux, P. "L'isagoge latine de M. Victorinus," in *Philologie et linguistique, mélanges offertes à L. Havet*. Paris, 1909, 290-310.
*142. Monroe, P. *A Brief Course in the History of Education*. New York, 1905.
*143. ———, ed. *A Cyclopedia of Education*. 4 vols. New York, 1911-13.
*144. Moore, C. H. "Latin Exercises in a Greek Schoolroom," *CP,* XIX (1924), 317-328.
*145. Moses, E. R. *Phonetics: History and Interpretation*. Englewood Cliffs, N. J., 1964.
*146. Moulton, W. G. "Linguistics and Language Teaching in the United States," *IRAL,* I (1963), 21-40.
*147. Newmark, L., ed. *Twentieth Century Modern Language Teaching*. New York, 1948.
*148. North, H. "The Use of Poetry in the Training of the Ancient Orator," *T,* VIII (1952), 1-10.
*149. Nostrand, H. L., D. W. Foster, and C. B. Christensen. *Research on Modern language Teaching (An Annotated International Bibliography 1945-1964)*. Seattle, Wash., 1965.
*150. O'Connor, P. *Modern Foreign Languages in the High School*. Washington, 1960.
*151. O'Donnel, J. R. "Coluccio Salutati on the Poet-Teacher," *MS,* XXII (1960), 240-257.
*152. Ohman, S. "Theories of the Linguistic Field," *Word,* IX (1953), 123-134.
*153. Oldknow, A. "Three Modern non-Roman Symbolaries." Paper delivered at the Annual Meeting of the Canadian Linguistic Association, 1965, MS.
*154. Ollman, M. J. *MLA Selective List of Materials*. New York, 1962.
*155. Ong, W. J. "Latin Language Study as a Renaissance Puberty Rite," in G. Spindler, ed., *Education and Culture*. New York, 1963, 444-466.
*156. ———. *The Presence of the Word, Some Prolegomena for Cultural and Religious History,* New Haven, Conn., 1967.
*157. *Oxford Classical Dictionary*. London, 1949.

*158. Paetow, L. J. *Guide to the Study of Medieval History.* London, 1931.
*159. ———. *The Arts Course at Medieval Universities.* Urbana, Ill., 1910.
*160. Psfort, E. "A Group of Early Tudor Schoolbooks," *Li,* Series IV, XXVI (1946), 227-261.
*161. Palmer, L. R. *The Latin Language.* London, 1954.
*162. Paré, G., et al. *La renaissance du XIIe siècle, les écoles et l'enseignement.* Paris, 1933.
*163. Parker, W. R. *The National Interest and Foreign Languages.* Washington, 1962.
*164. Passard, F-X. *La pratique du ratio studiorum.* Paris, 1896.
*165. Pattison, B. *English Teaching in the World Today.* London, 1950.
*166. Pederson, H. *Linguistic Science in the Nineteenth Century.* tr. J. W. Spargo. Cambridge, Mass., 1931.
*167. Pinloche, A. *La réforme de l'éducation en Allemagne au 18e siècle; Basedow et le philanthropinisme.* Paris, 1889.
*168. Plattard, J. *Guillaume Budé et les origines de l'humanisme francais.* Paris, 1923.
*169. Poole, P. L. *Medieval England.* London, 1958.
*170. Prator, C. H. *Language Teaching in the Philippines.* Washington, 1956.
*171. Quick, R. H. *Essays on Educational Reformers.* New York, 1897.
*172. Rand, E. K. "The Classics in the Thirteenth Century," *S,* IV (1929), 249-269.
*173. Reynolds, P. N. "Two Documents concerning Elementary Education in Thirteenth-Century Genoa," *S,* XII (1937), 255-256.
*174. Riché, P. "Le psautier, livre de lecture, d'après les vies des saints mérovingiens," *Etudes mérovingiennes,* II (1953), 253-256.
*175. Rickert, E. *Chaucer's World.* New York, 1948.
*176. Riemens, K. J. *Esquisse historique de l'enseignement du français en Hollande du XVIe au XIXe siècle.* Leiden, 1919.
*177. Rioux, G. *L'oeuvre pédagogique de Wolfgangus Ratichius.* Paris, 1963.
*178. Robins, R. H. *Ancient and Medieval Grammatical Theory in Europe.* London, 1951.
*179. Roger, M. *L'enseignement des lettres classiques d'Ausone à Alcuin.* Paris, 1905.
*180. Roy, A. *Les lettres, les sciences et les arts au Canada sous le régime français.* Paris, 1930.
*181. Russell, B. *A History of Western Philosophy.* London, 1946.
*182. Ryan, L. V. *Roger Ascham.* London, 1963.
*183. Salmon, V. "Joseph Webbe: Some Seventeenth-century Views on

Language Teaching and the Nature of Learning," *BHR,* XXIII (1961), 324-347.

*184. ———. "A Pioneer of the Direct Method in the Erasmian Circle," *La,* XIX (1960), 567-577.

*185. ———. "Language Planning in Seventeenth-century England; Its Extent and Aims," *Firth,* 370-397.

*186. Sandys, J. E. *History of Classical Scholarship.* London, 1921.

*187. ———. *Harvard Lectures on the Revival of Learning.* London, 1905.

*188. Sanford, E. M. "The Use of Classical Latin Authors in the *Libri manuales," Transactions of the American Philological Association,* LV (1924), 190-248.

*189. Sayers, D. L. "The Lost Tools of Learning," reprint from the *National Review,* New York, 1961.

*190. Schoell, F. L. "Un Humaniste francais oublié, Jean de Sponde," *RSS,* XII (1925), 361-400.

*191. Scott, P. D. "Alcuin as a Poet: Rhetoric and Belief in His Latin Verse," *University of Toronto Quarterly,* XXXIII (1964), 233-257.

*192. Seebohm, F. *The Oxford Reformers.* London and New York, 1914.

*193. Seiler, K. *Das pädagogische Wolfgang Ratkes.* Erlangen, 1931.

*194. Simonini, R. C. *Italian Scholarship in Renaissance England.* Chapel Hill, N. C., 1952.

*195. Sparrow, J. "Latin Verse of the High Renaissance," in ed. E. F. Jacob, *Italian Renaissance Studies: A Tribute to the Late Cecilia M Ady.* London, 1960.

*196. Squair, J. *The Autobiography of a Teacher of French.* Toronto, 1928.

*197. Ste-Beuve, C. A. *Port-Royal,* ed. M. Allem. Paris, 1934.

*198. Taylor, H. O. *The Classical Heritage of the Middle Ages.* New York, 1911.

*199. ———. *The Medieval Mind.* New York, 1919.

*200. Tell, J. *Les grammariens français depuis l'origine de la grammaire en France jusqu'aux dernières oeuvres connues.* Paris, 1874.

*201. Thorndyke, L. "Elementary and Secondary Education in the Middle Ages," *S* XV (1940), 400-408.

*202. Thurot, C. "Notices et extraits de divers manuscrits latins pour servir à l'histoire des doctrines grammaticales au moyen âge," *Notices et extraits des manuscrits de la Bibliothèque impériale,* XXII (Paris, 1868), 2.

*203. Tikkanen, F. *Die Psalterillustration im Mittelalter.* 2 vols. Leipzig, 1895-1897.

*204. Titone, R. *Foreign Language Teaching (An Historical Sketch).* New York, 1967.

*205. Tout, T. F., "Literature and Learning in the English Civil Service in the Fourteenth Century," *S,* IV (1929), 365-375.
*206. Tremblay, J. A. "L'enseignement des Jésuites," unpublished MS (Collège des Jésuites, Quebec, 1965).
*207. Turkevitch, L. B. "Soviet Education," *MLJ,* XLIV (1960), 113-117.
*208. Ullman, B. L. "Some Aspects of the Origin of Italian Humanism," *PQ,* XX (1941), 212-223.
*209. van Eenanaam, E. "Annotated Bibliography of Modern Language Teaching," *MLJ* annual.
*210. Vildomec, V. *Multilingualism.* Leiden, 1963.
*211. Wallach, L. *Alcuin and Charlemagne.* Ithica, N. Y., 1959.
*212. Watson, F. "Clenardus as an Educational Pioneer," *CR,* XXIX (1915), 129-134.
*213. Watts, J. B. "The Teaching of French in the United States," *FR,* XXXVIII (1963), whole number.
*214. Weisheipl, J. A. "Curriculum of the Faculty of Arts at Oxford in the Early Fourteenth Century," *MS,* XXVI (1964), 143-150.
*215. Weiss, R. *The Dawn of Humanism in Italy.* London, 1947.
*216. ———. *Humanism in England during the Fifteenth Century.* London, 1957.
*217. ———. "The Greek Culture of Southern Italy in the Later Middle Ages," *PBA,* XXXVII (1951), 23-50.
*218. Wieruszowsky, H. "*Ars dictaminis* in the time of Dante," *MH,* III (1943), 1-8.
*219. ———. "A Twelfth-century *ars dictaminis* in the Barberini Collection of the Vatican Library," *T,* XVIII (1962), 382-393.
*220. Winkler, S. *La doctrine grammaticale francaise d'après Maupas et Oudin.* Halle, 1912.
*221. Woodward, W. H. *Desiderius Erasmus concerning the Aim and Method of Education.* London, 1904.
*222. ———. *Studies in Education during the Age of the Renaissance.* London, 1904.
*223. ———. *Vittorino da Feltre and Other Humanist Educators.* London, 1904.
*224. Woolner, A. C. *Languages in History and Politics.* London, 1938.
*225. Wühr, W. R. *Das abendländische Bildungswesen im Mittelalter.* Munich, 1950.
*226. Zanfagna, Sister M. Laure. *Educational Theories and Principles of Cardinal Silvio Antoniane.* Washington, 1940.

INDICES

SUBJECT INDEX

AUTHOR INDEX

This index includes only those authors who are mentioned or quoted more than once.

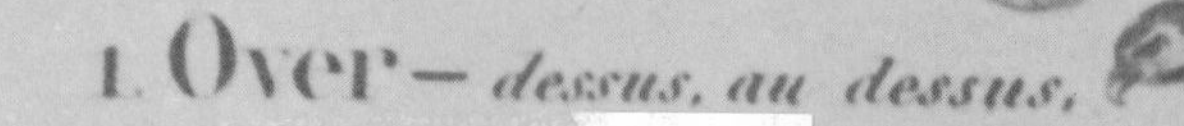

2 Under – sous, dessous,
dessous l'autre oiseau.

4. To – à, tendance vers...

7. In –
dedans

5. At – à, arrivé à

6. Into – dans, action d'entrer dans